APPLIED CONCEPTS
IN
MICROCOMPUTER GRAPHICS

Bruce A. Artwick

President
Sublogic Corporation
Champaign, Illinois

Prentice-Hall, Inc.   Englewood Cliffs, New Jersey 07632

Library of Congress Cataloging in Publication Data

Artwick, Bruce A.
  Applied concepts in microcomputer graphics.

  Includes index.
  1. Computer graphics. 2. Microcomputers. I. Title.
T385.A77 1984   001.64'43   83-10945
ISBN 0-13-039322-3

Production supervision: *Shari Ingerman*
Editorial supervision: *Ken Sessions*
Page layout: *Jill S. Packer*
Cover design: *Jeannette Jacobs*
Manufacturing buyer: *Gordon Osbourne*

IBM is a registered trademark of the International Business Machines Corporation.

Printed in the United States of America

10 9 8 7 6 5 4

ISBN   0-13-039322-3

Prentice-Hall International, Inc., *London*
Prentice-Hall of Australia Pty. Limited, *Sydney*
Editora Prentice-Hall do Brasil, Ltda., *Rio de Janeiro*
Prentice-Hall Canada Inc., *Toronto*
Prentice-Hall of India Private Limited, *New Delhi*
Prentice-Hall of Japan, Inc., *Tokyo*
Prentice-Hall of Southeast Asia Pte. Ltd., *Singapore*
Whitehall Books Limited, *Wellington, New Zealand*

Contents

Preface

Working with and programming today's graphically powerful microcomputers such as the Apple II, IBM Personal Computer, and Apple Macintosh, requires a working knowledge of computer hardware, software, and graphics methods. Specialized knowledge in the graphics hardware area that is not usually needed when working with nongraphics systems is also essential. Information concerning each of these topics is available from many scattered sources, but much sifting through often highly theoretical texts, articles, and cursory user's manuals is required to gain the required knowledge. My goal in writing this book is to consolidate all the practical information needed to work with and design graphics systems into one convenient volume.

In order to get the most out of a microcomputer's graphics facilities, one needs to know the theories and graphics techniques that are applicable to the desired graphics application. Animation, business graphics, simulation graphics, and computer-aided design all have appropriate techniques and "tricks" to get the job done. This book goes into specifics on these and other topics, and the methods described are not limited to simple screen displays. They are equally applicable to today's inexpensive and powerful graphics peripherals such as multicolor pen plotters and matrix printers.

Although this book briefly covers many of the interesting though seldom-used aspects of graphics, the major focus is on the practical aspects, with special emphasis on microcomputer applications and methods. This book's scope is intentionally broad—everything from what's available in the way of graphics systems and peripherals to the hardware details and specification sheets for display controller chips are presented. Graphics algorithms and programming are covered in depth.

The first few chapters make up an introduction to computer graphics. Presented first is an overview of the state of the art and what sort of equipment exists; this is followed by a chapter on software concepts and a chapter on basic graphics hardware. The first few chapters thus present what a student would learn in an introductory course on computer graphics.

The remaining chapters are more specialized; they cover in detail graphics software, hardware, and mathematical concepts. Many examples of the uses of the described techniques with relation to computer-aided design and simulation are given, thereby stressing the practical application of the concepts.

A chapter on the specialized though popular field of business graphics concludes the text.

So many concepts and specialized topics are used in computer graphics that it is difficult to remember all the methods and formulas. This book is also designed as a reference, to be consulted when specialized information is required.

Appendix sections are included to show foreign video standards and specialized graphics data for both Apple II and IBM personal computers.

Bruce Artwick

Chapter 1

Applications of Microcomputer Graphics

The origin of the old saw that one picture is worth a thousand words may be lost in antiquity, but the phrase well summarizes a picture's ability to transmit huge amounts of information rapidly. In many applications a picture is the best way to present information, and it is only logical that a computer (basically an information processing device) should be able to present results in the form of a picture or graphic display. Until recently, however, few computer installations used graphic displays. The old typewriter-style output dominated, and most people accepted the typewriter keyboard and printer (or at best, an alphanumeric TV screen display) as the standard computer input and output devices.

Ironically, the advantages of graphic displays contributed to this situation; they can present immense quantities of data to a user so rapidly that until recently most computers—especially those operating in time-sharing multiuser modes—were simply not up to the task. Graphic displays would have put too much of a burden on processor resources, memory, and communication channels. The costs were prohibitive.

Fortunately, two simultaneous developments have pushed aside all the roadblocks that previously put computer graphics out of most people's reach. These developments are the microprocessor (which solves the processing power problem) and low-cost solid-state memory that makes inexpensive systems possible.

Inexpensive display hardware has opened the world of computer graphics to fields where its use was not feasible or even considered a few years ago. Computer games and personal computers are predominantly graphics oriented, but graphic displays are also finding their way into business applications, art, and automotive electronics. Fields that have traditionally used computer graphics (science and engineering, for example) are using graphics more than ever, and on a much lower level.

Cheap high-performance computer graphics have arrived with such suddenness that while excellent hardware is available, applications information and operating software are not. Today it is possible to place an order for some low-cost graphics equipment and receive it in a matter of weeks; but making good use of that equipment in a specific application is not so simple and straightforward. The problems of display concepts—what you want to display and how—and the associated software to perform the required task must be considered.

TYPES OF GRAPHIC DISPLAYS

Display concepts, graphic techniques, and available hardware are subjects we must explore; but first it is good to take a look at today's computer graphics technology. Looking at some current products and applications may help answer these two basic questions: How can graphics benefit my application? What sort of display system will best serve my needs?

Graphic display systems come in many forms and sizes. There are graphics terminals that connect to larger computers, graphics terminals with built-in computers, and large graphics systems residing within computers that drive external display monitors. The most common form of graphic display is the *raster-scan* graphics terminal.

Raster-scan graphics terminals consist of (1) a color or monochrome cathode-ray tube (CRT) which serves as the display screen, (2) a keyboard, (3) an internal display generator, and (4) display memory to store the image.

The computer sends "drawing" commands to the terminal's graphics generator. Prewritten software or the user's custom graphics software running at the computer is in control of image generation. Raster-scan terminals can generate charts and graphs for scientific and business applications, medium-resolution line drawings for engineering drawings, and shaded images for life-like drawings and artistic use. High-performance color raster-scan terminals can in fact generate images that could be mistaken for photographs of real objects. Figure 1-1 shows a raster-scan graphics terminal.

Figure 1-1   Raster-scan graphics terminal. The vertical bars shown here in shades of gray are separate colors to show four separate sets of data: credit to banks, to credit unions, to finance companies, and to retailers. (Courtesy Ramtek Corp.)

2

Figure 1-2 Storage tube graphics terminal; this unit has internal graphics generation hardware and can semipermanently store complex screen images. (Courtesy Tektronix, Inc.)

Another common device is the storage-tube graphics terminal. This unit also contains a keyboard and internal graphics generation hardware, but instead of using a raster-scan CRT, a special storage tube that can semipermanently retain an image is used. The computer draws lines and characters on the screen in much the same way a draftsman draws lines with a pencil on drafting paper. Incredibly complex line drawings can be created on these devices, which makes them very popular in engineering and architectural applications where dense line drawings are required. Figure 1-2 shows a storage-tube display system.

Many applications require very complex imaging that is beyond the capability of simple graphics terminals. Large-scale graphic-display units that can be built into computer systems, and large graphics-generating and image processing computer systems fill these needs. The user communicates to the computer with a keyboard, data tablet, track ball, or other input device, and the computer generates, analyzes, and displays the results on an external monitor. Figure 1-3 illustrates an expensive high-end image processing system that falls into this "graphics computer" category.

Finally, there are special-application graphic displays. Storage tubes and CRTs are too expensive, not rugged enough, or simply inappropriate for such applications as automobile and industrial instrumentation displays. Light-emitting-diode (LED) arrays, liquid-crystal-display (LCD) arrays, and plasma panels are often used in these applications.

3

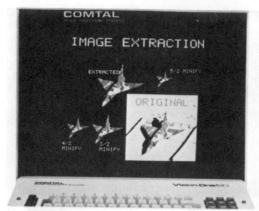

Object manipulation

Small area color manipulation

Color overview

Color zoom to second quadrant

Figure 1-3 An image-processing graphics terminal. Reproduced here in black and white, the displays are actually in full color. At top left an image from a scene (inset on screen) is extracted for manipulation; the color of any of the flowers (top right) may be manipulated as desired without changing the color on the rest of the bouquet. A portion of the color scene at lower left is reproduced in a zoom shot at right with no significant degradation of color quality. (Vision One/20 terminal photos courtesy COMTAL Corp., Altadena, California.)

GRAPHS AND CHARTS

The most basic form of computer graph is the simple plot or chart. A computer can plot an engineering or business graph on a graphic display device just as one would draw it on paper, as Fig. 1-4 illustrates. The computer-generated graph adds an element of interaction not found on a similar graph produced with pen and paper. The graph can be modified almost instantaneously by the computer to reflect changes entered by a user. An engineer using the filter response graph of Fig. 1-4 could change a capacitance value in the filter described by the graph, have the computer analyze the new filter response, and replot the graph in a matter of seconds. An engineer could in fact design the filter to meet his response specifica-

4

Figure 1-4 This circuit response graph appears exactly as it would had it been drawn manually on graph paper. (Courtesy Hewlett-Packard.)

tion by simply adjusting parameters in his computer-simulated circuit until the desired response curve appears. An added benefit of a computer-generated graph for this kind of design and analysis work is the ability to see the overall results of any situation at a glance. A short, drastic one-week sales slump in a yearly sales report or a detrimental resonance point in a circuit may go unnoticed while quickly scanning through tabular data; but in a graphic plot such anomalies become immediately evident.

STATUS AND CONTROL DISPLAYS

Indicator lights, gages (both digital and analog), and other indicators can be efficiently replaced by a graphic display. Many gages and indicators can be grouped onto one screen, and many screens can be used if necessary. The aircraft control panel shown in Fig. 1-5 is an example of computer graphics replacing the more traditional gages and lamp indicators.

Graphic displays have a few distinct advantages over conventional instrumentation beyond those we've just considered: One screen can display different instrument sets at different times, and important emergency conditions that occur infrequently can dominate the display as emergencies occur while not cluttering the display when everything is normal.

Cost is another advantage. Many gages and indicators, their mounting hardware, and the labor involved in constructing complex indicator panels are greatly reduced when the problem is reduced to mounting a display screen or two.

Figure 1-5   Computer graphics avionics system used in Boeing 767 aircraft. (Courtesy Boeing, Renton, Washington.)

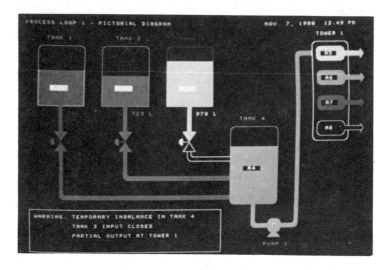

Figure 1-6   Industrial control graphic presentation, shown here in black and white, appears on screen with each tank's fluid content in a different color. (Courtesy Matrox Electronics, Montreal, Canada.)

Industrial control processes may be depicted in very visual ways using computer graphics, as the industrial control display of Fig. 1-6 illustrates. It would be difficult to show fluid levels changing in the tanks and chemicals flowing through ducts using conventional gages and instrumentation.

Radar, by its very sweeping nature, is well suited to the CRT display. But through the use of graphics, information may be superimposed on radar imagery, thereby giving it more meaning. Maps may be drawn, for example, to show the swept area, and color can enhance critical areas (such as thunderstorms on a weather radar display), as Fig. 1-7 shows.

Figure 1-7 Black-and-white reproduction of color graphic display of weather data. In this map display, colored sections are used to show moisture, temperature, thunderstorm areas, and other distinguishable parameters. (Courtesy Collins Air Transport Division, Rockwell International.)

COMPUTER-AIDED DESIGN

Engineers, industrial designers, and architects are increasingly using computer graphics to replace the functions of pencil, paper, and rulers in system and structure design and analysis. Graphics-oriented computer-aided design (CAD) systems allow a designer to manipulate a design at will using a quickly updated graphic display (raster-scan CRT or storage tube). Intelligence information may be attached to the graphics information. Final designs are drawn on large plotters or graphics printers, and "intelligence" information is analyzed. Bills of materials, cost, and critical stress points are a few items that the intelligence information may be reduced to. Figure 1-8 depicts a typical CAD system.

Computer-aided design systems are destined to become a major industrial design tool. As robotic technology emerges, computer-aided manufacturing (CAM) will dominate, and CAD systems are ideal for supplying information to CAM systems in computer-compatible form.

Figure 1-8 Graphics-oriented computer-aided design system allows immediate changes to be entered and displayed right at the work station. (Courtesy Summagraphics Corp.)

SIMULATING WITH GRAPHICS

Aircraft, automobile, oil tanker, and other vehicle simulations often use computer graphics. A 3-dimensional flight simulation display that depicts the world outside the windshield allows a student to become familiar with the visual cues encountered in the real world. While extensive 3D simulation is expensive and can involve multiple display generators and screens (one screen per window in an aircraft flight deck, for example), the cost is well worth it. The fuel and maintenance savings as well as the improved safety factor result in overall financial savings. Figure 1-9 shows a typical commercial flight simulator display system and a low-cost 3D flight simulation display used on personal computer systems.

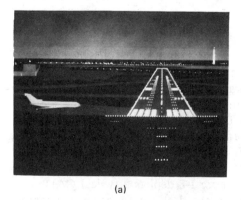
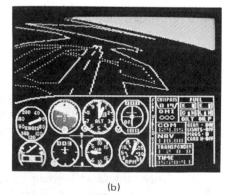

(a) (b)

Figure 1-9 Commercial (a) and personal-computer (b) displays in flight simulation systems. The commercial version has straight angled lines and shows runway markings. (Courtesy Evans & Sutherland and Rediffusion Simulations, and Sublogic Corporation.)

Chapter 2

Display Generation Basics

After reviewing the applications in the first chapter and seeing how desirable graphic displays can be, you might be tempted to rush immediately into the hardware and software aspects of getting some graphics running for your own application. It first is necessary, however, to get to know the basic concepts of computer graphics. The information in this chapter is enough to get you started in developing your own graphic displays. Specialized topics such as the mathematics of advanced graphics and the application of graphics for business are covered in depth in following chapters and may be referred to once the basic concepts of computer graphics are understood.

COORDINATE SYSTEMS AND CONVENTIONS

Before points, lines, and other more complex elements can be placed on a display screen, some method must be selected for determining where they start and where they go. Any system that maps a set of numbers (the computer's representation) to screen locations (the viewer's representation) is acceptable, but some systems are easier to work with than others.

CARTESIAN COORDINATES

The simplest and most popular screen mapping approach is the Cartesian coordinate system. The display screen is assigned an x axis (usually horizontal) and a y axis (vertical). Screen locations are specified by coordinate (x, y) pairs as shown in Fig. 2-1. This coordinate system is immediately familiar to most users because it is used extensively in graphing, mechanical drawing, and geometry.

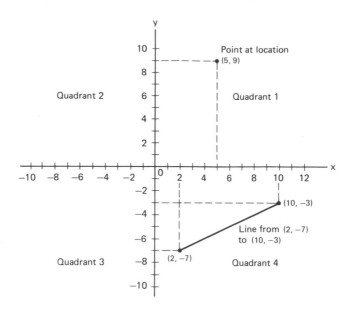

Figure 2-1   The Cartesian coordinate system. Note that coordinate pairs are shown with horizontal axis first.

Linearity

Linearity is a prime characteristic of the Cartesian coordinate system: a movement of 3 units in the *x* direction, for example, will have a similar effect no matter where on the screen it occurs. Another recognizable trait is axis independence. Movement on the *x* axis causes no *y* axis movement, and vice versa. In mathematical terms, the axes are orthogonal to one another.

The linear and orthogonal nature of the Cartesian coordinate system has one important real-world consequence: the properties make it similar to the space we live in. The display screen is represented as a 2-dimensional (*x, y*) plane in a 3-dimensional (*x, y, z*) space. It is therefore very easy to represent real-world data and images.

Direction and Origin

While there is wide agreement that the Cartesian coordinate system is the best way to define a point's screen position in most applications, there is often controversy over the direction and origin (*x* = 0, *y* = 0 point) of the point. Mathematicians, statisticians, and business people argue that the origin should be on the lower left of the screen, and the positive *x* and positive *y* directions should be to the right and toward the top of the screen, respectively—and this argument is based on the fact that geometric constructions, graphs, and charts are traditionally oriented in this manner. Engineers argue that the origin should be at the upper left with positive *x, y* being to the right and down, respectively, because this more closely corresponds to the physical operation of most common display devices. People who work with 3D graphics prefer the origin at the screen's center, forming a 4-quadrant coordinate system as illustrated in Fig. 2-2. The 4-quadrant center-origin system more closely corresponds to computer arithmetic, because it includes negative as well as positive values—something the other two coordinate systems ignore. The questions essentially boil down to these two: (1) Which direction should the positive y axis represent? (2) Where should the origin be placed? There is universal agreement that positive x direction movement is to the right.

The origin and direction choice is ultimately up to the user. It is easy to convert back and forth between these coordinate systems by simply negating the y values and adding appropriate biases to the x and y values to compensate for opposite direction sense and origin differences, so there is no need to worry about locking into the wrong coordinate system. Table 2-1 points out the advantages of the three common Cartesian coordinate forms. These factors should be considered before choosing a coordinate system.

The start-at-lower-left coordinate system is used for most examples in this text. The start-at-the-center form is occasionally used, especially in cases employing 3-dimensional graphics.

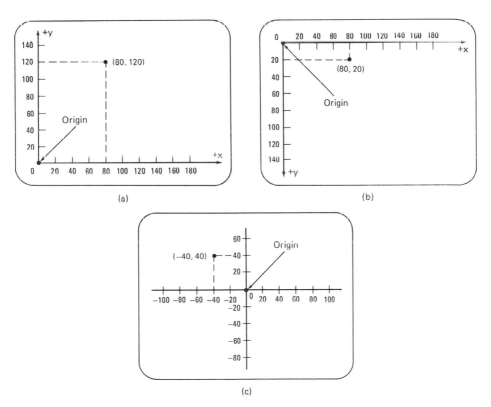

Figure 2-2 There are several coordinate conventions; the lower-left origin (a) and upper-right origin (b) show no "minus" values, while the center origin (c) depicts values to the left of center and below center as minus quantities.

Table 2-1   Common Coordinate Systems with Their Advantages and Drawbacks

Coordinate System	Coordinate Pair and Direction	Origin	Advantages	Disadvantages
Cartesian	x (+ = right) y (+ = up)	Lower left	Traditional for graphs	No negative coordinates
Cartesian	x (+ = right) y (+ = down)	Upper left	Matches display devices	Unconventional for graphs and charts
Cartesian	x (+ = right) y (+ = up)	Screen center	Matches 3D equations	Screen center 0 discontinuity
Polar	R (+ only) Theta (+ = counter-clockwise)	Screen center	Traditional for graphs	No correspondence to compass heading
Polar	R (+ only) Theta (+ = clockwise)	Screen center	Good for navigation	Unconventional for graphs

POLAR COORDINATES

In some cases, a graphics task can be simplified if the display screen's coordinate system is defined closely to match a physical situation. Cartesian coordinates correspond to the placement and movement of objects in the real world and are most often used. Next in popularity is the *polar coordinate system*, which corresponds to rotation in the real world. A circular sweeping radar display (while not always computer-driven) is an application that immediately comes to mind. Polar coordinates are also used to simplify the definition of closed polygons.

Screen location in polar coordinates is specified by a rotation angle and a distance from the origin (see Fig. 2-3). Polar coordinates' main advantage is the elimination of conversions from polar-oriented data to Cartesian coordinates. Polar coordinates' main disadvantage is its nonlinearity. A small angular change at a small distance from the origin results in a small screen movement, while the same small angular change causes a large screen movement at a large distance from the origin.

As with Cartesian coordinates, there are a number of controversial parameters. Screen center is generally accepted as the origin (radius = 0), but positive angular direction can be either clockwise or counterclockwise, and the zero-angle point can be either horizontal (to the right) or vertical (up). For computer graphing of polar mathematical functions, a zero angle to the right with positive counterclockwise movement is usually chosen. For applications dealing with compass direction (such as a navigation display), a vertical (upward) zero angle and positive clockwise movement are used to correspond to compass headings.

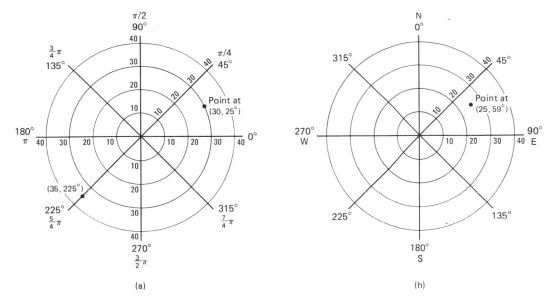

Figure 2-3 The polar coordinate system may be "right, counterclockwise" (a) or "top, clockwise" (b).

OTHER COORDINATE SYSTEMS

Cartesian and polar coordinates are by far the most common screen coordinate systems, but there is no reason why special, nonstandard coordinate systems can't be used to simplify the display of special functions. Logarithmically spaced Cartesian coordinates may simplify a particular graphing application, for example. You should select a screen coordinate system much as you would graph paper for a plot to be drawn.

COORDINATE SYSTEM MAPPING

Display systems are designed to represent coordinates on the screen in some particular way. The designers essentially build the display hardware around a coordinate system which in many cases will be inappropriate for your application. Once a working coordinate system for your graphics application is chosen, computer hardware or software can be used to convert this coordinate system, through scaling, translation, and bit-swapping, into a format acceptable to the display unit (the "display generator coordinate system").

The technique of *scaling* uses multiplication or arithmetic right and left shifts to match coordinate resolutions; that of *translation* involves the adding of offsets to match origins. *Bit-swapping* aligns rows and columns in out-of-sequence displays. More complex mathematics are required to convert from one coordinate system to another. Sines, cosines, and multiplication are needed to go from Cartesian to polar coordinates.

Conversion complexity and execution rate will often lead you into using a coordinate system that is similar to the display unit's for efficiency reasons. Mapping techniques (such as bit-swapping) are discussed in the display generation hardware section.

DISPLAY GENERATION, RESOLUTION, AND ASPECT RATIO

A hardware display generator produces a rectangular matrix of dots on a screen, called a bit map. Each bit or dot is the smallest resolvable *picture element* of any display (Fig. 2-4), and has been appropriately dubbed *pixel*. As shown, the rectangular matrix is assigned a Cartesian coordinate system, and each pixel has a unique *x, y* location. Computer software individually turns pixels on or off, thereby setting the pixels to white or black levels on the screen. The screen may be erased by turning all the pixels off, and images can be drawn by selectively turning them on.

"Vector" or stroke-writing displays don't have individually addressable pixels; they generate points and lines as single-stroke operations. The coordinates of the points and start and end positions of the lines must still be supplied to the display generator, and these positions are addressed in the same way as on the bit map—in *x* and *y* coordinates in an addressable (though nonexistent) rectangular dot matrix.

A display's dot size and matrix area determine its resolution, or detail-resolving ability. The display of Fig. 2-4 has a 256 × 240 (horizontal-by-vertical) resolution. Display resolution is thus a function of the display generator.

Aspect ratio is the relationship of a display screen's width to its height. Display screens are seldom square. The NTSC defines a standard television display's aspect ratio as 4:3 (4 units horizontal, 3 units vertical). But computer-driven display screens can vary from short and wide (found on many computer terminals) to tall and narrow (used extensively on specialized typesetting equipment). So aspect ratio is a function of display-screen (or panel) size.

Display resolution and aspect ratio must be considered when assigning a coordinate system to a display device. Two items to consider are display fit and squareness. In "fitting" a coordinate system to a display device, it is best to "cooperate with" the display system's characteristics rather than fight them. A coordinate system of 256 × 240 is well suited to the 256 × 240 resolution device of Fig. 2-4.

Multiples of resolution values are also quite easy to work with. If you prefer to work in a Cartesian coordinate system with larger dimensions than 256 × 240, a multiple such as 512 × 480 is a good choice. The 512 × 480 coordinate system can be "mapped" onto the 256 × 240 screen by simply having the computer divide all the coordinates' *x* and *y* values by 2 (which a computer can do quickly using an arithmetic right shift instruction). The coordinate mapping is:

$$\text{display } x = \text{coordinate } x/2$$
$$\text{display } y = \text{coordinate } y/2$$

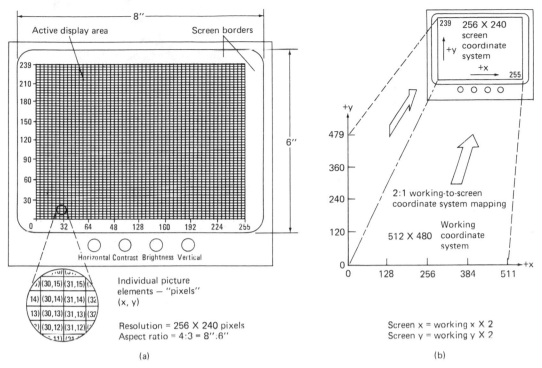

Figure 2-4 A 256 × 240 bit map (a) and a 512 × 480 working coordinate system mapped to a 256 × 240 bit map (b).

The display device still is limited to 256 × 240 resolution, but displayed images can be specified in the 512 × 480 coordinate system. The extra resolution is lost in the mapping (truncated in the divide-by-2 "right shift").

It would not be wise to attempt the mapping of a 400 × 400 coordinate system onto the 256 × 240 screen. The coordinate mapping would be:

$$\text{display } x = \text{coordinate } x/1.5625$$
$$\text{display } y = \text{coordinate } y/1.6666$$

The computer would have to resort to the time-consuming process of floating-point division or an equivalent complex computation to determine the display values. In addition, uneven point spacing problems would arise. Squeezing 400 coordinates into 256 pixels causes some pixels to correspond to two coordinates while others correspond to only one. Strings of points that are equally spaced in the coordinate system would appear unevenly spaced on the screen.

Display squareness must also be considered. A square with four equal sides ($x = 100$ by $y = 100$, for example) drawn in a 256 × 240 coordinate system being displayed by a 256 × 240 display generator will only be square on a display screen with an aspect ratio of 2.56:2.40. On a common 4:3 screen, the image would be rectangular. In some instances this slight distortion is acceptable, but if absolute squareness is needed, a compromise must be struck to obtain it. A 400 × 300 coordinate system, for example, could be used for perfect squareness on a 4:3 screen, but the mapping may be computationally wasteful.

15

Many display generators are designed to solve the squareness problem. Display generators with 640 × 480 display resolutions are quite common. The 640 × 480 resolution is proportional to a 4:3 aspect ratio. By using a 640 × 480 coordinate system with a 640 × 480 display generator and a 4:3 screen, squareness is maintained, but if your display screen doesn't have a 4:3 aspect ratio, the squareness problem again arises.

POINT MANIPULATION

Once a coordinate system is chosen, a way of specifying where picture elements are to be placed on the screen is defined. All that remains is to decide what you want on the screen and to place it there. The simplest of all elements that can be placed on a screen is the point. The point is in fact the central graphics element of the display, because more complex elements merely consist of many points.

POINT PLOTTING

Plotting a point on a display screen is a very display-dependent operation. It can range anywhere from turning on a single bit in memory in a shared program/display memory system, to a simple high-level-language point plotting statement such as:

PLOT 12,23

This statement is used to position a point at screen location $x = 12$, $y = 23$ on an Apple II microcomputer using Apple Integer BASIC. In this particular case, the resolution is 40 × 48, and the origin is in the upper left corner of the screen.

More than simple x, y locations must be specified in most situations. Different display systems require different parameters. In the Apple II's case, the point's color must be specified:

COLOR = 9

This statement precedes the PLOT command. Any PLOT commands that follow COLOR = 9 will plot a point of color 9 (color 9 is orange).

Other parameters that might be associated with a point are gray shade (for black and white systems), duration (how long the point will remain on), and fadeout rate. The particular display device's documentation specifies all the controllable parameters.

Once point plotting has been mastered, a crude form of graphics is at your command. It is possible to draw anything you want by erasing the screen (turning off all pixels in the bit map) and manually drawing lines, characters, circles, and shaded-in regions by turning on the proper pixels. Manually erasing the screen by turning off 61,440 pixels (for a 256 × 240 bit map) is cumbersome, however, and a small program that loops and sequentially turns off all pixels is faster and more appropriate. The same thing applies to line drawing, circle generation, and all the other high-level graphic functions; but on the lowest level, all functions end up plotting a series of points.

POINT READBACK

Many display devices allow you to "read" a pixel to determine if it is already turned on. This feature is useful for determining point or line intersections.

Point readback is useful from a graphics utility standpoint. One display screen can be copied to another by reading all the points on one screen and plotting the corresponding points on the other. Similarly, screen data can be transferred to a graphics printer or plotter. Selective erase methods that allow individual points or lines to be erased instead of the entire screen often rely on point readback.

LINE GENERATION CONCEPTS

Line generation techniques vary among display generators. Vector-oriented displays simply require that the line's start and end points be specified. The coordinates for the start and end points are sent to the display generator as they would be for two singular points, along with an additional indicator that this is a line instead of two single points.

But line generation on raster-scan equipment is not so easy. Raster-scan display units usually only accept points and have no internal line generation hardware.

LINE GEOMETRY

A series of points on a bit map can be strung together to form a line. A program to perform line generation is very useful in a graphics system. The complexity of such a program is dependent on desired line generation rate and display system capabilities. The complexity of a line generation task as performed by the display generation hardware can vary from complete line generation—where the start and end points of a line simply are submitted to the display hardware—to point plotting only, where the user's software must compute all the points that form a line and turn them on. Vector generators—usually circuit implementations of line-drawing software—are used in display hardware that is designed to draw its own lines.

Horizontal and Vertical Lines

Horizontal and vertical lines are special-case display elements that are easily generated. The program in Fig. 2-5 generates a horizontal line. First, the distance in the x direction between the start and end points of the line is computed by subtracting the start point's x value from the end point's x value. One is added to the distance to obtain the COUNT, which is the number of points that need to be plotted for this line. The horizontal line is then generated by beginning point plotting while moving in the x direction. Every time a point is plotted, the count is decremented by one. When the count reaches zero, all the points have been plotted and the horizontal line is complete.

This is a simple program, but there are a few important features that will be carried over to more complex line generators. Notice the line generation loop

```
; Plot the pixels for a horizontal line from
; STARTX,STARTY  to  ENDX,ENDY.
10    STARTX=15          ;Start point=15,20
20    STARTY=20
30    ENDX=27            ;End point=27,20
40    ENDY=20
50    COUNT=ENDX-STARTX+1
60    X=STARTX
70    Y=STARTY
80    GOSUB 1000         ;Plot the point X,Y
90    COUNT=COUNT-1
100   IF COUNT=0 THEN STOP
110   X=X+1
120   GOTO 80

;Point plot subroutine. Plots point at X,Y.
1000  COLOR=19
1010  PLOT X,Y
1020  RETURN
```

Figure 2-5 This program generates horizontal lines effectively so long as the end point is to the right of the start point.

(statements 80 to 120). Line generators all contain some form of loop that repetitively plots points. The line generator program thus is broken into two parts: the line generation setup section (statements 10 to 70) and the pixel generation loop (statements 80 to 120). The setup is done once per line and is thus called *line generation overhead*, while the loop is performed once for each pixel in the line. The time required to generate a line is thus:

$$\text{generation time} = \text{overhead time} + (\text{pixels} \times \text{loop time})$$

At the moment we are more concerned with generating lines than worrying about optimizing them for speed, but it is important to know from the outset that the loop time should be as low as possible. It is wise to trade off decreased loop time for increased overhead time, because the overhead operations are only performed once per line. This is the reason COUNT was used in the line generation. The end of the generation sequence could have been detected without using a count by comparing every plotted pixel with the ENDX end-point value, but a microcomputer can perform a decrement operation more quickly than a comparison. In this case, statement 50 was added to the overhead section to make the loop execute faster.

The program in Fig. 2-5 draws correct horizontal lines *as long as the end point is to the right of the start point*. If the x value of the end point is less than that of the start point, the count goes negative and the program no longer functions correctly. The program must be modified to compensate for these "backward" lines.

One approach is to make the program sign-independent. The overhead and loop sections can be modified to check for $-x$ movement and move to the right or left accordingly. A second approach is to check for a $-x$ line before the line

18

```
; Plot the pixels for a horizontal line from
; STARTX,STARTY  to  ENDX,ENDY.

10    STARTX=15       ;Start point=15,20
20    STARTY=20
30    ENDX=27         ;End point=27,20
40    ENDY=20

45    IF ENDX >= STARTX THEN GOTO 50
46    TEMP=ENDX
47    ENDX=STARTX
48    STARTX=TEMP

50    COUNT=ENDX-STARTX+1
60    X=STARTX
70    Y=STARTY
80    GOSUB 1000      ;Plot the point X,Y
90    COUNT=COUNT-1
100   IF COUNT=0 THEN STOP
110   X=X+1
120   GOTO 80

;Point plot subroutine. Plots point at X,Y.
1000  COLOR=19
1010  PLOT X,Y
1020  RETURN
```

Figure 2-6   Horizontal line generator program. Note the addition of statements 45 through 48, which allow for line reversal.

generation loop is entered, and then swap the start and end points if one is detected. This method is preferable because it only contributes to the overhead and not the loop time.

Figure 2-6 shows the "correct" horizontal line generator. Statements 45 to 48 have been added to correct for backward lines.

Vertical lines are generated in the same way as horizontal lines, but *y* is used to determine the count, and movement is made in the vertical direction.

Diagonal Lines

Horizontal and vertical lines can be perfectly drawn on a bit map. The vertical and horizontal columns and rows of bits in the matrix lend themselves to vertical and horizontal construction. Lines at odd diagonals are another matter. The closest we can come to generating diagonal lines on a bit map is to generate a stairstep approximation that most closely fits the desired diagonal line. If the display resolution is fine enough, the line will appear to be a smooth diagonal.

There are several methods that can be used to generate the stairstep line. We might be first inclined to use the line's equation to generate the line. The line's slope, which for simplicity we'll designate with a capital letter, is the change in *y* (Δy) divided by the change in *x* (Δx). Assuming that the line starts at the origin, the line's equation is:

$$Y = \Delta y / \Delta x \times x \quad \text{or} \quad Y = \text{slope} \times x$$

19

A line can be generated by simply plugging all the line's x values into this equation and obtaining the corresponding y values. Integer y values are needed, but the equation sometimes generates fractional results. By simply truncating or rounding the fractions, a reasonable line can be generated (see Fig. 2-7).

In terms of time, this line generation method is extremely expensive—especially for a microcomputer. The slope must be calculated, which involves a divide operation in the overhead, and a multiply operation is performed once per pixel in the line generation loop. Multiply and divide operations take 10 to 100 times as long as simple add and subtract operations on most microcomputers and should be painstakingly avoided as a matter of course.

What's worse is the fact that some sort of floating-point or fractional arithmetic is necessary because slopes are not always pure integers. This line generator works, but timewise it is out of the question.

Before moving on to more efficient line generation schemes, a few stairstep line characteristics should be examined. Line fit, symmetry, reversal, end-to-end overlap, and intensity consistency are the most important characteristics.

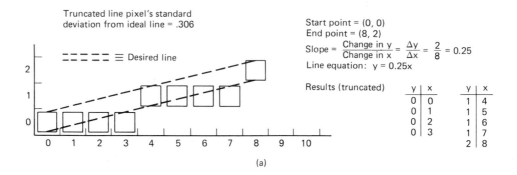

Figure 2-7   Bit map line generation using equations, with truncation (a) and rounding (b).

Line Fit. Line fit refers to the closeness of the stairstep to the desired diagonal line. All the points of the truncated line of Fig. 2-7 fall on or below the desired line. Some points are nearly a full unit off in the y direction. The rounded line is a somewhat better fit. The maximum y error is one half-unit. The standard deviation for the truncated and rounded lines are 0.306 and 0.283, respectively, which confirms the better fit of the rounded line.

Line Symmetry. This term refers to the conditions at the ends of the line. The truncated line in Fig. 2-7 starts with a horizontal step of 4 pixels, but it ends with a single pixel. The rounded line is more symmetrical. It begins with a 2-pixel step and ends with a 3-pixel step.

Line Reversal. A good line drawing system should draw the same pixels when generating a line from a to b as when generating a line from b to a; that is, it is capable of reversal. The lines of Fig. 2-7 are simply solutions of a parametric equation and will generate the same results regardless of order of generation, but other line generators may not.

End-to-End Overlap. Smoother-appearing lines can be generated if the stairsteps are allowed to overlap one another at their ends. Figure 2-8 illustrates end-to-end overlap.

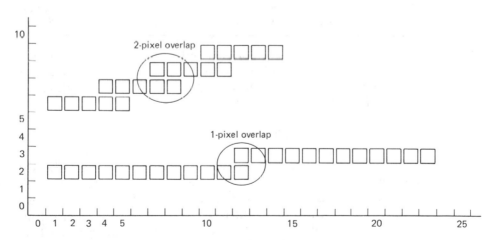

Figure 2-8   End-to-end overlap of generated lines results in a smoother line appearance when displayed.

Consistency of Line Intensity. A diagonal line with one y value for every x value will have the same number of pixels as a horizontal line of the same x distance, but it will be physically longer. The diagonal line will appear dimmer than the horizontal line because they both emit the same total amount of light (assuming equal pixel intensity). Line-intensity consistency can be achieved by increasing the pixel intensity on diagonal lines as the function:

$$\text{pixel intensity} = \text{line length} / \text{number of pixels}$$

If a bilevel (black or white only) display is used, there can be no pixel intensity control, so other methods must be used. End-to-end overlap can be used to add pixels to a line to intensify it.

DIFFERENTIAL LINE GENERATION METHODS

Multiplication in the line generation loop is the main problem with the line-equation system of line generation. Multiplication can be reduced to addition using "differential" methods. The equation for a straight line indicates that for a given change in x there is a proportional change in y. The line was generated by plugging equally spaced x values (1, 2, 3 . . .) into the equation. The y values could have been obtained by adding the proportional change of y to the previous point's y value. In mathematical terms:

$$\text{new point } x = \text{old point } x + 1$$
$$\text{new point } y = \text{old point } y + \Delta y$$

where Δy = change in y corresponding to change in x of 1 for given line.

The value of Δy is the slope of the line (y/x). To successfully implement this sort of differential method, one must keep track of the x and y values as running sums. Rounding or truncating is required for the y points before they are plotted, but the running sum should not be modified.

This differential method is certainly faster than the line equation generator, but there are still a few drawbacks. The running sum for y must be fractional (causing us to fall back on fractional or floating-point arithmetic again), and division still must be performed in the overhead.

Digital Differential Analyzer

The only way around the fractional arithmetic problem is to deal with the line's slope as a proportion of two integers, and two integers that meet the proportion requirement are Δx and Δy values of the line itself. Division can be avoided by dealing with these two values directly as well, because no slope calculation (y/x) need be performed. This leads us to the most common and efficient way to generate a line: the digital differential analyzer (DDA). This method combines the elements of differential line generation with operations that computers can perform quickly and easily (positive–negative determination, addition, subtraction, and branching).

The operation of the DDA is somewhat hard to visualize, but its mathematical basis is sound. A tracking sum (commonly called *line error*) keeps track of the amount of x and y movement that occurs as the line is being generated. As long as the sum is negative, the next point to be plotted is to the right of the current point (see Fig. 2-9). Every time an x move to the right is made, Δy is added to the error. When the error finally goes positive, enough horizontal movement has occurred so the next point to be plotted is above the previous one (a $+y$ movement). Whenever a $+y$ movement is made, Δx is subtracted from the error sum. The sum therefore oscillates about the zero value, with $+\Delta y$ making it go positive and $-\Delta x$ making it go negative. Because Δx and Δy are proportional to the line's slope, a proportional amount of time is spent on either side of zero—and thus a proper amount of horizontal and vertical moves are made, thereby generating a perfect line. When the line is finished, the error sum is zero (an error of zero also occurs whenever a plotted point falls exactly on the desired line).

Quadrantal DDA. There are a few variations that the DDA can take. Figure 2-9 illustrates the quadrantal DDA. There are four sets of movement rules that describe line generation, one set for each of the four quadrants.

Quadrant 1 rules:
  1. If error is negative, move $+x$ and add Δy to error.
  2. If error is positive, move $+y$ and subtract Δx from error.

Quadrant 2 rules:
  1. If error is negative, move $-x$ and add Δy to error.
  2. If error is positive, move $+y$ and add Δx to error.

Quadrant 3 rules:
  1. If error is negative, move $-x$ and subtract Δy from error.
  2. If error is positive, move $-y$ and add Δx to error.

Quadrant 4 rules:
  1. If error is negative, move $+x$ and subtract Δy from error.
  2. If error is positive, move $-y$ and subtract Δx from error.

The program implementation of these rules can be simplified by writing line generators for quadrants 1 and 4 and "folding" any quadrant-2 or -3 lines into quadrants 4 or 1, respectively, by swapping the start and end points.

The 4-quadrant DDA has perfect line reversal (if quadrants 2 and 3 are folded into 4 and 1) and 1-point end-to-end overlap. Line fit and symmetry are dependent on the initial value of the error parameter.

Lines generated with a DDA start a stairstep pattern from the start point and settle down to a repetitive pattern. The pattern may be three moves vertical, one move horizontal, three vertical, one horizontal, etc. Or it may be alternating—three horizontal, one vertical, two horizontal, one vertical, three horizontal, and so on, repeating the sequence. There may also be small perturbations along the line that disrupt the pattern as the line tracks the desired diagonal as well as it can.

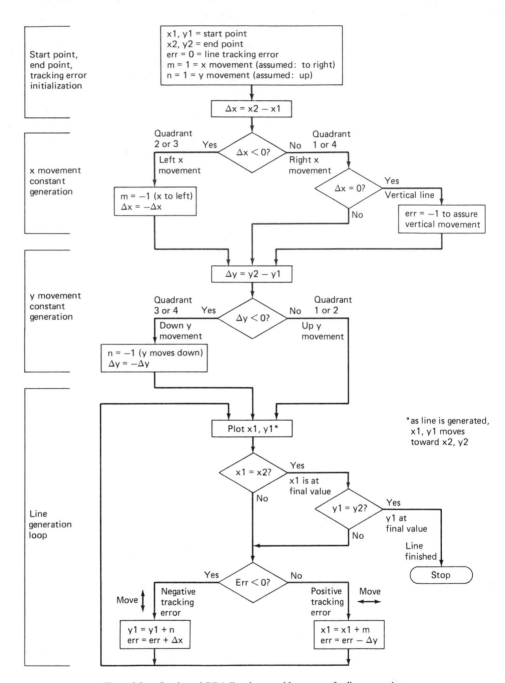

Figure 2-9 Quadrantal DDA line drawer with program for line generation.

24

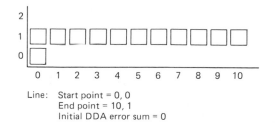

Line: Start point = 0, 0
      End point = 10, 1
      Initial DDA error sum = 0

	x	y	Error sum	Move	Add to err
Iteration 1	0	0	0	UP	$-\Delta x$
2	0	1	−10	RT	$+\Delta y$
3	1	1	−9	RT	$+\Delta y$
4	2	1	−8	RT	$+\Delta y$
5	3	1	−7	RT	$+\Delta y$
6	4	1	−6	RT	$+\Delta y$
7	5	1	−5	RT	$+\Delta y$
8	6	1	−4	RT	$+\Delta y$
9	7	1	−3	RT	$+\Delta y$
10	8	1	−2	RT	$+\Delta y$
11	9	1	−1	RT	$+\Delta y$
12	10	1	0	RT	done

(a)

Line: Start point = 0, 0
      End point = 10, 1
      Initial DDA error sum* = −5 = $(-\Delta x/2)$

	x	y	Error sum	Move	Add to err
Iteration 1	0	0	−5	RT	$+\Delta y$
2	1	0	−4	RT	$+\Delta y$
3	2	0	−3	RT	$+\Delta y$
4	3	0	−2	RT	$+\Delta y$
5	4	0	−1	RT	$+\Delta y$
6	5	0	0	UP	$-\Delta x$
7	5	1	−10	RT	$+\Delta y$
8	6	1	−9	RT	$+\Delta y$
9	7	1	−8	RT	$+\Delta y$
10	8	1	−7	RT	$+\Delta y$
11	9	1	−6	RT	$+\Delta y$
12	10	1	−5	RT	done

*Initial error sum is: IF $\Delta x > \Delta y$ THEN ERRSUM = $-\Delta x/2$
                        IF $\Delta x \leqslant \Delta y$ THEN ERRSUM = $\Delta y/2$

(b)

Figure 2-10   Quadrantal DDA line generator startup error: default zero error sum (a), and half long Δ error sum (b).

If a line is started with an error of zero, the pattern starts at the beginning of the stairstep. This can be undesirable, as Fig. 2-10 emphasizes. The line can be started in the middle of a stairstep by initializing ERROR to negative half the Δx value for long x steps, and half the Δy value for tall y steps. Notice in Fig. 2-10 that the x step breaks evenly in half and the error at the end of the line generation is no longer zero. The final error will always be the initial error in other than "zero" initialization cases.

Octantal DDA.   The line-equation system generated a line with no end-to-end overlap. Only one y value was assigned to an x value. The 4-quadrant DDA generated lines with 1-point overlap because movements were made in the vertical as well as the horizontal and diagonal direction during generation. The DDA can be modified to generate lines with no overlap by performing diagonal instead of vertical moves. The result is the *octantal* or 8-octant DDA (see Fig. 2-11), for which eight sets of rules are required. For lines from 0° to 45°, the slope is less than 1. In this case, many horizontal moves in sequence can occur; but no more than one vertical move can be made without having to perform another horizontal move. Two or more sequential vertical moves would constitute a line greater than 45°, which is out of the specified range. Because only one vertical move can be made at a time, it follows that every vertical move will be followed by a horizontal move. A vertical plus a horizontal move constitutes a diagonal move. By not plotting the point after the vertical movement is made, a single y value for every x value will result. In other words, a horizontal move is made between all pixels, and a diagonal move is made occasionally.

25

```
Entry Initialization
1 SCREEN 1,0
2 CLS

Start/End Point Submittal
3 LOCATE 1,1
4 INPUT "submit x,y - x2,y2";STARTX,STARTY,ENDX,ENDY

Eight Octant Line Generation
10 REM 8-octant line generator
20 REM on entry, startx, starty, endx, endy valid.
100 IF ENDX >= STARTX THEN GOTO 110
102 REM mirror quadrants 2,3 to 1,4
103 TEMP=STARTX
104 STARTX=ENDX
105 ENDX=TEMP
106 TEMP=STARTY
107 STARTY=ENDY
108 ENDY=TEMP
110 DX=ENDX-STARTX
120 DY=ENDY-STARTY
130 IF DY<0 GOTO 200
140 IF DY>DX GOTO 500
150 GOTO 400
200 IF -DY>DX GOTO 600
210 GOTO 700

400 REM Octant 1 Line Generation
410 CNTDWN=DX+1
412 ERRR=-DX/2
414 PSET (STARTX,STARTY)
416 CNTDWN=CNTDWN-1
418 IF CNTDWN<0 THEN GOTO 800
420 STARTX=STARTX+1
422 ERRR=ERRR+DY
424 IF ERRR<0 THEN GOTO 414
426 STARTY=STARTY+1
428 ERRR=ERRR-DX
430 GOTO 414

500 REM Octant 2 Line Generation
510 CNTDWN=DY+1
512 ERRR=-DY/2
514 PSET (STARTX,STARTY)
516 CNTDWN=CNTDWN-1
518 IF CNTDWN<0 THEN GOTO 800
520 STARTY=STARTY+1
522 ERRR=ERRR+DX
524 IF ERRR<0 THEN GOTO 514
526 STARTX=STARTX+1
528 ERRR=ERRR-DY
530 GOTO 514

600 REM Octant 7 Line Generation
610 CNTDWN=-DY+1
612 ERRR=DY/2
614 PSET (STARTX,STARTY)
616 CNTDWN=CNTDWN-1
618 IF CNTDWN<0 THEN GOTO 800
620 STARTY=STARTY-1
622 ERRR=ERRR+DX
624 IF ERRR<0 THEN GOTO 614
626 STARTX=STARTX+1
```

Figure 2-11   Octantal DDA line drawer program. (continued)

```
628 ERRR=ERRR+DY
630 GOTO 614
700 REM Octant 8 Line Generation
710 CNTDWN=DX+1
712 ERRR=-DX/2
714 PSET (STARTX,STARTY)
716 CNTDWN=CNTDWN-1
718 IF CNTDWN<0 THEN GOTO 800
720 STARTX=STARTX+1
722 ERRR=ERRR-DY
724 IF ERRR<0 THEN GOTO 714
726 STARTY=STARTY-1
728 ERRR=ERRR-DX
730 GOTO 714
800 REM Line Finished
810 GOTO 3
```

Figure 2-11 (continued)

For lines between 45° and 90°, the rules dictate that a vertical move be made between pixels and that a diagonal move be made occasionally. Again, folding can be used to reduce the 8 segments into 4. The left octants (3, 4, 5, and 6) fold into the right octants (7, 8, 1, and 2, respectively) by swapping the start and end points of lines.

Octant 1 rules:
  1. If error is negative, move $+x$ and add Δy to error.
  2. If error is positive, move $+x$ $+y$ diagonal and add $\Delta y - \Delta x$ to error.

Octant 2 rules:
  1. If error is negative, move $+x$ $+y$ diagonal and add $\Delta y - \Delta x$ to error.
  2. If error is positive, move $+y$ and subtract Δx from error.

Octant 3–6 rules:
  1. Swap start and end points of line and draw as octant 1, 2, 7, or 8

Octant 7 rules:
  1. If error is negative, move $+x$ $-y$ diagonal and subtract $(\Delta y + \Delta x)$ from error.
  2. If error is positive, move $-y$ and subtract Δx from error.

Octant 8 rules:
  1. If error is negative, move $+x$ and subtract Δy from error.
  2. If error is positive, move $+x$ $-y$ diagonal and subtract $(\Delta y + \Delta x)$ from error.

The 8-octant DDA has a few advantages over the 4-quadrant DDA. Lines are generated faster because less points are plotted, and $\Delta y + \Delta x$ (which should be calculated in the line generation overhead) is added to the error in one step instead of two. Lines also have a finer, more precise appearance. They have closer-to-ideal intensity characteristics for diagonal lines than the 4-quadrant-generated line. A 45° line, for example, should have 1.414 times as many pixels as a horizontal line of the same x distance for consistent line intensity. The 4-quadrant line has 41% too many pixels, and the 8-octant line has 29% too few.

The initial error value is calculated as it would be for the 4-quadrant DDA. Half the Δx or half the $-\Delta y$ value is used to start line generation in the middle of a horizontal or vertical step.

The COUNT value (number of pixels to plot) is $\Delta x + \Delta y + 1$ for the 4-quadrant DDA and $\Delta x + 1$ (for octants 1 and 8) or $\Delta y + 1$ (octants 2 and 7) for the 8-octant DDA.

Modular Overflow Vector Generator

There are a few other line generation methods that are rarely used; but they are sometimes appropriate in hardware vector generator implementations. The modular overflow vector generator (MOVG) falls into this category. Two sums (an x sum and a y sum) are used. The line's Δx and Δy values are added continuously and simultaneously to the x sum and y sum. The sums are stored in limited-size registers and are allowed to cyclically overflow. Whenever an x sum overflow occurs, an x move is made and a point is plotted. An overflow of the y sum initiates a y move and point plot. A correct line is generated because the Δx and Δy values are proportional to line slope.

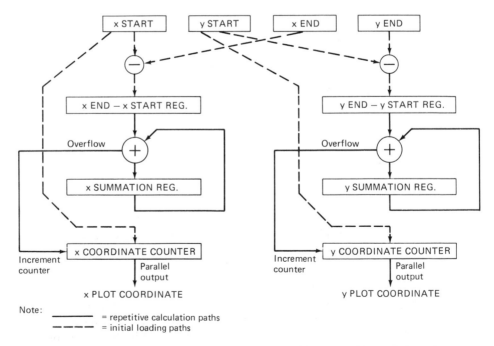

Figure 2-12 Modular overflow vector generator hardware, showing repetitive calculation paths and initial loading paths.

MOVGs are easy to implement on a hardware level because decisions don't have to be made as they do with the DDA. Simple additions are performed on each and every iteration. Microcomputers have conditional branching capabilities, so a MOVG is a waste of a microcomputer's resources. Also, MOVG-generated lines leave something to be desired appearance-wise. Either sum can overflow on any given iteration, so pure horizontal or vertical moves are usually made. At certain points, however, both sums may overflow simultaneously, causing a diagonal move. Some line segments will have one pixel end-to-end overlap while other segments will have none. Figure 2-12 depicts a MOVG line generator.

Midpoint Subdivider

While not particularly practical as a line generator, the midpoint subdivider does have its applications. This is an inefficient line generation method that involves complicated "bookkeeping" operations, which explains why it is so rarely used. Its principle, however, is a viable one and is often used in *clipping* operations (discussed subsequently).

The midpoint subdivider concept is based on the premise that a computer can quickly and easily generate an average of two numbers, as in the operation $(a + b)/2$. Division is time-expensive on a microcomputer, but division by 2 is a special case. An arithmetic right shift performs a divide-by-2, which takes about the same time as an addition operation. This operation, however, is rarely available in most high-level languages (although some languages such as "C" have it). The midpoint subdivider takes the average values of the start and end points of x and y:

$$\text{midpoint } x = (\text{start } x + \text{ end } x)/2$$
$$\text{midpoint } y = (\text{start } y + \text{ end } y)/2$$

The resulting position lies exactly between the start and end points. Points between the midpoint and start point and between the midpoint and end point can then be generated. And this is where the bookkeeping begins. You must keep track of all the points you have generated so you can continue generating new midpoints. Line generation ends when the line has reached a desired density. Line generation speed and density can be traded off with one another, which may be useful in some cases. End-to-end overlap is similar to the MOVG and can vary along the line, but it is dependent on line density. No overlap will result in a very sparse line (a line with few midpoints).

ANALOG LINE GENERATION METHODS

All of the line generation methods described so far have used some sort of summation (except midpoint subdivision), and there is no reason why an analog equivalent such as an operational integrator can't perform the same task (see Fig. 2-13). Integrators work with voltages and currents, and these can be used to

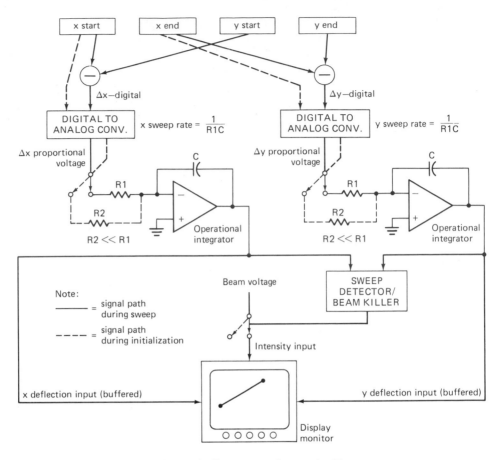

Figure 2-13   Analog line generator using operational integrator.

directly drive display systems. Separate integrators for the *x* and *y* screen directions can cause an electron beam to sweep smoothly across a display screen, thereby drawing an almost perfect diagonal line with no annoying stairstep effect.

Analog line generators bring all the advantages and disadvantages of analog hardware to a display system. They are fast, inexpensive, and can generate smooth lines, but they can drift with temperature changes, go out of calibration, and have trouble repetitively drawing exactly the same line at the same screen location. They are only suited to vector-oriented displays (displays that draw individual vectors on a screen) and are not usable with raster-scan equipment (the most common displays).

ABSOLUTE VS. RELATIVE LINE GRAPHICS

A 10-pixel horizontal line on one part of the screen is very similar to a 10-pixel horizontal line somewhere else on the screen, but their representations in an absolute screen coordinate system can be vastly different. The similarity between

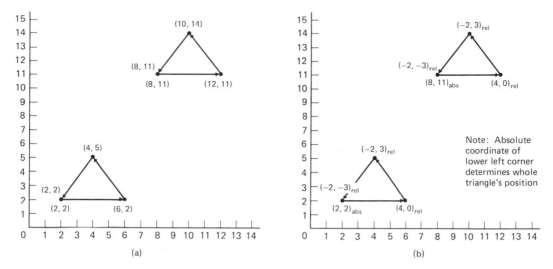

Figure 2-14   A simple triangle specified in absolute (a) and relative (b) coordinates.

these two lines is that their end points are at $x = 10$ and $y = 0$ relative to their start points (assuming their start points represent 0,0). Relative graphics uses this similarity as a basis for defining points, lines, and other graphic elements. Points are referred to with relation to previously defined points.

Relative graphics' main advantage is the ability to define objects on the screen and move them to other screen locations with a minimum amount of line definition change. The absolute and relative triangles in Fig. 2-14 illustrate this. The relocated triangle's shape and size are identical to the original, but the absolute definition is totally different. The relative definitions, however, are very similar with only the reference point changed to reflect the new location.

The starting point of the relative sequence of points and lines determines where on the screen a relative object will be placed (see Fig. 2-14).

Display devices rarely accept points in relative coordinates, so software must be used to convert relative to absolute coordinates. This software must continuously keep track of the current absolute position of generation as relative points and lines are specified. The absolute reference point can be used to initialize two tracking variables (abs$x$ or $|x|$, and abs$y$ or $|y|$, for example).

Initialize tracking variables:

$$|x| = \text{absolute reference } X$$
$$|y| = \text{absolute reference } Y$$

Relative-to-absolute conversion:

$$\text{screen } x = |x|$$
$$\text{screen } y = |y|$$

Tracking variable updating:

$$|x|' = |x| + \text{relative } x \text{ of next point}$$
$$|y|' = |y| + \text{relative } y \text{ of next point}$$

where $|x|'$ and $|y|'$ are the updated tracking variables.

COORDINATE SYSTEM BOUNDARY CONFLICTS

The screen's absolute coordinate system is limited by its definition. With absolute coordinates it is unlikely that an out-of-range screen point would be specified (unless some arithmetic error was made), but with relative coordinates the problem can arise. Figure 2-15 shows the triangle of Fig. 2-14, but in this case the absolute reference point is such that portions of the triangle fall beyond the area of the screen. These boundary conflicts must be handled in some reasonable manner.

Boundary conflicts can be handled on a mathematical basis using software, or they can be dealt with on a mathematical or electronic level by the display system. Some display systems allow you to submit out-of-range coordinates for lines and points even though they may only display those portions that fall within the screen perimeter. This operation is called *scissoring*. Without scissoring, boundary conflicts must be handled on a mathematical basis by the display hardware or software.

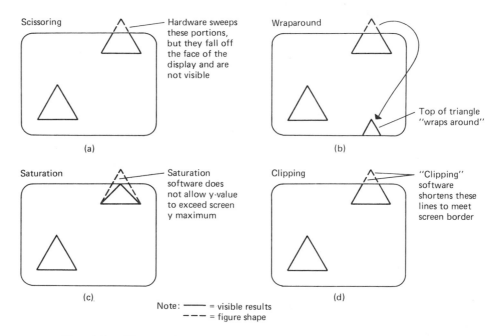

Figure 2-15 When a portion of an image extends beyond the screen border, there are several methods of resolving the conflict: scissoring (a), wraparound (b), saturation (c), and clipping (d).

WRAPAROUND

Wraparound is the crudest way of handling boundary conflicts. With this method, lines that run off the right of the screen continue at the left of the screen, and lines off the top resume on the bottom of the screen (see Fig. 2-15). This method is particularly easy to implement because most display systems have resolutions that are powers of 2. For these displays, you simply send the out-of-range value to the display system, which chops off the extra bits that have appeared as a result of the out-of-range condition. With displays that are not based on the power-of-2 concept, the results are less predictable—lines that fall off the right of the screen could resume at some odd location (perhaps near the center of the screen).

Relying on "automatic wraparound" is fine if your display device can perform it without any problems, but some displays (notably those that share screen display memory with a microcomputer system) can cause system problems if you exceed coordinate bounds. In memory-mapped systems a border conflict could cause the display unit to start writing outside of its display memory space and inside the processor's memory space, thereby destroying the program and crashing the system.

If automatic wraparound is not available, it can be performed manually. To do this, a "masking" operation is required. Assuming the display is a power of 2 in the x and y dimensions—or that it can at least accept coordinates within a power-of-2 range without drastic results—the binary value of the largest coordinate can be logically *and*ed with the point's x and y values. For a device with a resolution of 512×256 pixels:

$$\text{screen } x = \text{point } x \text{ } and \text{ } 511$$
$$\text{screen } y = \text{point } y \text{ } and \text{ } 255$$

But this method only works if you can easily perform a logical *and* operation, which rules out its use with some high-level languages.

SATURATION METHODS

Saturation methods can be used for other than power-of-2 displays as well as for power-of-2 displays. The idea is to "saturate" any value that is larger than the maximum coordinate so that it becomes that maximum value. This sort of statement can be used:

```
IF (SCRNX > 255) THEN SCRNX = 255
IF (SCRNY > 255) THEN SCRNY = 255
```

Compared with the wraparound method, the saturation technique has the disadvantages of increased execution time and less dramatic error results. A line that slightly exceeds the screen boundaries will certainly be noticeable if it pops up on the other side of the screen; but if it is saturated, the line looks fairly normal and the error may go unnoticed.

CLIPPING

The wraparound and saturation boundary-conflict resolving methods assume that objects that go outside of the defined coordinate system are in error and that the viewer will subsequently correct the error by modifying the generation program. These conditions need not be considered errors in all cases. The triangle in Fig. 2-15 is a good example. If the top of the triangle falls slightly off the screen, it would still be advantageous if we could see the remaining portion of it correctly with the out-of-range top clipped off. This sort of operation can be performed mathematically through the clipping process.

Two methods are commonly used for clipping: line equation solving, and midpoint subdivision. Line equation clipping makes use of the fact that partially offscreen lines cross the screen's border. The border and the line each have an equation. By solving the two equations for the line intersection point, the point where the line left the screen can be determined and used instead of the old off-screen end point. This operation is often called *pushing* because it "pushes" the end point to the screen boundary.

Pushing

Figure 2-16 shows the mathematics of the push operation. The equation is easily solved because the border is a vertical line with a simple equation. The pushed point's x value is, in fact, available immediately: it is the border's x value. A simple computer program that performs the simultaneous equation solution is derived from the equations in Fig. 2-16. Notice that the PUSHY and BIAS solutions can be reduced to a single equation, thus eliminating one multiply operation.

This sort of push program is the basis for all 2- and 3-dimensional line clipping, and in the simple case of Fig. 2-16 it is sufficient for clipping; but there are many possible ways in which a line can fall outside a border. Figure 2-17 shows some possible line clipping situations.

There are cases where both end points are out of bounds but the resulting line is in bounds. In the case of line B, the right side and then the left side would be pushed to its appropriate boundary. Line A is a line that may require two push operations. If the right point is pushed to the right border (notice that screen borders extend to infinity in all directions), the line is still partially off the screen and a second push to the top border is required.

Whole lines will occasionally end up off the screen (such as line C in Fig. 2-17). It is obvious at a glance that this line is totally off the screen, but the start and end points are numerically similar to line D's, which does intersect the screen. The computer must use mathematical rules to make the determination. In line C's case, a downward push to the top border makes it obvious that the line is off the screen.

After the push, both start and end points are to the left of the screen, so the whole line must be to the left of the screen. This is the kind of rule a computer can use to solve the problem.

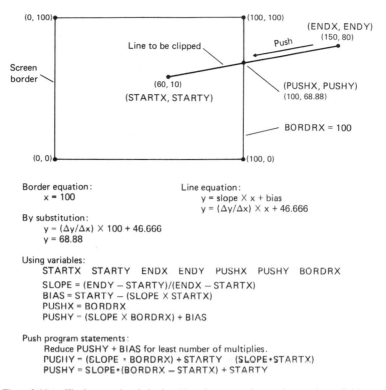

Border equation:
    x = 100

Line equation:
    y = slope × x + bias
    y = (Δy/Δx) × x + 46.666

By substitution:
    y = (Δy/Δx) × 100 + 46.666
    y = 68.88

Using variables:
    STARTX STARTY ENDX ENDY PUSHX PUSHY BORDRX

    SLOPE = (ENDY − STARTY)/(ENDX − STARTX)
    BIAS = STARTY − (SLOPE × STARTX)
    PUSHX = BORDRX
    PUSHY = (SLOPE × BORDRX) + BIAS

Push program statements:
    Reduce PUSHY + BIAS for least number of multiplies.
    PUSHY = (SLOPE × BORDRX) + STARTY − (SLOPE×STARTX)
    PUSHY = SLOPE×(BORDRX − STARTX) + STARTY

Figure 2-16   Clipping equation derivation. Note that one push operation requires a division, three multiplications, two additions, and two subtractions.

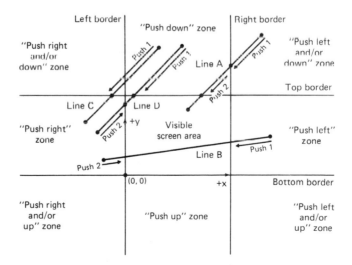

Figure 2-17   Four line clipping situations, in which the line to be generated falls off the visible screen area (center of drawing).

Two-Step Clipping

A generalized method and corresponding program to handle all of these cases is required for generalized clipping, and over the years many have been developed. Most of these methods break the clipping task into two steps: a decision-making step that determines if the line is off the screen and which action (what kind of push to which boundary) to perform if it is, and the actual push. The two-step process is executed repeatedly for multiple-push cases until the line is either totally within screen bounds or is off the screen entirely.

A generalized clipping approach is the Cohen-Sutherland method, in which the classic clipping algorithm is broken into two steps as outlined above. The "coder" determines whether a line is on, partially on, or off the screen, and the "pusher" clips it to the proper length. Figure 2-18 outlines the process.

First, a four-element code is generated for the start and end points of the line. These elements can take the value of true or false (1 or 0):

element 1 = point is to the right of screen
element 2 = point is to left of screen
element 3 = point is above screen
element 4 = point is below screen

If a point is on the screen, all elements will be set to false (0). Each of the nine areas defined by the screen boundaries (Fig. 2-18) has a unique 4-element code. Push decisions are made by comparing the codes of the start and end points on an element-by-element basis.

If two corresponding elements are true, the line is off the screen. If element 1, for instance, is a logic 1 for both points, both points are to the right of the screen and the whole line is therefore to the right of the screen. Similarly, if all elements of both lines are at logic 0, both points are on the screen and therefore the whole line is on the screen. If neither of these conditions is met, the line could be on or off the screen, and clipping is necessary to find out.

If one point is off the screen, it will be pushed. If both points are off the screen, either one may be pushed first. The code value of the point determines push direction. An element that is set to 1 is acted on. If element 1 is a logic 1, the point is to the right of the screen and a left push is in order. If more than one element is set to 1, either may be acted on.

The push is performed with push equations similar to those derived in Fig. 2-16. One routine for each push direction is used.

After the push, the pushed point again is coded. The on-or-off screen decision is made, and pushing is performed if the line's status is still ambiguous. This code–push process is repeated, for both points if necessary, until the line is clipped to the screen boundaries or is rejected as being off the screen.

Code elements can be handled as an array or as separate variables in a high-level language, but the most efficient way to handle them is as individual bits in one variable word or byte. The four least significant bits of a byte can represent elements 1, 2, 3, and 4. Using false = 0 and true = 1, if the byte equals zero (all

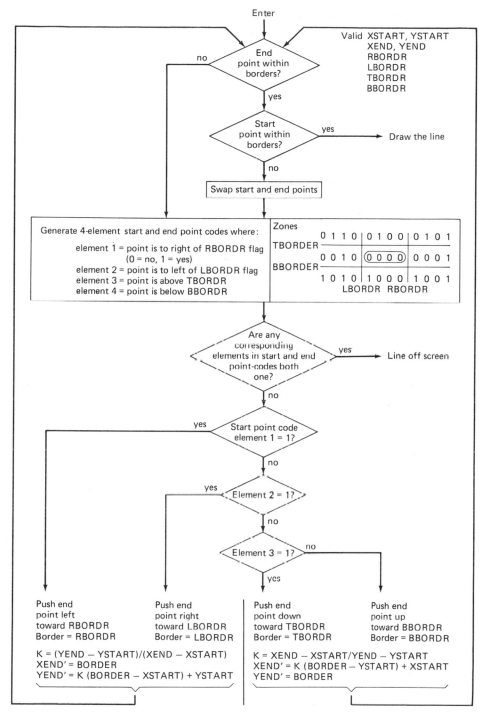

Figure 2-18 The Cohen-Sutherland two-step clipping algorithm, in which a four-element code indicates the position of a point (above, below, left of screen, and below screen).

elements = 0, the point is on the screen. If both points are off the screen, the two bytes' codes can be logically *and*ed. If the result is not zero, two corresponding elements contained a 1, indicating that the line is off the screen. If the result is zero and both codes are not at logic 0, the line must be pushed. Figure 2-18 outlines this byte-code method.

You can only take full advantage of the byte code if the language you are working with has logical *and*ing capabilities. This makes it well suited to nearly any assembly language but few high-level languages.

RESTRICTED-AREA DISPLAYS

A whole display screen is often used to display a single image, but in some cases it is desirable to use only certain portions of the display screen. A typical such instance might be one in which better display clarity is sought away from the screen's edges. Or a design constraint might impose a limitation, such as the need to restrict the graphics area to half the screen so text can appear on the other half.

VIEWPORTS

The area of the screen used for graphic displays is called a viewport, several examples of which appear in Fig. 2-19. Viewports can be square, rectangular, circular, or any other desired shape; and more than one viewport may be placed on one screen.

Points, lines, and other elements must be limited to fall within the desired viewport, and clipping can be used to perform this task. Clipping to a given rectangular boundary has been described and can be used on all rectangular viewports. Circular or other odd-shaped viewports require circular or other appropriate clipping methods which are not as simple and straightforward.

WINDOWS

The screen coordinate system is somewhat limiting. Elements defined in absolute screen coordinates are fixed in one screen location; they cannot easily be enlarged or reduced in size, and they maintain but one orientation (they cannot be rotated). A more versatile approach is to define lines and other elements in a separate coordinate system of your choosing—a working coordinate system. This coordinate system need not be display-dependent and can have very large dimensions ($65,536 \times 65,536$ x and y range, for example).

Using mathematical transforms, any portion of the image can be mapped into the viewport on the display screen. The area of the image that is being viewed is the window. Figure 2-20 shows the progression from working coordinates (also called *data base* coordinates or *world* coordinates), through a window, into a viewport. Notice that the window need not align itself horizontally or vertically with the image.

Translation, rotation, and scaling are used to map image coordinates to screen coordinates. These are display control operations.

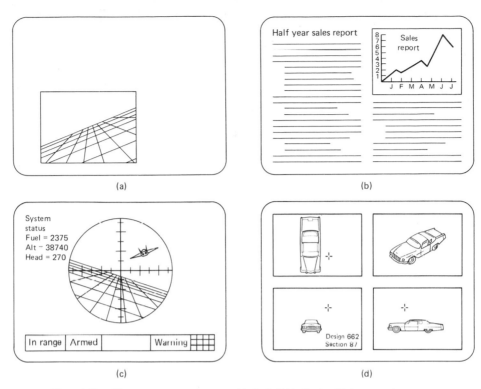

(a)

(b)

(c)

(d)

Figure 2-19 Viewports are screen areas set aside for individually viewable images such as an aircraft approach inset (a), a business graph (b) accompanied by text, a central-screen simulation with surrounding status displays (c), and a multiple-inset display showing various views of an element (d) used in CAD systems.

Figure 2-20 Use of a working coordinate system allows users to window in on a portion of a display and reproduce it as a viewport through rotation, translation, and scaling.

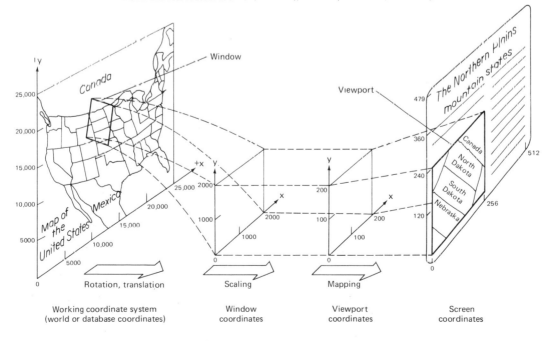

DISPLAY CONTROL

The concept of separate image, window, viewport, and screen coordinates raises many display manipulation possibilities. The displayed image may be controlled manually or by the program sequence. An image may be panned, scrolled, rotated, or scaled; or it may be selectively erased and redrawn to create a variety of effects, including animation.

PANNING

Panning is the process of smoothly translating a window over an image in image coordinates. This allows you to selectively view portions of the image and lets you easily find them using a scanning motion. Panning is usually performed by the user moving a control (joystick, table pen, or trackball) and having the window slide along the image in the direction of control movement.

Panning can be performed on the software level by drawing the image, erasing it, adding a new translation factor (based on the panning control setting) and regenerating the image. This method is feasible only if the image can be erased and redrawn quickly enough to produce a smooth scrolling action. Redraw rate is

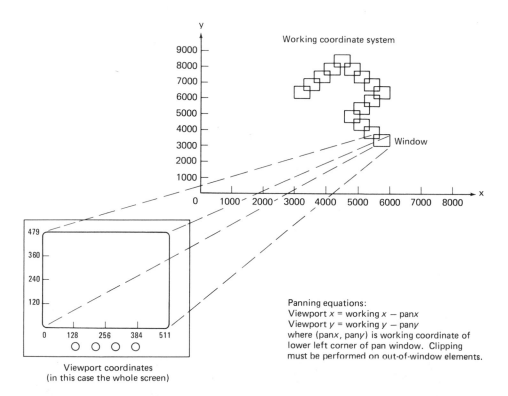

Panning equations:
Viewport x = working x — pan$x$
Viewport y = working y — pan$y$
where (pan$x$, pan$y$) is working coordinate of lower left corner of pan window. Clipping must be performed on out-of-window elements.

Figure 2-21 A panning capability gives users a means of selectively viewing any area of the working coordinate system by smoothly moving across it with the viewing window.

a function of processor power, the display's maximum redraw rate, display erase time and discontinuity (some displays emit large flashes of light during erase, which would tend to break up the smooth panning action), image complexity, and the number of transforms being performed. Figure 2-21 illustrates panning and the associated mathematics to perform it in software. Offset values are added to the window x and y reference values, resulting in a new translation. The image is then regenerated.

ROAMING

Some manufacturers have overcome panning image regeneration problems by building special display devices. Such displays typically have a large addressable image area, but only a small portion of it can be displayed at once on the screen. A 1024 $\times$ 1024 resolution area may be drawn on, for example, but only a 512 $\times$ 512 portion is displayed on the screen at any one time. On the display generator level, it is a simple matter to "window in" on any portion of the 1024 $\times$ 1024 image area. This only requires a new horizontal and vertical scan start address to change the window location (especially on raster-scan displays). A complex image can be panned at the screen refresh rate (usually 30–60 frames per second). This sort of hardware panning is called *roaming*.

SCROLLING

Because roaming is memory-intensive, it is an expensive solution to the panning problem. Raster-scan bit maps require vast amounts of memory (1 million bits for a 1000 $\times$ 1000 display) to provide even modestly sized roamable areas. Scrolling can bring many of roaming's advantages to a display without requiring as much memory.

Scrolling displays always have their full image area on the screen, but the point where $x = 0$ and $y = 0$ can be moved about. As pixels overflow due to this movement, they "wrap around" to the other side of the screen (top to bottom and left to right). This would seem to be of limited use; as images move off one side of the screen during the scroll panning, they appear again on the opposite side. But there is a clever software solution to this problem.

The edge of the picture can be updated for each scrolling step. It takes a lot less processor time to update an edge of a picture than the whole screen. An auxiliary memory or large-capacity (and low-cost) Winchester disk can store a larger image area than can be panned through using scrolling plus software edge-updating. Figure 2-22 illustrates scrolling.

Scrolling has its limitations. It is difficult to enter discrete lines and points into an image area that physically resides on a disk, because the disk would have to be accessed for every line entered. Scrolling is more appropriate for applications requiring alphanumerics that can be generated easily at the edges of the display or for large shaded areas that can be generated on the visible screen portion and then scrolled off onto a disk.

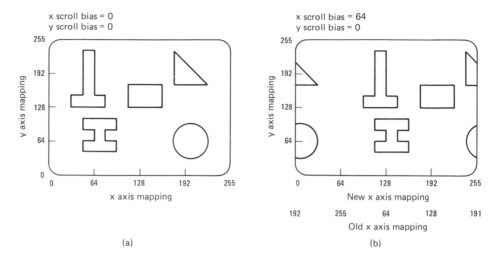

Figure 2-22   Scrolling is achieved by biasing axis points. The screen image with no bias (a) appears to have moved to the right with a horizontal bias (b). Note that with the shown bias of 64, an element mapped at an *x* location of 128 appears with an *x* location of 128 + 64, or 192.

ROTATION

It is often desirable to view items in different orientations, and rotation allows you to do this on a display screen. As with panning, hardware or software methods can perform rotation.

Display systems usually contain a CRT that "draws" an image by shooting an electron beam at the phosphor-coated face of the tube (the screen). The electron beam is deflected and swept across the screen by controlled magnetic or electrostatic fields. Some displays have the ability to control these fields in a way that "twists" the path of the electron beam to cause an image to be generated in a new orientation on the screen. Smooth rotations of a whole image can be made quickly and easily if such a facility is available, but this is an analog rotation method and has all the disadvantages of analog hardware.

Hardware rotation methods are also somewhat limited in the rotations they can perform. A whole screen can be easily rotated about its center, but off-center axes of rotation and independent-element rotation are beyond this method's capabilities.

For truly versatile rotations, mathematical methods must be used. Rotation equations are derived from trigonometry, as shown in Fig. 2-23. The equations reduce to two simple formulas that can be used to generate a rotated *x, y* point (ROTX, ROTY) from an initial *x, y* point and a rotation angle.

$$\text{ROTX} = x \times \cos(\text{angle}) - y \times \sin(\text{angle})$$
$$\text{ROTY} = x \times \sin(\text{angle}) + y \times \cos(\text{angle})$$

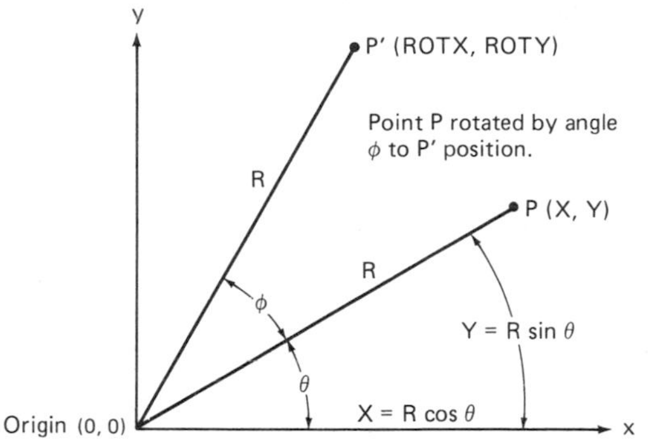

Figure 2-23 Rotation derivations in equation and matrix forms.

The figure shows:

P′ (ROTX, ROTY)

Point P rotated by angle ϕ to P′ position.

P (X, Y)

$Y = R \sin \theta$

$X = R \cos \theta$

Origin (0, 0)

$$ROTY = R \sin (\theta + \phi)$$
$$= R (\sin \theta \cos \phi + \cos \theta \sin \phi)$$
$$= (R \sin \theta) \cos \phi + (R \cos \theta) \sin \phi$$
$$= Y \cos \phi + X \sin \phi$$

$$ROTX = R \cos (\theta + \phi)$$
$$= R (\cos \theta \cos \phi - \sin \theta \sin \phi)$$
$$= (R \cos \theta) \cos \phi - (R \sin \theta) \sin \phi$$
$$= X \cos \phi - Y \sin \phi$$

Note: $X = R \cos \theta$ $Y = R \sin \theta$ where R = radius length of rotation arc

Rotation equations:

$$ROTX = X \times \cos (ANGLE) - Y \times \sin (ANGLE)$$
$$ROTY = X \times \sin (ANGLE) + Y \times \cos (ANGLE)$$

Rotation equations in matrix form:

$$[ROTX, ROTY] = [X, Y] \begin{bmatrix} \cos (ANGLE) & \sin (ANGLE) \\ -\sin (ANGLE) & \cos (ANGLE) \end{bmatrix}$$

$$ROTX \text{ solution} = [ROTX, -] = [X, Y] \begin{bmatrix} \cos (ANGLE) & \text{———} \\ -\sin (ANGLE) & \text{———} \end{bmatrix}$$

$$ROTY \text{ solution} = [-, ROTY] = [X, Y] \begin{bmatrix} \text{———} & \sin (ANGLE) \\ \text{———} & \cos (ANGLE) \end{bmatrix}$$

Figure 2-23 also shows the matrix form of the rotation equations. A matrix representation isn't really necessary for such a simple set of equations, because two simple program statements such as those shown can perform the operation; but as translations and rotations are combined and 3-dimensional rotations are introduced, matrix representation becomes the easiest way to handle things. The matrix is shown to give an example of where the matrix elements come from in equations; it is not so obvious when equations get very complicated.

The rotation equations rotate a point about the 0, 0 point. If a point is to be rotated about another point (rotation axis), the point must be translated so the rotation axis becomes 0, 0, rotated about the axis, then "untranslated" back to the old coordinate system reference frame. The following equations perform rotation about the axis Ax, Ay.

$$ROTX = Ax + [(x - Ax) \times \cos(angle) - (y - Ay) \times \sin(angle)]$$
$$ROTY = Ay + [(x - Ax) \times \sin(angle) + (y - Ay) \times \cos(angle)]$$

The above equations rotate single points, but because larger elements consist of many points—and their outlines can be defined by start and end points of lines—whole elements can be rotated by applying these equations. Lines remain lines before and after rotation, so a line may be rotated by rotating its start and end points around a common rotation point.

43

SCALING AND ZOOM

It is often necessary to look more closely at an image to see detail, or to shrink an image to get more of the total scene on the display screen. Sometimes one display dimension (the *x* screen direction, for instance) must be stretched or compressed to compensate for nonsquareness. Scaling is used to perform such operations.

Multiplication can be used to make display elements larger. Multiplying all the displayed points in an image by a scale factor of greater than 1.0 will cause them to move radially away from the origin (point 0,0). Multiplying only one coordinate dimension (such as all *x* values on all the points) will cause expansion in only one direction (stretching). The statement for scaling may be expressed:

$$BIGX = X \times SCALEX$$
$$BIGY = Y \times SCALEY$$

where SCALEX and SCALEY are the *x* and *y* dimension scale factors.

Scale factors of greater than 1 *increase* an element's size, and scale factors of less than 1 *decrease* it.

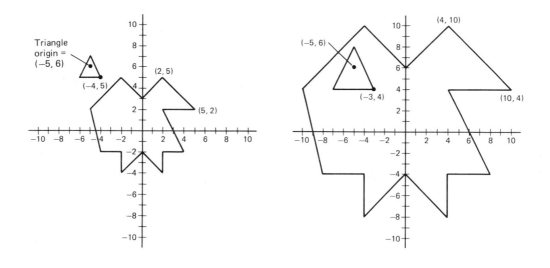

Scaling equations used to expand odd shaped polygon about (0, 0):
 BIGX = X × 2 = X × SCALEX
 BIGY = Y × 2 = Y × SCALEY
where scale factors = SCALEX = SCALEY = 2

(a)

Scaling equations used to expand triangle about its own origin (−5, 6)
 BIGX = CNTRX + ((X − CNTRX) × SCALEX) = −5 + ((X + 5) × 2)
 BIGY = CNTRY + ((Y − CNTRY) × SCALEY) = 6 + ((Y − 6) × 2)
where center of scaling = (CNTRX, CNTRY) = (−5, 6)
and scale factors = SCALEX = SCALEY = 2

(b)

Figure 2-24   Even a complex image shape can be scaled for reduction or expansion about its own origin. Here a closed polygon adjacent to a triangle (a) is expanded to include the triangle (b).

Expansion or compression will occur about the 0,0 point. Translation methods are used to scale elements about other points (an element's center, for example). The following equation statements are used to scale an element about its center (CNTRX, CNTRY):

$$BIGX = CNTRX + [(X - CNTRX) \times SCALEX]$$
$$BIGY = CNTRY + [(Y - CNTRY) \times SCALEY]$$

Figure 2-24 illustrates scaling. When scaling is performed to all elements in the x and y screen directions about the screen's center, the result is "zoom."

Many raster-scan display systems have hardware zoom capability. This feature is similar to roaming in that display counters are manipulated to display different portions of the image based on user control. You are allowed to home in and examine any portion of the display area. Hardware zoom is normally limited to powers of 2. Zoom factors of 2, 4, 8, etc. are easily obtained by manipulating the low-order bits of the display generator counters (see display generation hardware section). Complex mathematics using multiplication is necessary for other than power-of-2 zoom factors (at least on a binary-oriented system), and additional hardware is required.

DISPLAY ERASE AND FILL

A display screen must be erased before an image is generated and between images (frames) in an animation sequence. A screen may be erased to its natural "off" color (typically black or green), or it may be filled to a solid color such as white if elements of a different color will be generated. Lines and characters are often drawn in black on a white background to give the effect of pen on paper. This is achieved through the *white erase*, or "fill."

A screen can be erased by individually setting all the display pixels to the desired color, but this takes a long time (65,536 pixels would need plotting for a 256×256 display). Most display systems have internal hardware that performs screen erases and fills with a single command. This reduces screen erase time and makes a display system more desirable for animation.

Word-Oriented Erase and Fill

Display systems without erase hardware often have a mode that allows multiple pixels to be written simultaneously. Raster-scan display systems often allow 8–16 pixels (representing a byte or word in the display's memory) to be written in one step, thus reducing erase time by a factor of 8 to 16. This erase method is more versatile than hardware screen erase, because it allows selected screen areas as well as the whole screen to be erased. The byte/word-oriented erase method is often faster than hardware screen erase; this is because most raster-scan erase hardware cleans the screen by turning bytes and words off as they are displayed, which takes a total time of 16.6 ms at a standard 60 Hz frame rate. A processor can usually fill a display's memory in less than half this time, especially if a relatively low-resolution display (256×256, for example) is used.

Selective Element Erase

A single display element can be moved around on an otherwise blank display screen by erasing the screen and regenerating the element in its new location. When other objects are on the screen, however, they too must be regenerated, whether they moved or not. This takes time and can slow an animation sequence to an unacceptably slow speed. This problem can be avoided by selectively erasing the moving element instead of the whole screen and redrawing it in its new location.

A screen area containing the object to be erased may be erased or filled if selective-area erase is available on the display hardware. But this causes problems if other display elements happen to fall totally or partially within the erase area. A more restrictive erase is needed.

Individual lines can be erased by drawing them in the background's color: a white line on a black background is effectively erased when a black line is drawn over the white line. This erase method restricts erasures to the point where any element can be selectively erased as long as the lines it consists of never intersect those of another element. Upon erasure, all intersections are erased and other elements may be left with gaps in their lines, as Fig. 2-25 illustrates. A single animated line that sweeps across a screen would erase everything in its path using this method, which is certainly unacceptable.

Special techniques are needed to make selective erasure usable in every situation. General selective erase methods are based on line intersection restoration. Lines are erased by redrawing them in the background color, but all intersections with not-to-be-erased elements are restored to their original condition. Screen point readback typically is used to perform the restoration.

The most obvious way of selectively erasing over line intersections is to record all line intersections that were made when the selectively erasable element was generated. This can be done by reading each screen pixel before plotting over it. If the pixel is not a background color, its location and color are added to a list of "overwritten pixels." When the lines are erased, each intersection point is restored to its original color by regenerating all pixels in the overwritten pixel list.

It may seem tempting to perform this operation as a two-step process of erasing all lines and then regenerating intersections; but a problem arises with this concept. If two lines of the erasable element cross one another, an entry in the overwritten pixel list will be made. Upon selective erasure, a point will be regenerated where none existed before. This can be avoided by associating intersection points in the overwritten pixel list with the lines that caused the overwriting.

Line erasure should be performed in the inverse order of line generation, and intersection regeneration should immediately follow every line erasure. Any falsely generated intersections will eventually be erased by the erasure of the other selectively erasable line that caused the false intersection problem.

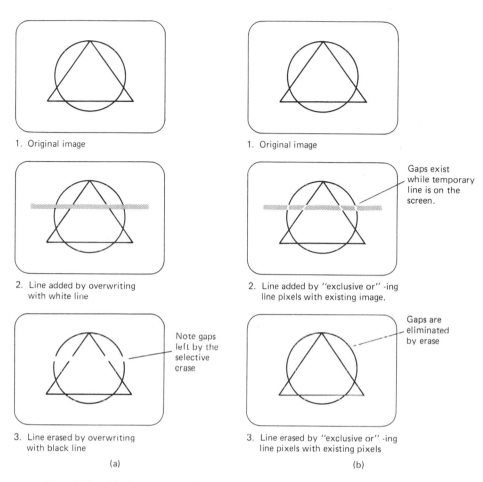

1. Original image

1. Original image

2. Line added by overwriting with white line

Gaps exist while temporary line is on the screen.

2. Line added by "exclusive or" -ing line pixels with existing image.

3. Line erased by overwriting with black line

Note gaps left by the selective erase

Gaps are eliminated by erase

3. Line erased by "exclusive or" -ing line pixels with existing pixels

(a)

(b)

Figure 2-25   Selective erasure can be achieved as in (a) by overwriting a line in the color of the background, but this leaves gaps at line intersections. Exclusive-*or* erasure (b) restores the line intersections.

Toggling and Exclusive-*Or* Erase

The overwriting method requires extensive bookkeeping to keep track of all the intersections. This uses up processor time and memory. Fortunately, there is an effective way of actually storing all this bookkeeping information on the display screen itself. This method results in mild degradation of the quality of the display element if intersections do occur, but it has the advantage of leaving intersected elements intact after selective erasure. The exclusive-*or* element generation method is primarily applicable to bilevel displays but can be used for multicolor displays with proper planning and some ingenuity. Again, screen readback is required. The following paragraph outlines this method.

An element can be generated by plotting pixels in an unconventional way. Instead of simply setting a pixel to logic 1 to turn it on, a 1 can be exclusive-ored with the current screen pixel and the resulting bit plotted. In other words, if the pixel is off, then turn it on; if the pixel is already on, then turn it off. On a blank screen the generated image would look identical to an element generated in the conventional way, but when intersections with other lines occur, the intersection of the lines is turned off (usually black) as shown in Fig. 2-25.

A line generated in this manner can be erased by drawing it again in the same way. All the turned-on pixels will be turned off (thus erasing the white line on the black background), while all the turned-off intersections will be turned on again, thus restoring any erased intersections. The image degradation is caused by gaps at the line intersections (which is essentially the bookkeeping information that is stored on the screen). This degradation is nearly unnoticeable if only a small number of intersections occur, but images with many intersections can cause problems.

Line erasure order is not important with exclusive-or line erasures, because the intersection is simply being toggled on and off and not restored permanently to a screen color. It also makes no difference how many lines of an element go through an intersection point. The intersection will be toggled between black and white as each line intersects it. The point will be toggled from black to white an equal number of times as each line is erased, so the intersection will eventually be correctly restored.

CURSORS

Unless you generate drawings by manually computing all the numerical values of the start and end points (perhaps using graph paper and a pencil) and feeding pure numbers to the computer, you will eventually require a means of physically indicating specific locations on the screen in much the same manner as you would use a handheld pointer to indicate to a classroom audience a specific position on a wall map or a blackboard. Pointers generated on a computer screen are known as *cursors*. A few of the more common types are illustrated in Fig. 2-26.

A principal characteristic of a cursor is selective erasability, to enable it to be moved about on the screen. And so selective erase methods must be used to generate cursors. Cursors are usually under user control, their mobility controlled by moving a pen on a digitizer tablet, rotating a track ball, moving a "mouse," or specifying movement with keyboard commands. Figure 2-26 illustrates a cursor "tracking loop" that takes commands from an input device such as a digitizer tablet and controls a cursor.

The location of the cursor on the screen can be sampled at any time by simply looking at the current CURSX and CURSY values. Cursor data can be used in a number of ways. The cursor can be allowed to track until the user gets it to the desired position, at which time a button (a keyboard key or a switch on the digitizer tablet, perhaps) can be pushed to indicate that this is the desired point. Control software can then plot the point or set it aside to be used as the start point of a line.

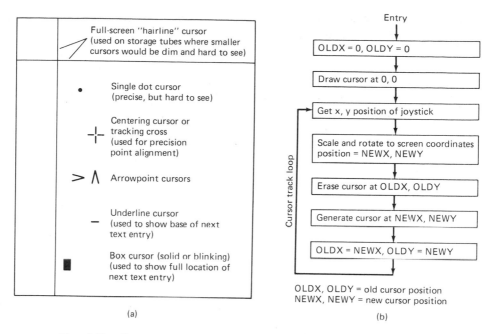

Figure 2-26 Cursors may take the form of intersected horizontal and vertical lines, a single illuminated point, a tracking cross, arrowheads, an underline, or a character-sized illuminated or blinking box, as in (a). A cursor tracking loop (b) accepts commands and controls cursor position.

Cursor data can also be used in a continuous mode. The cursor's *x* and *y* position can be taken on every sampling and used to perform point plotting or line drawing. A digitizer tablet or other input device can be made to act as a "pencil" using this technique. As the user moves the cursor, a line is left behind its position on the display screen. This is known as the *stream* mode of cursor tracking.

GRAPHICS DATA COMPRESSION

A high-resolution display screen can contain an enormous amount of data. A 1000×1000 screen with 16 colors per pixel (4 bits per pixel) contains the equivalent of half a million 8-bit bytes of computer memory. The amount of data and processing needed to generate a dense picture on such a display is also large. Data compression techniques are often used to reduce memory and program size on both the hardware and software levels.

CELL-ORGANIZED DISPLAYS

Display generator memory requirements can be reduced in two ways: Display resolution can be decreased, resulting in a smaller dot matrix; or the resolution can remain the same if the number of combinations of pixels that can be turned on simultaneously is limited.

The second method can be accomplished by breaking the overall matrix into smaller submatrixes, or *cells*. Figure 2-27 illustrates a 256 × 256 display that is broken into 32 × 32 pixel cells. The whole display consists of 8 × 8 of these cells.

Memory savings will result from limiting the combinations of on and off pixels within a cell. This is done by choosing desired patterns of pixels and assigning codes to them. As long as the code size is less than the number of pixels in the submatrix, memory savings will result. Images can be drawn by piecing the predefined pixel patterns together.

A game display specifically designed to provide images of chessmen is a good candidate for cell organization (see Fig. 2-27). A high-resolution display is desirable to portray detailed pieces, but a 256 × 256 general-purpose graphic display is hardly justifiable for an inexpensive game. Only 12 graphic elements are ever going to be drawn on the display (6 types of pieces with distinctions for black and white), so 12 cell types can be defined. A 256 × 256 display can be broken into 8 × 8 cell positions (representing a chessboard) with cells of 32 × 32 pixels. Twelve chesspiece configurations can be designed in the 32 × 32 pixel cells, and a 4-bit code can represent which of the 12 men are to be displayed for each of the 8 × 8 cell locations on the screen. Four additional codes are possible in the 4-bit code (4 bits = 16 combinations), so a solid white and solid black cell (to represent board positions) as well as two other cell designs can be defined.

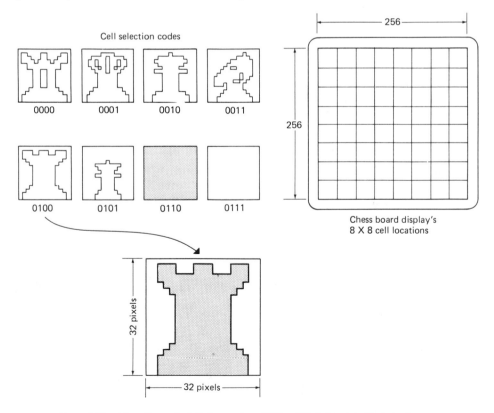

Figure 2-27   The cell-organized display consists of 256 × 256 pixels—eight 32-pixel cells across and eight 32-pixel cells vertically. The 32 × 32 cells accommodate images of chess pieces.

Character Set (80-FF) Quick Reference

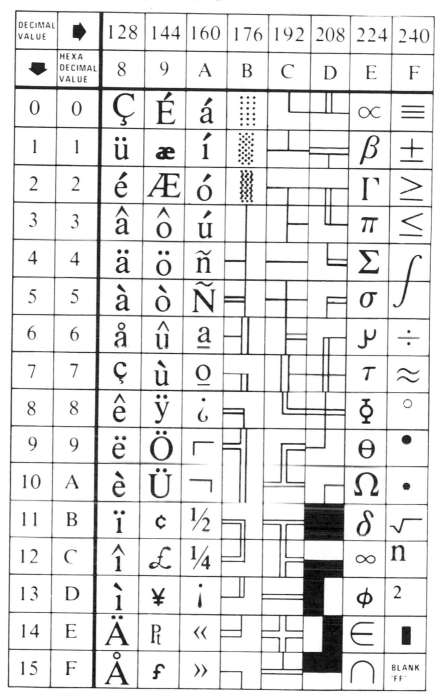

DECIMAL VALUE ➡		128	144	160	176	192	208	224	240
⬇	HEXA DECIMAL VALUE	8	9	A	B	C	D	E	F
0	0	Ç	É	á	▦	╚	╨	∝	≡
1	1	ü	æ	í	▨	╔	╤	β	±
2	2	é	Æ	ó	▩	╩	╥	Γ	≥
3	3	â	ô	ú	│	╦	╙	π	≤
4	4	ä	ö	ñ	┤	╠	╘	Σ	∫
5	5	à	ò	Ñ	╡	═	╒	σ	∫
6	6	å	û	ª	╢	╬	╓	µ	÷
7	7	ç	ù	º	╖	╧	╫	τ	≈
8	8	ê	ÿ	¿	╕	╨	╪	Φ	°
9	9	ë	Ö	⌐	╣	╤	┘	θ	•
10	A	è	Ü	¬	║	╩	┌	Ω	·
11	B	ï	¢	½	╗	╦	█	δ	√
12	C	î	£	¼	╝	╠	▄	∞	n
13	D	ì	¥	¡	╜	═	▌	φ	2
14	E	Ä	₧	«	╛	╬	▐	∈	▪
15	F	Å	ƒ	»	┐	╧	▀	∩	BLANK 'FF'

Figure 2-28   Some character sets offer a broad number of commonly used patterns (such as those under decimal values 176, 192, and 208 here), but combining them effectively requires complex software; cell organized displays are memory-expensive. (Courtesy IBM Corp., Boca Raton, Florida.)

The overall result of this display is a high-resolution chessboard with detailed chessmen but very little memory. A 4-bit code replaces a 32 × 32 (1024 bits total) cell, resulting in a 256:1 memory savings. The 256 × 256 cell-organized display requires 256 bits versus 65,536 (256 × 256) bits for the general purpose of display.

Reduced versatility is the price paid for cell-organized displays. The chessboard display is fine for chess games, but there is no way to draw even such a simple graphic element as a line on it. Some cell-organized displays attempt to trade memory size for versatility by offering commonly used pattern combinations such as horizontal and vertical lines through the cell, 45° diagonals, and right angles for corner generation (see Fig. 2-28). These displays can generate impressive high-resolution graphics for special applications, but putting together the proper cell combinations requires complex software or programming tricks.

Cell organization is performed on the display hardware level. The programmer is told which cells are available and how to specify and place them on the display screen. In some display generators, the cell definition library is "writable," allowing you to define your own cells for a limited set of codes. Usually 128 or 256 codes (the number of codes in a 7- or 8-bit byte) are available.

The most common form of cell-organized display assigns character definition to 7-bit codes. These cells are typically arranged 80 across and 24 down. These displays are the basis for alphanumeric computer terminals, and the codes most frequently used correspond to ASCII, the standard alphanumeric code set for data communications.

CHAINED LINES

When two lines are drawn end-to-end, they share a common end point. Time and memory can be saved by specifying the set of two lines to the display device as a line string or chained lines. A start point, a continue point, and a second continue point describe two lines, as shown in Fig. 2-29. The same two lines require two start and two end points if specified with standard start and end points.

Large line strings can define more complex graphic elements, but as elements get more complex, the chance of painting yourself into a corner increases. A square with an 'X' in the middle (from corner to corner) is a good example. Five of the six required lines can be drawn as a line string, but the last line never starts where the fifth one ends.

The *ray* is a solution to this problem. A ray point specifies where a line will be drawn from the last continue point in a line string, but the continuation of the line string after the ray is from the old continue point instead of a new ray point. The square with the 'X' can be drawn by specifying the two diagonal lines as rays as the outer square is drawn with a line string.

Chained lines and relative graphics are a useful combination. Each continue point is specified with relation to the previous point. Complex elements generated using relative line strings can be translated on the display screen by moving the string's start point.

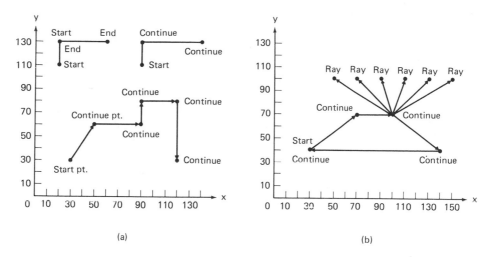

Figure 2-29 Complex graphics elements can be specified with chained lines. Where the image consists of an unbroken line it can be described with a *start* point, *continue* points, and an *end* point (a); images requiring elements that are not defined by a continuous line are constructed using rays (b).

A line string's definition can be reduced even further by assigning default line lengths and standardized angles of line drawing. Figure 2-30 illustrates a display made up of equal-length line segments limited to 8 directions of movement. Each line in the string is specified by a 4-bit code that indicates direction of movement or if the line is finished. The beginning of each line string must be fully specified in absolute coordinates.

Strings of equal-length line segments have speed as well as memory advantages. A minimal amount of data must be sent to a display if the display incorporates strings of equal-size lines, and complex DDA line generation techniques can be avoided if line directions are limited to horizontal, vertical, and 45° angles (all special-case lines that are easy to generate). Scaling and zooming are also faster. A new size for a default line changes the size of the entire image.

Relative angles can further increase an equal-size-line string's versatility. Instead of specifying absolute line angles, angles are specified with relation to the last line's angle. A 90° "right turn" would continue the line to the screen's right if the previous line was vertical, but the same 90° movement would cause a 45° downward line if the previous line were at a 45° upward angle. The absolute direction of the first line must be specified. A whole image can be rotated by starting the first line in the string in a new direction.

Equal-size-line strings are often used in map displays where jagged borders, ground features, and coastlines must be specified in a limited-size memory and generated quickly.

53

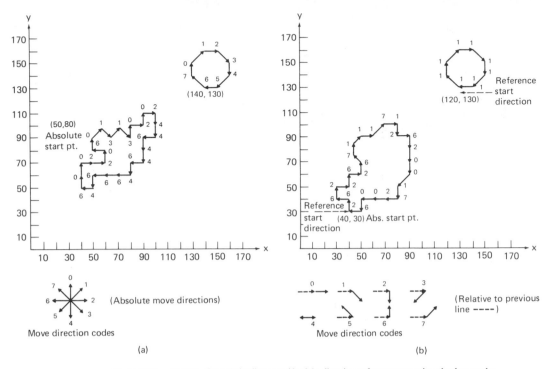

Figure 2-30 Strings of equal-size lines specify eight directions of movement using absolute angles (a) and relative angles (b). The use of relative angles increases the versatility of equal-size-line strings, since each line section is specified with respect to the previous line's angle.

SHAPE TABLES

When a display has the same graphic element repeated many times, a common definition of the element can reduce data storage requirements. A transistor in a circuit diagram, for instance, may be used a dozen times, and 12 different sets of lines that define the universal symbol for a transistor are wasteful. Shape tables can help solve the problem of multiple definitions.

A shape table is a list of graphic elements (usually chained lines in a default-length, relative format) that is stored in a computer's memory. The list defines a commonly used shape or symbol. When the symbol is used, the program driving the display refers to this table to generate an element on the screen. The program determines where the element will be placed (by selecting the absolute start point of the relative string), and the shape table defines the element.

Shape tables work in the display system's coordinate system and define fixed-size elements. The concept of shape tables can be expanded to let the computer program rotate and scale the element defined by the shape table. Versatile placement of an element is called *instancing*, and shape definitions that are manipulated by instancing are *subpictures*. Instancing and subpictures are detailed in the chapter on mathematics for advanced graphics.

54

ALPHANUMERICS GENERATION

Letters and numbers are often overlaid with graphics on a display screen. Special techniques are available to generate alphanumeric information on raster and vector screens.

CELL DEFINITION

The most common alphanumeric generation method uses "cell definitions." A character cell consists of a small submatrix of dots, as shown in Fig. 2-31. Cell size depends on desired character size, complexity, and detail. Common cell sizes are 5 × 7 and 7 × 10.

A *font*—a complete character set of a particular style—is stored in computer memory as a character table or "font library." Characters can be placed anywhere on the display screen as needed. Characters are stored as a series of bytes that represent the character cell. Five 8-bit words, for example, are used to store a 5 × 8 character cell.

Odd-sized cells don't always fit nicely into bytes or words, so the cell must be packed into a series of words. A 7 × 10 cell requires 70 bits for its definition, so nine 8-bit bytes could be used to define it (with two bits left over). Software is used to transfer the cells in the character table to the display screen.

Odd-sized cells that are packed into bytes require additional software to unpack them. In many cases, when an odd-sized cell is nearly able to fit nicely into bytes without resorting to packing, a bit in each character-definition byte can go unused to simplify software and result in an overall memory savings. A 9 × 7 cell may be defined by nine 8-bit bytes instead of eight packed 8-bit bytes.

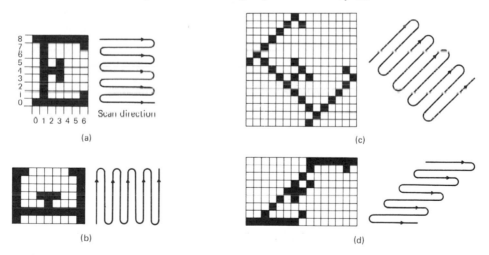

Figure 2-31 Character cell drawing methods: horizontally scanned 7 × 9 submatrix (a), vertically scanned 7 × 9 submatrix (b), horizontally defined cell scanned at a 45° angle (c), and a horizontally scanned cell with a bias of 1 pixel per row for slant (d).

Additional bits may be included in the character table to define special features about characters. A bit in a cell definition might indicate that the character should be shifted two rows downward to generate a character with a *descender*, or character portion that drops below the text baseline (such as lowercase g, q, and y).

Characters are positioned on the display screen by specifying the screen coordinates of one of the corners of the cell and the character to be generated (using a character code such as ASCII) to the character generator software. The software then proceeds to transfer the matrix defined in the character table to the screen at the specified location.

Cell definition characters have several restrictions:

1. They are limited to use in horizontal (or vertical if row and columns are swapped) text strings.
2. They are limited to power-of-2 sizes of the definition.
3. They are limited to use on raster devices (unless special hardware is used).

A few variations to standard horizontal and vertical character cell placement increase the versatility of dot-matrix character sets. Characters can be "scanned-out" diagonally at exact 45° angles with no loss of resolution. Adjacent rows may be skewed by one or more pixels to create slanted characters. Figure 2-31 shows a few of these variations.

VECTOR DEFINITION

Characters may also be generated using vector definitions. A character table again is used, but the table consists of definitions of the lines (instead of pixels) used to draw each character. Character definitions are usually in relative representation, and the size of character-table entries varies, based on how many lines are required to define a character. The variable-size entries can cause an indexing problem for the software that uses the tables, so an index to the table (Fig. 2-32) is often used.

Vector definitions take up more memory space than cell definitions, but versatility is increased. Characters are in a standard graphics form so they can be scaled, translated, and rotated as a graphic element. Slanting, mirroring, and stretching are also possible using *text placarding* (dealt with in the chapter on high-performance graphics).

The choice of cell or vector definition should be based on the application. In situations where many horizontal rows and columns of graphics are required, such as alphanumeric computer terminal applications, small-sized cell definitions are the best choice. Large cells are appropriate where many horizontal rows of finely defined characters of various fonts are used (typesetting, for instance). Vector definitions are superior in applications where text and dimensions are written at many angles and in many sizes as on an engineering drawing.

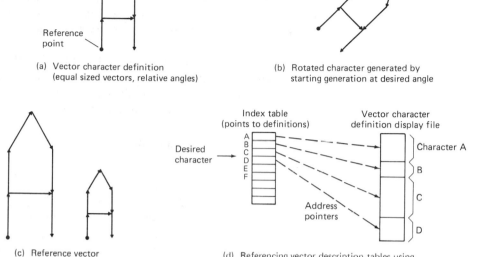

(a) Vector character definition
(equal sized vectors, relative angles)

(b) Rotated character generated by
starting generation at desired angle

Index table
(points to definitions)

Vector character
definition display file

Desired character

Address
pointers

Character A

B

C

D

(c) Reference vector
length changed

(d) Referencing vector description tables using
an evenly spaced index table.

Figure 2-32   Vector character generation: character definition with equal-size vectors and relative angles (a) simplifies character rotation (b) and permits scaling by changing reference vector length (c). Vector description tables are referenced using an evenly spaced index table (d).

PRACTICAL WAYS OF USING GRAPHICS

Point plotting, line generation, shape tables, and character tables can be used to draw just about anything you can imagine, but these individual methods and programs must be integrated into a form that can readily be used. On a bits-and-pieces basis, graphics generation is cumbersome and time consuming. Graphics calls, languages, and display files make graphics more usable.

GRAPHICS CALLS

Most engineering, scientific, and business programming is done in a high-level language such as BASIC, PASCAL, or FORTRAN. These languages all have subroutine calling capabilities, and one way to bring graphics capability to these high-level languages is to introduce a few subroutines that allow graphic functions to be performed by a simple subroutine call or *graphics call*. These subroutines can be—and often are—written by the user; or they can be incorporated into the language itself, in which case the language is usually given a name such as "Extended Graphics BASIC."

DISPLAY FILES

A screen image can be thought of as a "list" of individual graphic commands such as "draw a circle," "draw a line," and "plot a point." Lists of graphic commands can be built sequentially in a computer's memory and handled as a file that represents a picture.

A display file is similar to a computer program in that it is a list of instructions for a processor to perform. The display processor can take the form of a program that sequentially reads the display file and draws the graphics instructions, or it can be a hardware item that is designed specifically to read the display file out of computer memory (or local memory with a graphics display device). Figure 2-33 shows a display file and some representative commands.

Command name	Command (decimal)	Command (hex)	Arguments	Function
PNT	00	00	x lsb, x msb, y lsb, y msb, z lsb, z msb	Define 3D point
SPNT	01	01	x lsb, x msb, y lsb, y msb, z lsb, z msb	Define 3D start point
CPNT	02	02	x lsb, x msb, y lsb, y msb, z lsb, z msb	Define 3D continue point
RAY	03	03	x lsb, x msb, y lsb, y msb, z lsb, z msb	Define 3D ray
CLPSW	04	04	n where $n = 0$ clipper on, $n = 1$ clipper off	Clipper control switch
EYE	05	05	x lsb, x msb, y lsb, y msb, z lsb, z msb, P, B, H	Viewer's x, y, z, P, B, H
LIN2D	06	06	x_1, y_1, x_2, y_2	Draw 2D line from point 1 to 2
DISP	07	07	n where $n = 50$ set graphics $\quad n = 51$ set text $\quad n = 52$ clear mixed $\quad n = 53$ set mixed $\quad n = 54$ page 1 set $\quad n = 55$ page 2 set $\quad n = 56$ clear HI-RES $\quad n = 57$ set HI-RES	Display screen select
ERAS	08	08	n where $n = 00$ erase page 1 $\quad n = 01$ erase page 1 $\quad n = 02$ fill page 1 $\quad n = 03$ fill page 2	Erase screen
DRAW	09	09	n where $n = 00$ draw page 1 $\quad n = 01$ draw page 2	Write screen select
PNT2D	10	0A	x, y	Plot 2D point
JMP	11	0B	A lsb, A msb where A is the jump address	Interpretive jump
LMODE	12	0C	n where $n = 00$ normal line $n = 01$ exclusive or line	Set line drawing mode
ARRAY	13	0D	A lsb, A msb where A is output array start address	Turn on output array generation
SCRSZ	14	0E	Screen width, screen height, x center, y center	Screen size selection
FIELD	15	0F	axr lsb, axr msb, ayr lsb, ayr msb, azr lsb, azr msb	Field-of-view selection
INIT	16	10	none	Easy initialize
NOP	17	11	none	No operation

(a)

Hexidecimal memory address	Contents	Results
1000	08, 00	Erase the screen to black (00)
1002	06, 0, 0, 20, 0	Draw 2D line from 0, 0 to 20, 0
1007	06, 20, 0, 20, 30	Draw 2D line from 20, 0 to 20, 30
100C	06, 20, 30, 0, 30	Draw 2D line from 20, 30 to 0, 30
1011	06, 0, 30, 0, 0	Draw 2D line from 0, 30 to 0, 0

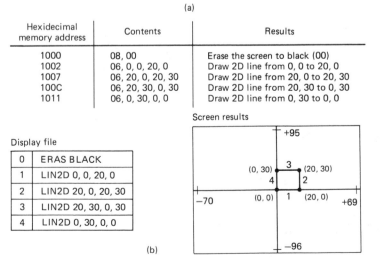

Display file

0	ERAS BLACK
1	LIN2D 0, 0, 20, 0
2	LIN2D 20, 0, 20, 30
3	LIN2D 20, 30, 0, 30
4	LIN2D 0, 30, 0, 0

(b)

Figure 2-33   3D animation reference card showing display file commands (a) and an example display file (b).

58

There are four categories of display file commands: element generation, display file flow control, display system control, and element and viewer location and manipulation. Element generation commands are similar to graphics calls that are often added to high-level languages, such as "plot a point" and "draw a line."

Display file flow-control commands direct the interpretation of the display file in the same way that control commands affect the execution of a computer program. Commands such as GO TO and CALL SUBFILE tell the display processor where to continue interpreting the display file. These commands make it possible to set up display programs that loop and call other smaller display files. All the nesting and recursion techniques that apply to a computer language apply here also.

Display system control commands are used to control the display hardware. Display resolution (on multimode displays), color, gray scale, DMA addresses, and other parameters must be initialized and occasionally changed on most display systems, and display file commands that can be placed in line in a display file are very convenient for performing the task.

Finally, viewer and element manipulation commands allow the user to change the location and orientation (translation, scaling, and rotation) of individual objects and to select the viewer's "eye location" and "viewing angle." These, when combined with flow-control commands, make animation possible.

Display file command formats are similar to assembly language program statements. Each command has an "opcode" followed by a string of "argument words." A PNT command, for example (see Fig. 2 33) plots a point at the location specified by its argument words X, Y, and Z. This command is interpreted by the display processor (a software program called A2-3D1 in this case) as the location of a point in space. The point is transformed and plotted accordingly on the display screen.

LANGUAGES FOR GRAPHICS

A common computer programming language such as BASIC, FORTRAN, or PASCAL with a few simple graphics calls often is not enough for a complex graphics application. And display files, like assembly language on a data processing computer, are adequate but cumbersome to work with. Graphics languages are appropriate in these applications. A graphics language is a programming language that is built around graphics. Graphics commands are compiled (or interpreted) directly rather than through the use of subroutine calls, and more extensive element manipulation and transformation capabilities are usually included.

Chapter 3

Working with
Display Generation
Hardware

The many available display generation devices range from raster-scan to such exotic devices as LCD (liquid-crystal display) arrays and plasma panels. The raster-scan display is the most widely used computer-driven type; but this is more the result of its ready availability than its superior performance or ease of use.

Raster-scan techniques have evolved in the television industry over decades, and innovative manufacturing methods, technological advances, and mass production techniques have brought these displays down to a price and availability level that no other display technology can match.

This chapter examines display generation hardware. Basic principles of the common as well as the not-so-common display devices are covered. Raster-scan techniques are stressed, since this is the most common and economical form of display technology; the advantages of other display types are outlined to help you compare capabilities and perhaps select another type of display device when necessary.

RASTER-SCAN CRT DISPLAYS

The CRT is the central component in most television receivers and computer terminals. This tube consists of an electron "gun" that shoots a fine beam of electrons at a phosphor-coated screen. Under this electron bombardment, the struck phosphor glows. Since each struck phosphor takes some time to decay after illumination, an entire picture can be "painted" on the screen by selectively energizing the electron beam as it scans the tube face. Lines, circles, or any other type of figure may be traced on the screen by moving the beam over the phosphors in straight or circular motions. Figure 3-1 illustrates these concepts.

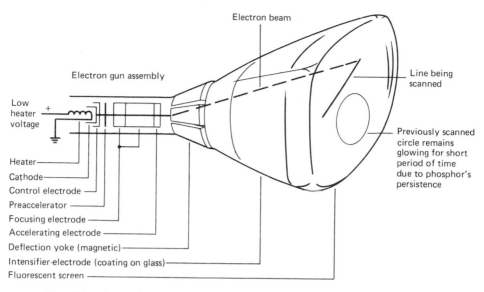

Figure 3-1 Construction of cathode-ray tube with magnetic deflection yoke. The electron beam traces images on the screen, which persist for a brief period before decay. Tubes with electrostatic deflection are similar in construction but have vertical and horizontal deflection plates to direct the beam.

The basic monochrome CRT is a simple device. There are, of course, tube variations, but the concept of sweeping an electron beam over a phosphor-coated screen remains the same.

Before effective image generation techniques can be employed under various conditions of color, intensity, and animation, it is important to understand a few characteristics of CRTs and their phosphor-coated "screens."

1. A phosphor glows when it is being struck by the CRT's electron beam. When the beam is removed, the glow gradually fades away. Glowing under beam excitation is a phosphor's *fluorescence*, and the glow after beam removal is its *phosphorescence*. Fluorescence and phosphorescence of a phosphor *are not necessarily the same color.*

2. The fadeout time is known as the phosphor's *persistence*. Some phosphors fade out at a slower rate than others.

3. The electron beam intensity determines the brilliance of the phosphor's glow. A low-intensity beam creates a dim glow; a high-intensity beam creates a bright glow. An electron beam of too high an intensity *will damage the phosphor* permanently, leaving an unusable spot on the screen in its place. A damaged phosphor is said to be "burned." A rapidly pulsating high-intensity electron beam that is above the phosphor's burn level will not damage the phosphor but will be averaged out to an intensity equal to a low-intensity beam.

4. Phosphor damage is a function of the average energy reaching the phosphor over a long time period. An *unchanging image of low intensity will burn the phosphor eventually,* just as a beam of excessive intensity will cause rapid phosphor damage.

We may draw a few conclusions from these properties. A single sweep of a line on the screen with an electron beam is not adequate to continuously display it, because the phosphor fades out shortly after the beam passes. This problem can be resolved by repeatedly resweeping the line at a very fast rate. If every glowing area on the line is rebombarded by the beam (refreshed) before the phosphor has time to fade, it will appear to glow continuously. The line will appear much dimmer than a glowing dot struck by a constant beam of identical intensity, because the beam energy is averaged over the whole line; but the dimming can be compensated for by increasing the beam intensity. The intensity will usually have to be above the phosphor's burn level to get a bright enough line. This presents no problem, however, because the beam intensity will be averaged out to a nonburn level *as long as the beam never stops moving.* Obviously, then, a stationary beam must be avoided at all costs.

Points, lines, and a wide variety of other graphic elements can be drawn in this way, but there are problems with this method. In the first place, beam intensity must constantly be modified to compensate for the number of lines being drawn on the screen, and in the second, the beam must never stop scanning.

Raster-scan displays sweep out an illuminated screen made up of a raster of lines as shown in Fig. 3-2. Lines are rapidly swept from left to right, and they are sequentially drawn below previous lines from the top to the bottom of the screen until the resulting raster fills the entire screen. The intensity of the beam is controlled as it sweeps from left to right. When the beam is in the high-intensity mode, the line is bright; in the low-intensity mode it is dark. An image can be generated by putting bright and dark spots on appropriate lines to result in an image. A diagonal line, for example, can be drawn by intensifying points of raster lines that are above and to the right of the previously intensified points.

A raster-scan display repeatedly scans the same set of raster lines (usually at a rate of 25 or 30 full screens per second). Images are changed by changing beam intensity at different screen locations. There is no danger of burning the phosphor on a raster-scan display because the beam never stops sweeping.

A standard raster-scan display that produces 525 lines per raster 30 times per second with a screen that is 12 in. wide results in the beam sweeping across the screen at approximately 10,000 miles per hour. Beam sweeping speeds of this velocity would normally require *electrostatic* (as opposed to *electromagnetic*) deflection if random lines are to be displayed, because a deflection coil (electromagnet) is an inductor and resists quick changes in its driving current and magnetic field. It is much easier to overcome the small capacitances associated with an electrostatic deflection system. But if identical lines are to be scanned at a constant frequency, a magnetic deflection system can be tuned and optimized for that frequency, thereby saving the cost and complexity of an electrostatic CRT.

The basics of raster scan are simple enough, but there are standardized terms that are often referred to in regard to CRTs and raster-scan systems, and a passing familiarity with the terminology is prerequisite to understanding performance or operation descriptions. For monochrome systems, the terms to know are listed below. (Color displays involve a number of additional terms, which are introduced later.)

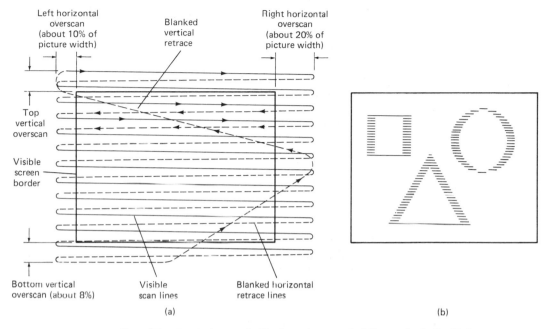

Figure 3-2 A raster is scanned with a beam that traces the full screen line by line (a); by selectively turning the beam on and off during the scanning process, images are generated on the screen (b).

Horizontal retrace is the action of the electron beam returning to the top of the screen after sweeping one scan line.

Retrace blanking is the shutting off of the electron beam as it returns to the left or top of the screen after a full screen sweep.

Overscan refers to the distance the electron beam sweeps off the edges of the display tube.

Linearity is a measure denoting the extent of equality in the spacing of raster lines and pixels on the screen.

Spot size refers to the size of the glowing phosphor dot struck by the electron beam on the CRT. (The spot size should be just large enough so the scan lines don't overlap, but not so small as to cause gaps between scan lines.)

Field describes the screen of the CRT from the left to right and top to bottom borders. A "scanned field" refers to filling a screen with raster lines (that may have gaps between them). One, two or more fields may be scanned to produce a full image.

INTERLACE

A complete CRT image consists of a sufficient number of raster lines to produce an apparent screen, but they may not all be displayed on one full sweep. With a 525-line screen, for example, one field of 262½ lines may be displayed in one field with gaps between the horizontal scan lines, and a second field with the remaining 262½ scan lines can then be scanned to fill in the gaps.

This interlacing technique has the dual advantage of increasing the overall screen display scan rate and reducing the noticeability of the scanning process. The scanning of the display from top to bottom appears as flickering when less than about 40 (depending on the phosphor's persistence) fields per second are scanned. Of course, the same 525 lines would be scanned onto the screen in the noninterlaced case, but the interlaced image usually appears more stable.

Standard transmitted television images (in the U.S.) are interlaced as just described. Thirty full pictures are scanned per second. Each picture consists of two full fields of 262½ lines per field.

Interlace Flicker

A 1-second string of 30 frames of 60 interlaced fields presents a solid, flicker-free display of conventional television images, but the same interlaced field rate can produce annoying flickering and shimmering effects when computer-generated displays are used. The image content is the cause.

Computer-generated graphic displays usually contain horizontal line segments that are only 1 pixel in height. Lines in wire-frame graphics, portions of characters in text displays, and dividing lines in business charts all contribute to the number of these line segments. Interlace techniques rely on the eye's ability to average two nearly identical lines above one another into one solid line. In normal television scenes, scan lines above one another differ very slightly, and the eye averages the alternately scanned fields so they appear as solid surfaces; but a single horizontal line with no matching line on the alternate field flashes at a 30 Hz rate.

Flicker Reduction

Interlace flicker can be reduced by using monitors with long-persistence phosphors or by strategically placing and carefully generating lines. In applications involving graphic displays, high-persistence phosphors are undesirable because they tend to make the picture appear smeared: the image from a prior scan persists during succeeding field scans.

Whenever more than two pixels appear next to one another in a horizontal line segment, matching pixels above or below them on the alternate field should be generated also. This reduces the annoying 30 Hz flicker. Diagonal lines of greater than 45° (from horizontal) can have individual pixels with no alternate field matching. The eye tends to average diagonally as well as vertically.

Interlace flicker does not affect color displays as much as it does monochrome. Flicker is still slightly noticeable, however, where horizontal line segments are severely unmatched.

RASTER GENERATION USING BIT MAPS

Creating an image on a raster-scan display may seem an impossible task. Portions of raster lines must be intensified, and you must somehow determine which portions of which scan lines to intensify. This is difficult enough for one simple

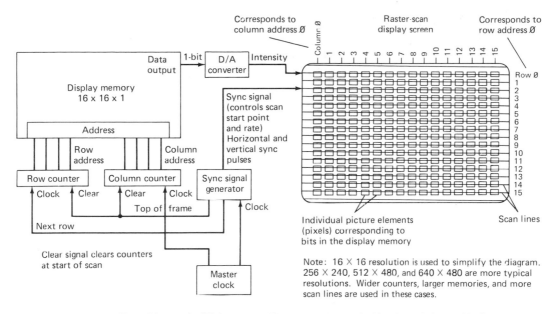

Figure 3-3 A simplified raster-scan bit map system. Note the 16 × 16 resolution used in the display screen, which is used here for ease of presentation; a typical resolution might be 256 × 240 pixels, or even 640 × 480.

diagonal line, let alone a whole picture with hundreds of lines, curves, and shaded regions. Fortunately, however, there are techniques that make the task quite simple indeed.

Television camera tubes perform the task by acting as raster-scan displays in reverse. The desired picture is focused on a target with a lens. An electron beam scans the image just as the CRT of an ordinary TV receiver is scanned. A detector detects the intensity of the electron beam (light or dark) as it bounces off the target and produces an intensity signal with each scan.

The image is then generated on the CRT. Digital raster-scan display generation systems control the beam intensity by reading a stream of 1s and 0s out of the display memory and turning the beam on or off accordingly. Bits are read out of memory at equal intervals, so a matrix of dots results. These dots can be turned on or off to generate the desired image. Figure 3-3 shows a raster-scan bit map.

DISPLAY MEMORY MAPPING

Plotting pixels on a raster-scan system amounts to turning display memory bits on and off under computer program control, and the key to easy use lies in the interface to the display memory. Some manufacturers simplify the task of writing to memory by building in hardware to do the display memory mapping for you. A bit on the screen is turned on by sending an *xy* coordinate to the display device. The hardware then determines which memory bit to turn on and does so.

In many cases, the display memory is integrated with processor memory and can in fact be used as a general-purpose memory if desired. In these cases, you must do the mapping yourself.

Manufacturers of display devices tend to take one of two approaches when assigning memory bytes to specific pixels on the screen: they either strive to make the interface easy to use and perhaps use a few extra parts (or gates if the display generator is a single-chip device) in the process, or they go for pure economy and parts savings and leave the mess for the graphics programmer to clean up.

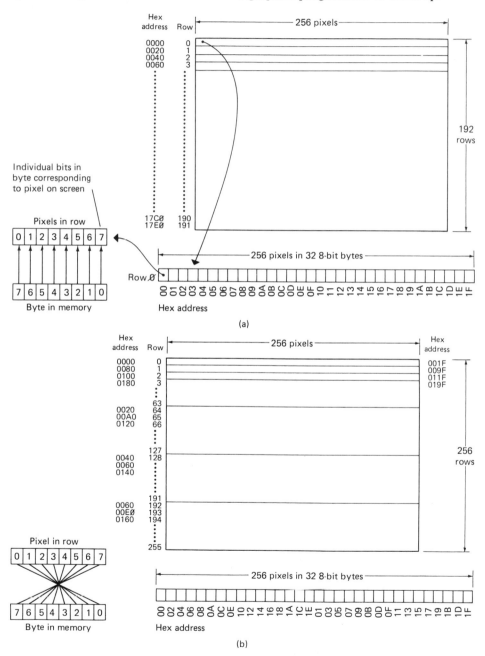

Figure 3-4   A linear arrangement (a) is easy to map to, but a nonlinear display (b) makes mapping a real chore.

Linear Method

Figure 3-4 shows two memory mapping methods. The *linear* method is quite easy for mapping a display coordinate system. Assume that coordinate 0,0 is in the upper left corner of the display. The *x* range is 256 pixels across and the *y* range is 192 pixels down. For any given *xy* coordinate, the byte associated with it can be found by the following method:

1. Take the *y* value and multiply it by 32 (because there are 32 bytes per line). This represents the number of 32-byte blocks of memory you must skip over to get to the line that the *y* value corresponds to.

2. Take the *x* value and divide it by 8 (because there are 8 bits per byte on the line). This shows how many bytes you must advance across the screen to get to the desired *x* location. Ignore any remainder.

3. The *byte address* is the result of steps 1 and 2.

4. The bit in the byte is the remainder of the division of *x* by 8. In mathematical terms:

$$\text{byte address} = y \times 32 + x/8$$
$$\text{bit in byte} = \text{remainder } (x/8)$$

where 0 is the bit corresponding to the leftmost pixel
on the byte.

The mapping equations involve time-expensive multiply and divide instructions, but in most cases the operations will be powers of 2. Arithmetic left and right shifts can replace the multiply and divide operations in assembly language implementations, resulting in vast performance improvements. Figure 3-5 illustrates the program required to map to this display device.

```
Integer
BASIC (that truncates)
or FORTRAN                          8080 assembly language
; on entry:                         ; on entry %D = x; %E = y
;   x = x coordinate, y = y coordinate   ; on exit %HL = memory address, %A = memory
; on exit:                          , byte bit number
;   addr = address, msk = memory byte
;   bit number where 7 = MSB, 0 = LSB        MVL    H, 0      ; y X 32
                                              MOV    L, E
        addr = y X 32 + x/8                   DAD    H
        msk = 7 − x − x/8 X 8                 DAD    H
                                              DAD    H
                                              DAD    H
                                              DAD    H
                                              MOV    A, D      ; x/8
                                              ANI    0F8H
                                              RAR
                                              RAR
                                              RAR
                                              ADD    L         ; +
                                              MOV    L, A
                                              JNC    . . OK
                                              INR    H
                                  . . OK      MOV    A, D      ; bit number
                                              ANI    07H
                                              CMA
                                              ADI    8
```

Figure 3-5   These program elements map to the linear display shown in Fig. 3-4 (a).

Nonlinear Method

The second display in Fig. 3-4 is not such a simple matter to map to. In cases such as this, you must analyze what is going on in the display memory addressing scheme.

Notice that when you reach the end of the first line, the next sequential data byte appears one fourth of the way down the screen in the *y* dimension. This would seem to indicate that one of the low-order bits in the screen coordinate address has been mixed into one of the high-order memory addressing bits. A number of bits may be "scrambled" in this way, and the best way to sort it all out is to use a chart that shows bit alignments of graphics memory to coordinate address space (a *Martin diagram*).

Figure 3-6 illustrates the Martin diagram process. Getting the proper diagram is a trial-and-error process. You must check to see if it acts as the screen addressing does, and modify it appropriately until it is correct. When a correct diagram is obtained, you can write an assembly language routine to move and shift the bits of the desired coordinate into the proper screen address.

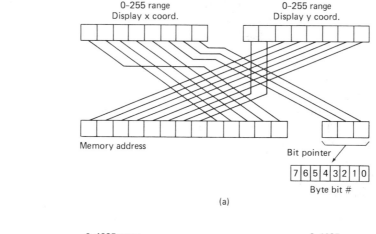

(a)

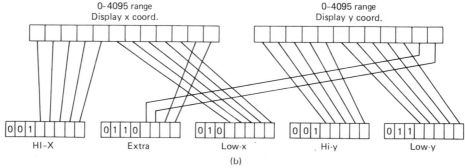

(b)

Figure 3-6 Martin diagrams are helpful for mapping display memory addresses to screen addresses. The nonlinear display of Fig. 3-4(b) is mapped using a pointer to indicate the appropriate bit (a). The mapping for a 4096 × 4096 display (Tektronix 4014-1) specifies a coordinate with five sequential bytes (b).

```
# Lookup table initialization. Called once
# at program start.
10 DIM A (256)     #row table
11 DIM B (256)     #column table
12 DIM C (8)       #mask table
20 FOR I=1 TO I=64 STEP 1
20 J=(I-1)*128
30 A(I)=J                    #for rows 0-63
40 A(I+64)=J+32             #for rows 64-127
50 A(I+96)=J+64             #for rows 128-195
60 A(I+128)=J+96            #for rows 196-255
70 NEXT I
80 FOR I=1 TO I=128 STEP 1
90 J=((I-1)/8)*2
91 B(I)=J                   #for columns 0-127
92 B(I+128)=J+1             #for columns 128-255
98 NEXT I
100 C(1)=1 : C(2)=2 : C(3)=4 : C(4)=8 #mask table
110 C(5)=16 : C(6)=32 : C(7)=64 : C(8)=128
120 RETURN

# Get address of coordinate (X,Y).
# Get mask to be "or"ed with screen byte.
200 ADRS=A(Y+1)+B(X+1)
210 MASK=C(Y-(Y/8*8)+1)
220 RETURN
```

Figure 3-7   Table lookup program to map screen of the nonlinear display shown in Fig. 3-4(b) to display memory.

Table Lookup

Table lookup methods can be used for plotting to out-of-sequence memory mappings. These methods are quite efficient and are applicable to high-level as well as assembly language programs. The idea is to initially build a table or array that contains all the addresses of the beginning byte of each scan line.

Figure 3-7 performs mapping to the out-of-sequence display of Fig. 3-4. Each element in the array MAP is the address of the first byte in the scan line corresponding to the y coordinate used to index the array. A y value of 23, for instance, produces a reference to table entry MAP (23) which contains the address of the first byte address on line 23. The value for x is computed in the same manner, and the two results are added together to produce the byte address.

Table lookup methods are fast and efficient, but they are memory wasteful. A lookup table for 512 scan lines takes 512 table entries of 16 bits (or 2 bytes) each. One kilobyte is required for the table alone, not to mention the table lookup routines.

MULTILEVEL DISPLAYS AND GRAY SHADES

Until now the discussion has been restricted to a raster-scan displays that consist of a scanned matrix with pixels that can be turned on or off. These are known as *bilevel* displays, and logic 1s and 0s can be made to represent black and white. In many applications, however, it is desirable to control pixel intensity and display gray levels.

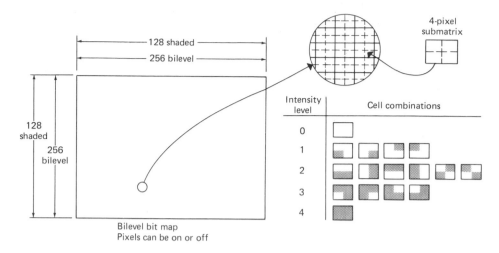

Figure 3-8   Representation of varying shades of gray may be achieved by appropriate control of pixel illumination within submatrixes of four pixels each.

Pixel Blocks

It is not always necessary to achieve a gray level by varying pixel intensity. One way of generating gray is to control small submatrixes of pixels. A block of four pixels (see Fig. 3-8) can represent four levels of gray. All pixels off can represent black, one to three on can represent gray shades, and four glowing pixels can represent white.

By choosing a coordinate system with half the x and y range of the display unit's limits and plotting the four-pixel submatrixes based on the desired intensity, gray shades can be produced. This method has a few obvious drawbacks. While four bits of memory can indicate 16 separate codes, only five intensity levels are available. Further, resolution is halved in both x and y directions.

Resolution can be maintained to a certain degree by attempting to match the edges that run through any given 4-pixel block with the pixels that are turned on for intensity control. If a line happens to run horizontally through the top of a 4-pixel cell, for example, and a 2-pixel gray shade is required, the two top pixels of the cell are the obvious choice for the submatrix. A picture must be analyzed before display using this method, and there are a number of techniques that are commonly used.

Pixel Intensity Control

Another method of creating a gray scale is to directly control the display intensity for each pixel. A display generator that stores two or more memory bits for each pixel can store more than just an indication of on or off. Two to four bits per pixel are commonly used in display generators that generate gray scale. This results in 4 to 16 possible gray levels for each pixel. More than 16 gray levels per pixel are usually only used for special applications (such as image processing) or color generation, because 16 levels produce adequate shading for most pictures.

COLOR DISPLAYS

Color raster-scan displays are readily available at low cost because the display technology is the same as that used in conventional television reception. Color displays are based on color CRTs.

The classic color CRT consists of three electron guns that represent red, green, and blue (the three additive primary colors), and a screen with triads of red, green, and blue phosphor dots. The electron guns are positioned in a similar triad at the base of the CRT. A "masked" screen with one hole per phosphor triad is placed between the CRT face and the guns. The holes in the screen cause the electron beams from the three triad-spaced electron guns to fall only on the phosphor dot of the color they represent. The display monitor section describes this and other color display tubes in detail.

Red, green, and blue can be mixed to form a wide selection of colors. From a distance, the eye tends to blend the distinct color triads into the proper colors. A close examination of an operating color CRT reveals the three color triads especially in areas that appear to be white from a distance. White is a balanced mixture of red, green, and blue.

Before examining how computer graphic displays can control the red, green, and blue dots, it is necessary to understand the basic principles of colorimetry. This will help explain the limits of the 3-dot color system so that you will know how much to expect from a graphics system based on it.

Colorimetry and Chromaticity

The human eye can see colors ranging from a wavelength of about 390 angstroms (violet) to about 750 angstroms (red). The eye is most sensitive to wavelengths between these two vaues at 560 angstroms (green).

Pure or "saturated" colors are colors of one specific wavelength. The only pure colors are those of the prismatic spectrum. All other visible colors are "unnatural" in that they are simply mixtures of two or more different wavelengths.

The ICI (International Committee on Illumination) standard chromaticity diagram (Fig. 3-9) is commonly used to describe all visible colors. The horseshoe-shaped line indicates the pure colors and their wavelengths in angstroms. All visible colors are found within this horseshoe (down to the straight magenta line). White is roughly in the center of the horseshoe.

Two pure colors, when mixed, create unnatural colors that appear within the horseshoe. The color can be determined by finding the two pure colors on the horseshoe and drawing a straight line between them. The resulting color lies at a location along this line which is related to the relative mix of the colors. For example, an equal mix of blue and green produces cyan (see Fig. 3-9). If green is of higher amplitude than blue, the resulting color takes on a greener hue and gets "pulled" toward the green point on the horseshoe.

A few interesting observations can be made from this chart. First, magenta is a very interesting color—a mix of red and violet, two colors that are about to go off the visible spectrum at opposite ends. Any colors below the magenta line are a mix of ultraviolet and infrared; they are unnamed and invisible to us.

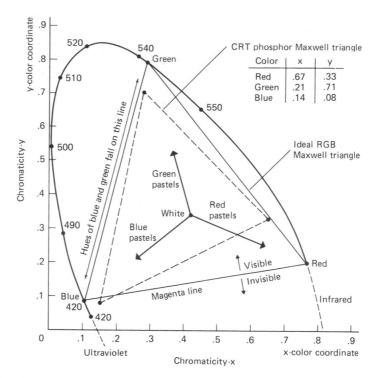

The figure contains the following table:

Color	x	y
Red	.67	.33
Green	.21	.71
Blue	.14	.08

Figure 3-9 ICI standard chromaticity diagram shows color range of CRTs with idealized (solid-line) and actual-response (broken-line) Maxwell triangles.

Another characteristic of the color system is that you can take any two pure colors that can be connected with a straight line through the white dot, mix them in the proper proportions, and obtain the color white.

This "line-between-two-points" mixing method doesn't stop at the mixing of two pure colors. You can create a color hue point inside the horseshoe by mixing two pure colors, and mix it with a third pure color to obtain a hue that is on the line connecting the third pure color to the originally created hue point. Using this three-pure-color generation method, you can create all the colors within the triangle connecting the three pure colors. This triangle is called the *Maxwell triangle.*

Pastel colors are pure, saturated colors mixed with varying degrees of white. Red is a pure color, and its pastels are pinks. You can draw a line from any pure color on the horseshoe to white to determine where the pastels of a given color are.

The ICI chromaticity diagram has important implications to the color television and color graphics display user. Colors on CRTs are created using the Maxwell triangle method. Three pure colors of red, green, and blue are the triangle's three corners. Color television R, G, and B (red, green, and blue) signals are generated in color TV cameras using three camera tubes with pure red, green, and blue filters over them. Filter manufacturing technology is advanced enough to provide filters that are, for all intents and purposes, "pure" (the color purity of transmitted television signals is, in fact, excellent and exceeds the best color printing and photography in color fidelity). Outputs from a computer graphics display generator can also be pure simply by letting the graphics user define them as such.

72

Unfortunately, phosphor technology isn't yet capable of producing pure-color phosphors (at least not on a production basis). The Maxwell triangle for a color CRT using a standard P22 phosphor is:

Red	$x = 0.67$	$7 = 0.33$
Green	$x = 0.21$	$y = 0.71$
Blue	$x = 0.14$	$y = 0.08$

This triangle is outlined in dashes in Fig. 3-9. A color CRT can produce all the colors within this triangle. By the NTSC's definition of color transmission (the solid Maxwell triangle), only three pure colors (red, green, and blue) can be produced, and pastels of all colors can be generated. A color CRT (with its impure-color phosphors) can only produce a limited set of pastels (those within the dashed Maxwell triangle), and no saturated colors at all.

The mix of colors within the phosphor's triangle are adequate for producing excellent computer-generated graphics, but these limitations should be kept in mind when working with or purchasing color systems.

Display Generation

Computer graphics color display generators often consist of display memories with three bits per pixel. The bits are assigned to the colors red, green, and blue. These systems are referred to as RGB displays. Each of the colors is either turned on or off for any given pixel, resulting in 8 possible colors: black, red, green, blue, yellow, magenta, cyan, and white.

Another approach to color displays uses a color encoder. Any number of bits can be assigned per pixel, but the bits don't control the red, green, or blue guns directly. Instead, the pixels bits represent a color code. The code is fed to a color encoder which controls the display system guns. A system using two bits per pixel, for example, has four possible codes per pixel. A color encoder could assign the colors black, green, orange, and white to the four codes. The encoder takes care of turning the color code into the appropriate combination of red, green, and blue.

In some applications black, green, orange, and white may be a good color combination for a system using two bits per pixel. In other situations, black, purple, yellow, and blue may be more appropriate. The encoder may be modified to generate either of these combinations.

Encoders often allow the user to select between a number of color combinations under computer control. Each set of colors is called a *palette,* and the encoders are often referred to as palette mixers. Figure 3-10 shows the two common color graphics systems.

More than eight colors can be obtained by assigning more bits per pixel. A 64-color system can be created using 6 bits per pixel—2 for red, 2 for green, and 2 for blue.

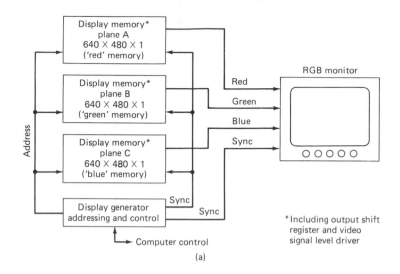

(a)

*Including output shift
register and video
signal level driver

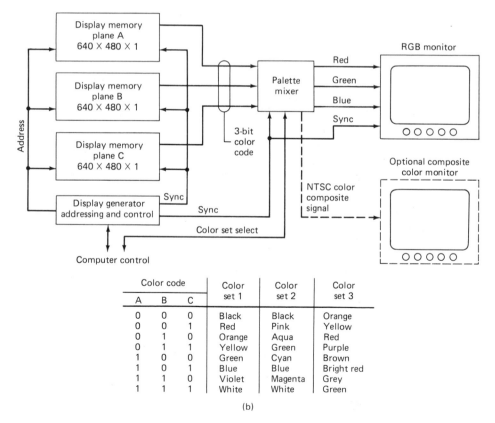

Color code			Color set 1	Color set 2	Color set 3
A	B	C			
0	0	0	Black	Black	Orange
0	0	1	Red	Pink	Yellow
0	1	0	Orange	Aqua	Red
0	1	1	Yellow	Green	Purple
1	0	0	Green	Cyan	Brown
1	0	1	Blue	Blue	Bright red
1	1	0	Violet	Magenta	Grey
1	1	1	White	White	Green

(b)

Figure 3-10 Screen displays of color graphics can be achieved with the RGB system (a) or with a palette mixer system (b).

DISPLAY MEMORY ORGANIZATION

Multilevel and color display systems have one thing in common: both use multiple memory bits to represent each pixel on the screen. The low cost of LSI memory has made these high-performance displays affordable, and the display memory configurations can be quite complex.

Memory Planes and Controllers

Simple bilevel displays have a single memory and the required counters, shift registers, and video encoders to sequentially shift the memory contents onto the screen. In such simple displays these functions tend to be integrated into one functional unit, as shown in Fig. 3-11. Multibit-per-pixel displays require multiple display memories, but common control logic suffices.

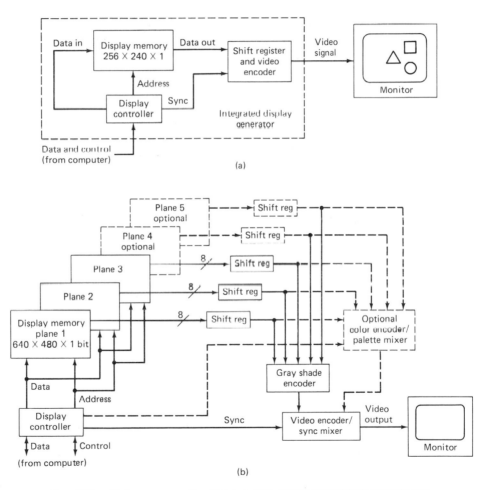

Figure 3-11 Display memory configurations in a simple, integrated bilevel display (a) and a complex modular color system (b).

A common approach taken in multilevel display design is to separate the component hardware into modules (see Fig. 3-11). A common controller is used to control memory addressing for a number of graphic memory planes. As the image is scanned on the raster screen, all planes are simultaneously cycled through a common address sequence. The bits of planes 1, 2, and 3 (plus 4 and 5, if you purchase the two optional memory-plane modules) represent a 3-bit (or 5-bit) gray-scale code. The baseline system with memory planes supplies 8 gray levels; the 5-plane system provides 32 levels for more critical applications.

This modular approach is economical in that it permits the user to buy only the hardware required for a given application; but the system may be upgraded with ease when the need arises. The standard 3-plane system of 8 gray levels (Fig. 3-11) can be upgraded to a 5-plane (32-color-level) system by adding two additional memory planes and color encoder/palette mixer.

Memory Partitioning and Address Manipulation

Controller logic is often designed to perform operations that are more complex than simply cycling through memory addresses. By cycling through memory in nonsequential order, and by selectively displaying single memory planes, many graphic effects can be produced.

A 3-plane system such as that of Fig. 3-11, for instance, can display a 640×480 8-gray-level image. A second display mode could allow the user to selectively display plane 1, plane 2, or plane 3 individually. Partitioning the display memory into three separate display buffers allows one to "build" an image in one buffer while displaying another. A command to the controller to display the new buffer allows the screen image to be instantly switched from one frame to another with no visible screen erasing or image building. This technique, known as double buffering, multibuffering, or screen ping-ponging, is useful in setting up animation sequences.

Display memory address manipulation is used to provide hardware, pan, scroll, zoom, and roam functions. These functions are useful and look quite impressive on a display screen, and they are quite easily performed. The example 16×16-bit display screen of Fig. 3-12 illustrates how these special effects are achieved. The arithmetic and logic operations are the same for high-resolution systems, but the address fields are wider.

The 16×16 display consists of 256 memory bits that are shifted out of memory in sequential order as the raster is scanned (resulting in the numbering shown in Fig. 3-12). The Martin diagram shows how an 8-bit sequential counter cycles through memory to display the normal mapping. Notice how the address conveniently breaks into a 4-bit row and a 4-bit column address.

The first two address manipulation examples are those of horizontal and vertical scroll. A value is added to the row or column address, thereby shifting the row and column positions on the screen. The addition is cyclic and overflow is ignored in these cases; but in some systems the overflow bit is used to blank the screen when it is active. On such systems, parts of images that go off the screen to the right or bottom are blanked instead of wrapped around to the other side of the screen.

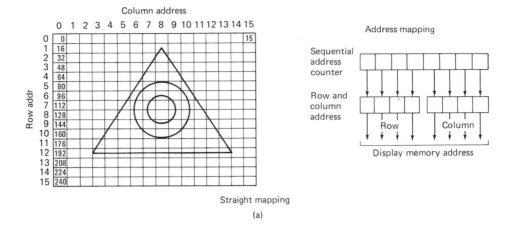

Straight mapping

(a)

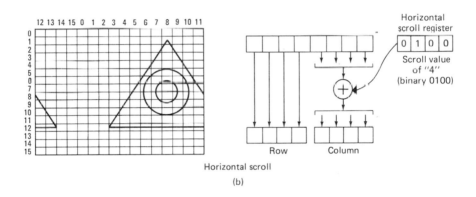

Horizontal scroll

(b)

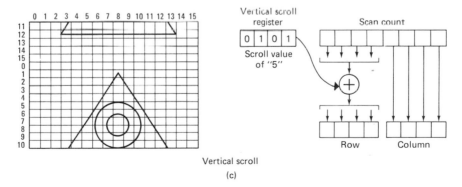

Vertical scroll

(c)

Figure 3-12 Several methods for memory address manipulation: straight mapping (a), horizontal scroll (b), vertical scroll (c), power-of-2 zoom (d), and zoom and pan (e). (continued)

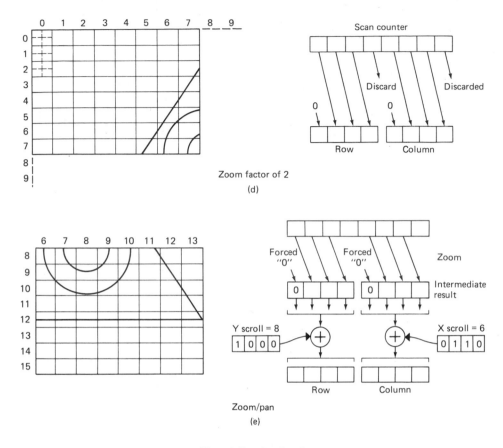

Zoom factor of 2

(d)

Zoom/pan

(e)

Figure 3-12 (continued)

Zoom is performed by shifting the row and column address by one place to the right (essentially dividing them by two). This restricts memory addressing to the upper left corner of the image in memory. The scan counter still clocks along at its normal rate, but it takes two clock cycles before the actual memory address is changed. (Notice that the least significant bit is discarded.) The same pixel is displayed in two consecutive column positions. The same holds true in the vertical direction: the pixel occupies two row positions. The overall result is the upper left 64 pixels in memory being mapped over the 256 pixel locations on the screen, or a 2:1 zoom. A single shift creates a 2:1 zoom, a double shift a 4:1 zoom, etc. Different power-of-2 shift factors can be used independently on rows and columns, resulting in image stretching in the x or y direction.

Users require more versatility than simply a zoom into the upper left corner of the display memory, so the scroll feature can be combined with zoom to allow zooming into any desired portion of the screen, as the final illustration of Fig. 3-12 shows. By incrementing the x and y scroll registers while maintaining a zoom factor, the user can pan or roam through display memory.

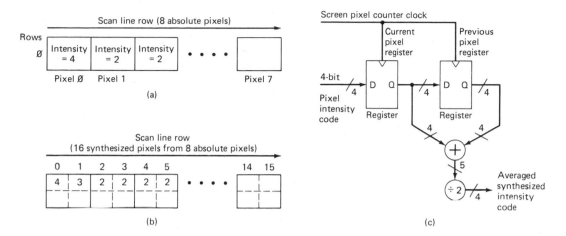

Figure 3-13 A normal scanned line with absolute intensity levels (a) is synthesized using averaged intensity levels (b) with a pixel-averaging synthesizer (c), and the result is a hardware zoom capability.

There are two factors that display designers must consider when building hardware that performs hardware zoom and pan: display resolution reduction, and display refresh. When zooming in on a display memory, each pixel is displayed many times. In the 2:1 zoom, for example, each pixel was displayed four times. viewable resolution essentially drops when this occurs (it dropped from 16 × 16 to 8 × 8 in the example display).

Figure 3-13 illustrates one synthesizing method that would apply to the 8 × 8 image described above. Two registers store current and previous pixel intensity values, and an adder keeps a running average of the pixels. This approach permits smooth blending of the pixels.

More complicated algorithms that border on those used in signal processing are used in some of the more expensive graphic systems and in nearly all image processing systems.

Dynamic memories are typically used in display planes, because they are less expensive, consume less power, and contain more bits per chip for any given device technology; but they must be refreshed by periodically reading through every memory row. (Memory chips are internally organized into rows and columns just as are graphics display screens.)

In full-screen display modes, refreshing is no problem because all memory rows are rapidly being scanned, but in zoom modes, only a portion of the memory is accessed. Designers often incorporate special circuitry that refreshes unreferenced locations during zoom. With respect to memory access, this poses no timing problems, because a memory access cycle can be "stolen" from every displayed pixel to perform the required read operation. (In zoom modes, single pixels are read many times in a row, while a single read operation is all that is necessary.)

Multiport Memory Access

Display memories have a unique requirement that is not often applicable to general-purpose computer memories: they must be shared between the computer and the graphics controller on a real-time basis. Direct memory access and interleaving techniques are commonly used to share memory between devices on nongraphics-oriented computer buses, but these methods assume that any device can wait for an arbitrary length of time between memory access operations. A display memory controller must access memory as the screen electron beam scans across the CRT—*without exception.* If a controller can't access memory when it needs to, the screen image is ruined.

Display system memories are usually made independent of the computer's memory to avoid access conflicts. The display generator has control over the display memory and can access it while the computer is busy using its own memory. Provisions must be made for the computer to access the display memory to manipulate images. The display memory must therefore be a multiport type—that is, it must be capable of being addressed and accessed by two devices at once.

Memory Interleaving

Commonly available memories are single-port devices; and although true multiport memories with two sets of address and data lines exist, they are usually low capacity (contain few bits) and are designed for small temporary storage memories in processors. Normal memory with control circuitry to make the memory look like a multiport memory must be used instead—memory interleaving is a simple and effective way of achieving this.

With interleaving, alternate memory cycles are assigned for accessing the processor and the controller. This method is particularly appropriate with microprocessors that share a memory with a display generator. The display controller can read memory on odd cycles, and the processor can read it on even cycles. No processor time is wasted because processors usually require time between memory access operations to perform internal computation.

Interleaved memories are wasteful in that they require memory integrated circuits that are twice as fast as would be required if a processor or controller alone were using the memory. The extra speed is not wasted if the processor and the controller both use every memory access to advantage; but in most applications, the display controller "outruns" the processor by a factor of at least 10:1, thus wasting about half the access cycles. This problem is avoided by employing *cycle stealing* methods.

Cycle Stealing

A display controller doesn't actually use a display memory 100% of the time. Memory accesses are not performed during horizontal and vertical retrace; nor are they performed while an image portion is being overscanned or when a portion of the image falls on a visible but undisplayed screen area. So a memory controller can be designed to "steal" these memory cycles away from the display controller and offer them to the processor.

A processor is often given free access to a display memory. In such cases the processor access has priority over the display access; and if display controller and microprocessor get into an access conflict, the microprocessor wins.

Status Signals. A status signal that tells when the display controller is not using the memory is sent to the microprocessor (usually in a status word that can be read by the microprocessor). The microprocessor uses this signal to avoid access conflicts. In this scheme, memory access stolen from the display controller during critical screen display times will result in the controller substituting the wrong display pixel value for the pixels currently being scanned. This results in "snow" on the screen. Graphics programmers must therefore be sure to keep track of the status signal and avoid interference with the display processor.

Stack Blasting. Some display designers go so far as to tie the "memory being used by display controller" status signal to the microprocessor's "wait" input, thus causing the processor to wait until the display memory is available before performing memory input/output operations. But this is wasteful because the microprocessor can be performing important calculations using its own independent memory during the wait interval.

Generating a vector, for example, requires many calculations to determine the value of a single pixel. These calculations can be performed while the display controller is scanning a visible portion of a scan line. The identification of pixels to be plotted can be saved on a stack. When the memory is available for processor access at the end of a scan line, the identified pixels can be "blasted" to the screen memory sequentially. Significant performance improvements can be made using this stack-blasting technique.

MONOCHROME VIDEO SIGNALS

An image from a television camera or display memory can be sent to a CRT to form an image. The act of sending the image involves synchronizing the display's scanning to the transmitting device and controlling electron beam intensity to match the transmitter's level. The signals sent to the display device to perform these tasks are referred to as video signals and are broken into two broad classes: *synchronization* and *intensity* signals.

Synchronization Signals

A raster-scan display must be synchronized to the display generator for proper image generation. The horizontal scan of each raster line must begin at the same instant for both devices (horizontal synchronization), and the specific line locations on the screen must match (vertical synchronization).

A separate sync signal is often generated by the display generator for synchronization of display devices. This signal consists of short pulses that represent the beginnings of scan lines, plus a long pulse that indicates the beginning of a new display frame. This is depicted in Fig. 3-14. The display device's sweep circuits are tuned to be near the synchronization frequency, so they readily lock onto the sync signal. Raster displays are tolerant of sync frequencies (number of sync pulses per second) that are a few percent away from the tuned frequency in either direction, and controls (horizontal hold and vertical hold) vary the tuned frequencies to more closely match the sync signal if it falls outside of the locking range.

Intensity Signals

Display generators that send sync signals also send intensity signals to control the intensity of the synchronized beam as it scans each scan line. This is simply an analog level signal that uses voltage to represent white (high-voltage levels), gray shades (medium-voltage levels), and black (low-voltage levels), as shown in Fig. 3-14.

In color systems, three intensity signals are generated—one for each of the color guns.

Display monitors using the separate sync method have two inputs: one for sync and one for intensity. Color monitors have four inputs: one for sync and three for intensity.

Video Bandwidth

A raster-scan display unit typically scans 59.94 frames of 262½ lines per second. This works out to a frequency of 15,734.264 sync pulses per second. This value is standard in the television and graphics display field. Crystals that are multiples of this frequency are often used to drive display generators (and even the microprocessors in graphics-oriented microcomputers) to simplify digital generation of sync frequencies. The high-pitched whine that emanates from low-quality monitors and televisions, as a matter of fact, are the sounds of coils and transformers oscillating at this frequency.

The 15.734 kHz sync signal is in the audio range and is quite easy to deal with. Transmission line losses are minimal, and impedance matching is not particularly critical. In essence, it is a digital signal, and the monitor can either lock to it or it can't; the signal can tolerate a bit of noise with no image degradation.

The intensity signal frequency depends on what is being displayed. A typical display of 512 pixels across a screen in a bilevel display can effectively create a square wave with 256 cycles per scan line by turning alternate pixels on and off. A scan line is 63.6 μs in duration (1/15,734.264 second), but display generators are designed to put all 512 pixels within a narrower portion of the scan to avoid the retrace and overscanned invisible portion of the scan line. A 50 μs intensity window on each scan line is typical. The resulting frequency is 5.12 MHz, which is well into the rf (radio frequency) range. Odd harmonics of 15.36 and 25.6 MHz also abound, especially in bilevel displays that create square waves with their alternating black–white intensity stream.

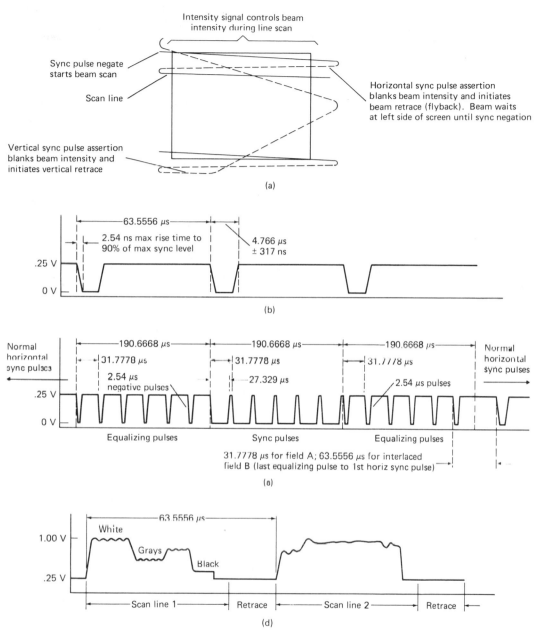

Figure 3-14 A scanned screen display (a) results when the video signal contains the appropriate information, which consists of horizontal sync pulses (b), vertical equalization and sync pulses (c), and appropriate intensity signals (d).

Intensity signals require good rf transmission lines and shielding. These are analog signals, and any noise or ringing caused by impedance mismatches and inductive pickup affect electron beam intensity; they are clearly visible on the screen as smeared and bright-edged pixels.

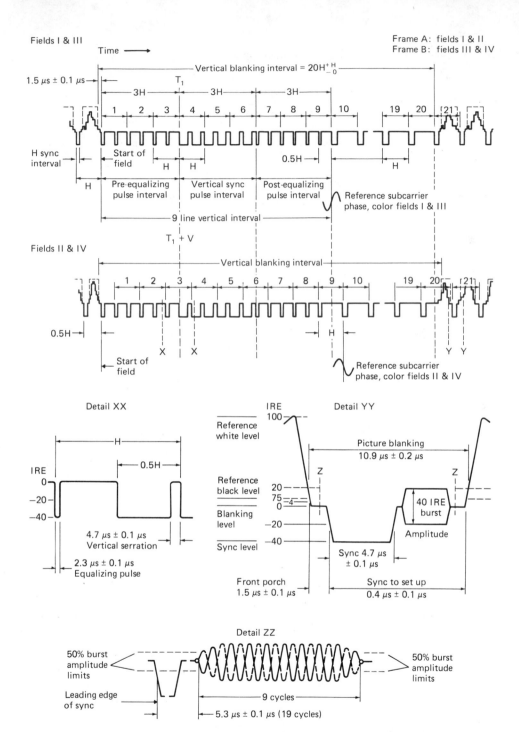

Figure 3-15 RS170 color/monochrome video signal standard, with detail provided for marked portions of scanned fields. The start of color fields I and III is defined by a whole line between the first equalizing pulse and the preceding H sync pulse; the start of color fields II and IV is defined by a half-line in the same position. (The standard includes a comprehensive set of specifications given as accompanying notes that are not presented here.)

Video intensity signals have a wide bandwidth. The 5.12 MHz signal was derived from a worst-case situation (alternating on and off pixels). A totally white screen results in the intensity signal being high all the way across the screen. Assuming that the intensity signal is made "black" during horizontal retrace, the resulting signal is that of the sync signal (15.734264 kHz). The signal thus ranges from 15.734264 kHz to 5.12 MHz—a 5 MHz bandwidth. It is this wide bandwidth that makes it necessary for the FCC to allocate 6 MHz of the rf spectrum for each designated television channel.

Composite Video

Separate sync and intensity lines are fine if a display generator or television camera is only a few meters from the monitor; but what about cases where a monitor is situated at some distance from the signal source? Obviously, it would be desirable to have all required signals combined into a single entity.

Television standards have been adopted by computer graphics display manufacturers in the use of one standard "composite video" signal.

Figure 3-15 illustrates the NTSC standard, which is used in the U.S. and Canada. The definition of the NTSC signal is very rigid, but most monitors will accept signals that vary widely, as shown in Fig. 3-16. The baseline of the signal is the *reference black* level. Sync signals are often said to fall in the *blacker than black* region. Appendix A describes video signals used in other countries. Differences include inverted signal sense, scan rate, and resolution.

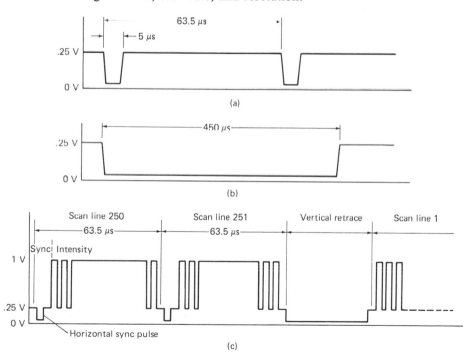

Figure 3-16 Typical crude video graphic signals that most monitors will accept: simplified horizontal (a) and vertical (b) sync signals are shown with a composite video signal (c).

Interlace

Much of the complexity in the composite video signal is the result of the vertical retrace interval. This interval alternates between two waveforms on a frame-to-frame basis to accommodate interlace.

The vertical sync interval has been designed to make construction of interlaced displays as simple as possible, and this explains some of the intricacies of the waveform as well as why the two interlaced fields are 262½ scan lines each instead of one field with 262 and one with 263 scan lines.

Scan lines on a raster-scan display are not truly horizontal. The beam is continuously sweeping downward while each horizontal scan line is swept. The beam reaches the bottom of the screen after about 230 to 240 scan lines have been swept (the remaining 22 to 32 lines are swept with the electron beam blanked during the vertical retrace). The spot size is such that scan lines will be half as wide as the vertical distance the beam drops per scan line. The consecutive scan lines will therefore be two beamwidths apart, forming a gap of one beamwidth between scan lines.

Assuming that scan lines are numbered consecutively (1, 2, 3 . . .) starting at the top of the screen, the gaps between the scan lines can be considered scan lines 1½, 2½, 3½, etc. If all vertical retrace interval sync signals were identical, the beam would always be moved to the top of the screen and begin scanning downward at the same instant with relation to the horizontal sweep across the screen. The first scanned line would always begin at precisely the same spot on the screen, and subsequent lines would be overwritten. By modifying the retrace interval waveform slightly on the second field, the start of the horizontal sweep on the next field can be delayed by half a scan line's time, thereby allowing the beam to drop to line 1½ before horizontal scanning again begins. The second field therefore scans lines 1½, 2½, etc. and fills in all the first field gaps, resulting in interlacing. When the second field is fully scanned, the first field's vertical retrace interval (with the appropriate equalizing pulses) causes the first field to begin on line 1, and the two-field process is repeated.

Most computer terminals using CRTs with short-persistence phosphors don't use interlace. The composite video signal repeats the same vertical retrace interval for every field, resulting in a 240-visible-horizontal-line display that is refreshed 60 times per second. More complex graphic displays that require greater than 240-unit vertical resolution use interlace-generating sync and composite video signals.

Color television camera sync-generator integrated circuits (such as the National Semiconductor MM5520) are quite inexpensive due to their wide use in the television industry and are often used in interlaced graphic display systems to avoid building all the complex waveform generating circuitry required for interlaced displays. Figure 3-17 is a block diagram of the chip showing signal inputs and outputs.

Video Voltage, Polarity, and Impedance

The NTSC television standard defines signals as ratios of peak-to-peak signal level instead of in absolute voltage levels. This is sensible because the waveform, when used in the television industry, is modulated and transmitted. Black levels are

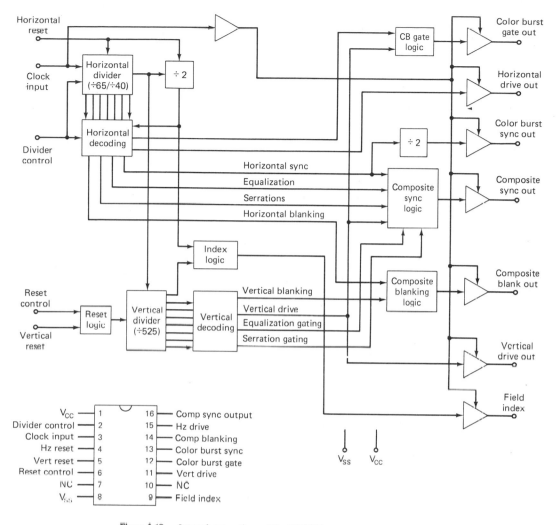

Figure 3-17 Internal connections of the MM5320 camera sync generator chip, with a top view of the dual inline chip identifying its pin connections. (Courtesy National Semiconductor Corp.)

represented by a "zero carrier" and white levels by "maximum carrier." It is up to the receiver to decode the modulated signal and turn the signal into the voltages it requires. As long as the proportions are correct, the signal can be decoded.

Standards for sending video signals directly via cables have also evolved. Most monitors accept signals that are 1.0 V ($\pm 10\%$) peak-to-peak. Cable impedance is usually 75Ω.

Video signals are sometimes drawn with black levels higher than white and other times white higher than black. This is dependent on whether the diagram is depicting voltage levels or percentages of carrier modulation. When video signals are sent via a coaxial cable, the center conductor is the signal and the shield is the "ground." Using the ground as reference, the waveform is a positive voltage, with white being 1 V and blacker than black (sync) being 0 V.

COLOR VIDEO SIGNALS

The desirability of a single video signal instead of intensity and sync signals extends to color video as well as monochrome. The need for four separate signals (three for the colors and one for sync) make a single signal even more attractive, because four signal lines can be replaced by one; but combining four signals into a composite color signal poses many problems.

The sync signal and intensity signals combine quite easily in the monochrome case because they occur in two isolated time intervals (intensity is always 0 during sync interval, and sync is never present during a line scan). Color, on the other hand, requires the mixing of three separate signals that occur simultaneously. The fact that black-and-white television standards were established before the introduction of color television compounds the signal mixing problem because a signal that portrays color on a color monitor must also be useful on a monochrome monitor that includes no provisions for ''unmixing'' a combined color signal.

The NTSC established the color television signal standard that is used in the United States, while other countries have adopted their own standards.

The computer industry has adopted yet another television industry standard for use with computer display devices. The display generation methods used for color graphics, however, differ greatly from those used in the television industry. Color video signals are quite versatile, and many electronic tricks can be employed to synthesize colors, as we shall see.

Color Burst and Phasing

There are two components in a monochrome video signal: the sync component to synchronize the scan, and the intensity component to control screen brightness as the beam scans across the visible scan line. Figure 3-18 shows two gray lines being scanned using a monochrome video signal.

A color video signal is very similar, but a new component is added—the *chroma* or chrominance component. Figure 3-18 shows this component added to the basic monochrome video signal.

Chrominance. The chrominance signal is a sine wave of 3.579545 MHz. The average intensity of the scan line remains the same as in the monochrome case, and in a color system this is called the ''luminance'' level.

Color monitors use the chrominance signal to generate colors. The color's saturation is determined by the amplitude of the chrominance sine wave with relation to the luminance level. A relatively low-amplitude chrominance signal produces pastel shades and a high-amplitude signal produces deep, saturated colors.

Phase Shift. The color itself is specified by the phase shift of the chrominance sine wave. Figure 3-18 shows the effect of chrominance amplitude on saturation. A reference signal is shown with a phase shift of 0° as well as the phase shifts of a few common colors. As the phase shift increases, the specified color changes smoothly from one color to the next, forming a smooth spectrum of pastel or nearly saturated colors.

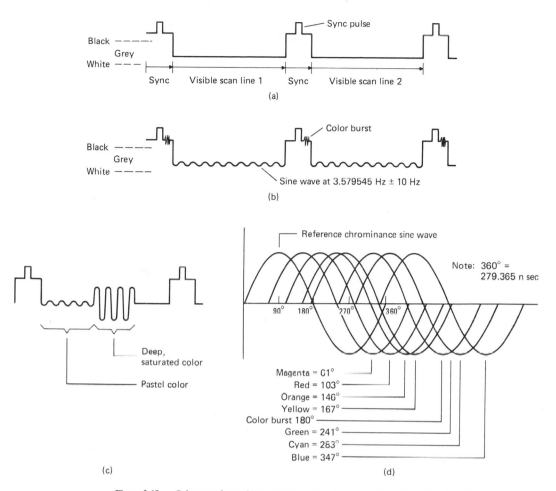

Figure 3-18 Color waveform phase concepts: monochrome (gray) scan lines (a), chrominance component and color burst added (b), color saturation based on chrominance amplitude (c), and a reference chrominance sine wave with its phase shifts to indicate color (d).

The monitor decoding the chrominance signal must have a reference chrominance sine wave on which to base its phase comparisons, and the reference must correspond to the display generator's reference sine wave for colors to be interpreted correctly. This is where *color burst* enters the picture.

Color Burst. The color burst consists of eight cycles of the chrominance reference sine wave positioned on that portion of the horizontal sync signal known as the *back porch* (Fig. 3-19).

The display generator positions its reference signal and the monitor locks onto it. The monitor has its own 3.579545 MHz oscillator, and once it locks onto the reference at the beginning of the scan line, it must stay synchronized all the way across the scan line. This explains the close tolerance of ±10 Hz for this multimegahertz signal. There are about 180 cycles of the chrominance sine wave in

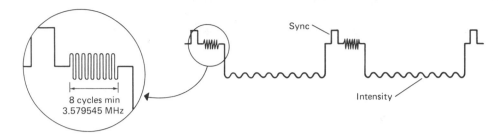

Figure 3-19   The color burst (inset) appears on the back porch of the video waveform.

a 50 μs scan line, so a maximum error difference of 10 Hz corresponds to a phase error of 0.18° by the time the scan reaches the end of the line—the color error would be unnoticeable.

Color Killers. The color burst serves a second function by "informing" the monitor that the signal is indeed a color signal. A monochrome signal with many rapid black-to-white transitions across a scan line (perhaps caused by a complex scene) can fool the color decoders into thinking that color information is present. The resulting picture would be a mass of smeared colors if it weren't for the "color killer" circuits in the monitor that turn color decoding off when the color burst isn't present.

Color Limitations. From these qualitative basics of color signals, a few conclusions can be drawn.

First, a monitor must generate its colors by locking onto the color burst and then decoding the 180 cycles of chrominance information across the screen. With only 180 cycles of chrominance information to work with, it is impossible to specify hundreds of color changes across a scan line; a monitor's electronics has but a limited color tracking ability.

A 640 × 480 resolution color graphics system that allows you to change colors 640 times per scan line could not live up to its full potential using an NTSC composite color monitor. This is why high-resolution color systems usually stick with separate RGB monitors which can handle high resolution using three separate wide-bandwidth video signals—one each for red, green, and blue, resulting in a combined bandwidth of 18 MHz or more (compared to 6 MHz for an NTSC composite).

A much higher chrominance subcarrier frequency (20 MHz, for example, instead of the standard 3.579545 MHz) could easily solve this problem; but the FCC frowns on signals that use up 25 MHz of spectrum. The lower-bandwidth signal does a reasonably good job for the purpose it was intended (television programming and advertising).

Why doesn't the chrominance signal's large sine wave, when added to a solid gray scan line, chop the line into a series of black and white dots on monochrome monitors? The answer lies in the clever choice of the chrominance signal's frequency. The chrominance subcarrier frequency is 3.579545 MHz, which is an odd multiple of half the horizontal scan frequency (15.734264 kHz). The chrominance signal does, in fact, chop the line into pieces, but on alternate fields the signal is out of phase, which visually cancels the effect. This is essentially interlacing on a vertical line basis.

For all frequencies

Luminance	$= E'_Y = .3\,R + .59\,G + .11\,B$
In-phase chrominance	$= E'_I = -.27\,(B-EY) + .74\,(R-EY) = .6\,R - .278\,G - .3217\,B$
90° out-of-phase (quadrature) chrominance	$= E'_Q = .41\,(B-EY) + .48\,(R-EY) = .213\,R - .5251\,G + .3121\,B$

Note: $R = E'_R$ = gamma-corrected red-level voltage
$\quad\quad G = E'_G$ = green-level voltage
$\quad\quad B = E'_B$ = blue-level voltage

Composite video = sync signal + E_Y + $E_Q \sin(\omega t + 33°)$ + $E_I \cos(\omega t + 33°)$

$\underbrace{}_{\text{sync}}$ $\underbrace{}_{\substack{\text{luminance} \\ \text{(monochrome} \\ \text{portion of signal)}}}$ $\underbrace{}_{\text{chrominance}}$

---

or for color differences below 500 kHz

Composite video = sync signal + E_Y + $\dfrac{1}{2.03}(B-Y)\sin\omega t + \dfrac{1}{1.14}(R-Y)\cos\omega t$

$\underbrace{}_{\text{sync}}$ $\underbrace{}_{\text{luminance}}$ $\underbrace{}_{\text{chrominance}}$

Note: gamma correction rules for color picture tubes with chromaticities of:

	x	y
Red	.67	.33
Green	.21	.71
Blue	.14	.08

$R = E'_R = E_R^{1/\lambda} = E_R^{1/2.2} = E_R^{.46}$

$G = E'_G = E_G^{1/\lambda} = \quad\quad = E_G^{.46}$

$B = E'_B = E_B^{1/\lambda} = \quad\quad = E_B^{.46}$

where γ (gamma exponent) = 2.2 and $E_R\ E_G\ E_B$ are linear intensity voltage levels

Figure 3-20 Equations for conversion of composite color signal from RGB to NTSC.

RGB-to-Color Conversion

Color television cameras and computer graphic displays generate red, green, and blue output signals. These are primary colors, and a wide selection of colors can be generated by mixing them in the proper proportions. Composite NTSC color signals, on the other hand, define colors using one signal with a luminance level to specify *brightness,* a chrominance signal amplitude level to specify *saturation,* and a chrominance signal phase shift to specify *color.* A set of equations that relate RGB signals to composite video signals exists. This set of equations is implemented in hardware to generate composite color signals from RGB inputs. Figure 3-20 outlines these equations.

Gamma Correction. The equations outline how the red, green, and blue voltage levels of the three independent voltage signals are mixed with the reference chrominance signal. The voltages are specified as *gamma corrected.*

Gamma correction refers to a nonlinear scaling (compression) that the normal red, green, and blue voltage levels must be put through to compensate for the nonlinear screen brightness increase in a CRT corresponding to a linear beam intensity increase. The NTSC reasoned that it was much more efficient to compensate for these picture tube nonlinearities at the relatively few transmitting stations instead of in the millions of television receivers across the country, so "gamma units" must preprocess the R, G, and B signals before mixing begins. The gamma correction rules look complex, but they simply nonlinearly amplify the R, G, and B voltage levels by raising them to a specific power fraction.

Color Difference Information. The composite video signal is composed of sync, luminance, and chrominance components whose voltages are simply added together. The sync is the normal monochrome sync with an 8-cycle color burst added on the back porch (Fig. 3-19), and the luminance is a proportional mix of red, green, and blue voltages.

The chrominance component is where the actual phase shifting information is generated. The reference chrominance signal is phase-shifted according to the in-phase chrominance level E_I' which is a proportional mix of R, G, and B, and the 90°-out-of-phase (quadrature) chrominance level E_Q' (a different proportional mix of R, G, and B).

Both E_I' and E_Q' can be expressed in terms of separate R, B, and G voltages, but it is convenient to deal with two *color difference* signals instead. These signals are "blue minus luminance" $(B - E_Y)$ and "red minus luminance" $(R - E_Y)$. These two color difference signals are used extensively in color video applications and can be found as outputs on color graphics controller chips such as the "6847" described in the graphics generator section.

Figure 3-21 shows the resulting vector diagrams for the mixing equations. In Fig. 3-21(a) the in-phase portion (representing a sine wave in phase with the reference chrominance sine wave) is added to the quadrature (a sine wave that is 90° out of phase from the reference). The resulting vector is rotated 33° and projected onto the E_Q' and E_I' axes in Fig. 3-21(b), resulting in the chrominance voltages that are added to the luminance and sync to produce the composite video.

Figure 3-22 illustrates the hardware implementation of the mixing equations. The gamma correction feature requires special nonlinear amplifiers, but the proportional mixing can be simply performed using resistive dividers. The diagram of Fig. 3-21(b) shows a simplified mixer that suffices for computer graphic displays. With the proliferation of personal computers, video games, and home-entertainment color television cameras, it is not surprising that a number of integrated circuits

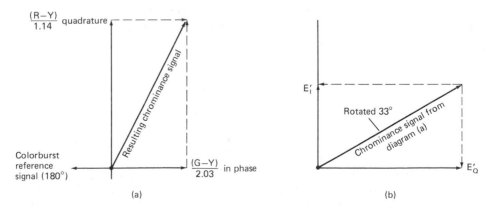

Figure 3-21 Vector diagrams of color video signal: chrominance signal generated by mixing R − Y and G − Y signals (a), and vector created by rotation and projection of chrominance onto the E_Q and E_I axes (b); the resulting chrominance voltages are added to luminance and sync information to produce a composite color video signal.

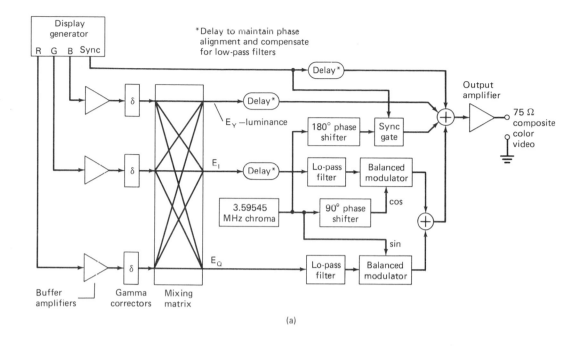

(a)

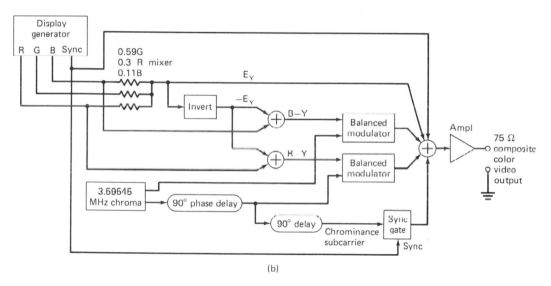

(b)

Figure 3-22   Hardware implementation of RGB-to-color conversion: a standard color converter (a), and a simplified system for computer graphics applications (b).

(e.g., National Semiconductor's LM1889 and Motorola's MC1372) are available to perform the balanced modulation and mixing functions required in such converters. These chips typically accept $R - E_Y$ and $G - E_Y$ inputs and bias signals. Figure 3-23 shows a complete RGB mixer using the LM1889.

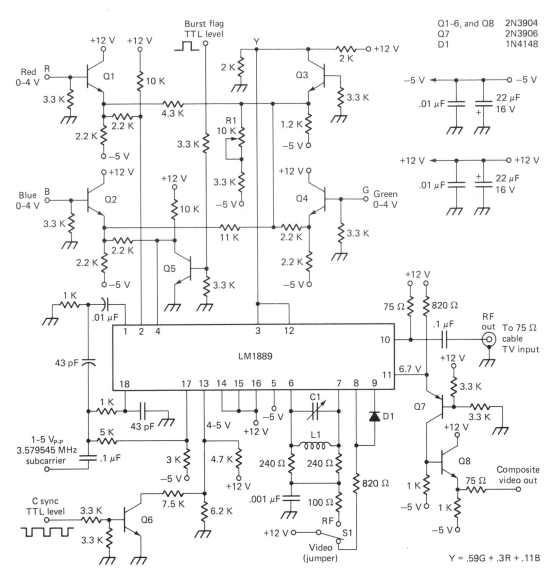

Figure 3-23 RGB mixer accepts RGB and sync signals and produces composite video. (Courtesy Matrox Electronics, Montreal, Canada.)

Color Tricks

Color is a desirable feature to add to a display system, even if the added color has limited capabilities. There are a number of techniques for adding color to a graphic display system economically, and many have found wide use in video games and personal computers. These methods entirely avoid using mixing matrixes and balanced modulators.

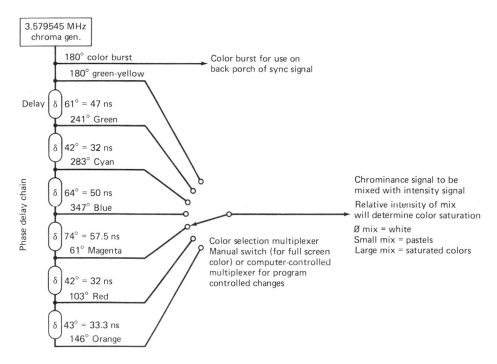

Figure 3-24 Crude color generator based on phase shifts (delay); the delay and multiplexer selection choices are broad, and can be based on a tunable delay line or simple logic gates (CMOS or TTL) that have inherent propagation delay. Equal delays between stages may be used for economy, yet a wide selection of random colors will result.

Color Burst Shifting. One of the most primitive techniques is to change the color of the whole screen by simply adding a color burst to the back porch of the sync signal and mixing in a little of the color burst frequency into the scan line. The generated color corresponds to the phase difference between the color burst and the mixed signal.

By simply adding a slight delay between the color burst signal and the mixed signal (through insertion of a CMOS gate or amplifier between the two signals), a phase shift is generated—and so is a new color. A few gates can in fact be strung together to provide selectable amounts of delay and thus a wide selection of screen colors. Figure 3-24 shows such a color generation scheme. It requires only an inexpensive crystal oscillator, a few gates, and a few miscellaneous mixing resistors and transistors. This kind of color generation is crude, but it can make the difference between a green and a gray playing field on a video football game!

Employing Artifacts. Monochrome television signals contain no color burst, and the "color killer" circuitry in color monitors turns off the color decoders if none is present. This avoids rapid black-and-white transitions from being interpreted as color information, thus avoiding a mass of smeared colors.

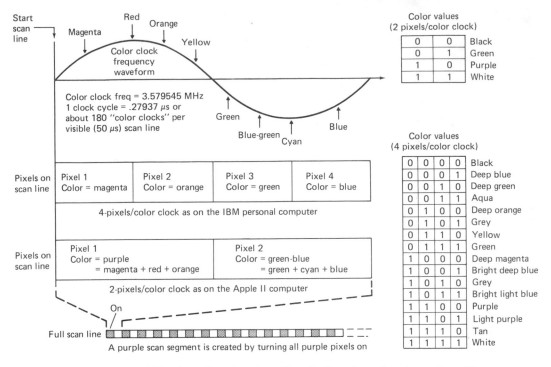

Figure 3-25 Generating colors using artifacts. (Artifact colors only work on systems with identical color-burst phase from frame to frame.) The color values shown in the inset charts are based on results with the first pixel falling on magenta; if it does not, a different set of colors results.

Many personal computers make use of the fact that monochrome signals can be interpreted as color signals if the monitor's color decoders are somehow switched on. And of course the decoder can be turned on by putting a color burst on the back porch of the sync pulse. The scan line will thus be interpreted as having color information.

Display system designers make the number of pixels across the screen be a multiple of the burst frequency. By turning on pixels in a phase-strategic manner, the color monitor can be "tricked" into thinking a chrominance signal is being generated. Figure 3-25 is an example of this method.

If *odd* pixels are turned on, a phase shift of 241° results and the line is green. If *even* pixels are turned on, a phase shift of 61° results, producing a magenta scan line. If all pixels are turned on, a reference white level is produced; and no pixels turned on results in black. The pixels are thus broken into pairs that can be set to white, green, magenta, or black. Colors generated in this manner are called *artifacts*. No chrominance data is mixed with the luminance signal, yet controllable color is produced.

White, green, magenta, and black may not be a desirable color palette in many applications, but a simple modification can be made to yield a choice of color sets. The color burst is the color phase reference, and by simply delaying it (phase shifting), a color set of any two colors that are 180° apart (in phase) can be selected. Such color combinations as red and cyan or orange and blue are thus easily achievable.

The artifact technique has a drawback (some would call it an advantage): Because the bit map remains the same from scan field to scan field, the synthesized chrominance waveform does not cancel itself on successive frames when viewed on a monochrome monitor. A colored scan line appears as a broken string of dots on a monochrome monitor instead of the gray shade that an equivalent true chrominance signal would have generated. Proponents of this effect argue that this is advantageous, because those who have monochrome equipment can then individually turn these dots on and off to achieve a double-resolution display. This is fine from a theoretical standpoint, but color graphics programmers often swap programs with monochrome users and people ultimately end up looking at chains of broken dots on monochrome monitors and smeared color messes on color monitors. It is questionable whether the advantages of artifact usage outweigh the disadvantages.

Mixing Video Signals

It is often necessary to mix the output from a character display with that of a graphic display. If no provisions for mixing the signals prior to the video generation circuitry have been made, the video signals themselves must be mixed.

The first step in mixing video signals is to synchronize the display generators to one another. A monitor can only lock to one sync signal, so a common signal must be used. Display generators usually have inputs for external sync signals, and they produce sync output signals. When two or more display generators' outputs are to be mixed, one display generator sync signal should be connected to the external sync inputs on the other generators. One generator is the master, and the others are slaves.

The intensity portions of the signals must then be mixed. If separate intensity signals are available, a simple resistor mixing circuit (Fig. 3-26) can be used. Buffer

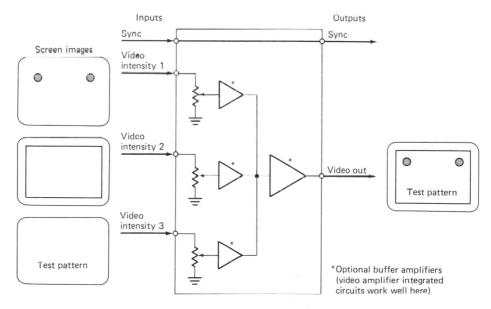

Figure 3-26   Simple resistive mixer for combining intensity signals.

amplifiers may be necessary to minimize cross effects between generators and reduce video noise. Composite video signals can also be mixed in this manner. The intensity interval of the waveform will be a mixture of two or more images, and the common sync intervals (which are identical in the master–slave mode) will add together to form a recognizable, if somewhat higher in amplitude, sync interval.

The mixing of color signals is slightly more complex. Sync signals must be synchronized; in addition, the color subcarrier signals must be synchronized between generators. This is usually done by running all generators from a common 3.579545 MHz source. This restriction only applies to NTSC composite signals, however, and RGB signals can be mixed using standard monochrome methods.

Video Modulators

Modulating a video signal at a standard television frequency would seem to be a topic that is more appropriate to a text covering the principles of television transmitters; but with the proliferation of complex video games and personal computers, the topic is equally appropriate to computer graphics. The huge sales volume of such products indicates that the vast majority of computer graphic displays today are using standard color television sets as monitors, and video modulators that turn the video signals into rf signals are required to do so.

A video modulator consists of a carrier frequency oscillator (usually in the channel 3 or 4 range) and a circuit to vary its amplitude as a function of the video signal's intensity (to amplitude-modulate it).

Figure 3-27 depicts a simple single-transistor modulator. This circuit is actually a low-power television transmitter; it is capable of transmitting color as well as monochrome signals. The ability to handle color has nothing to do with the transmitter itself, because a color video waveform is simply a modified monochrome video waveform.

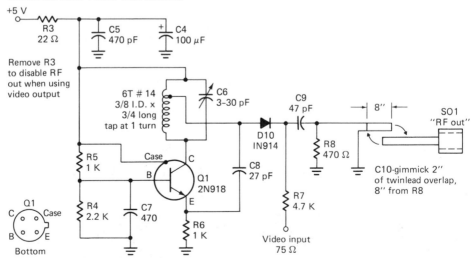

Figure 3-27   Video modulator circuit. The output signal is coupled to the VHF input of TV through a gimmick made by overlapping a couple of inches of 300Ω twinlead spaced 8 in. from resistor R8. (Courtesy Radio-Electronics magazine.)

Integrated circuit chroma generator–video modulators (such as the National Semiconductor LM1889) that combine the chrominance generation and video modulation functions into one chip are typically used in video games. A tuned circuit consisting of a coil and capacitor must be connected to these chips to act as the resonant circuit or "tank."

It's important to remember that video modulators are television transmitters and are treated as such by the FCC. If transmission power limits are exceeded, or if the transmitter emits interference-causing harmonics or spurious radiation, the FCC can (and often does) take action. Shielded transmission lines and metal enclosures must be used to confine rf signals to the local computer display.

VIDEO NOISE

Any quality of image generated on a raster display is enough to satisfy most users—until they see another system's cleanly generated image. Gray lines between pixels, hum bars that sweep down the screen, smeared colors on color displays, and snow in the picture can make an otherwise excellent display system look poorly built or badly designed. Cleaning up a video signal to improve an image is certainly desirable, and isn't very hard to do.

Identifying Noise Problems

Video noise can cause the anomalies just mentioned. This noise is added to the intensity of the electron beam that scans across the screen, thereby changing the image. Video noise can cause regular patterns to be formed on the screen because lines are scanned at precise intervals. Computer systems, display generators, and even other raster-scan display systems near the display generator are capable of generating noise that synchronizes with the display system's scanning rate. Poorly designed display system electronics can also add noise to the display, and in many cases one can tell a great deal about the design of a raster-display generator (how many pixels there are across the screen, how wide the intermediate shift register is) just by looking at the noisy picture.

Scan-line intensity is controlled by the intensity portion of the video waveform. In bilevel displays a logic 1 generates an intensity corresponding to a solid white level, and a 0 generates a black level. On an electrical level, voltages corresponding to white and black are produced at the electron gun in the CRT. There are a multitude of gates, registers, amplifiers, cables, etc. between the binary 1 that is supposed to represent a white level and the electron gun; the desired "solid" white can be modified by any of these electronic components. The intensity portion of the video signal is an analog signal and is susceptible to noise.

Clock Noise. Display generators have many internal clock signals that control display generation. There typically is a master clock signal that shifts the bits out of the memory (or an intermediate shift register) onto the display screen. There are also divided-down clock signals that perform less often recurring functions such as horizontal and vertical line and frame counting and loading the intermediate shift register. Any of these signals can crosstalk their way into the final analog intensity signal if proper design practices are not followed by the display generator designer.

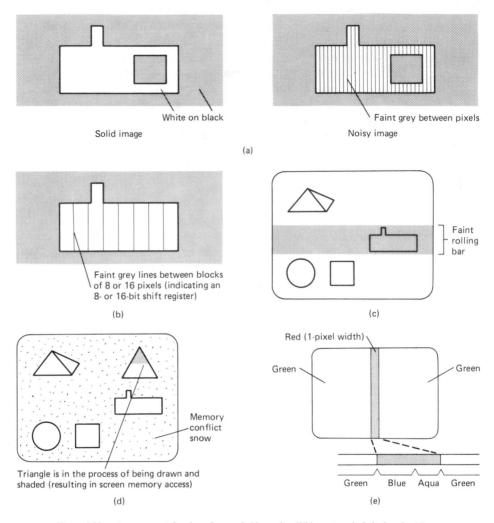

Figure 3-28 Appearance of various forms of video noise: With master pixel clock noise (a) solid end-to-end pixels have gray separations; intermediate shift register noise results in gray lines between pixel blocks (b); line-voltage hum causes a faint bar (c) that gradually traverses the screen vertically; memory-conflict noise results in "snow" typical of a faint transmitted TV image (d); color-vector tracking noise (e) causes pixel-wide color anomalies because shifting from green to red over one pixel width is too fast for the monitor's response.

The most common form of crosstalk occurs with the master clock signal. Solid white scan lines (end-to-end white pixels) appear to be broken into individual pixels by faint gray lines (Fig. 3-28).

Register Load Noise. A load noise from intermediate shift registers is also common. Display generators with intermediate shift registers typically load these registers with fresh data every 8 or 16 pixels. If noise from the loading process finds its way into the intensity signal, blocks of 8 or 16 pixels will be separated by faint gray lines as in Fig. 3-28.

100

Any event that synchronizes with the generation of scan lines can also degrade an image. If a noise pulse is introduced at the same location in every scan line, a gray vertical line will appear on the screen.

Clock noise is most noticeable in large, solid white areas of the screen. This type of noise therefore has a small effect on graphic displays—especially those with large shaded areas.

Line-Frequency Noise. Display generators are often situated next to power supplies that run on 50 or 60 Hz line current (50 Hz in Europe, 60 Hz in the U.S.). If the display generator—or any cables that connect it to the display monitor—are not properly shielded 50 or 60 Hz noise can be introduced into the intensity signal. Signals of 60 Hz are low in frequency compared to the 15.734264 kHz scan frequency and the 3–25 MHz pixel display frequency, and noise of this frequency is not noticeable along any individual scan line.

Low-frequency noise tends to put a slightly different voltage bias on each scan line. The bias varies at the 60 Hz rate as scan lines are scanned. This noise typically occurs in the form of a sine wave, so the resulting effect is slight intensity changes from line to line as the intensity is biased by it. The 60 Hz frequency closely corresponds to the 59.94 Hz frame display rate of most monitors, so the image goes through one light-to-dark bias interval (caused by the 60 Hz noise) per scanned frame. The result is a slight intensity difference between the upper and lower part of the screen. This effect is quite noticeable on a pure white field as a dark, smoothly blended-in, horizontal "hum" bar that runs across the screen.

Hum bars are not noticeable if they are faint enough, but even faint hum bars can be extremely annoying if they sweep down the screen at a rate of once every few seconds. This sweeping is caused by a very slight difference between the noise frequency and the display's frame rate. When subjected to 60 Hz noise, a display generator with a 59.75 Hz frame rate (close enough to 59.94 Hz for proper display operation in monochrome mode) will display hum bars that sweep down the screen at a 0.25 Hz rate (one sweep every 4 seconds).

Memory Conflict Snow. Graphic display generators usually share a display memory with the computer that generates the graphic images in the memory. The display generator must access the memory as the electron beam scans the CRT, and the computer should only access it when the display generator does not need to. If the computer is using the display memory when the display controller requires access, the controller may receive false data; this results in a glitch in the picture. Random computer–display generator memory access conflicts result in random pixel flashings or *snow*. This problem can usually be pinpointed by watching the graphics system while images are being generated. If snow appears while images are being generated, but the display is "solid" while the computer is idle or performing nongraphics tasks, memory conflicts are probably at fault.

Vector Tracking Noise. Color video monitors that accept NTSC composite video signal have internal decoders that convert the composite signal into separate red, green, and blue signals that drive the CRT guns. These decoders convert the phase-encoded information into appropriate mixes of R, G, and B by synchronizing to the color burst and then locking onto the actual chrominance signal of the scan line. The decoder "tracks" the chrominance signal as it phase-shifts and produces colors corresponding to these phase shifts.

There is a limit to how fast the chrominance signal tracking circuit can respond to the color phase shifts (the color vector), and if this limit is exceeded, erroneous colors are generated as the circuit tracks. This effect is most noticeable on rapid shifts from high to low (241° green to 103° red, for example). A very steep waveform (high slew rate) is required to produce the phase shift in a short time interval, as Fig. 3-28 illustrates. High slew rates create high-frequency signal components that can in fact be beyond the bandwidth of the receiving circuit and amplifier's range, so these signals may never even reach the color decoder properly in the first place.

Color vector tracking noise results in incorrect color generation at pixel edges and during whole pixels if they are short enough. A single pixel of red totally surrounded by blue pixels, for instance, may be generated as green or yellow.

Noise Reduction

Most noise problems can be dealt with by implementation of specific procedures. The correction methods, of course, must be determined by the types of noise experienced.

Dealing with Clock Noise. Clock noise in a video signal is usually the result of poor display generator design. Digitally oriented designers often don't realize or know how to deal with analog signal problems. One often overlooked fact is that digital integrated circuits have large amounts of crosstalk between elements within the same package.

Four independent *nand* gates, for example, work independently on a logical basis, but the input of one gate can cause analog noise on the outputs of another. This noise is no problem to digital signals so long as the output remains within the logical 0 or 1 voltage ranges, but too many designers use the output of a shift register or gate to directly drive an analog amplifier to create a video intensity signal. If a clock or timing signal is running through another gate in the same package, clock noise is introduced into the signal.

Clock noise can be reduced within the display generator by channeling the digital pixel bit stream of 1s and 0s through a saturating video amplifier (operational amplifiers would be ideal, but they are not usually fast enough). Input noise that previously was on the input signal is eliminated if the tops and bottoms of the noise pulses fall within the saturating range of the amplifier. The resulting output signal can be mixed with a similarly filtered sync signal to produce a clean waveform and good picture.

Gray level and color displays pose more of a filtering problem because their signals consist of more than just single voltage levels for black and white. Saturation techniques can't be used on the composite intensity signal. The point to attack clock noise problems on multilevel displays is where the digital signals are mixed to form the composite.

A fast digital-to-analog converter is ordinarily used to mix a few digital signals. The mixed output, of course, is only as clean as the digital inputs, unless the converter has built-in filters on the digital inputs. Saturating filters can be introduced before signal mixing to result in a clean mixed output.

Eliminating Hum Bars. The first step is to identify the source of the noise so it can be isolated from the video signal. Line-frequency noise is usually caused by one of the following:

- Poor common ground connections between monitors and display generators.
- Poor shielding between the power supply and either the display generator or the monitor electronics.
- Poor shielding of cables leading from the display generator to the monitor.
- Power supply ripple within the display generator.

Proper grounds, better shielding, and better power supply filters usually solve the problem.

Another approach to eliminating line-frequency noise is to synchronize the display generator frame rate with its 60 Hz power source. If a very faint hum bar is somehow introduced onto the screen, it will be stationary and will (hopefully) go unnoticed.

A method for doing this involves deriving the display clock from the line frequency using a phase-locked loop. An inexpensive phase-locked loop integrated circuit can be used as the display generator's oscillator instead of the more conventional crystal oscillator.

Designing Snow Out of Displays. Memory conflict snow can be the result of a poorly designed display memory controller that cannot inform a processor when the memory is free for computer access. A graphics program that ignores such information if it is available will also bring on the snow. Graphics display generators that don't inform the computer when it can access memory can be modified to do so.

Display generators have many internal signals that can be used to indicate unused memory time. Horizontal and vertical retrace signals are two examples. These signals can be attached to a status register that the computer can read, or they can be tied to the computer's interrupt system to interrupt the computer when display memory is free for use.

Once a status signal that indicates free memory intervals is available, either the graphics generation program or the hardware will have to be modified to use the signal, but there are some design considerations.

There will be situations, for example, in which the status signal will have no safety margin and will indicate "memory being used by display" within a microsecond of the actual display memory access. This can pose software problems: The signal may be read by the computer just before the memory becomes busy, and the computer will go ahead with a data transfer to the display memory a few microseconds after it received the misleading "not busy" status signal. This causes a processor–display generator memory conflict that usually shows up as snow near the top or left edge of the display when vertical and horizontal retrace intervals are used as the status signals.

The problem can be corrected by determining the maximum number of pixels that can safely fit into a free memory interval and never exceeding it. A software loop that generates the pixels acts as a timer. This method also reduces the number of times the status signal must be sampled. A single sample at the beginning of the free interval is enough. It allows you to squeeze a few more memory accesses and pixels onto the screen in the allocated time.

Solving Vector Tracking Problems. Color vector tracking noise is the result of exceeding a monitor's color tracking limits. The problem can be cured by either obtaining a monitor that can track color changes as fast as the display generator can produce them, or by reducing the number and rate of color changes along the scan line.

On rare occasions, a display generator may be at fault and may not be producing the color phase shifts correctly. Rapid phase shifts cause high slew rates and high-frequency components to be added to the waveform. The output mixers and amplifiers on a poorly designed generator may not handle the added bandwidth. In these cases, wider range mixers and amplifiers are in order.

If an extremely large number of color changes per scan line are absolutely necessary in your graphics application, it may not be possible to find a monitor that can accurately display the desired image. If this is the case, the composite signal must be abandoned in favor of more expensive RGB monitors and display hardware.

GRAPHIC DISPLAY GENERATORS

Now that display memory organization, video waveforms, and techniques for reducing video noise have been covered, it is appropriate to examine hardware that controls display memory and generates video output signals. Graphic display generators perform these tasks.

Graphic display generators can be separated into two groups: discrete and LSI. Discrete display generators are built with small-scale and medium-scale integration, and the chips are referred to as SSI and MSI packages. Such generators contain counters, gates, and shift registers to perform graphics generation. The more complex circuits using large-scale integration (LSI) are simpler in the sense that all of the required counters, gates, and shift registers are contained on one ship, which usually comes in a 40-pin package.

With the advent of LSI controller chips, one wonders why anyone would still bother to build graphic generators from discrete components. The answer is versatility and performance. LSI controller ships usually are intended for large-volume applications (video games, personal computers, and low-end video terminals). These are low-performance applications where resolutions of 256×192 with a few simple colors and a single set of alphanumeric characters are considered adequate.

More complex high-resolution graphic controllers are used in low-quantity, high-performance applications. The market demand traditionally hasn't justified advanced LSI display controller chip development and production costs. This situation is changing, however.

Without question, the display designer is offered more flexibility with a discrete design. If the application requires that a special hardware function such as a vector generator or half-screen scroller be built, the additional hardware can be accommodated with ease in a discrete design. With LSI controllers, you must eigher settle for what the chip already has or choose another chip.

Discrete Graphic Controllers

The best way to get familiar with a graphic controller is to examine an actual product. The Matrox ALT-256 graphic display generator card has a 256 × 256 display resolution and is designed to plug into the popular S100 microcomputer bus. It can be considered a first-generation display device because it is built entirely with SSI and MSI circuits (excluding the LSI memory chips) and has a minimum of features.

This display controller was subsequently upgraded to a 512 × 256 version with many more features and higher-density memory chips (the ALT-512), and the evolving technology led to the more powerful second-generation RGB-GRAPH display unit which combines SSI, MSI, and LSI controller technology to produce 512 × 512 × 4-pixel color displays. The ALT-256 serves as a good example of a basic display generator controller, however, and is in fact very similar to what can be found inside today's LSI controller chips.

Figure 3-29 shows a block diagram of the ALT-256. The center of activity is the display memory. This is where the image is stored. Surrounding circuits let the computer access the memory and read the memory onto the display screen.

Display memory can be accessed by two sources: the scan counters for display scan access and the x and y registers for computer access (the left side of the diagram). The address is selected by the RAM address multiplexer and RAM read–write control circuitry, which performs memory cycle interleaving to avoid memory access conflicts between the computer and scan access sources.

The scan counters are driven by an 11.066 MHz clock. Their continuous count generates display scan addresses that cycle through memory as the raster is produced on the screen. These counters also act as sequence counters that keep track of the generator's current scan position. Horizontal and vertical video timing logic, driven from these counters, generates horizontal and vertical sync signals based on them.

The upper right portion of the diagram shows the video mixer system that takes the pixel bit stream that flows from memory (driven by the scan counter system) and mixes it with the sync signal. A shift register is used to temporarily buffer the memory data so the display memory can perform other tasks—computer accesses and subsequent scan data accesses—while the old scan data is being shifted onto the display screen a pixel at a time.

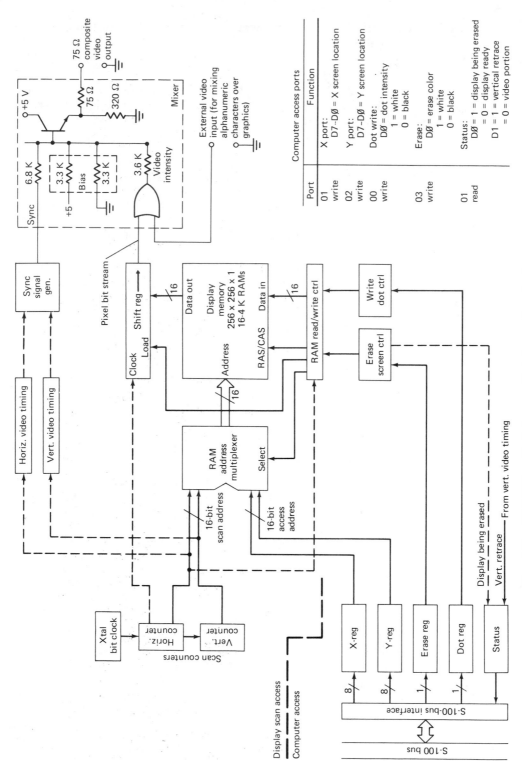

Port	Function
01 write	X port: D7–DØ = X screen location
02 write	Y port: D7–DØ = Y screen location
00 write	Dot write: DØ = dot intensity 1 = white 0 = black
03 write	Erase: DØ = erase color 1 = white 0 = black
01 read	Status: DØ = 1 = display being erased = 0 = display ready D1 = 1 = vertical retrace = 0 = video portion

Computer access ports

Figure 3-29 ALT-256**2 graphic display system block diagram. (Reproduced courtesy Matrox Electronics, Montreal, Canada.)

The final mixer stage is simply a resistor mixer that mixes proportional amounts of intensity and sync signal to form an NTSC composite video signal. The single-transistor emitter follower acts as a buffer–amplifier that drives the 75-ohm composite video output.

Two additional features are the erase system and external video mixing system. The erase system turns off (or on) all the display memory pixels by writing them with all 1s or 0s as the display is scanned. This erases the screen more rapidly then would be possible by setting all the pixels individually using computer memory accesses.

The video mixing system simply mixes another pixel bit stream with the video pixel bit stream before mixing it with the sync signals to form a composite video signal. This allows a synchronized alphanumeric generator board (the compatible ALT-2480 board, for example) to mix alphanumerics onto the image.

The computer access ports are outlined on the lower right of the block diagram. Writing a pixel into memory is a matter or writing the desired x and y values into the x and y registers, followed by writing the desired intensity into the dot register (Fig. 3-30).

Erasing the screen is performed by writing a 0 into the erase register. It is important not to write any pixels onto the screen until the screen is fully erased, because this disrupts the erase system's cycle. A software loop that introduces a delay of 33 ms (maximum erase time) can be used to "time-out" a wait, or the status register's "D0" bit (display being erased) can be read until it indicates that the erase is finished. Figure 3-30 lists a program that performs an erase using the status register.

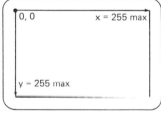

Matrox ALT-256**2 screen addressing

8080 assembly language
Program to write white pixel at (27, 35)

```
mvi a, 27 ; x reg = 27
out 01
mvi a, 35.; y reg = 35
out 02
mvi a, 01 ; dot = white
out 00
```

(b)

Matrox ALT-256 features

Resolution: 256 x 256 x 1 (256 x 240 x 1 jump-selectable)
I/O: 4 sequential output ports
    1 input port
Erase: single instruction — 33 ms max
Screen coordinate system: Cartesian, upper left origin
Color: multiple boards can be synchronized for
    multiplane color operation
Memory access: scan/computer access interleaving
Sync: internal or external

(a)

Program to erase screen

```
          mvi a, 0     ; erase = black
          out 03
Wait:     IN 01        ; check erase done bit
          ANI 01
          JNZ WAIT     ; if not done, loop
Done:                  ; if done continue
                         with program
```

(c)

Figure 3-30 Characteristics and programming data for ALT-256**2 display generator. (Reproduced courtesy of Matrox Electronics, Montreal, Canada.)

There are a few subtle points to note about this display generator. First, because it has vertical resolution of 256 pixels, interlace is not used. This results in a very solid image, even on short-persistence monitors. Another feature is the ability to decrease the number of displayed lines from $y = 256$ to $x = 240$. Monitors that follow the NTSC 525-line standard only display about 240 lines (the others are lost in retrace). Pixel addressing remains the same in both modes, and the bottom 16 lines simply are not displayed in the $y = 240$ mode.

Finally, a *vertical retrace in progress* status bit is available in the status register. This allows you to update images while a frame is not being displayed, count the number of displayed frames, and synchronize events to the display scan cycle. This feature is useful in creating smooth and glitch-free animation sequences.

Low-End LSI Graphic Controllers

The motorola MC6847 (Fig. 3-31) is a low-cost LSI controller that is gaining wide acceptance in low-end color graphics, personal computers, and instrumentation displays. This controller, like most LSI display controllers, is part of a microprocessor family (in this case, 6800/68000 family). It is designed to interface directly to the 6800 microcomputer bus. It can be interfaced to other buses as well, but additional interface hardware is required.

The 6847 is designed to share memory with a microprocessor. It has built-in direct memory access circuitry that takes control of the bus when the microprocessor is not using it. On the 6800, this occurs once every clock phase, thereby allowing the 6847 and microprocessor to alternate memory accesses.

Straightforward memory mapping is used. The display memory's first address corresponds to the upper left corner of the display screen, and the memory address is sequentially incremented as the raster is scanned from left to right and top to bottom. The amount of memory scanned and the way it is interpreted are dependent on the display mode of the controller.

The 6847 has 12 display modes, which offer a wide selection of display resolutions, display memory sizes, display characteristics (alphanumerics, cell-organized graphics, or high-resolution graphics), and color combinations.

The display mode is selected by applying the appropriate combination of logic 1s (5 V) and 0s (0 V) to 7 control pins on the chip (A/G, A/S, INT/EXT, INV, GMO, GM1, GM2). Figure 3-32 outlines these display modes.

Low-end users such as video game manufacturers usually choose the low-resolution colorful modes that require the least amount of memory. Mode 3 (Alpha Semigraphics-4), for example, produces a 64×32 display with 8 colors per pixel and uses only 512 bytes of memory. The "semigraphic" modes, however, are cell organized and are harder to map than the true graphic modes (5–12).

The mode control pins are usually hardwired in low-cost video games and instrumentation displays, but in personal computers and video terminals, the mode control pins are often connected to a register that the microcomputer programmer can control. The programmer can thus select whichever mode seems appropriate for a given application. Figure 3-32 outlines the 6847's graphic modes and shows how each byte of display memory is interpreted on the display.

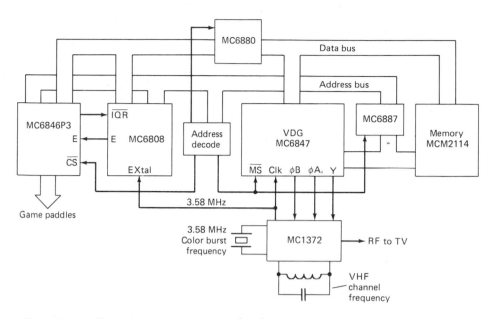

Mnemonic	Pin numbers	Function
V_{CC}	17	+5 V
V_{SS}	1	Ground
CLK	33	Color burst clock 3.579545 MHz (input)
DA0–DA12	22, 23, 24, 25, 26 13, 14, 15, 16, 18, 19, 20, 21	Address lines to display memory
DD0–DD5	3, 4, 5, 6, 7, 8	Data from display memory RAM or ROM
DD6–DD7	2, 40	Data from display memory in graphic mode
ϕA, ϕB, Y	11, 10, 28	Chrominance and luminance analog (R–Y, B–Y, Y) output to RF modulator
CHB	9	Chroma bias; reference ϕA and ϕB levels
$\overline{RP}$	36	Row preset — output to provide timing for external character generator
$\overline{HS}$	38	Horizontal Sync — output to provide timing for external character generator
INV	32	Inverts video in all alpha modes
$\overline{INT}$/EXT	31	Switches to external ROM in alpha mode and between SEMIG-4 and SEMIG-6 in semigraphics
$\overline{A}$/S	34	Alpha/semigraphics; selects between alpha and semigraphics in alpha mode
$\overline{MS}$	12	Memory select forces VDG address buffers to high-impedance state
$\overline{A}$/G	35	Switches between alpha and graphic modes
$\overline{FS}$	37	Field synchronization goes low at bottom of active display area
CSS	39	Color set select; selects between two alpha display colors
GM0–GM2	30, 29, 27	Graphic mode select

Figure 3-31 Block diagram of video game application using the MC6847 video display generator as a low-end graphic controller. Mnemonics and pin functions are also given. (Courtesy Motorola Semiconductor Products, Inc.)

Before choosing a low-cost controller, it is important to consider the applications for which it was intended. The MC6847/MC1372 display generator and TV chroma–video modulator chip set is inexpensive and offers excellent performance for the money, but video quality is not as high as might be desired. Clock noise is often plainly visible when using a high-performance video monitor (this is not the

TABLE OF MODE CONTROL LINES (INPUTS)

$\overline{A}/G$	$\overline{A}/S$	$\overline{INT}/EXT$	INV	GM2	GM1	GM0	Alpha/graphic mode select
0	0	0	0	X	X	X	Internal alphanumerics
0	0	0	1	X	X	X	Internal alphanumerics inverted
0	0	1	0	X	X	X	External alphanumerics
0	0	1	1	X	X	X	External alphanumerics inverted
0	1	0	X	X	X	X	Semigraphics - 4
0	1	1	X	X	X	X	Semigraphics - 6
1	X	X	X	0	0	0	64 x 64 color graphics
1	X	X	X	0	0	1	128 x 64 graphics
1	X	X	X	0	1	0	128 x 64 color graphics
1	X	X	X	0	1	1	128 x 96 graphics
1	X	X	X	1	0	0	128 x 96 color graphics
1	X	X	X	1	0	1	128 x 192 graphics
1	X	X	X	1	1	0	128 x 192 color graphics
1	X	X	X	1	1	1	256 x 192 graphics

SUMMARY OF MAJOR MODES
MAJOR MODE ONE
TABLE OF ALPHA MINOR MODES

Mode no.	Title	Memory	Colors	Display elements
1	Alphanumeric (internal)	512 x 8	2	
2	Alphanumeric (external)	512 x 8	2	
3	Alpha Semig-4	512 x 8	8	Box ⎯ Element
4	Alpha Semig-6	512 x 8	4	Box ⎯ Element

MAJOR MODE TWO
TABLE OF MINOR GRAPHICS MODES

Mode no.	Title	Memory	Colors	Comments
5	64 x 64 color graphic	1K x 8	4	Matrix 64 x 64 elements
6	128 x 64 graphics*	1K x 8	2	Matrix 128 elements wide by 64
7	128 x 64 color graphic	2K x 8	4	elements high
8	128 x 96 graphics*	1.5K x 8	2	Matrix 128 elements wide by 96
9	128 x 96 color graphic	3K x 8	4	elements high
10	128 x 192 graphics*	3K x 8	2	Matrix 128 elements wide by 192
11	128 x 192 color graphic	6K x 8	4	elements high
12	256 x 192 graphics*	6K x 8	2	Matrix 256 elements wide by 192 elements high

*Graphics mode turns on or off each element. The color may be one of two.

Figure 3-32   Display modes of the MC6847 graphic controller chip. (Courtesy Motorola Semiconductor Products, Inc.)

case using an inexpensive color TV set). And the display almost always has a big green or buff border around it in the graphic modes in order to strategically place the 256 pixels per scan line on the 3.579545 MHz chrominance subcarrier to aid in NTSC color generation. The 6847 is an LSI controller, so little can be done to improve display quality or increase the number of graphic features once the chip is chosen. In most low-end applications the 6847 is fine; for high-end applications a more expensive LSI controller or a discrete design should be used.

High-Performance LSI Graphic Controllers

Some manufacturers feel that market growth in high-performance graphics (simulation, CAD, and image processing) combined with the low cost of memory and high-performance microprocessors will create a large market for high-performance displays. These manufacturers have therefore gone ahead and developed high-performance LSI display controllers for graphics. The uPD7220/GDC by Nippon Electric Company (NEC) is a good example of such a chip.

The uPD7220 resembles high-performance discrete controller designs not only in the way it handles display memory but in its selection of features. Figure 3-33 outlines ithe 7220's features.

The 7220, like other high-performance graphic systems, requires a separate display memory. Memory is not shared with the microprocessor, although the 7220 can access the microprocessor memory using DMA to fetch commands and data.

When display memories as large as 256K words are used, display scanning of memory occurs at such a rapid rate that it would totally tie up (if not overrun) a microprocessor bus. The final assembly of data from the memory into a video

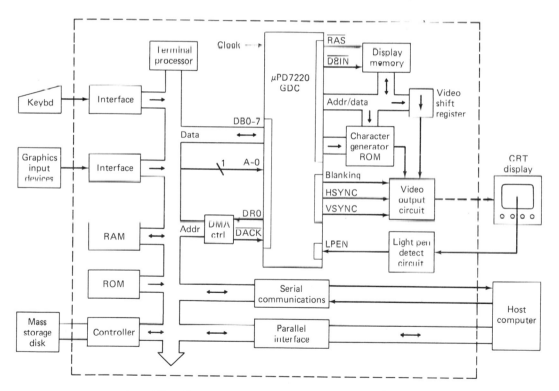

Figure 3-33   Block diagram of a graphics terminal using the high-performance μPD7220 graphic display controller; the direct connection of peripherals illustrates the capabilities of this chip. (Courtesy Nippon Electric Company.)

signal is not performed by the chip. Instead, it is left to external shift reegisters and video output circuitry; this allows the designer to configure the output in a customized way. Control signals are generated by the controller to help control whatever shift registers and mixers are ultimately used. (Blanking, horizontal and vertical sync, and a clock for shift register clocking are available).

Before using the 7220, you must consider its intended application. NEC states that the uPD7220/GDC "is an intelligent microprocessor peripheral designed to be the heart of a high-performance raster-scan computer graphics and character display system." It is easy to get interested and excited about such a high-performance chip, but in most everyday applications, this chip offers too much performance for too much money; separate display memories, shift registers, video mixers, and DMA controller chips must be used. This adds to overall system size and cost. The 7220 belongs in high-performance systems and should be used ac - cordingly.

RASTER-SCAN MONITORS

A monitor is a CRT and the associated electronics that convert video signals into a screen image. Monitors can be bought in stripped-down OEM (original-equipment manufacturer) form for integration into cabinets, terminals, or consoles. They also are readily available in enclosures that range from rugged sheet-metal cabinets to stylish television-style units.

Monitor Characteristics

There are a few obvious characteristics that must be considered when choosing a monitor. These include screen size, color display versus monochrome, type of input, and cost.

The most common shape is rectangular with a 4:3 aspect ratio (4 units wide, 3 units high), which is a direct result of the television industry's NTSC standard. Monitor screen size is usually measured diagonally, but on sizes other than those defined by a 4:3 aspect ratio, the side dimensions are given. When only a diagonal measure is given, a 4:3 ratio is assumed. Common diagonal screen sizes are, for color: 5, 7, 10, 12, 13, 15, 17, 19, and 26 inches. For monochrome: 9, 12, and 17 inches.

Nearly all other sizes from 3 in. to 30 in. are available, but costs tend to be higher for odd sizes. It is also getting hard to find large, inexpensive monochrome monitors because large television sets are rapidly switching to color.

Monitor manufacturers often offer a choice of two factory-wired modes of operation for a 4:3 monitor: conventional (horizontal) and page (vertical 3:4 ratio). Large quantities of page monitors are bought by word processing and phototypesetting system manufacturers who attempt to make their displays more closely resemble the dimensions of a printed page.

There are a few different monitor input configurations to choose from, and the selected type depends on the output capabilities of the graphics generator. Inexpensive monitors usually have composite video inputs that conform to EIA–RS170 standards. The input impedance is 75Ω, so 75Ω cables and appropriate connectors (usually easily obtainable PL-59 or BNC plugs) should be used.

Proper impedance matching is advisable, and properly assembled cable–connector sets improve a system's appearance, ruggedness, and performance—and of course sound interconnections result in reduced radiation of signals.

The result of cable problems will normally be visible on the monitor's screen. Image sharpness suffers if the cable is too capacitive, and black–white image intensified or attenuated when impedances are mismatched.

Another input configuration consists of separate intensity and sync signal inputs. These inputs are usually 75Ω also, but one requires an intensity-only signal (3 separate intensities for red, green, and blue on color monitors), and the other a sync signal. There is often a switch on these monitors (especially the monochrome models) that allows you to feed an NTSC composite signal into the intensity input and avoid using the sync signal input—which is ideal for users who intend to upgrade to a separate sync system in the future.

Multiple monitors can be driven by one video signal by using the chainthrough feature found on most monitors. There is usually an output jack that corresponds to every video input jack on a monitor. The first monitor's input is fed directly by the display generator, and subsequent monitors are driven by the previous monitor's output jack (Fig. 3-34).

Internally, each monitor acts as a high-impedance input and takes the signal it requires from the low-impedance signal that is passed through it in parallel from the input to the output jack. The final monitor in the chain must have a 75Ω ter-

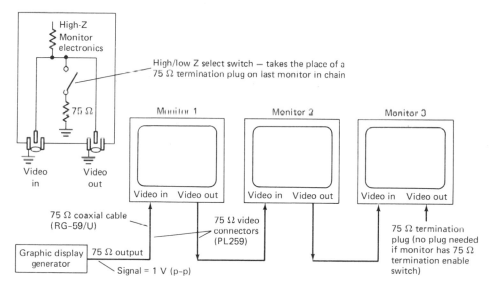

Figure 3-34   Chained video monitors. Cables may be very long if low-loss cables of the proper impedance are used. At video frequencies (5—10 MHz) standard RG-59/U coaxial cable attenuates signals no more than 1 dB/100 ft.

mination, which can be a resistive device that plugs into the last output jack. Some monitors have a switch that connects a resistive 75Ω termination across the line when turned on, eliminating the need for the termination plug.

Monitor cost is largely a function of the quantity a manufacturer sells. A large popular color monitor may be far less expensive than a small, exotic monochrome unit. Phosphor type usually affects cost and delivery times. Standard phosphors (such as P4, the type found in most monitors and monochrome TV receivers) pose no problems, but less often specified phosphors, such as P34 and P39 green, are usually special-order items. Manufacturers usually assemble special monitors as the need arises, and this results in longer lead times and additional cost.

Monitors with RGB inputs are very expensive. It is not uncommon to spend a few thousand dollars for one. This seems unjustified because the RGB monitor is conceptually less complex than a monitor that accepts composite video signals. A composite monitor must accept a composite signal and use additional decoder circuitry to break the signal into R, G, and B outputs to be fed to the R, G, and B amplifiers and guns (which are common to both RGB and composite-only monitors).

Production volume plays a large role in the high cost of RGB monitors. The demand for such equipment is negligible, and so smaller, more specialized industrial monitor manufacturers must charge more than the large television manufacturers who use their consumer television production resources to lower costs.

RGB monitors are designed for the industrial market, and their quality is usually very high. They are rugged, and few cost-cutting compromises are made in the circuitry, so the higher cost also buys higher quality. This also holds true for monochrome monitors manufactured by the small, industrial market companies.

Monitors have many performance characteristics that must be considered for display graphics.

Bandwidth

The rate at which a monitor's amplifiers and electron beam respond to an input signal determines its bandwidth. Bandwidth may be specified by frequency, lines of horizontal resolution, or characters per screen. Specification by lines of horizontal resolution gives the user a better idea of a monitor's display capabilities; but this is not a true measure of bandwidth, because frame rate and number of horizontal lines are not accounted for.

A monitor's bandwidth determines the number of pixels or characters that can be displayed legibly. A graphic display scan line with 256 pixels, or a character display scan line with 32 8-pixel-wide characters, requires a monitor with at least 256 lines of horizontal resolution. Each pixel should be visible, and single pixels (a white pixel with three black pixels on either side, for instance) should be visible and not faded on such a monitor. Standard television receivers have a bandwidth of about 4 MHz, which corresponds to about 300 lines of horizontal resolution. Microcomputers, video games, and other graphic displays that use receivers as monitors are thus limited to about 300-pixel or 40-character horizontal resolution.

Monitor bandwidth β is a function of display, aspect ratio, number of scan lines, and frames per second. To obtain the value of β in hertz:

$$\beta = \tfrac{1}{2} k \alpha n^2 \times F$$

where

α = aspect ratio w/h
n = number of horiz. lines in picture
F = frames per second
k = constant (1.8 frames/line squared)

This equation assumes equal horizontal and vertical resolution for any square portion of the screen (resulting in the αn^2 terms). For computer graphics involving more horizontal than vertical resolution (512×240 displays, for example), this equation is more appropriate:

$$\beta = \tfrac{1}{2} k H V F$$

where

H = horizontal resolution in lines
V = vertical resolution in lines
F = frames per second
k = constant (1.8)

It is important to note that noninterlaced displays on standard 525-line monitors have a 60 Hz frame rate (which corresponds to 240 vertical scan lines), while interlaced displays have a 30 Hz frame rate.

The horizontal lines of resolution depend on bandwidth. For standard 525-line monitors with a 4:3 aspect ratio, the resolution and characters per line are given for four bandwidths:

Bandwidth	Horizontal Lines of Resolution	Characters/Line (6-pixels wide)
4 MHz	280	46
8 MHz	560	93
12 MHz	840	140
20 MHz	1400	233

Bandwidth is measured somewhat differently on color monitors. The advertised bandwidth of color monitors is usually three times what an equivalent resolution monochrome monitor would be, because three beams are used in the color tube. An RGB monitor that can display 1400 lines of horizontal resolution, for example, must have three electron guns, each capable of handling a 20 MHz signal. The monitor is therefore claimed to have an incredible 60 MHz bandwidth. It's important to remember this $\times 3$ factor when evaluating color monitor specs.

Scan Rates

The standard NTSC television scan rate (525 lines, 30 frames per second) is by far the most common for monitors. This rate is adequate for low- to medium-performance graphics systems. For high-resolution graphics, where many lines of vertical resolution are required (such as high-resolution CAD and phototypesetting displays), nonstandard scan rate monitors must be used. Horizontal scan frequency is the parameter that determines a display's number of lines of vertical resolution. Larger vertical resolutions require faster scanning to maintain a flicker-free rate of 30 frames per second.

High-performance monitors (with resolutions of up to 1000×1000) have horizontal frequencies in the 25–50 kHz range as opposed to the standard 15.734 kHz. The frequency is usually adjustable over a wide range (± 10 kHz or more) to give display designers the option of specifying the exact number of scan lines for their systems. In many high-vertical-resolution applications, the increased scan rate is used to increase the number of frames per second to above 30 for less flicker. In these situations, interlace is usually not used, and interlace flicker (a problem that affects computer graphics more than television pictures) is avoided.

Phosphors and Persistence

Phosphors are the materials deposited on the inside face of a CRT that create a visible glow when struck by the scanning electron beam. There are a number of compounds that have phosphorescent and fluorescent properties, and their properties vary according to their mixtures.

Phosphors used in CRTs exhibit two important properties—fluorescence and phosphorescence. Fluorescence refers to the glowing of the phosphor when being bombarded by the electron beam; phosphorescence is the glow that remains after the electron beam is removed. Figure 3-35 illustrates these two properties.

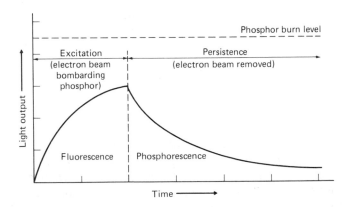

Figure 3-35 Fluorescence and phosphorescence in terms of light output versus excitation and decay time.

116

It takes a given length of time (the excitation time) before a phosphor fluoresces at full intensity, and the phosphorescence decays after the beam is removed. The rate of decay is called the persistence. A phosphor's fluorescence and phosphorescence are not always the same color.

Body color is another phosphor property. A phosphor appears to be a certain color (usually white) when struck by normal light. This property determines the color of the face of a CRT when it is turned off or when no beam is striking a given area.

Persistence and color are the two most important characteristics to consider when deciding which phosphor should be used in the monitor for a given application. Phosphors ranging from blue to red are available, and mixes of red, green, and blue phosphors that glow white (as used on monochrome TV receivers) can be used where white is needed.

A CRT with a relatively long-persistence phosphor can be used to reduce flicker on displays that are not refreshed very often. Persistence is officially defined as the time it takes for a phosphor's phosphorescent light output to fall to 10% of its initial value, and ranges of decay rates are defined as follows:

Persistence	Decay
very short	Less than $1 \mu s$
short	$1 \mu s$ to $10 \mu s$
medium short	$10 \mu s$ to 1 ms
medium	1 ms to 100 ms
long	100 ms to 1 s
very long	more than 1 s

Phosphors are assigned special numbers or P-values. (See table of phosphor characteristics in Appendix A.) A P4 phosphor has a medium–short persistence that is a good tradeoff in most applications. The persistence is long enough so 60 Hz frame rates do not cause flicker, yet short enough to keep dynamic displays from smearing in animated sequences.

In graphic displays that are refreshed at 30 Hz when interlace is used, a P4 phosphor is sometimes not adequate, and noticeable flicker is introduced. A higher-persistence monitor using P39 (green in color) solves the problem. This phosphor is fine in dense text-oriented character displays, but it is next to useless in dynamic graphic displays. Slow-moving objects are smeared, and fast-moving objects become unrecognizable.

DC Restoration

One often overlooked but very important monitor characteristic is that of dc restoration. This refers to a monitor's ability to correctly align itself to the "reference black" portion of the video waveform. Many monitors have a tendency to lose track of the proper black signal level when the screen is mostly white. This is usually caused by capacitive coupling between monitor amplifier stages, which causes a waveform (and thus the reference black level) to be averaged closer to the white level of a video waveform.

Circuits that restore the reference black level to the monitor's black recognition level are used to combat this problem. One common approach is the *back-porch lock* that samples the voltage level of the back porch of the sync signal. The waveform is only sampled in this time window, so line intensity has no effect on white and black reference levels.

Lack of dc restoration is particularly troublesome in graphic displays where large white areas can be generated. Character displays are rarely affeced by dc restoration problems. Lack of dc restoration results in a solid white screen appearing gray, black, or sharply white on the left edge of the screen, fading into gray or black levels toward the right.

Intensity

Screen intensity is measured in candelas per square meter (cd/m^2). An average P4 white monitor puts out about 137 cd/m^2. Lower outputs are common, especially on single-color phosphors such as P39, but it should be remembered that the human eye's maximum spectral sensitivity is in the yellow-green portion of the spectrum and 65–70 cd/m^2 in this range can appear as bright or brighter than blue, red, or even white at 137 cd/m^2. Tube intensity should be carefully considered, especially if screen filters are going to be used. *[Ed. Note: Some U.S. manufacturers still use footlamberts as the measurement of luminous intensity. To convert footlamberts to candelas per square meter, multiply by 3.426269.]*

Linearity

Vertical linearity is a monitor's ability to evenly space the raster scan lines across the face of a CRT. Wide gaps and curved lines that fall off the screen at the top and bottom are signs of poor linearity. Horizontal linearity is the measure of the equality of spacing between adjacent pixels in the horizontal direction on a scan line. Poor horizontal linearity results in pixels being compressed on one side of the screen and expanded on the other.

Inexpensive monitors often have linearity problems, and this should be checked before deciding on a monitor that requires good linearity over the entire screen. Linearity is often measured in dot error per specified reference dot density. A linearity in the range of 12 dots horizontal or vertical at 120 dots per inch reference (or 5 dots at 50 dots per centimeter) is considered to be very good linearity.

Overscan

In many applications it is necessary to fill a screen completely with a picture. Television and computer graphics are two examples where this is necessary. Monitors are designed to be able to accommodate this type of display. The beam sweep is started before the left edge of the screen and is ended past the right side of the screen. This causes each horizontal line to sweep the full width of the screen and eliminates nonlinear start and end points of the line where the beam is accelerating and decelerating as it begins and ends its sweep.

As much as 25% of a scan line can be off the edge of a screen in the horizontal direction, mostly on the right. Inexpensive monitors are notorious for having large amounts of overscan; expensive monitors sometimes have an underscan switch that allows you to decrease the raster width by about 20% to see full raster lines.

Overscan also affects the vertical direction where about 8% of the raster lines fall off the screen. Standard 525-line monitors typically show only 449–480 scan lines.

Color Monitor CRTs

There are a few additional features that must be examined when selecting a color monitor. The color CRT is more complex than a simple monochrome type, and a few variations are used.

The two most common color CRT types are the delta-gun and the inline-gun CRT. The delta gun has three guns arranged in a triangular pattern plus a shadow mask with alignment holes spaced in triangular patterns, with red, green, and blue phosphor dots also spaced in triangular patterns. The inline-gun type has three guns arranged in a horizontal row, a shadow grille with many vertical slits, and vertical stripes of red, green, and blue phosphors.

Until recently, delta-gun systems were almost universally used. It was prohibitively expensive to produce inline-gun systems because it's difficult to fit three guns side-by-side in the neck of a CRT. Advanced techniques involving the use of miniature guns, the mounting of guns at angles, and the implementation of magnetic fields to linearize the beams have helped make the inline-gun CRT common.

Inline tubes have a few advantages over delta tubes. A shadow grille has no vertical "structure," so vertical brightness change is limited only by the scanned lines themselves. This results in a sharper-looking image. Inline systems are easier to keep properly adjusted, and they require only 4 dynamic convergence adjustments as opposed to a delta system's 12. (Dynamic convergence adjustments keep the beams striking the proper phosphor dots and stripes at the screen edges where the beam's incidence angle is different than at the tube's center).

One disadvantage of inline tubes is that the shadow grille with its vertical slits can only bend cylindrically and not spherically as the delta shadow mask can. This makes tube construction and design more difficult. This drawback affects the manufacturer more than the user, however, and most of the manufacutring problems have been solved. Figure 3-36 shows both both inline and delta tubes.

The inline tube's sharpness superiority is evident in inexpensive monitors, but most of today's best color monitors still use the delta configuration. Expensive "fine pitch" shadow masks and dot triads make incredible sharpness possible.

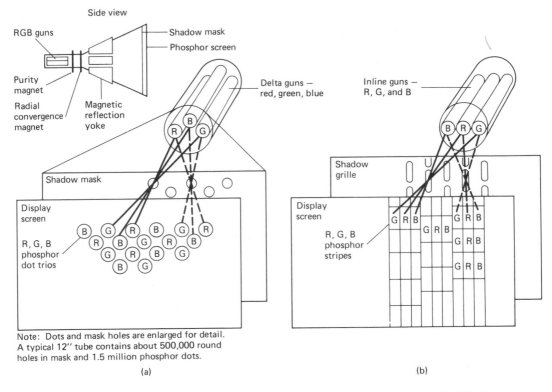

Note: Dots and mask holes are enlarged for detail.
A typical 12" tube contains about 500,000 round
holes in mask and 1.5 million phosphor dots.

(a)

(b)

Figure 3-36 A color monitor CRT may have an internal construction based on the delta (a) or the inline (b) gun configuration.

Screen Reflection Reduction

Monochrome and color monitors have contrast ratios that are better than 50:1 in a totally dark room. This ratio is more than adequate for nearly all television and computer graphic applications. But users seldom view monitors in totally dark rooms, and ambient light reflecting off the face of a CRT can reduce contrast to a 10:1 ratio, which may be inadequate in many situations. Screen reflection of ambient light can also change saturated colors into pastels on color monitors, and can distract the user if the reflections are not diffused. A user may see a faint mirror image of the surrounding room on the face of a glass CRT.

A number of techniques are used to combat the reflectivity problem. Dull-finished nonreflective CRT faces are available—and are desirable in a monitor. This eliminates sharply defined reflection problems. The feature is usually enough to solve reflection problems on character displays where readability and lack of user distraction are more important than perfect color fidelity and contrast.

Screen filters are used in more critical applications. Filters have a transmission index τ value that specifies how much light gets through the filter. A τ of 0.25 means that one quarter of the light passes through the filter. Filters of $\tau = 0.5$ (usually gray in color) are often placed over CRTs to decrease reflection and

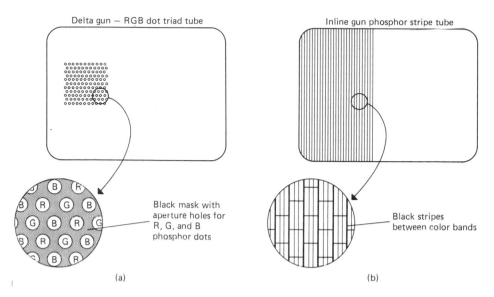

Delta gun — RGB dot triad tube

Inline gun phosphor stripe tube

Black mask with aperture holes for R, G, and B phosphor dots

Black stripes between color bands

(a)

(b)

Figure 3-37   Black masking arrangements for delta-gun (a) and inline-gun (b) CRTs.

increase contrast. The monitor's intensity is cut in half by such a filter, but only one quarter of the ambient light striking the face of the monitor is reflected, because it has to pass through the filter twice (when entering and leaving the filtered CRT).

Color CRT designers attack reflection problems at the source: the white body color of the phosphor itself. Most of the light output from a color CRT comes from the centers of the color dots on the screen (the center of the stripes on inline tubes). Designers intentionally avoid letting the electron beams get too close to the phosphor dot edges for fear of the beam striking adjacent dots of the wrong color. Designers take advantage of this situation by depositing a black opaque layer of material with tiny aperture holes where the center of the phosphor dots will eventually be deposited on the inside face of the CRT. Tubes using this technique are known as "matrix" CRTs. A combined area of about half the screen ends up being black using this technique, so a matrix tube can cut screen reflection in half. This gives as much contrast advantage as a gray glass filter of $\tau = 0.5$ but with no display intensity loss due to absorption.

Designers of inline tubes use the same technique and put black stripes between the phosphor stripes. No electron beam can ever illuminate the striped areas that are blocked by the shadow grille's slit cross supports, so the designers put black there too to make the screen as black as possible. Figure 3-37 illustrates matrix and black striping techniques.

Selecting a Monitor

The characteristics just described should be matched with the display generator requirements, and some consideration should be given to viewing conditions in the intended application before choosing a monitor. Pay particular attention to the factors that affect the user.

The image should be sharp and free of noise, and there should be no annoying reflections. The monitor should not emit a high-pitched whine (of the horizontal oscillator frequency). High voltages (25–35 kV) are used in color monitors, so X-ray emission specifications should be checked and kept well below maximum safe levels.

Technical specifications that affect the display generator design and adjustments and graphics programming are important also; but always keep the user in mind, for this is the individual who will be forced to live with the machine on a day-to-day basis.

VECTOR REFRESH DISPLAYS

The process of directly drawing lines by sweeping an electron beam over the surface of a CRT was brought up in the raster-scan section. There is a class of display devices known as *vector* or *refresh graphic* displays that use this technique. A typical system contains a graphics memory that holds a display file of line segments to be drawn on the screen. The display processor repeatedly cycles through this list of lines, thereby refreshing the screen.

In more advanced refresh displays, character generators are used to interpret character codes in the display file and draw them on the screen, thereby eliminating the need to store common characters as large strings of line segments.

Refresh displays require CRTs with high-speed deflection capability to enable quick random electron-beam sweep direction changes; and high-speed memories store the display list to accommodate fast refreshing.

The graphics quality from a vector display can be excellent if a small number of vectors are drawn. A small number of vectors can be refreshed at rates of hundreds of times per second (versus a raster-scan display's 50 or 60), thus creating a very solid-looking image. Diagonal lines appear straight, with none of the stairstep characteristics typical of the raster-scan type.

As image complexity grows and more vectors are introduced into the display list, the refresh rate drops—and display quality begins to deteriorate. The screen may flicker noticeably. The flicker is less bothersome than that of a raster-scan display, however, because no screen sweeping from top to bottom is performed. All elements on the screen seem to pulsate in unison, which distracts the eye much less than a sweeping motion.

Vector displays are particularly desirable in animated or dynamic graphics. Erasing single elements from the display is simply a matter of removing it from the display list. A whole image or selected parts of an image can be changed without worrying about selective erase problems or large bit-map memory clearing-out times.

STORAGE-TUBE DISPLAYS

The vector refresh display's primary disadvantage is its inability to display a large number of vectors without flickering. High cost is another disadvantage, but this is primarily a result of attempts by designers to solve the flicker problem. Expensive deflection amplifiers, electrostatic deflection tubes, high-speed yokes, beam positioning circuitry, and high-speed memories are required to keep refresh rates high.

The refresh problem can be totally eliminated using a special CRT that permanently retains an image once it has been written by the electron beam. This storage capability is the central feature of the storage tube display.

A storage-tube display is a vector display in that individual lines can be drawn directly on the CRT, but the complexity of the image can be increased without introducing flicker. Extremely dense pictures can be drawn on such devices, and line quality is extremely high, because the straight, nonstairstep lines are combined with a flicker-free display.

Storage tubes find application in areas that require extremely dense drawings but none of the dynamic capabilities of the refresh vector display. Computer-aided design is an example of such an application. (From an application standpoint, it is important to note that a storage tube will produce a bright green flash as it is erased.)

Vectors may be drawn on the storage tube in a nonstoring mode by reducing the writing beam intensity to a level below the storing intensity. Some storage-tube display devices incorporate a *writethrough* mode that allows small amounts of refresh vector information to be mixed with stored information. This may seem like the ideal solution to mixing simple dynamic graphics with a stored background image, but there are a few pitfalls to writethrough modes.

The major disadvantage is that vectors are written at a very low intensity to avoid permanently storing them on the screen; so a dim image results. Another drawback is that a storage tube's deflection systems are typically not as fast and accurate as in vector-refresh systems (an economizing measure), and the image is thus not as steady as might be desired.

Writethrough modes for storage-tube displays are therefore best suited for limited graphics such as screen cursors and status information.

STATIC-MATRIX DISPLAYS

Display devices discussed up to this point have been of a dynamic nature, where images are scanned with electron beams. Static-matrix displays form another class of display device. A rectangular matrix of individually controllable light sources such as light-emitting diodes are used to form a viewing screen. Each light source corresponds to a pixel in the screen coordinate system; graphic elements are generated by selectively turning on pixels.

Liquid-crystal arrays, LED arrays, and plasma panels are all static-matrix displays. These devices and others of the genre have a few common characteristics.

Usually the display is formed on a flat panel. There is no need for a long tube-neck structure as in the CRT, because the matrix consists of small independent elements.

Such displays are also rugged. There are no shock-sensitive precisely aimed electron guns or shadow masks to get out of alignment, and the principal limiting factor is the ruggedness of the individual display elements themselves—which is usually quite high.

From a graphic programmer's standpoint, static matrix displays are nearly identical to CRT-based display devices. The display manufacturers work out the interfaces to the computer system so that the individual pixels can be turned on and off by submitting x and y coordinates. Since these displays seldom share memory with the computer that drives them, there is rarely a need to use software to map into a shared display-processor memory.

PLASMA PANELS

Neon bulbs can be used as display elements in a static matrix display. A 512 × 512 display would require 262,144 individual bulbs. Assembling such a matrix with hundreds of thousands of physical bulbs is obviously impractical; so methods are used to overcome this problem.

One such approach is to manufacture a panel with a matrix of individual neon cells sandwiched between two layers of glass. Voltage must be applied to each glowing element.

Again, a wire volume involving 262,144 pairs individually routed to appropriate switching devices or circuits is impractical. Instead, each row of cells is given a common positive voltage line and each column a negative line. Wires run along the rows and columns and are nearly invisible because of their almost microscopic size. The number of wires is thus reduced to 512 x lines and 512 y lines. An individual cell can be turned on by applying appropriate positive and negative voltages to the x and y lines that correspond to the cell's intersection point.

This scheme is fine for selectively turning on a single cell, but when many cells in the matrix are to be turned on, and some cells don't share common x or y axes, unwanted cells start turning on. If the cells at coordinates 2,2 and 4,4 are selectively turned on, for example, the cells at coordinates 2,4 and 4,2 also glow. A solution to this problem is needed, and this is where the physical properties of neon gas enter the picture.

Neon requires a potential of about 90 V to glow continuously; but to trigger a glow requires a firing potential of 120 V. A continuous 90 V potential can be applied continuously across all cells in the panel. In this way, all *off* cells will remain off, and all *on* cells will continue to glow.

Individual cells can be selectively toggled between glowing and nonglowing states by manipulating voltages at cell intersections—just enough to pass the trigger voltage but not enough to affect other cells in the given row or column.

The plasma panel is therefore a memory in itself. All cells can be erased by dropping the sustaining voltage below neon's glowing voltage.

LED, LCD, AND INCANDESCENT MATRIXES

Any form of glowing element can be used to make a display matrix, but unless each cell has memory characteristics such as the neon cells in the plasma panel, the contents of the screen at any given time must be stored in an auxiliary memory. It is impractical to have wires running from each memory cell to each display element in a large matrix, so a multiplexing method must be used to transfer display memory data to the matrix.

Display scanning performs the memory-to-display transfer in many LED and LCD display matrixes. All LEDs in each row are connected to a common x wire, and all LEDs in each column connect to a common y line. A counter is used to sequence through memory addresses and read single bits of the display memory; a decoder driven by the same counter selects which x and y wire to drive.

If a memory bit is a logic 1, the LED is turned on; if it is a 0 it is not.

LED displays scanned by this method rely strictly on the eye's ability to average many short light pulses into one steady glow. LEDs have no persistence whatsoever. This fact can be observed on an LED-display calculator by rapidly moving the display back and forth. The scanning is very noticeable. LCDs, on the other hand, are very slow in changing from one state to another and thus work well with scanning methods.

Chapter 4

An Introduction to Peripheral Graphic Devices

There is a lot more to computer graphics than simply displaying an image on a display screen. The information to be displayed (the data base) must somehow be entered into the computer in an efficient and user-interactive manner, and final display results must be output onto paper or film for later reference, public display, or printing. In many cases, a graphics display unit and computer system are not up to the desired display performance levels, and performance must be increased.

Peripheral graphic devices are pieces of hardware that perform these mundane but important tasks. Digitizers, joysticks, printers, plotters, and performance boosters such as arithmetic processors all fall into this category. These devices usually come in small, modular packages, and they attach to graphic-generation systems through standard interfaces. Normally, they can be added to a display system as the need arises.

This chapter examines these peripheral graphic devices, some of which are illustrated in Fig. 4-1. A broad spectrum of devices is covered to give you an idea of what is available and what is appropriate to common applications. A good knowledge of peripheral graphic devices will enable you to set up a very powerful, efficient, and easy-to-use computer graphics system.

INPUT DEVICES

Digitizing is the process of entering data into a computer graphics data base. The complexity of the task can range anywhere from the control of a screen cursor (simple x and y movements so the user can position the cursor and point to objects on the screen) to the conversion of an existing drawing such as a map or blueprint into computer-usable form. Devices that aid in performing such tasks are graphics input devices. They convert real-world positions and movements into computer-usable form.

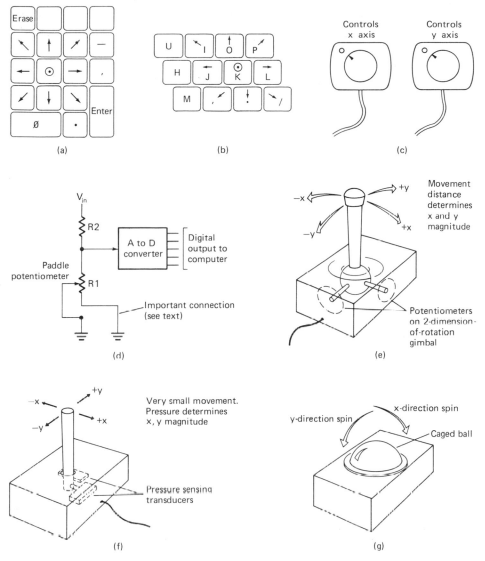

Figure 4-1 Input devices for microcomputer graphics: cursor control keys on keypad (a), control diamond (b) using portion of keyboard, potentiometers, or paddles (c), variable-resistance-to-digital converter (d), joystick (e) using gimbaled potentiometers, force stick (f), and track ball (g).

SWITCHES AND KEYBOARDS

Simple control of a cursor in left–right and up–down movement is often all that is required, and equally simple input devices are appropriate. Special graphics cursor control keys on a computer terminal's alphanumeric keyboard, or separate keypads or pushbuttons off to the side of the main keyboard are ideal for limited cursor control. Using existing keys eliminates the need for additional peripheral boxes and thus reduces system cost and complexity.

Step Control

Keyboard keys are usually assigned to control cursor movement rate or stepping rather than absolute position. One approach uses four keys in a horizontal row on the keyboard for up, down, left, and right cursor movement. A screen cursor can be stepped up, down, left, or right by pressing the appropriate key and holding it down for a specific time (more than 500 ms, for example).

Releasing the key stops cursor movement. This sort of cursor movement control is popular in text-handling operations. The horizontal step size is one character width and the vertical step is one text line. Programs that allow you to enter text into a computer by positioning a cursor on the screen and typing in text lines (screen editors) use this cursor control method.

Rate Control

Stepping is practical for text processing because there are usually only about 80×24 character-row positions, but cursors for graphics may be positioned on coordinate grids that are thousands of units in the x and y directions. Here, cursor movement rate control keys are required. Arrow-labeled left, right, up, and down keys are used here too, but the travel is much faster. Pressing an arrow-labeled key starts the cursor slewing in the selected direction at a preselected rate. The cursor can be stopped by pressing the opposite-direction arrow.

The preselected rate is a tradeoff between easy fine positioning and delay until the cursor reaches its destination. Fast slewing moves the cursor to the general destination area, but accurate positioning of the fast slewing cursor is not easy.

Multiple slew rates are one solution to the problem. One cursor arrow push can cause slow slewing while two or more presses can activate higher slew rates.

A *cursor freeze* key that instantly stops cursor slewing is a virtual necessity with multiple-rate cursors. The user must not be forced to remember how many rate presses are currently in effect.

Key Positioning

Cursor control key positioning is important, especially in multiple-rate cursor systems. The user must be able to place one hand on the keyboard and control cursor movement while watching the screen. Special keypads are available, as shown in Fig. 4-1(a), or existing ASCII keyboard keys may be used.

The control diamond shown in Fig. 4-1(b) is a good arrangement. The "diamond" can be set up in the middle of an alphanumeric keyboard, with the letter K corresponding to the center of the diamond.

Use of a separate keypad may be inferior to simply centering the control diamond around the K key because the user must constantly switch between keyboards to position the cursor and add text. With K as the center key, the user's hand is in the proper position to type in text when necessary.

Rollover

A keyboard's rollover characteristics can be used to make the keyboard cursor control system easier to use. Keyboard rollover refers to the way keyboards react when multiple keys are pressed simultaneously. A two-key rollover characteristic describes a keyboard where you may press a second key while the first key is pressed and still generate the proper pair or two characters. This feature allows fast typists to overlap keystrokes without being penalized. Many of today's keyboards have three-key rollover, and some have *n*-key rollover, where many keys may be pressed simultaneously. One seldom-advertised fact is that many keyboards have two-key rollover in *decreasing* ASCII code sequence but three-key rollover in *increasing* sequence. In other words, the overlapped pressing of an A,B,C sequence may register correctly while a C,B,A sequence would not.

Some keyboards' rollover and keypress scanning systems (notably those that are scanned directly by the system microprocessor such as that used in the Radio Shack TRS-80) allow the computer software to determine that two keys are being pressed simultaneously and determine which keys they are. This feature can be used to advantage by allowing the user to hold the cursor freeze key down while tapping a directional movement key. This lets the user make very small cursor adjustments without starting the cursor slewing across the screen.

POTENTIOMETERS AND PADDLES

One or more rotating knobs can be used to position cursors and control other graphic functions such as scrolling. Two knobs, one for *x* and one for *y* positioning, are typically used. These controls are often placed in small, handheld units called paddles, as illustrated in Fig. 4-1(c).

Absolute Positioning

Paddles are set up to send a number to a computer system based on the absolute position of the control knob. A 0 may represent full counterclockwise rotation, while 255 may represent full clockwise rotation. A wider range of values (greater than an 8-bit 256-step range) is possible, but precision and repeatability are limited by the mechanics of the paddle itself (usually a potentiometer).

The software can use the number returned by the paddle for any purpose, but the most common use is that of specifying absolute screen position. Two paddles with ranges of 0 to 255 can be mapped to the *x* and *y* coordinate system of the display device and the cursor can be positioned accordingly.

Paddles have the advantage of being true absolute position controls, and they are inexpensive. A screen position can be specified quickly with a quick turn of a knob or two. Once a user gets the feel of a paddle, he can easily determine just how much of a quick turn is required to get to the desired position. Low cost, fast (though nonprecise) response, and the capability to double as a nongraphics control (as a throttle, steering, or gun-elevation control, for example) has made paddles very popular on computer games.

It makes little sense to waste the paddle's money savings on sophisticated position-to-number conversion hardware such as expensive analog-to-digital converters, so manufacturers use a few tricks to reduce costs in this area as well. These ploys may have serious performance impacts and should be considered before using this hardware.

Input Data Conversion

One of two methods is used to convert a paddle's position to a usable number: a true analog-to-digital (A/D) converter or a timer. The true A/D conversion method uses the paddle's potentiometer as a variable resistor in a voltage divider. As indicated in Fig. 4-1(d), the paddle is thus a variable voltage source, and an A/D converter is used to convert the voltage into a digital number. The A/D converter's digital output is software-readable through an input port or predefined memory location. Conversion rates of 50 conversions per second are more than adequate, as a paddle is a mechanical device that can only be moved so fast. Low-cost, low-speed A/D converters can be used. True A/D conversion systems constantly make the paddle position available to the software, and software performance is unaffected.

Even low-performance one-chip A/D converters are expensive ($2–$3 is considered expensive to a video-game manufacturer!), so less costly methods involving the use of timers are often employed. The paddle's potentiometer serves as the resistance in a timer's RC (resistor–capacitor) control circuit.

The timer is periodically triggered under software control and the period that elapses before the timer "times out" is proportional to the RC time constant and thus the paddle's position.

The microprocessor counts up a value that begins when the timer is triggered and ends when the time elapses. This value is used by the software as the paddle's position. This method heavily loads the microprocessor, because it must count a value while waiting for the timer to complete its timed period. No other useful processing can be performed during this interval.

Sampling rate must also be cut to reduce the load on the microprocessor. And interrupts must be disabled during paddle timer counting to avoid disrupting the count; so any interrupt-based graphic devices must be made to wait temporarily. Paddles using this conversion technique are fine for low-cost games, but they have no place in a high-performance graphics system.

Linearity

When selecting potentiometers for custom-built paddle systems, carefully evaluate the specifications. Potentiometers come in *linear* and *logarithmic* tapers. A linear taper indicates a linearly increasing resistance throughout the rotation range. A log taper's resistance per degree of turn increases toward one end of the rotation. Linear units are appropriate to most paddles using the variable voltage divider with an A/D converter. The chosen resistance of the potentiometer should be small compared to the other resistor in the voltage divider to maintain good linearity. Voltage divider output is:

$$\text{paddle voltage} = \frac{V_{IN} \times R_1}{(R_1 + R_2)}$$

where

V_{IN} = voltage divider driving voltage
R_1 = paddle potentiometer resistance (variable)
R_2 = other resistor's resistance (fixed)

The larger R_2 is, the more linear the response will be. Large R_2 values will require higher input voltages for equivalent output. Figure 4-1(d) illustrates the paddle voltage divider. If V_{IN} exceeds the A/D converter's safe operating input voltage, the grounding of one resistive and as well as the potentiometer's tap becomes very important. This protects the converter from voltage spikes caused by contact noise that may develop with heavy use.

CONTROL STICKS

The joystick is a vertical lever that can be pushed from side to side and up and back, thus providing two dimensions of control movement. The x and y movements of the stick can be made to correspond to x and y screen-cursor motion, scrolling, or other control movement. As shown in Fig. 4-1(e), joysticks generate x and y position information with two potentiometers connected to the stick's rotating gimbal. One responds to x stick movement while the other responds to y movement.

Self-Centering

All joysticks perform in basically the same way; variations in features are what set one joystick apart from another. The most important feature to watch for is self-centering. Many joysticks' gimbals are spring-loaded so that the stick returns to center when released. This type of stick is good for control applications and cursor slew rate control. Self-centering sticks are a poor choice for absolute cursor control because you must constantly hold the stick to keep a steady cursor position. Self-centering sticks can usually be converted to noncentering by simply removing the springs on the gimbals.

Trim control is a desirable feature on self-centering sticks; this consists of two controls for finely adjusting the x and y center position of the stick. Separate trimmer potentiometers or gimbal spring tension adjusters perform this task. It's possible to perform trim functions in the computer's software, but on-stick trim will save you from having to modify software if your joystick's center position is slightly off-center.

Mechanical Considerations

Joysticks are mechanical devices, and smooth, precise operation depends on construction quality. Sloppy gimbal movement and excessive free play should be watched for. A joystick may have a "swing" of only 50–60° from side to side. Potentiometers usually have 270° movement, so direct gimbal-to-potentiometer-drive joysticks use but a small portion of potentiometer range.

Some manufacturers attempt to gain resistance precision by matching the small joystick rotation to the large potentiometer rotation using gear drive. This sounds like a good idea on paper, but it works poorly in practice. The slightest bit of gear backlash results in an annoying and hard-to-use joystick. Gear backlash increases with time and wear, so the stick constantly gets worse. This type of stick should be avoided.

Position Sensing

Joysticks are used extensively on graphics-oriented games as well as on serious display systems. Ruggedness and cost effectiveness are the watchwords of computer games, and the switch stick, a variation on the conventional joystick, has found wide use in this field. A switch stick has a two-dimension movement lever, but four switches (left, right, up, back) are used instead of potentiometers to sense stick position. The stick position information is usually relayed to the computer as four bits of data (one bit per switch), and no analog-to-digital conversion is required. This is particularly convenient because two switch sticks (ideal for a two-player game) can be interfaced to a microcomputer using a single 8-bit port. Switch sticks usually have a pushbutton on the top of the stick or mounted on the case, for use as a gun control in game applications. The switch turns on two bits of the 4-bit stick code (right and left, for example) which would be physically impossible for the control stick to perform.

Rate and Movement Control

Switch sticks control movement or rotation rates and rate increases. Holding the stick forward may cause the cursor to increase its forward movement speed, while a movement to the right causes rotation and a change in movement direction. Switch sticks can be very effective control devices, and through the proper uses of springs and rubber damping, users can be made unaware that they are really only controlling four switches.

The force stick is an interesting joystick variation that solves many of the cursor positioning and overshoot problems of conventional joysticks. It can control a cursor as a joystick can, but speed and directional movement are controlled by the force and angle applied to the stick rather than by its absolute position. This device is illustrated in Fig. 4-1(f). Stick movement is almost imperceptible, and the device is self-centering. The Sanders Associates 5787 force stick is a good example of this device. Maximum force makes the cursor move across the screen in a second, while lower forces are used for fine positioning. A "bump" mode allows the cursor to be incremented by one position (on screens that are typically 2048 × 2048 resolution) by simply tapping the stick in the desired direction.

TRACK BALLS

A track ball is a captive rotating ball that can be spun in a desired direction to move a screen cursor in a corresponding direction. Movement rate is proportional to ball spin rate. This device is unique in that a single, fine movement rate is acceptable and doesn't hinder fast cursor positioning because it is easy to make the cursor move fast (by giving the ball a good, quick spin).

GRAPHICS TABLETS

Graphics work has traditionally been performed using pencil and paper; and because many people prefer to generate drawings in this manner, the graphics tablet has gained wide popularity. A graphics tablet is a large flat surface on which you move a stylus to indicate absolute *x,y* position to the computer. The stylus often has a ballpoint pen built into its tip so the drawing can actually be seen on a piece of paper placed over the tablet, as shown in Fig. 4-2(a).

Figure 4-2 Graphics tablets and control devices: small graphics tablet (a) with stylus pointer, drafting table (b) with digital coordinate display, and typical stylus pen and cursor (c).

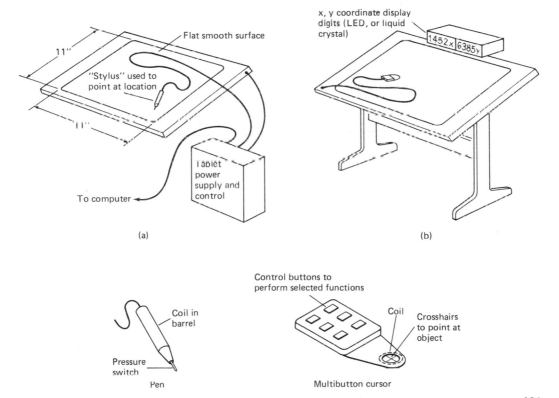

Tablets come in many sizes, ranging from the popular 11 in. square size that fits nicely next to a microcomputer on a desktop, all the way up to 60 by 40 in. Large tablets are in fact used as drafting tables in large CAD systems, where the operator can lay a large drafting sheet on the tablet and trace out the drawing into computer-usable form (digitize the drawing). The drafting-table tablet is shown in Fig. 4-2(b).

A number of techniques have been used in tablet construction. High-frequency sound with linear microphones at the tablet edge (known as acoustic tablets), resistive sheets of material with a stylus acting as a point pickup, and tablets with thousands of x and y grid lines that are capacitively coupled to the stylus have all been tried; but most modern tablets use the transmitter-and-antenna technique, in which the stylus is a transmitter coupled to the tablet (as the antenna). This arrangement results in an easy-to-manufacture, extremely accurate, and maintenance-free input system. Two variations of input transmitters are illustrated in Fig. 4-2(c).

Below the smooth plastic surface of the tablet antenna lie parallel conductors for the x and y axes. The conductors are usually spaced about 0.2 in. apart, with the x and y conductors etched on opposite sides of a large printed circuit board. This is illustrated in Fig. 4-3. A square tablet of 11 in. on a side has 64×64 grid lines. The grid lines, tied together on one end of the tablet, are fed to multiplexers on the other end. Any one of the grid lines can be electronically selected and examined.

The circuitry electronically scans across the tablet, producing an output when it senses a stylus signal.

Simple level detection circuitry is used to judge which x,y grid lines the stylus is near. More complex analog circuitry (a buffer amplifier, phase detector, active filter, and zero-crossing detector) is often used to determine the position of the cursor between two grid lines by comparing the received signal's phase angle with that

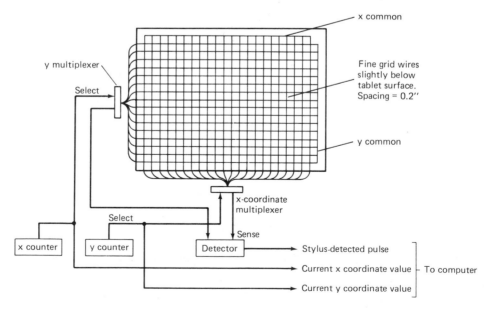

Figure 4-3   Transmitter-and-antenna tablet construction.

of the originally transmitted signal. The scanning system and analog circuitry set up a scanning wave that travels across the tablet surface. The zero-crossing detector issues a voltage pulse at the precise instant the scanning wave passes the stylus.

A digital counter begins counting as the scan begins and is stopped by the stylus-detected pulse. The counter value then reflects stylus position. The counter typically counts about 200 counts per inch, giving an 11 × 11 in. desktop tablet a resolution of about 2200 × 2200 units.

The stylus-transmitter/grid-receiver principle can be reversed, resulting in a grid-transmitter/stylus-receiver tablet. This arrangement is used often in modern tablet designs.

The following specification terms apply to tablets and should be considered for the application at hand:

Resolution refers to the number of points per inch that the tablet can resolve. Low-cost tablets typically resolve 200 lines per inch, while high-performance tablets approach 1000 lines per inch.

A tablet's specified *accuracy* is the precision of the distance between two selected points on the tablet. This is primarily a function of the quality of the spacing between the grid lines in the tablet. Accuracies of ±0.01 in. and ±0.025 cm are common, but higher accuracy (of ±0.005 in. and ±0.0013 cm) is usually available as an option.

Electrical noise and other nonideal conditions can cause slightly different phase angles to be detected from one scan to the next, causing different results for the same stylus position from scan to scan. *Repeatability* is a measurement of this variation, and is about ±0.001 in. for a high-quality tablet.

It takes time to perform an *x,y* tablet scan, and a tablet can only generate results when a scan is complete. *Repetition rate* indicates how many coordinate *x,y* pairs of new data can be supplied per second. A repetition rate of 100 coordinate pairs per second is a typical value.

Pickup proximity refers to the maximum distance the stylus can be from the tablet surface and still accurately register position. This is important if the tablet is going to be used to trace out data from thick documents. A typical value is ⅜ in. maximum.

Tablets operate in many modes, the most common of which are described below.

In the *point mode,* a coordinate pair is sent to the computer when a button on the stylus or tablet is pressed.

In the *run mode,* data is sent whenever the tablet can accurately determine stylus position (when the stylus is near the tablet) at maximum repetition rate. The *stream* or *track* mode is similar to the run mode, but a stylus button must be pressed before data is sent.

In the *incremental mode,* data is only sent when the stylus position exceeds a certain preprogrammed changed distance.

In the *remote* mode, the tablet submits coordinate pairs to the computer when the computer asks for them.

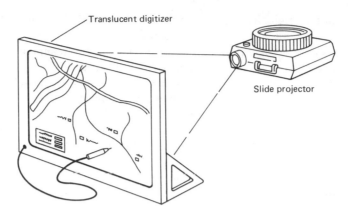

Figure 4-4 Translucent tablet for back-projection; in this case a slide projector is used to view a map for digitizing.

Other tablet features include translucent tablet surfaces for rear projection and backlighting (ideal for tracing photographs, slides, and X-rays), as shown in Fig. 4-4.

Large CAD tablets (and even some inexpensive desktop models) have display readout options. A peripheral box with LED or LCD readouts monitors the stylus position so the operator can position the stylus to exact numerical values.

Tablets are wide-range devices. A large tablet can produce x and y coordinate pairs with 16-bit precision. Tablets usually have parallel TTL-level data outputs with *data-valid* strobes for reading the data. Many modern tablets, in particular the inexpensive desktop models, now have built-in microprocessors to perform data conversion (from "tablet numbers" to fractions of an inch or millimeters), sampling, mode control, and formatting. The Houston Instrument "HIPAD" tablet, for example, generates binary or BCD codes in inches or metric values and sends them in standard ASCII using an RS-232 interface. This output can be connected directly to a standard terminal interface, and software can assemble the data into usable form as if a user were typing it in.

This mode of operation certainly simplifies software and interfacing, but it can seriously bog down a processor. It takes from 6 to 14 characters to indicate the coordinate pair, and sampling rates of 100 samples per second can push a communication line to 1400 characters per second. High-speed (19,200 or 38,400 baud) communication lines are required for full rate output in highly formatted serial modes.

Output is usually "bursty" as well. The tablet scans, performs its conversions, then dumps the data all at once. This sort of output is best handled using interrupts on the host processor system; but again, interrupt latency and processing (especially when using complex operating systems) can seriously load the processor. For high-performance applications, parallel output is preferable to formatted serial output.

LIGHT PENS

Cursors that are controlled by potentiometers, track balls, and data tablets can be used to point to objects on a display screen, but this is an indirect approach—the user holds the knob, ball, or stylus, and the screen cursor does the pointing. A more direct approach involves use of the *light pen,* a stylus with a photodetector that can be used to directly point at an object on the screen. Light pens are great for pointing and selecting objects, but they are limited in their drawing capability.

A light pen simply distinguishes between light and dark screen areas. This information is made available to the computer as a single bit of information. It is up to the computer to determine which light or dark area of the screen the pen is pointing to. There are a few ways for the computer to do this. Screen areas can be toggled between black and white, and the computer can compare the toggling to the light pen output. When the pen output starts to toggle, the computer knows that it has found the right area of the screen. This method is useful when "menu" selections are performed. A question with multiple-choice responses could be asked, and the user could point the stylus to the proper answer. The light pen software could toggle the answer choices at an unnoticeably high rate, and the light pen would respond when the answer it was pointing to was toggled.

More complex hardware methods are often used to determine pen position. Raster-scan and vector refresh displays have scanning electron beams that only illuminate a small portion of the screen at a time. Phosphor persistence tends to average the electron beam energy into a fairly solid glow, but the light pen's sensitivity can be adjusted to sense the slight intensity variation as the beam passes by. The instant this happens, the light pen can trigger auxiliary hardware that captures the current pixel scan address in the case of a raster-scan display or the current display list address in a vector refresh display.

Timing is quite critical using this method, and capture tolerance must be in the 100 ns range to be successful with raster scan hardware having 512-horizontal-line resolution. Microprocessors are limited by their inability to respond at such speeds.

Tracking a light pen as a user draws an image on the screen is not a trivial task. The pen must first be "found" by computer (by sending a "tracking dot" down the screen until the pen position is sensed). The pen must then be tracked by moving the tracking dot's position to keep it locked into the light pen as the user moves the pen. If tracking is lost, the pen's position must again be found.

TOUCH PANELS

The touch panel is a screen pointing device that consists of a square frame around the display screen with light sources (usually infrared LEDs) on the right and top edges and light sensors on the left and bottom edges. The user specifies screen position by touching the screen at the desired location. This breaks one or more of the horizontal and vertical beams of light that cross the screen. The touch-panel hardware or software determines position by sensing which of the screen traversing beams of light are broken.

Touch panels are low-resolution devices. A common touch-panel size is 64×64 units, because this is about the best resolution that can be hoped for using a finger to break the beam.

Touch panels are most often limited to applications in which the user points at objects or selects from multiple-choice menus. Position tracking poses no hardware or software difficulties, but drawing using a touch panel as an input device is rarely done because of the limited resolution.

AUTOMATIC DIGITIZERS

All of the input devices discussed so far have required an operator to enter data into the computer. In some industrial applications there may be a huge number of drawings that must be entered directly into a computer with no physical changes—they simply must be digitized. An operator could spend hours or days on a single complex map using conventional data tablet techniques. Automatic digitizers are devices designed to take existing data bases and digitize them automatically with little or no operator assistance.

Vector Generating Devices

Most large CAD systems work with vector-oriented data bases, and vector-generating autodigitizers must be used. These are large devices that consist of a flat bed on which the drawing is laid and a motor-controlled head that scans the drawing. Fine light beams (incandescent or laser) illuminate the drawing, and photodetectors receive the reflected light. Position information is noted by the computer when lines are crossed. The rest of the process is software controlled.

The computer must control scan head movement, sense lines and other shapes, determine end points, and add them to the data base. This is an extremely complex task and a large minicomputer or mainframe is usually used to perform it.

Automatic digitizers and their software are not yet fully perfected. After digitizing, an operator must physically check the drawing for errors and oversights and correct them using manual CAD techniques. Advances in artificial intelligence and pattern recognition will ultimately improve automatic digitizers to the point where human intervention is unnecessary.

Frame Grabbers

A frame grabber is a device that takes a single frame of a television image, "freezes" it into a display memory, and makes the memory's contents available to the computer for storage or analysis. Frame grabbing is useful for digitizing photographs or direct television images, or editing films or television presentations.

Frame grabbers are raster-scan display generators that can synchronize their scan to that of the input television camera. As data flows in from the camera, a fast A/D converter digitizes the image into gray scale or color levels. Final digital results are written into the display memory as the raster is scanned.

Frame grabbing is usually a feature that is built into a graphics display generator. Features to watch for are number of gray or color conversion levels, conversion speed, triggering method (make sure it is right for your application), and the ability to view the digitized output (the output of the A/D converter put back through a D/A converter) before grabbing the frame.

Phototriggers

The eye smoothly blends the scanning action of a raster-scan display into a solid image, but a camera has a better view of reality. Photographs taken at less than 33 ms (the approximate frame rate of a standard video display) will only contain a portion of the screen image. If higher exposure times are used, light color bands appear where the frame was scanned one more time than the rest of the picture.

The diagonal or horizontal scanning movement of the camera's shutter plane only compounds the problem. One solution is to use a very long exposure time and go for the averaging effect. This works well with static pictures, but dynamic graphics pose problems. Also, the filming of animation sequences can take too long if a second or two is spent on each frame.

The phototrigger provides the solution. This is a display generator feature or a pheripheral device that blanks the display screen (usually under software control) and waits for a trigger pulse from a camera. When the trigger signal is received, the display generator waits until the beginning of the next frame, then scans out a single complete frame.

The camera's shutter should be open for the duration of the single frame scan. The result is a photograph with no scan bars or shutter-plane effects. The "X" contacts on most cameras (designed to trigger an electronic xenon strobe) can be used to activate the phototrigger. The timing of the X contacts is perfect for this application because xenon strobe photography uses precisely the same principle: open the shutter and flash the image.

PERFORMANCE-BOOSTING PERIPHERALS

Computer graphics is one area of computer science where multiple and parallel processors are applicable in a very practical way. Unlike general-purpose data processing, which must be performed in a step-by-step manner, graphics processing easily partitions into multiple, independent tasks. One processor can perform line drawing and screen mapping for the current display frame while another performs 3D rotations for the next.

A bank of 10 processors can in fact process (translate, rotate, and clip) 10 independent lines with little or no synchronization or data dependency penalties. The overall processing will be performed at 10 times the rate of a single processor. This property of computer graphics has resulted in the availability of a wide variety of general and specialized peripheral processors that improve display performance.

GRAPHIC FUNCTION MICROPROCESSORS

Many new display generators contain on-board microprocessors that perform general-purpose graphic functions. These range from 10 MHz (8085) and 6 MHz (Z80) microprocessors on S100, Multibus, and other popular buses to custom 16-bit high-performance bit-sliced processors in expensive graphics work stations (such as Megatek's *Wizard* system). The idea is to let the on-board microprocessor perform functions such as screen erase, vector generation, geometric shape generation, and text generation, thus freeing the host microprocessor or minicomputer to perform other processing tasks.

Graphics commands instead of pixel coordinates are sent to the "intelligent" graphics board. Drawing a line becomes no more complex than sending the following bytes to the microprocessor:

byte 1 = 23 = command code for DRAW A LINE
byte 2 = 05 = start point x
byte 3 = 43 = start point y
byte 4 = 97 = end point x
byte 5 = 43 = end point y

After receiving such a command, the graphics microprocessor executes a line drawer program stored in its on-board ROM complement.

It takes time for the on-board processor to perform line drawing and other commands, so a status signal that can be read under host processor control lets you know when the graphics board is ready to accept another command. It is best to divert program execution to other tasks while the graphics processor is busy. Busy status checking can be performed occasionally in the program, or interrupts can be used to inform the program when another graphics command may be substituted.

Before choosing a display generator with an on-board microprocessor to increase graphics performance, it is important to look at the performance specifications. The performance will not be better than the software being executed by the processor. In many cases, the on-board software may time wasteful. This can be the result of poor graphics programming knowhow or the desire to squeeze too many graphic features into a limited ROM space. In any event, some graphic functions could more efficiently be performed by the host computer.

If your application requires extensive screen data manipulations (such as hit detection in games or image processing), the on-board processors tend to isolate the display memory from the user; and a complex, time-consuming command protocol must be followed to access it.

ARITHMETIC PROCESSORS

Three-dimensional graphics and other graphics that involve many multiplications, divisions, and trigonometric functions for rotations and scaling quickly use up a byte-size microprocessor's processing power. Powerful 16-bit processors with multiply and divide capabilities partially solve the problem, leaving only the trigonometric functions to slow down processing. Arithmetic capability can improve performance greatly on 8-bit processors and to a slight extent on 16-bit processors.

One general-purpose arithmetic processor currently in use in many microcomputer systems (and even built onto some graphic boards) is the Advanced Micro Devices 9511. This chip is designed to interface easily to a microprocessor bus. The unit has an internal stack that you push operands into. Operands of 16 and even 32 bits are required, so 2 to 4 bytes must be pushed into the chip by sending bytes to a memory-mapped address or I/O port for each operand.

Once an operation code and all necessary operands are sent to the chip, it performs the operation and lets the processor know when it is done by clearing a busy bit in the chip's user-readable status register (which also contains zero, sign, carry, and error code bits). A hardware signal called END also issues a pulse when processing is finished. This is often connected to the processor's interrupt system.

When performing simple functions such as double-precision addition and subtraction and even multiplication, the time savings due to the arithmetic chip may not be as great as initially thought. Routines to send data to the chip, interrogate busy status, and take data from the chip are required, and these use up time. Another point is that most graphics-oriented tasks consume time with simple data moves, adds, subtracts, compares, and branches (especially if line drawing is performed by the processor). Arithmetic processors offer no advantage on these operations. Multiply- and divide-weighted graphic tasks typically execute 30% faster using an arithmetic processor with an 8-bit machine.

MATRIX MULTIPLIERS AND ARRAY MULTIPLIERS

Scaling, projection, and rotations require many multiplications, and external hardware that speeds up multiplication improves processing rate. The arithmetic processor helps in this regard, but time is also wasted by formatting data and sending it to the arithmetic processor chip. Matrix multipliers and array multipliers eliminate this overhead by taking large blocks of memory containing many operands, performing arithmetic operations on them, and placing them back into memory using DMA. High-performance processor chips such as the TRW MPY16 multiplier, which performs a 16 × 16 multiply in 200 ns, make sense in these applications because the processing power isn't wasted by 5 or 10 μs of I/O time. The multiplier and DMA system can sequentially step through memory-reading operands and write results as quickly as memory will accept it (usually 300–500 ns per 16-bit operand).

Matrix multipliers and array multipliers are not off-the-shelf peripherals that can be bought and plugged into a system. The market demand for such high-performance hardware doesn't justify mass production. This sort of feature can be designed into a new graphics system, and should be watched for in high-performance graphics hardware.

CLIPPER DIVIDERS

Users are inclined to think that complex matrix multiplications account for most of the processing time in complex two- and three-dimensional graphics. In most applications, however, this is not the case. One 3D graphics program for flight simulation, when analyzed, was found to be spending only 5% of its time performing matrix multiplication operations. Small percentages of time were also going for projection, data-base manipulation, line drawing, and other mundane functions; but the largest block of time (23%) was spent on clipping. Three-dimensional clipping involves multiplication as matrix multiplying does, and it also requires divisions, comparisons to determine if the line is on or off the screen (coding), and repeated iterations until the line is pushed entirely onto the screen. Clipping is not a simple task from a control standpoint as matrix multiplication is. Operations to be performed are dependent on data. Processing method and time varies from line to line.

The clipper divider is a piece of hardware that performs clipping. You feed it a line start and end point (3D or 2D) and it returns a start and end point of the line clipped to the predefined boundaries.

HARD-COPY OUTPUT DEVICES

Graphs and designs plotted on pen plotters, images generated on paper by matrix or laser printers, and digitized photographs projected onto film by a film recorder all fall into the "hard copy" category. Permanent records on paper or film are necessary in many applications, and hard-copy output peripherals are used to produce it.

MATRIX PRINTERS

The most recent entry into the computer graphics hard-copy field is the matrix printer. This printing technology cannot yet produce graphics copy of as high a quality as other output devices, but this method is rapidly becoming the dominant graphics printing method because of its low cost and versatility. It's necessary to understand a dot matrix printer's mechanics to realize its advantages and limitations.

Operational Characteristics

A matrix printing system is the mechanical equivalent of a raster-scan display system. A print head with a vertical column of wire hammers (usually 7 or 9) scans across a piece of paper. Electromagnets (one for each hammer) drive the hammers into the print ribbon and onto the paper, leaving a series of dots across the page. These dots are arranged to form characters in the same way that characters are generated on a CRT by a raster-scan display system.

The impact matrix print head and the microprocessor make a good combination. The print head is simple and reliable, and the microprocessor is ideal for performing the data crunching and timing necessary to convert an ASCII character string into a dot matrix pattern of corresponding characters and firing the hammers as the head scans across the page. Paper advance and head movement are usually controlled by stepping motors that are also easily controlled by the microprocessor.

Graphics Capability

Hundreds of printers with this ideal combination of matrix print head, microprocessor, and stepper motor have been introduced. To be competitive in the marketplace, many manufacturers add extra features to their printers, and one of these features is a graphics capability.

The dot patterns produced by the printer can be thought of as graphics pixels; and images can be created by simply reprogramming the printer's microprocessor to accept direct pixel-control information instead of a character stream. Manufacturers claim that "with proper software, beautiful graphic images can be generated." "Proper graphics software" is the catch. An examination of the numbers involved reveals why.

Impact matrix printers are capable of printing extemely dense dot patterns. There is no persistence or scan-rate limit as there is in a CRT display system, and densities (measured as dots horizontal by dots vertical per inch) are as high as 216 × 120 dots per inch on economy model printers that cost less than $700. Much higher densities arc available on high-cost printers. A standard 8½ × 11 in. printed page thus has a "display" density of 1836 × 1320—denser than that of most high-cost raster display systems.

Matrix printers require no internal memory to store the image, because the image is permanently stored on the page as it is printed. The pixels on the page, however, are not randomly accessible, because the printer scans the page serially. The most common way of printing an image on a matrix printer is thus to first use a large memory in the computer to format the image, then serially dump the memory to the matrix printer. An image of 1836 × 1320 dots requires 2,423,520 bits or 302K bytes of storage to hold it, and most computers (especially those driving low-cost printers) simply don't have this much memory. This results in the need for complex user-written software to break up the image into horizontal strips and use a technique involving format, print, format, print. . . .

Time between strip formatting and printing must be kept as low as possible. Ideally, the printer should not stop printing throughout the generation of a complete image. This increases print speed, but more importantly it keeps dark or light strip separation lines from forming due to paper and mechanism settling and start-up acceleration. This problem is more critical on electrostatic printers than on impact matrix types.

Another problem concerning graphics on a matrix printer is print head temperature. Print heads must be small and light so they can move fast, and they must have 7–9 high-power electromagnets to drive the ballistic print wires at high rates. The result is a small, hot-running print head.

Many heads have aluminum cooling fins to dissipate the heat, but most are designed to print text that requires a low duty cycle on the print head magnets. Wide letters such as "W" require up to 4 impacts per pin as the character is scanned, while the letter "I" only requires 1 or 2. Impact duty cycle averages out to 25–40%. Print heads are designed to print text as fast as possible without burning up the print head. A large black area in a graphics image, however, will result in a 100% printer duty cycle.

Some printers (such as the Heath H14) have circuits that monitor print head temperature by measuring electromagnetic coil resistance while a carriage return is being performed. Such devices will stop printing until print head temperature reaches a safe level. Other printers simply burn up. Stopping the printing process in the middle of an image is not good, because a horizontal strip line will result. Modern matrix printers often use heavy-duty print heads or slow their print rate in graphic modes to eliminate this problem.

Matrix Printer Variations

There are variations of the impact matrix printer that also use dot matrix techniques. The three most common are electrostatic, thermal, and electrosensitive printers.

Electrostatic printers use high-voltage sources and electrodes to place a charge on paper. The paper is passed through a toner–developer to turn the charged areas black. Thermal printers use small heating elements that heat temperature-sensitive paper, resulting in black dots (no developer is required). Electrosensitive printers use electrodes to blacken dots on conductive electrosensitive paper (usually shiny silver in color).

All three printers require special, and often expensive, papers. This is their major disadvantage. Another disadvantage of electrostatic printers is the need for a developer solution.

When it comes to text printing, impact matrix printers are superior to these methods, and manufacturers have to rely on simplicity, reliability, and—most importantly—silent operation (a very desirable feature in a printing terminal); but when graphics are involved, electrostatic technology has an edge. The reason lies in the way the image is generated. Electrostatic elements are small and cheap. It makes more sense to simply mount a row of hundreds or thousands of them and let the paper pass over it while controlling them electronically than to use 7 to 9 of them on a moving print head. The print mechanism is therefore mechanically simple and reliable.

There is no moving print head that scans horizontally in an electrostatic printer, so no carriage return or print head reversal is needed. Also, the paper can be passed over the electrostatic elements in a smooth continuous motion, as opposed to the ratcheting line-at-a-time motion a print head requires. The result is perfect vertical dot alignment (something that is nearly impossible to get on an impact matrix printer).

Electrostatic printers (such as those made by Versatek) have gained wide acceptance in the graphics field. They are made in very wide models (up to 60 in. paper width is used) and can produce line drawings comparable to those of a pen plotter. In addition, they can quickly and accurately produce dot matrix text fonts of typesettable quality—something even the best pen plotters are not capable of.

PEN PLOTTERS

If the matrix printer can be considered the mechanical equivalent of a raster-scan display system, the pen plotter is the mechanical equivalent of a vector display system. This device has a computer-controlled moving pen that draws images on paper in the same way a draftsman would draw it with a pencil or pen. Like the vector display, the pen plotter is superior to the matrix printer for performing line drawings; but shading and rapid drawing of extremely complex images and character sets are best handled by the matrix printer.

There are two basic types of pen plotters: flat-bed and drum. The flat-bed plotter has a flat surface that the paper is laid on. A pen tip is mounted on a moving bar that passes over the paper under motor control, providing x movement. The pen slides back and forth on the bar, resulting in y movement. Flat-bed plotters are good for small drawings on standard paper.

Drum plotters come in two varieties: those that handle a single sheet and those that use a roll of paper. The single-sheet drum plotters have a moving pen attached to a stationary bar that runs across the width of the paper (for x pen movement). A sheet of paper is mounted to a cylindrical drum that rotates under the stationary bar to provide y movement. Single-sheet drum plotters, like flat-bed plotters, only handle standard sizes of paper and are more economical than flat-bed plotters because they are less complex. Economy is their only real advantage, and they tend to be bulkier and harder to use than flat-bed plotters.

Paper-roll drum plotters have an elaborate paper feed mechanism that continuously feeds a large roll of paper across a drum. A pen on a stationary bar provides x movement, and the paper passing over the drum provides y movement. Unlike the single-sheet drum plotter, paper length is not restricted to the circumference of the drum but can be any length. This is limited only by the length of the paper roll and the plotter's ability to keep track of where it is in an extremely long drawing.

Plotters of this type are used extensively in CAD applications where large-size drawings are plotted.

Paper-roll drum plotters are the most expensive and complex plotters because of their elaborate feed mechanism, which must be able to pull a large paper area back and forth over the drum many times while maintaining positional accuracy. The shear size of large paper-roll plotters makes them expensive. Drum widths of 34 in. or more are quite common. These plotters require special paper with sprocket holes to maintain accurate paper alignment.

Plotter Communications

Plotters are usually incremental devices. You must tell the plotter to step repeatedly in the x or y direction to move the pen. Steps can be made in x and y directions simultaneously. Pen movement is thus restricted to eight directions (x, y, and $45°$ movements), but step size is usually much smaller than the pen's line width (0.002 in. or 0.05 mm steps are common) so even lines at odd diagonals look perfectly straight with no stairstep effect.

Two additional commands that must be sent to a plotter are PEN UP and PEN DOWN. These are commands to lift and lower the plotting pen. On more expensive plotters, multiple pens of different colors are available, so commands such as LOWER RED PEN and LIFT GREEN PEN are used. When writing plotting software, you must take pen lift and lowering times into account. A 50 ms delay is a standard pen lifting or lowering time requirement.

Plotters (especially low-cost models) accept data at a low rate of a few hundred to a few thousand steps per second, so serial communication over standard RS-232 computer terminal lines is possible. Some manufacturers equip their plotters with serial RS-232 interfaces and recognize ASCII characters as plot commands.

Plotter Characteristics and Features

A few important characteristics to consider before deciding on a plotter are plot size, speed, resolution, accuracy, and repeatability. Plot size is limited by the maximum size of paper the plotter can handle and the freedom of movement of the pens. If full-sheet color plots are desired, you must make sure that all pens can plot the full plotter area. In many cases, pens are mounted side-by-side and all colors can't reach the edge of the sheet.

Plotting Rate. Plotting speed is measured either in steps per second or in inches or centimeters per minute. Low-cost plotters that plot about 400 steps per second at 0.005 in./step can only plot 120 in./min. At the high end, expensive plotters can plot a few thousand inches per minute. Plotting speed is very important in large and complex drawings. Some complex mechanical and architectural drawings and cartographic maps take hours to plot on high-speed plotters.

Resolution. Plotter resolution is similar to display CRT resolution and indicates the number of distinguishable points per unit distance (centimeter or inch) that can be plotted. Plotters seldom perform dot graphics, but this figure is useful in determining how close parallel lines may be drawn and still be individually distinguishable. This characteristic is limited more by the tolerance of the plotting pen than the pen movement mechanics and step size.

Repeatability. Accuracy and repeatability characterize the plotter's ability to accurately position a pen and to return to that position. Repeatability is especially important, because it insures that the drawing geometry will remain stable and that polygons will close properly. Modern plotters use computer-controlled stepping motors that reduce accuracy to step size and make repeatability "absolute."

Plotter Materials. Just as a draftsman has many pen–paper options, so does a pen plotter. For CAD, architecture, and other applications requiring a large selection of plotting materials, it is important that the plotter be able to handle the desired materials. Paper and Mylar are two standard materials that most plotters can handle. Most plotters use ballpoint and fiber pens, but much better resolution can be obtained using tube-fed ink pens. Ink pens, however, tend to clog, dry up in the middle of a plot, and bleed if held still.

Exotic plotting "pens" such as light heads that record on film with a precise light beam or laser, and cutting heads that can cut patterns in paper or cloth are also options on some plotters.

Plotter Software. Plotter software can be simple or complex, depending on the desired performance. Software that simply takes a display file of vector start and end points and issues the proper pen commands is fairly straightforward. To simplify this software, long delays for pen lift and minimum stepping rates can be used. High-performance pen software can get very complex.

Head or drum acceleration can be taken into account when writing plot software. Long step times are required to accelerate a pen from rest, but higher rates may be used as the pen accelerates. Deceleration must also be accounted for to avoid overshooting lines and "jumping steps" on the stepping motor.

Another technique used to increase plotter performance is to sort line sequences and direction to reduce pen repositioning. Two parallel lines, for instance, can be drawn more quickly by drawing one from left to right and the other from right to left than drawing both in the same direction with a pen positioning command in the middle. Short lines in nearby plot areas can be grouped together to reduce movements between line drawing operations.

The amount of sorting performed depends largely on the desired plot performance, but a certain amount of sorting is necessary in all cases. A circle that is composed of 64-line segments, for example, should always be drawn with end-to-end segments without lifting the pen. Even the best plotters have trouble producing a smooth circle if the pen is repeatedly lifted and repositioned while drawing. This property is caused by the paper and ink characteristics as much as by mechanical tolerances in the plotter.

Chapter 5

Interactive Design
Elements and Intelligence

Having the ability to produce every letter of the alphabet doesn't qualify a person as a writer, even if the individual can construct words and sentences with alphabet characters. Similarly, being able to draw circles, squares, ellipses, and other geometric shapes doesn't make an artist, despite the fact that every drawing consists solely of these elements. In both cases, however, knowledge of the basic elements—the alphabet in the case of the would-be writer and geometric shapes in that of the prospective artist—must precede their effective implementation.

This philosophy applies equally to microcomputer graphics. Before a system can be used for creative image generation or animation, a good working knowledge of the tools and techniques involved must be acquired.

When implementing graphics in practical applications, the user's interface with the graphics system becomes as important as the graphics. Lines, circles, and other graphic elements must be submitted to the graphics system in an easy-to-perform way. The user must not be forced to think in terms of the graphics process, but must be left free to think about the application at hand. User interaction encompasses more than just submitting graphic elements. The user will want to correct errors and change designs, so methods for finding, deleting, and moving groups of graphic elements on the screen must be considered also.

DESIGN ELEMENTS AND THEIR SUBMITTAL

Graphic images, complex though they may sometimes appear, are nothing more than selectively positioned design elements such as lines, curves, circles, and ellipses. Learning to specify and submit these relatively few elements is the key to preparing image-generating software.

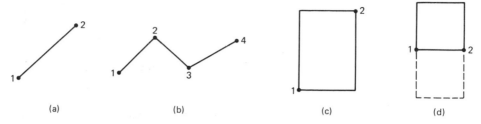

Figure 5-1 Submittal formats for straight-line figures (numerals indicate sequence of entry). Examples are a line (a), a line string (b), a rectangle (c), and a mirrored square (d).

STRAIGHT LINES

Simple lines (with two end points) are added to a design by specifying a line command (using the keyboard or a menu and cursor) followed by the start and end point. The point submittal button (on the keyboard or tablet stylus) is pressed once for the start point and once for the end point, as indicated in Fig. 5-1(a).

Line Strings

Strings of lines appear often in designs, and most systems have an end-to-end line string command. The command is selected, and the cursor is placed at the start point followed by the sequential continue points of the string sequence. The stylus button is pressed once for each end point; the last point is specified by selecting a new command. This is illustrated in Fig. 5-1(b).

Single-precision line key-in submittal modes are often used, as are x and y coordinates, but the user must typically submit an angle and length through keyboard entry.

Previewing Input Lines

Continuous feedback of what a line will look like before it is submitted to the system is very helpful, and *rubber-band* lines—that is, lines that are continuously updated as the cursor is moved about the screen during end-point selection—help in this visualization. The availability of this function is dependent on system hardware. A display system that can selectively erase lines very quickly is required. Storage tubes sometimes have a special mode (called *writethrough*) that allows a rubber-band line to be refreshed continuously without storing an image on the screen. The line is usually dim, but this is better than nothing at all.

Line Weights and Styles

Conventional designs use many types of lines. Wide lines are used to emphasize certain features, and broken lines are used for hidden edges or as coded borders. Most display systems—especially those used in expensive design systems—are capable of generating a few different types of lines. The width of the line is known as the line weight and the pattern is known as its style.

149

The user should have control of what line style is to be used. Menu boxes that allow selection of weights and style should provide the most recently selected style and weight until a new style is specified. All elements entered should use that line style.

Many design systems let you choose from a wide number of line weights, some of which can't be represented on the screen. These weights are used by plotters that can handle wide ranges of line weights. A substitute line weight is used when drawing on a display device, but the correct weight code goes into the graphic element in the design's data base.

SQUARES AND RECTANGLES

Rectangles are nothing more than line strings of four simple lines, but they are used so often that separate interactive entry commands are used. The most common rectangle sequence is "bottom left corner, top right corner," as shown in Fig. 5-1(c). In other words, we specify the rectangle's diagonal. Rectangles specified in this way are assumed to be vertical or horizontal.

There is no standard way of specifying a square, and the methods used are usually arrived at with some application in mind. A square can be specified by submitting its base or any of its sides. For any specified side, two squares can exist; the desired square, and its mirror image. The side to be chosen must either follow a predefined convention or the user must submit a third point that indicates the submitted side on which the square is to appear. This is shown in Fig. 5-1(d).

CIRCLES AND ELLIPSES

The most common circle parameters are center, radius, and diameter. Circle submittal formats use these parameters. The most common form is "circle center and radius." The cursor is used to specify circle center as illustrated in Fig. 5-2(a), and cursor placement at the desired radius from the center (in any direction) is used for the radius. Interactive systems often allow a user to key in the radius.

Diameter specifications are sometimes used. The diameter of the desired circle is submitted in the same way a line would be, and the circle is drawn around the desired diameter, as shown in Fig. 5-2(d). This method allows the "fitting" of circles between two borders or points.

Ellipses are quite a bit more complex than circles. Not only do they have two radius-type parameters (semimajor and semiminor axes), but they have an orientation angle as well. Unless an ellipse is going to be oriented horizontally or vertically, it is hard to visualize just where it will appear once orientation points are specified. Automatic fitting techniques are ordinarily used for ellipses, but manual submittal methods are sometimes used. The most common involves specifying the center and two points that will fall on the ellipse itself, as shown in Fig. 5-2(e). A second method lets you define one axis of the ellipse as you would a line or circle diameter, followed by a point on the ellipse, as in Fig. 5-2(d).

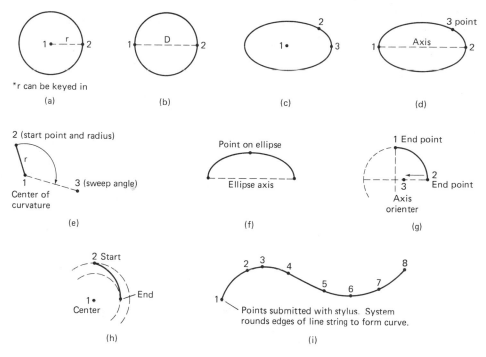

Figure 5-2 Interactive element submittal formats for curved-line constructions. For a circle (a), the cursor may be used to locate the circle center and then repositioned to specify radius; or a circle may be specified with a straight line to denote diameter (b), which is useful for fitting circles between image areas. An ellipse may be submitted manually by specifying the center plus two points that fall on the ellipse border (c), or by specifying one axis as if it were a circle (d) and adding a point that defines the ellipse boundary. A partial circle may be submitted by specifying a center, a radius, and a sweep angle (e). A partial eclipse is submitted by specifying one axis and a point on the ellipse (f) or, in the case of a quarter-ellipse (g), by specifying the start and the end point and an orientation point. A spiral segment (h) requires specification of a center of rotation, a start point, and an end point. Random curves are submitted with point-by-point entry (i), and a smoothing function is used to round the edges.

PARTIAL CIRCLES AND ELLIPSES

When only a partial circle or ellipse is desired (while rounding-off corners, for example), information regarding where the circle starts and ends, as well as which side of the circle to generate, is required. Interactive submittal formats combine the generating and limiting information in a way that one usually expects when manually drawing an arc.

Partial circles are specified by submitting a center of curvature, a start point (which also happens to be the radius), and a sweep angle (defined by the center point and the third-specified point). This is illustrated in Fig. 5-2(e). A clockwise or counterclockwise convention determines which way the partial circle will be generated.

A start point, a midpoint (along the circle), and an end point is another convenient way to specify partial circles.

In engineering applications, precise and uniform radius values are required, so radius key-in along with partial circle start-, end-, and center-point specification is used. The specified start and end points actually represent the start and end of the sweep angle, not points on the circle itself. The circle is generated at they keyed-in radius distance away from the center.

Full ellipses are difficult enough without having to specify where partial segments of them start and begin. Partial ellipse specification is therefore limited to special cases that appear often in designs. One common method is to specify one of the axes and a point on the ellipse, as in Fig. 5-2(f). Half an ellipse is always generated. Another often-used segment is the quarter ellipse. The start and end points (which correspond to the ends of the axes) and an axis orientation point (that defines the direction of one of the axes) must be specified, as shown in Fig. 5-2(g).

Odd-sized portions of arbitrary ellipse segments are very rarely used, so specification methods are not standardized.

SPIRAL SEGMENTS

Designs and maps that require decreasing radius functions on mechanical parts or curves will be easier to design if a spiral segment command is available. A center of rotation, a start point, and an end point are specified, as shown in Fig. 5-2(h). Unlike the partial circle command, where one point represents the true radius and the other a simple sweep angle, both points represent the spiral's radius at the specified points. The spiral's expansion rate is calculated mathematically and the segment is drawn. Spirals of Archimedes (spirals with linearly increasing radii) are the most common. Logarithmic and hyperbolic spirals are seldom required. (The word *spiral* implies linear spiral on design systems unless stated otherwise.)

CURVES

Curves are defined as lines that follow a nonstraight course, but with no rigid mathematically defined boundary. Curves, therefore, are not generated using a few guiding points and a predefined fitting formula and generation equation. Instead, curves are submitted in the same way as line strings. You submit the general shape of the curve in a sequential point-by-point manner, and a smoothing function is used to round the rough edge when the curve is finally generated. Figure 5-2(i) illustrates such random-curve generation. Smoothing procedures vary from simple blending functions to quadradic and spline curve fitting functions.

TEXT ELEMENTS

Most designs require some sort of text, and some require it in many styles, sizes, and orientations. Text submittal interaction is therefore quite important. The submittal and placement capabilities depend not only on the hardware but on the definition of the font sets. Vector-defined font sets are more versatile—they fit into limited spaces, and can be placed at odd angles more easily than dot-matrix font sets—but dot-matrix font sets with their solid typeface look are often used instead of or in addition to vector fonts. A few types of text interaction modes may exist on one system.

Fitted Text

If vector text generation is used, fitted text at any angle can be interactively entered. The text baseline is specified with two points, and a third point specifies height, as shown in Fig. 5-3(a). The third point can also be used to indicate slant, as in Fig. 5-3(b). It is trivial to perform this sort of text fitting using the "text placard" generation method.

Uniform Text

Fitted text is versatile, but uniform text is preferable in most situations. Identical character geometry and size (or a few standard sizes) generate a better-looking display. Positioning standard text requires only one point (two if a nonstandard angle is used). The standard text height, width, and spacing determine the area the text will occupy. There are a number of ways to specify the "text orientation dot." Figure 5-3(c) shows common positioning. Single lines of text can be right, center, or

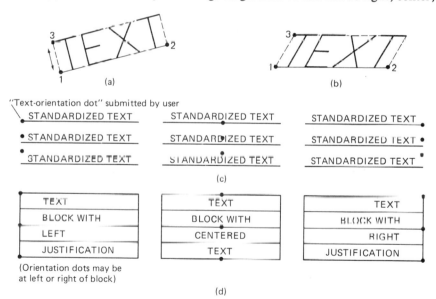

Figure 5-3 Interactive text placement methods. Vector text may be upright (a) or slanted (b) by specifying the baseline with two points and the slant with a third point. Lines of uniform text can be placed using a text orientation dot at the start, center, or end of each line (c), and the dot may be at the text baseline, its center, or at the character-height point. For appearance, text blocks (d) may be displayed as quad left (where all lines of copy are moved to the left copy-start position), quad center, or quad right.

left justified. Text often is written as a series of a few lines, so *text blocks* are a good interactive feature. Text blocks offer standardized vertical spacing between lines, which adds to the professional look.

Fitting a text block requires that block orientation be specified with an orientation dot; it also requires internal block justification, as shown in Fig. 5-3(d).

Text Entry

The system's alphanumeric keyboard is the logical choice for entering the text strings themselves.

Text entry involves a lot of switching back and forth between input devices. The stylus is first used to specify where to place the text. The user must then move to the keyboard to type it in, and subsequently return to the stylus. If 100 cities were to be entered on a map, this would mean 200 movements between peripherals—a real waste of the user's time. Sequential text entry can minimize this problem.

In the interactive mode, many text placement points (next to cities, for instance) are specified. The system then automatically sequences through the text points, requesting the user to submit the text for each submitted point. With this mode the user locates and specifies the graphic location of all 100 cities, then moves to the keyboard and sequentially types in their names. Nearly 200 operator movements are saved.

SYMBOLS, CELLS, AND SUBPICTURES

Every field of design has its own set of symbols and standard shapes. Electronics has resistor, capacitor, transistor, and many other symbols, while cartography has symbols that indicate mine or quarry, church, school, or any of a large number of other specially designated elements. In most designs, certain nonstandard shapes (perhaps a window frame in an architect's design or an outline of a locally common house shape on a map) are used over and over again throughout a single design. Whether it's a standard symbol or an often-used shape, the situation is the same: there's no sense in drawing out the whole thing every time you want to use it again. Conventional drawing technology attacks this problem with templates, decals, and overlays. Computer-based design systems solve the problem with symbols, cells, and subpictures.

The definitions of the terms *symbol, cells,* and *subpicture* are not standard, and their use is often interchanged due to poor understanding of the differences between them.

The *symbol* is a small graphic shape that is stored and manipulated in the same way that a text character is manipulated. A symbol's representation is very compact, and the symbol is placed and oriented by specifying its center (or one of its corners) and an orientation angle. Basically, it is a character that is designed to look like a standard design symbol.

The *subpicture* is a small design (or even a moderately large one) that consists of elements such as lines, circles, and other standard elements. It is designed in its own reference frame. The subpicture is "called" in much the same way a subroutine is called in a computer program, and the variables passed to it are the offset and orientation (its "instance") in space. Many calls to the subpicture with different offsets and orientations can result in a display with many copies of the design scattered throughout the screen, but only one copy of the design exists in the data base. Any changes made to any element of a subpicture will show up in every occurrence of the subpicture on the screen.

The *cell,* like the subpicture, is a small design consisting of standard design elements; but unlike the subpicture, the cell's primary purpose is to be copied repeatedly into the data base. Cells are copied, not called. This allows for custom modification on individual copies of the cell, but prohibits simultaneous changes on all copies with one simple change on the master cell.

There are two interactive sequences that must be performed in systems using symbols, subpictures, and cells: definition and placement.

Symbol Design

Symbols are similar to characters, and most systems use character generation hardware and software to present them. Symbols are thus designed in the same way fonts are: usually with a font editor—a small interactive program that puts up a design grid of the standard character matrix size (5 × 7 dots, 9 × 14 dots, and larger). The font editor allows you to specify dots in the matrix to be turned on or off for raster graphics. For vector-oriented generators, the font editor permits specification of vectors to plot between the grid intersections.

Symbols are usually treated as part of a character set, and unused character codes are used to specify them. The ASCII uses 96 out of 256 possible codes in an 8-bit byte for upper- and lower-case alphanumerics. This leaves 160 unused codes. The 32 codes from 0 to 31 correspond to control characters and have functions assigned to them, so symbols that represent these control functions are somewhat standardized. The 128 codes from 128 to 255 are normally used for special characters and symbols. This range of characters is unusable in data transmission because the most significant bit of the 8-bit byte is used for parity. Within a design system, however, full 8-bit bytes are available and thus 128 additional codes are available.

Symbols are often programmed into ROM on popular microcomputers and some display terminals.

In some applications, a much larger set of symbols is needed. In these cases, a 16-bit code can be used, and symbol libraries (that are stored on disk or in large areas of random access memory) can be set up to reference all the symbols efficiently. Figure 5-4 shows a font editor used to design symbols as well as text fonts.

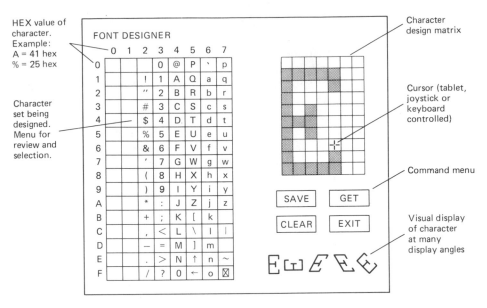

Figure 5-4   Raster-scan font editor display. Commands are selected by positioning cursor on command menu or design matrix position and pressing cursor button or keyboard key.

Cell and Subpicture Design

Cells and subpictures consist of standard graphic elements; they are designed by manually specifying lines, circles, parabolic fillets, etc. The user either chooses an unused area of the overall image space and designs the cell in that location or turns part of an existing design into a cell or subpicture.

Cells and subpictures are usually manipulated, rotated, and stretched more than symbols, so orientation points are also defined in the cell definition. These points align with placement points when the cell is placed into a design. Figure 5-5 shows the representation of a door that can be oriented with two points.

Symbol Placement

Symbols are placed in the same way as characters. The screen cursor is moved to the appropriate location on the screen and a placement point is specified. The point usually corresponds to the lower left corner of the symbol. Sometimes rotation options are available, in which case an additional orientation point (a point defining the baseline of the cell or a keyed-in angle value) is needed.

The user must also select which symbol to place. The symbol name or number can either be keyed in (a poor choice if many symbols are available), or menu boxes with rough pictures of the symbols can be selected with the tablet stylus (for tablet menus) or the screen cursor (for screen menus). Menu selection is the preferred method.

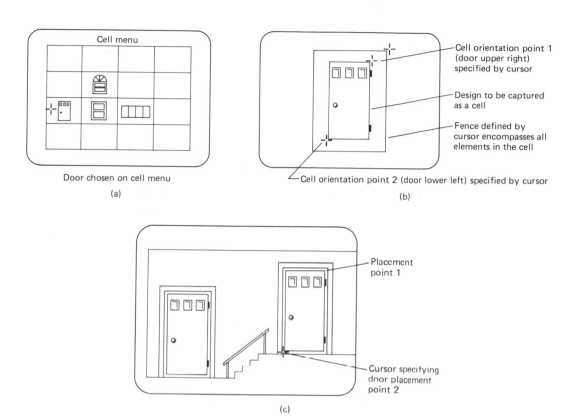

Figure 5-5 The cell or subpicture to be placed is chosen from a cell menu (a) and then positioned using the cursor to specify the element's orientation points (b). Using this approach, the element may be positioned more than once on the screen in different positions (c).

Cell and Subpicture Placement

Cells and subpictures are placed by selecting the cell using key-in or menu selection and by specifying placement point locations. Multiple orientation points are often required to match portions of the cell with portions of the design. A good approach to cell placement is to have a master orientation point that must always be specified (the bottom left corner of a door, for instance), and optional alignment orientation points (say, the door's upper right corner). The optional alignment points can use a prespecified or standard default value if no placement points are submitted. Vertical door placement would be an appropriate default in the door-cell case.

LOCATING AND DELETING ELEMENTS

Changes and corrections are always made in any design process. A design system must have ways of modifying, moving, and deleting elements as well as simply adding them. Before an element can be manipulated, however, it must be found;

this, unfortunately, is not such a trivial process. The advantages of storing graphic information in a computer as a numerical data base (precision, opportunities for analysis, etc.) have been stressed throughout the previous chapters, but when it comes to finding elements, this method becomes a barrier.

FINDER SYSTEM

There are a few ways to find an element. The simplest ways are the worst, and the hardest ways are the best. Very little software is required to implement a simple "user query" finder. With this system, the same software that draws the display is used, but instead of drawing it as quickly as possible, it draws it one element at a time. After each element, the user is asked if this is the element to be deleted. If not, the next element is drawn. This method is acceptable for data bases of only a few elements.

Modifications of the user query system can be effective for larger data bases (up to a few thousand elements). The system can draw elements at a rate of about 10 per second, and the user can press a keyboard key to interrupt the process when the proper element flashes onto the screen. The user can then step backward through the elements until the precise element is again displayed and thus found. The process can be sped up by having the user initially declare what kind of element to search for. If a circle is to be deleted, all the lines, text strings, curves, and other elements can be bypassed in the element scan. This scheme starts adding complexity to an already cumbersome method.

Clipping Windows

The best way to find an object is to use the cursor to point to an element on the screen and tell the system to find that element. What we actually tell the computer to do in numerical terms is to find all the elements that intersect a small viewing window near the center of the cursor. A small clipping window can be set up, based on the cursor's position.

The size of the window depends on how precise you want the pointing to be. Too large a window may encompass multiple elements, while too small a window will make it necessary to position the cursor with difficult-to-obtain accuracy. Figure 5-6 shows a reasonable-size clipping window set up around a cursor's coordinates.

Once the window is chosen, the system can scan through the data base, clipping to the small window until something intersects it. Instead of drawing it at this point, the element number or address can be recorded for use by other routines (such as the delete routine).

Once the system finds a candidate element for deletion, it should ask the user to verify that this is indeed the proper element. If the user says no, the scan should continue until another intersection is found or the end of the data base is reached. This is especially important in dense designs where pointing at just one element is particularly difficult. The element can be overwritten on a storage tube system to make it flash as a verification indicator, and the element can be repeatedly erased and redrawn on raster displays with selective erase.

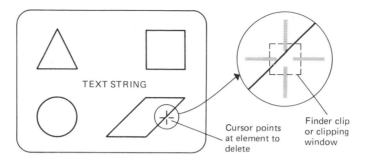

Figure 5-6   To delete an element, the cursor may be used to define a clipping window or finder clip (inset), which may then be positioned as desired to locate the element from the data base.

Finding an element under worst-case conditions can take nearly as long as redrawing the whole design on the screen, but it's better to let the computer do the scanning than to do it manually with a user query system.

Fences

The window-clipping method of finding elements can be used to find whole groups of elements. Instead of creating a clipping window around the center of the cursor, however, a larger window can be specified on the display screen. A "rec tangle" command is ideal for specifying the clip window. The finder routines (modified drawer routines) can find all elements that fall within the rectangle and make a list of their numbers or addresses for use by other routines. In this case, the rectangle is known as a *fence*.

Identifying groups of elements in this way is good for deleting large numbers of elements, but it has much broader capabilities. Once a list of elements is grouped together, all the elements in the list can be put through manipulation processes. A group of 100 lines that define a door on an architect's design, for example, can be moved a few millimeters to make room for hinges. Or it can be copied to 20 other door openings, creating 20 new, identical doors. Fence identification methods are necessary to fully utilize the computer's manipulation power.

The fence must have element capture rules associated with it to handle elements that are only partially within the fence. When using a fence to extract a portion of a design, anything that intersects the fence, even partially, is included. When using a fence to define a subpicture or cell, partially intersecting elements are not included. Elements are rarely clipped to a fence boundary, then manipulated.

ELEMENT DELETION

A graphic element may be deleted easily in two ways. The user may selectively erase it on the screen or he may eliminate it from the design file or display list. Deletion is simply the generation process in reverse.

159

DISPLAY INTELLIGENCE

Some of the advantages of attaching information to graphic elements instead of having them represent only pixels on a display screen include the ability to put elements together into meaningful groups, to manipulate groups, and to perform analysis and costing of designs.

Tagging

In order to attach information to graphics, it is necessary to have a list of the graphic elements to attach it to. This rules out generation by high-level graphics languages and necessitates the use of display files. Display files are lists of graphic elements stored in memory or on disk that describe an image.

A display file element contains a numerical description of the graphic structure and properties of an element. Figure 5-7(a) shows a circle element that contains center, radius, and color information as well as a code that identifies the element as a circle when the element is placed in a list of many elements.

Word number	Function	
1	Circle code	
2	x coordinate of center	Pure
3	y coordinate of center	graphics
4	Radius	information
5	Color code	
6	Material code	Intelligence tag

(a)

Word number	Function
1	Circle
2	x coord. — center
3	y coord. — center
4	Radius
5	Color code
6	Intelligence group tag number

(b)

Word	Function	
1	Tag number to be defined	Tag 1
2-10	ASCII text string containing tag meaning	
11	Tag number to be defined	Tag 2
12-20	ASCII text string containing tag meaning	
.	.	
.	.	
.	.	
N	End of file marker	

(c)

Word	Function
1	Intelligence element code
2	Tag being defined
3	Words in tag meaning string
4-N	Tag meaning text string
.	.
M	Intelligence element code
.	.
.	.

(d)

Figure 5-7 A display file element with intelligence information. The display file contains information that identifies the element to be displayed, and an intelligence tag may be added to attach a fixed-meaning appendix to the code (a). By using an intelligence dictionary to form a descriptor group, the intelligence tag becomes more flexible (b). The intelligence dictionary is similar in structure to a display file, but it contains intelligence elements rather than graphic elements—the entry lengths may be fixed (c) or, better yet, variable (d).

Information can be attached to the circle element by adding a code word that has some nongraphical meaning to the end of the element. Perhaps the material that the circle is made of needs specifying, so the following codes might be used:

Code Number	Material
1	cloth
2	steel
3	glass
4	wood

Every element in the display file can have a material code attached to it; the routines that handle the elements can be written to recognize the specific word in the element as a material code, as depicted in Fig. 5-7(b).

Even this crude intelligence information allows us to selectively display all the steel components in the design, calculate the glass area, calculate the weight of all the wood components (or of the whole design based on each material's volume and material weight), or determine how many square yards of each color cloth will be required.

This tagging method can be improved. First, it is too rigid in its definition. A material code may be fine in one application, but another may require a tensile-strength entry. Word 7 of the circle definition could be reserved for this; but before long, each element would have innumerable tag words after it describing many properties, most of which would be unspecified for any given element.

A solution to this problem is to remove the default meaning of the tag word. We will no longer consider word 6 to be a material code, but rather just a code. The new codes will be:

Code Number	Meaning
1	cloth
2	glass
3	steel
4	wood
5	tensile strength 1000 pounds
6	tensile strength 2000 pounds
7	1000Ω resistor
8	8087 numeric data processor

The tag word can now be used to define an element in almost any way. It is unreasonable to change the element handling programs to recognize the meaning of every new code that is introduced. This problem is solved by creating a sort of dictionary that defines the meaning of all the codes, as shown in Fig. 5-7(c).

The intelligence tag dictionary can be arranged in the most convenient format for a given application. In the example, ASCII text strings were used to actually write out the names of the tags. Integer, floating-point, or BCD numbers may be more appropriate for numeric fields with no text.

Another point to note about the dictionary is that fixed entry lengths are used—9 words or 18 ASCII characters are reserved for each tag. Some tags names will be shorter (thereby making the data meaning storage inefficient), and some will be longer (making meaning storage impossible). A variable-length dictionary definition is more useful, and the best way to handle this is with a display-file structure that has intelligence elements rather than graphic elements.

The intelligence element has a code identifying it as such, and the tag it is identifying is word 2. Variable-length *meaning* text strings are used, so word 3 tells how long the meaning string is. This concept is illustrated in Fig. 5-7(d).

An alternative approach is to use an end-of-string character (for example, *ASCII 13—carriage return*).

A word count is preferable, however, because the only way to find an intelligence element in an intelligence file (assuming there is no corresponding index file) is to scan through it. With word counts, we can skip over meanings of unwanted tags as we scan the file without having to read each string to find its end-of-string code and thus the next intelligence element.

Keys Within Tags

A 16-bit tag word can identify 65,536 groups of information. This may seem like enough for most applications, but it is not. It's true that a user will be unlikely to specify 10,000 different types of woods, metals, and steels, but a mapmaker may want to identify the names of all the families or street addresses in a map of a city of 100,000 people. A 32-bit tag would fill the need, but this is not very practical. The mapmaker's broad classification is "family names" or "street numbers." Resistance values on an electronics schematic is another case in point. The broad classification is "resistor" while the subdefinition is its value in ohms. Tolerance, manufacturer, wattage, and coefficient of temperature would also be considered subdefinitions.

If a 32-bit tag were given to each of 100,000 families represented by a map (tag names such as JOHN R. SMITH), their names would exist in the design file, but the fact that they are family names would be missing. When the mapmaker requests an alphabetized list of all families on MAIN STREET (another tag name), the system would have no way of separating family names from street names, house addresses, and fire hydrants.

The problem of too many tags (and consequently, lost information) is solved using keys within the tag. These are subelements within the tag element that further describe the intelligence element. Figure 5-8 shows the structure of a tag element with internal keys for a resistor. In this example, the tag selected by the user was RESISTOR. From this information, the system built the intelligence element with a group number that will be attached to the graphic element instead of the tag itself. The group contains all the key entries that are asked for and must be entered pertaining to the resistor.

The group number is a 32-bit number because every resistor (there could be thousands) must be uniquely identified, but only one tag—RESISTOR—was used to specify them all. The 32-bit group number is invisible to the user who goes on thinking of the group by its tag name. The group element that corresponds to the

Word	Function	TAG1 = resistor
1	Intelligence element code	
2 & 3	Group number being defined (32-bits)	
4–10	12-character group name	
11	key code = 1 resistance	
12	number of words in string	
13	resistance value (16-bit integer — ohms)	
14	key code = 2 tolerance	
15	number of words in string	
16	tolerance value (16-bit integer — percent)	
17	key code = 3 manufacturer	
18	number of words in string	
12–21	manufacturer name (20-ASCII character string)	
22	End of keys marker	

Figure 5-8   Keys within tag elements can further describe the intelligence element. In this case, the tag is a resistor.

resistor now has all information that a user would want to access. A count of all resistors could be made by searching for resistance keys. A resistor list by resistance value is also possible. All parts by a given manufacturer could be reported and all 5% error-tolerance resistors could be listed. The keys tell the system what characteristic is being defined while the following text strings or integers define it in detail.

TAG ACCESS METHODS AND LINKS

Tags and group intelligence elements are great for organizing vast amounts of information, but they are stored in large files that must be accessed sequentially to extract the information. To find all the lampposts in a map of a city, the whole graphics file would have to be scanned for elements with lamppost tags. This might take 10 s or more for a large design. For information reporting this is acceptable, but in some cases instantaneous response is required.

Object manipulation is one of these cases. There may be 20 line elements grouped together under the DOOR1 tag. To move the door, all elements of the group must be found, translated, and rotated. This action falls under user interaction and must be performed very quickly, so normal tagging methods can't be used. Links are designed for these cases.

A link is a pointer that indicates a graphic or intelligence element. The element's disk address (record number and offset) or any other convenient pointer can be used. Links can be used to set up manipulative groups. An intelligence element can define the group by containing a list of links that point to all graphic elements in the manipulative group.

All the elements in the manipulative group likewise contain a link back to the intelligence element that defines the group. Moving a manipulative group such as DOOR1 requires that the user find any element on the door. The link is then used to find the intelligence element.

Once the intelligence element is found, its links are used to locate all elements in the group, which then can be translated and rotated. No file scanning or searching is involved in the process.

The price paid for the rapid access time of links is element size. A list of links must be stored in the intelligence element where only a tag number was previously required.

163

Chapter 6

Design and
Simulation System
Interaction

Drawing complex images with dense alphanumerics in multilevel tonal gray or perhaps color on a high-resolution graphics display screen or matrix printer is quite an accomplishment, but the final result is not different from what could have been performed by a skilled draftsman or artist. What practical role can computer graphics fill, then, other than being a replacement for rulers, pens, and paper? A closer examination of the computer graphics generation process gives us our answer.

Computer images are generated from a numerical data base in a computer's memory. The computer adds to this data base as the image is being entered (digitized), and quickly dumps the data base to a display generator or hard-copy device when a display or physical copy is required. The two characteristics that set computer graphics apart from conventional graphics are the numerical data base and display generation speed. Unlike the conventional drawing, the computer drawing or display has a numerical data base that can be manipulated, analyzed, and copied with a computer's error-free precision. The final result can be produced 10,000 times more quickly than the conventional drawing. Nearly instantaneous display generation makes presentation of intermediate graphic results feasible; and when combined with a computer's ability to accept user input this feature makes user interaction possible.

Display interaction is one aspect that sets computer graphics apart from more conventional forms of drawing. A second aspect is that of display intelligence. A computer's information processing resources can be utilized not only to store graphic elements for display purposes but to attach meaning to those elements. A line element in a graphics data base may consist of the line's start and end points as well as some intelligence information such as, "10 in. steel I-beam, 35 lb/ft." The

164

computer can later perform such functions as scanning through a whole design and making parts lists of all the materials needed to construct a design as well as how much the materials will cost and weigh. And the computer can analyze the structure to determine critical stress points.

It becomes apparent that the computer graphics system is taking on the roles of design analysis engineer, accountant, parts lister, draftsman, and artist. The results are performed with computer precision and thoroughness. With proper software, no stress point will go unanalyzed or misanalyzed, and the cost will be accurate to the penny—with no costs overlooked.

Display interaction and intelligence are what makes computer graphics useful, and the two most active areas of computer graphics—CAD and simulation—rely heavily on these properties. Display interaction and intelligence are what set "design" systems apart from simple "drawing" systems.

DESIGN SYSTEM INTERACTION

There are a number of ways a user can generate an image on a screen. There is the familiar graphics language approach, where commands such as PLOT 25,35 are used to plot points, and subroutines that call the PLOT routine are used for more advanced functions. One can hardly expect an architect or engineer to sit down and write a huge graphics program using this sort of computer language or even higher-level graphics languages (which might include commands such as CIRCLE centrex, centery, radius) when designing a house or mechanical part. The graphics language approach is impractical for design systems.

Another method that is more reasonable in design systems involves use of a prewritten control program that accepts simple graphics commands and generates results on the screen. The keyboard can be used as an interactive input device that results in immediate image generation as commands are typed in rather than as a means of entering programs that will later be run to generate an image.

Figure 6-1 lists a small interactive control program that accepts 3 commands:

Command Code	Function
1	draw a line
2	draw a circle
3	stop

The user runs the program and can then start thinking about the design. This program is in fact an extremely primitive CAD system. When the program is run, it prompts the user to submit a command. If the user wants to add a line to the design, he types 1. The system will then ask for the start and end points of the line. When submitted, the system will draw the line, then ask for the next command. Circles work in a similar manner, with circle center and radius being submitted.

It is much easier to interactively design with this program than by using a programming language, but the user still has to think too much in terms of the computer system. In order to submit screen points, the screen coordinate system must be used.

```
3        SCREEN 1
4        CLS
5        LOCATE 1, 1
6        PRINT "SUBMIT A COMMAND"

10       INPUT COMAND
20       IF (COMAND = 1) THEN GOSUB 100
30       IF (COMAND = 2) THEN GOSUB 200
50       IF (COMAND = 3) THEN END
60       GOTO 5

100      PRINT "SUBMIT LINE (X1, Y1, X2, Y2)"
110      INPUT X1, Y1, X2, Y2
120      LINE (X1, Y1) — (X2, Y2)
130      RETURN

200      PRINT "SUBMIT CIRCLE (X, Y, R)"
210      INPUT X, Y, R
220      CIRCLE (X, Y), R
230      RETURN
```

Figure 6-1   Interactive graphics command interpreter for the IBM personal computer. This type of program is a primitive form of computer-aided design system because of the prompts associated with the commands.

The user must remember the location of coordinates and never exceed their valid ranges (0 to 319 x and 0 to 199 y on the IBM personal computer).

The commands are also too cryptic. Commands 1, 2, and 3 can be remembered easily, but an expanded set of 50 or more graphic functions would pose problems.

The first step in making this sytem more usable is to "hide" the screen coordinate system from the user. Designers think in terms of shapes and locations rather than numbers. A user-movable screen cursor is ideal for this purpose. The cursor could be controlled through keyboard commands using one of the input devices (e.g., control diamond, joystick, graphics tablet) described earlier.

Assuming that a graphics tablet is used to position the screen cursor, line submittal takes the form of pressing the 1 command (to indicate a line) followed by moving the tablet stylus (and thus the screen cursor) to the desired start and end points of the line and pressing the appropriate button to indicate that you are submitting the points. The user can forget about coordinates entirely and simply specify lines using the tablet.

Another good idea is to adopt short, easily remembered abbreviations instead of the command numbers. The commands L for line, C for circle, and S for stop are appropriate, for example.

Alternatively, the graphics tablet can be used to submit commands as well as controlling the cursor. This is done using "menus." An area of the tablet can be set aside as a menu area, and a few rectangles with graphics function names can be printed on a thin plastic card that goes over this area. When the user wants to enter a line in the design, he simply moves the stylus to the proper menu box, presses the stylus button, then moves the stylus to the start and end points of the line on the screen to submit it.

Most large CAD systems use precisely this technique. Menu cards such as the one pictured in Fig. 6-2, with hundreds of graphics functions, may be used. Menu-driven systems have a few advantages over key-in systems. Function names need

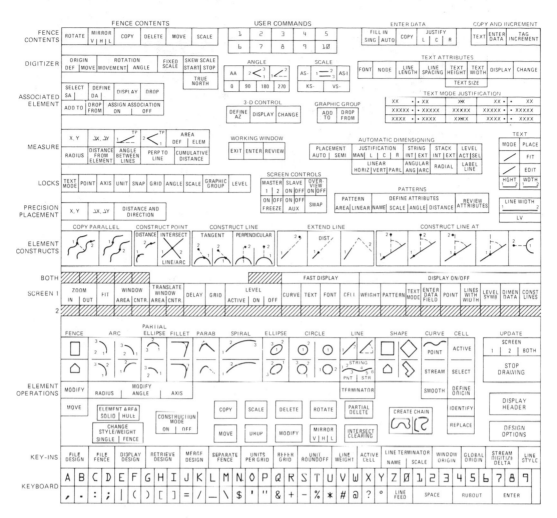

Figure 6-2 The degree of reduction necessary to reproduce this menu card for a large CAD system makes many of the entries unreadable, but it is easy to see the very broad specification of functions that can be stipulated with such a menu. An alternative menu arrangement is to display the data on the screen so elements can be specified with a screen cursor.

not be remembered because they appear on the menu. The user also does not have to keep alternating between the keyboard and graphics tablet to submit graphics information. The user must still divide his attention between the tablet and the screen, however. But even this problem can be eliminated by placing the menu information on the screen and letting the user move the screen cursor to commands as they are needed.

Menu schemes have their disadvantages. Users get to know the menu well with extensive use, and finding commands becomes quite simple; but short, 2- or 3-letter keyboard commands are also easily memorized. Many experienced users prefer the keyboard entry method because it is faster and eliminates the need to look over at a tablet menu or move the cursor (which may be in a strategic location for the next command) across the screen to a screen menu box.

167

Figure 6-3   This CAD system employs two screens—one for graphic displays and one for menus, character displays, and low-resolution graphics. (Courtesy Summagraphics Corporation.)

Tablet menus do look very impressive, and most manufacturers stick with them (although some companies have equivalent keyboard commands and screen menus for more practical users.) One of the main arguments *for* the tablet menu is that it frees the user from having to use an alphanumeric keyboard; but when text generation capabilities are added to a CAD system, the user again must alternate between tablet and keyboard.

Figure 6-3 shows a large CAD system that uses screen menus and a tablet for command and graphic point submittal. Like many other CAD systems, two screens are used. One is a high-resolution screen (4096 × 4096) for graphic displays, and the other is a lower-resolution raster-scan unit for menus, character displays, computer terminal functions, and low-resolution graphics.

DESIGN AIDS

A display system can draw a straight line and generate perfect circles and squares, but these capabilities take the place of nothing more than a draftsman's straightedge and templates. For serious design work, precision placement, angles, and constructs are required. The design system needs the equivalent of ruled paper, triangles, and a T-square.

Units of Resolution

Nearly any design represents a physical object, so designs must have real-world dimensions associated with them. So far, the only numerical values discussed were those associated with the design space. Screen coordinates do not have the necessary range and resolution for design purposes, so windows are used to view 16-bit, 32-bit, or even floating-point design spaces. The smallest definable distance in a design space is called a *unit of resolution,* or UOR. A 16-bit design space has a range of 65,536 UORs in the *x* and *y* (and *z,* if it is a 3D system) dimensions.

For a cartographer's mapping applications, a UOR of 1 m might be a good choice for a unit definition. This would give a design range of 65 km in all directions. If the map were to precisely define small lot property lines, however, the resolution may be too coarse, and a unit assignment of 10 UOR/m would be more appropriate. Property lines could be defined to the nearest 10 cm, but range is reduced to 6.5 km in all directions.

As this example illustrates, tradeoffs must be made in choosing a unit's relation to UOR. To make a system useful in any application, user-definable units are a must.

A user should be allowed to work with a few different units while designing. Three or four units of linear measure for any measurement system are usually enough. When keying in lengths, the user can specify the length and unit of measure (234 mm, 45 cm, 1.5 m, for example).

Grids

Once units are defined, the design system's equivalent of graph paper—grids—can be set up. Grids should be definable in units. A design grid with 1 mm grid spacing in the *x* and *y* dimensions might be good in the design of a small mechanical part. As with the UOR, the user must decide what grid spacing is right for the task at hand.

Most display systems don't allow very dim grid lines to be drawn, and drawing a dense design grid at full intensity severely clutters the screen. Symbols such as •, ×, +, etc. are drawn at grid intersections instead. The choice of crosses or dots depends on the display screen. Both may be used simultaneously to simulate the effect of standard drafting coordinate paper. Crosses can represent the coarse coordinates, with dots used for the fine divisions (4—10) between them, as shown in Fig. 6-4.

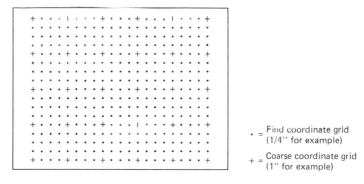

Figure 6-4 Representation of a design grid with dots and crosses to depict fine and coarse coordinates. The coordinates may be locked to grid points.

169

The number of grid points that the system must generate is the square of the linear density. A fine grid of 200 units across the screen requires 40,000 grid points to be drawn before design work can begin. This takes a long time. Most grid systems have density limiters that suppress the generation process if the grid gets too dense and would take too long to generate. This kind of system works very well when multiple levels of grids are used. Only the coarse grids appear as the operator zooms out on the image, and fine grids appear on closeups when performing detailed design work.

Graphics Locking

In interactive design systems, a technique called *locking* is used to position entered elements with precision automatically. Locking is a software-implemented feature applicable to a number of display functions.

Axis Lock. One of the main differences between a rough sketch and a precision drawing is that elements of the design are "squared up" in the precision drawing. In mathematical terms, vertical lines run parallel to the y axis and horizontal lines run parallel to the x axis. *Axis locks* serve this function in an interactive design system. When the user draws a line with the axis lock turned on, the system assumes that a perfectly vertical or horizontal line is desired and sets the y or x difference of the roughly specified line to zero, locking it into a horizontal or vertical orientation. The line's start point or a previously defined point are used as the proper x (for vertical) or y (for horizontal) axis value.

End-Point Lock. The ends of lines or other linear elements that join together in a precision design must be produced with 100% accuracy. End-to-end alignment is important on conventional drawings, but it is even more important in computer-generated drawings because of the revealing nature of the zoom-in feature. Two lines that approximately come together may look fine on a large overview, but they'll come apart when a closeup view is selected. End-point lock is used to perfectly join end points of lines and other linear elements. The user selects the point to lock to, and this point is used as the beginning (or some other defined point) of the new element.

This scheme can be implemented using the finder system discussed in the previous chapter. The user points to the line, and the finder finds it. Once the user verifies that this is the correct element, the end-point lock software analyzes the element to obtain the element's end point closest to the user's cursor position. The x, y, and z values of this point are then used as the first input point of the new element.

Grid Lock. Grids permit size visualization and serve as an element construction guide. Most drawings end up with many of the design lines running up and down the grid lines. Grid locks allow a designer to interactively lock design lines to the grid.

A grid lock causes lock element end points to be "snapped" to grid intersection points. This allows construction of lines that run up and down the grid lines, but it also serves the function of horizontal, vertical, and point lock. Two lines with end points snapped to a common grid point have perfect end-to-end alignment.

Grid locks also aid in construction of standard-radius circles by snapping center and radius points to grid intersections. Precisely aligned arrays of elements (circles, squares, etc.) can be created by snapping them to grids at equally spaced intervals.

Angle Lock. Lines at standard angles other than 0° and 90° are often used, and angle locks help construct them with precision. The desired angle is usually keyed in and stored as the "standard" angle. Many lines can then be drawn locking to the standard angle. A start point (often snapped to the end of another element) is chosen, and a distance is either keyed in or approximately specified with the cursor. The line is generated starting at the start point and extending in the direction of the standard angle.

AUTOMATIC GEOMETRIC CONSTRUCTION

Just about anything can be designed with better than conventional drafting precision using the grid, angle, end-point, and axis locks. The computer's numerical precision and analytical capabilities are starting to be utilized. But the computer is capable of a lot more than just locking to a few grid points and finding and snapping to end points. It can be used to figure out exactly how to place elements (one, or many simultaneously) by interactively getting an idea of what a user wants and performing the necessary computations. Automatic geometric construction software and coordinate geometry software perform these functions. The power of this sort of capability is best described with an example.

Street intersections on city planning maps create a lot of "busy work" for civil engineers and mapmakers. The streets must intersect, and lines in the center of the intersection must be removed. The resulting street corners must be rounded with curves or fillets. Using a design system, the designer can identify the four corners of the intersection, key in the street-corner radius, and let the automatic geometric construction system do the rest (Fig. 6-5).

First, the intersection lines are removed. Then fillets of the proper radius are placed at each corner. Finally, the extension lines are removed.

A computer must go through a number of computations to perform such functions. The original 4 elements are deleted and 12 new ones are specified and generated automatically. This computation takes perhaps 1–2 s—a long time on computer time scales—but it only needs to be performed once. Once the elements are automatically specified and generated, they remain in the data base as manually specified elements would. Automatic geometric construction software can therefore take advantage of all the powerful, but slow-running, high-level language features (powers, roots, trig functions, logarithms, double-precision floating point) without affecting display and redraw performance.

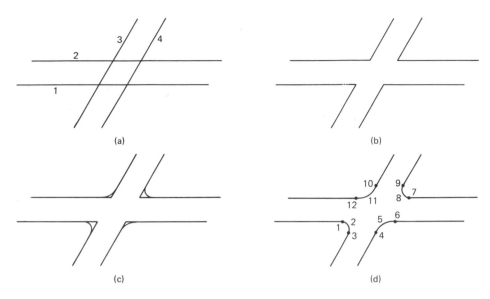

Figure 6-5   The design system automates geometric construction. In this case the four corners of an intersection are identified (a) and the radius of the corners is keyed in; the computer eliminates the lines within the intersection (b), adds the fillets (c), and removes the extension—resulting in an intersection display (d) with the 12 elements shown.

Perpendicular Extension

A line perpendicular to another line can be drawn by specifying the line to which the result will be perpendicular and a point at the desired location away from the basis line. The computer must calculate the point on the basis line that results in a perpendicular intersection and use this point along with the user-specified point to draw a line. Figure 6-6(a) shows this method.

Parallel Projection

A line parallel to a basis line can be interactively specified by submitting a point on the basis line (to identify it) and a point away from the basis line through which the parallel projection is to run. The parallel line is a projection, so the corresponding end points of the parallel lines, if connected, would form perpendicular projections. As shown in Fig. 6-6(b), it is a perfect rectangle consisting of the basis line, the projected line, and the two perpendicular projections.

Parallel line strings and curves (smoothed line strings) are also quite useful, especially in the areas of mapmaking, where rivers and winding roads must be depicted. Figure 6-6(c) shows a parallel curve. It is specified by choosing the basis curve and a point away from it to be used as the parallel distance. Parallel curve generation involves more computation than a single line because simply paralleling every line in the string yields a string of overlapping and broken lines where inner and outer angles exist. Line extension is used to solve the problem.

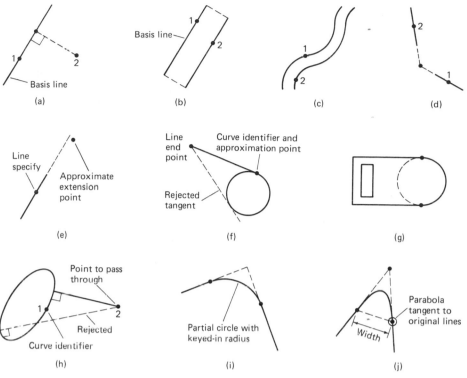

Figure 6-6 Common elements for automatic geometric construction: the perpendicular extension (a), parallel projection (b) and curve (c), automatic line extension to point of intersection (d), single line extension (e), tangent to a curve (f), the deletion of an element portion using two tangent points as reference (g), perpendicular to a curve (h) in which a portion is rejected because it passes through ellipse interior, fillet (i) with sharp corner replaced with rounded radius, and parabolic fits (j).

Line Extension

It is sometimes necessary to extend two lines to their point of natural intersection; but there is no way of knowing exactly where the point is until the lines are already intersected and extended. Automatic geometric construction can be used to extend the lines and form the intersection. Figure 6-6(d) shows line intersection. The computer simply determines the equations of the two lines and solves them simultaneously. Element modification to physically extend both lines (and perhaps convert them into a line string) is then performed.

Figure 6-6(e) illustrates a simpler form of line extension, which involves only single lines. A line can be made longer by instructing the design system to add a given amount to the line through a key-in command (in whatever units are desired), or the cursor can be used to approximate the position. The system must calculate the equation of the basis line and find a point that satisfies that equation at the approximate or keyed-in distance. The element must then be modified.

Tangents to Curves

A tangent to a circle or ellipse can be interactively specified by submitting a curve identifier point (to indicate which ellipse to use) and a point outside the circle or ellipse. Any point outside a circle or ellipse has two possible tangents that can be generated, so the curve identifier point can double as a "side of the circle" indicator, as shown in Fig. 6-6(f). It is useful to have the system save the tangent–ellipse intersection point after generating the tangent line. This point may be useful later when part of the ellipse must be deleted, as illustrated in Fig. 6-6(g).

Perpendiculars to Curves

The specification of perpendiculars to ellipses, circles, and general curves is accomplished by specifying the curve and a point away from the curve that the perpendicular line is to intersect, as Fig. 6-6(h) illustrates. Two perpendicular intersection points exist on every closed ellipse and circle (one on the near and one on the far side of ellipse), but it is generally assumed that the perpendicular is not to pass through the ellipse's interior.

Fillets

Most mechanical designs require rounded inner and outer corners. Fillet commands can be used to round corners interactively. The user specifies the corner to be rounded by picking two intersecting lines that represent the corner, then keys in a radius (the cursor can also be used to indicate radius), as in Fig. 6-6(i). The system then calculates the equation of a circle (or ellipse, if that function is available and specified) that is inscribed by the two borders. A new corner is formed, and the portions of the two initial line segments that formed the sharp corner are removed. The remainder of the circle that is "inside" the corner is not generated, and a partial circle element is entered into the data base as the round corner.

A parabolic fit function is also a useful feature, since the parabola is a very natural shape. To submit a parabola, the two intersecting lines must be identified, and a parabola geometry function must be specified as in Fig. 6-6(j). The width of the parabola at the intersection with the lines is an often-used parameter and lends itself well to key-in entry.

Curve Fitting

Random curves that can't be defined by relatively simple mathematical functions are usually defined by submitting line strings and having the computer smooth the edges as described previously. The interactive way of entering the curve into the system is identical to that of submitting a line string. The curve is approximated with the cursor and multiple stylus button presses. The curve generation equations follow these approximate points and lines.

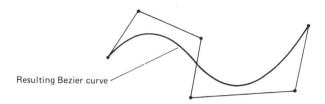

Resulting Bezier curve

Figure 6-7   Control-node method for generating a Bezier curve. The pictured points are user-submitted in an interactive procedure requiring immediate user feedback.

There are other interactive ways to submit curves. One common approach uses curve control nodes. Instead of submitting line segments or points that fall along an approximation of the curve, points located away from the curve itself influence the curve and cause varying degrees of bending as they are moved around. Control nodes define curves in the same sort of way that the gravity of a number of planets (gravity nodes) might influence the curved course of a spacecraft (although the equations used to generate them bear no relationship to gravity equations). Bezier curves are generated using control-node methods (Fig. 6-7).

Control-node methods can create very smooth-flowing, esthetically pleasing curves, but their entry method demands user interaction and immediate feedback. A raster screen can use selective erase, and a storage tube can use its writethrough mode to modify the curve in real time until the desired curve appears.

The absolute end points of node-generated curves are specifiable, so end matching by trial and error is avoided.

AREA PATTERNING

Area patterning is the process of filling a predefined area on a display screen with a selected pattern. This is a method that is primarily used on systems that don't have shading capabilities. Patterning is also well suited to plotters that perform shading. Patterns are used to fill in an area; they consist of lines at regular intervals.

Patterns identify areas of a graphics image as being solid areas or holes. Or they attach some significance to a given area as described by a legend on the drawing (maps are good examples). Patterns are thus usually not transformed but are of a fixed size on a display screen. A crosshatched pattern, for instance, would begin to look like a big grid of some design significance during a zoom-in on a section of a drawing where the pattern expands to only two horizontal and two vertical lines across the whole screen.

Patterns, like cells and subpictures, must be defined and placed. The computer has a much larger role in placement, however, because it must fit the pattern into a closed boundary.

The simplest approach to user interaction with patterns is to have a set of standard patterns from which the user can select by means of a menu or by keying in pattern names and numbers, as shown in Fig. 6-8(a). The user selects the pattern,

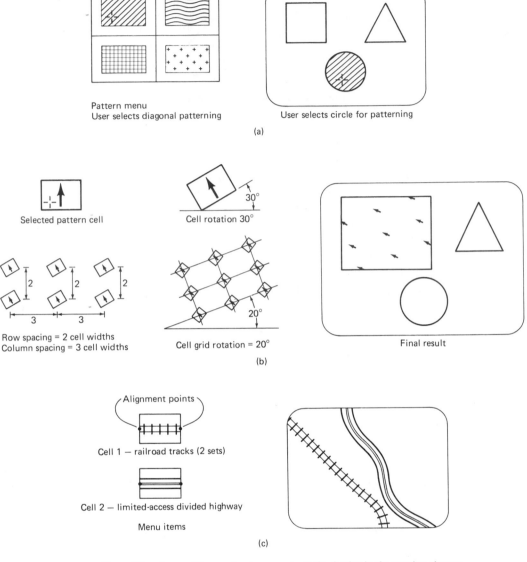

Pattern menu
User selects diagonal patterning

User selects circle for patterning

(a)

Selected pattern cell

Cell rotation 30°

Row spacing = 2 cell widths
Column spacing = 3 cell widths

Cell grid rotation = 20°

Final result

(b)

Alignment points

Cell 1 — railroad tracks (2 sets)

Cell 2 — limited-access divided highway

Menu items

(c)

Figure 6-8   Area and linear patterning concepts. In the simplest implementation, the user
selects a pattern from a menu and picks the element to be patterned with a screen cursor (a). A
more complex capability results when the user specifies generation parameters (b), with a default
pattern value to be displayed in the absence of a specification. Linear patterns (c) are simpler,
but they must be shaped to follow curves and bends, which affects the linearity to some extent.

followed by selecting an interior point within the area to be patterned. The design
system does the rest. Patterns for this method can be predefined, or a small *pattern
editor* program can allow a user to design a pattern within a pattern sample box or
cell. The resulting pattern is generated by copying the box or cell repeatedly in adjacent rows and columns, clipped by the area's boundary.

176

A second approach to area patterns gives the user much greater control of pattern generation. Pattern sample boxes are defined in the same way as the first method; but when placing the pattern, the user must specify generation parameters, such as row-to-row pattern cell spacing, column-to-column pattern cell spacing, pattern scale factor, pattern cell rotation angle, pattern grid (formed by rows and columns) rotation angle. This allows total control over pattern slant and density, and it lets the user take a defined pattern and make countless variations of it (different scales, slants, spacings, etc.). The best way to handle the extra parameters is to have standard default values if the parameters aren't specified. The user may then interactively change the default values. Figure 6-8(b) shows how control of generation parameters affect a simple pattern.

Linear Patterning

Railroad tracks and interstate highways on maps, isogonic lines on flight navigation maps, and keyed bus lines on electronics drawings are good examples of applications for linear patterning. In these and other cases, long winding lines or perimeters of areas need to be patterned to represent something. Linear patterning performs this task in a design system.

Linear patterning is similar to area patterning, but pattern cells are defined somewhat differently. Two ends of the cell have alignment points where the pattern will connect with an identical adjacent cell. Cell definition is a matter of designing the desired linear pattern between these two alignment points. Cell placement is performed by the user selecting the pattern (from a menu), then selecting the lines to be patterned.

A useful option is to allow the user to specify the start and end points on the line to be patterned for applications where a pattern must change partway down a single line, line string, or curve.

As far as the software is concerned, linear patterning is a bit simpler than area patterning, because the pattern doesn't have to be clipped to a border, but generation still is not a trivial process. The main problem is coping with curves and bends in lines. The pattern must be mathematically "bent" to follow curvatures, as illustrated in Fig. 6-8(c); ends of pattern cells must be shortened and extended, because they tend to break apart and overlap when joined on a curve.

Shading and Color Specification

Most design systems based around raster-scan display equipment have shading or solid-color generation features. There are a number of ways to interactively apply shading and color.

The first is an extension of the area patterning method. The user selects a color or gray-scale tonal value from a color menu, and specifies an area's interior point. The area is then totally filled with color or a gray shade. This action is called color filling or *painting*. This method is adequate for most serious engineering design systems where color is used primarily for identification of parts.

More artistic methods of applying colors are common on design systems aimed at less technical but more creative users. The concept of painting an area is often implemented to simulate the way an artist paints. The user is given a color menu (usually called a palette, and sometimes even shaped like a painter's palette) and is allowed to select a brush width. Painting is then achieved with a tablet-controlled cursor. A push on the stylus botton simulates the brush touching the canvas.

Airbrushes are also simulated. The user decides what width and intensity of "spray tip" to use, and can then start "spraying" color pixels onto the screen.

Artistic color submittal methods are quite easy to implement and involve considerably less mathematical computations than design graphics that shade areas within borders automatically.

Mirroring

Mirroring is useful when a design requires symmetry about an axis. A user interactively performs mirroring by specifying an axis and selecting the elements on the side of the axis to be mirrored—with a fence, individually, or as they are entered. The mirroring software then mathematically computes the location of the element in a mirrored position on the other side of the selected axis.

A mirror plane must be specified for 3D mirroring. Three points can define the plane, or a plane parallel to the x,y, x,z, or y,z plane can be used.

VIEWING AND MOVEMENT IN SPACE

A display screen in a design system is only a window that looks into the design space. The user must have interactive control over the window's size and where it is pointing.

Bidimensional View Control

The basic interactive view controls are pan and zoom. The viewer must be able to access any part of the design with a wide range of scales. Panning can be controlled with a joystick or track ball or by using the coordinates of the graphics tablet, as illustrated in Fig. 6-9(a). These methods require that the display be erased and updated fast enough to track with reasonable smoothness. If the image can be generated only once in a period of greater than 1 s, real-time panning becomes too hard to control.

Large design systems work with such large data bases that display refresh time is usually above the critical limit, and so other methods must be used. The "center and zoom" method of Fig. 6-9(b) controls both pan and zoom. With this method, the user places the cursor at the location on the design that is to become the center of the new view, and then keys in (or selects from a menu) a zoom factor. A keyed 1 indicates the same size, 0.5 means zoom-in 2:1, and 2 means zoom out 1:2.

The "sides method" shown in Fig. 6-9(c) is good when the user has an overview of a design and knows the precise area to zoom in on. With this method, the user chooses the lower left and upper right corners of the area to view (essentially putting a rectangular fence around it). The computer will then zoom in on the area and make sure that everything within the rectangle is on the screen. The view most likely won't be exactly the rectangle described by the fence, because it would probably

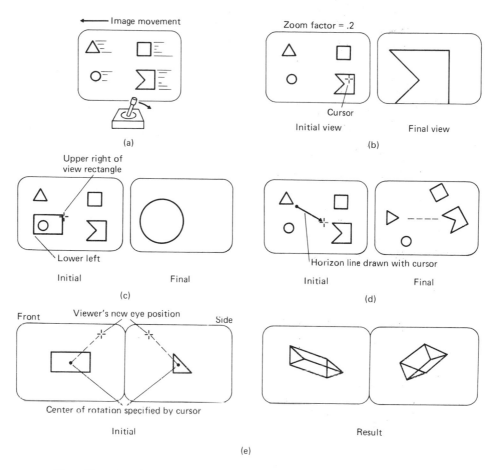

Figure 6-9   Screen displays may be manipulated in many ways: The screen may be used as a moving window (a) by panning with a joystick (panning to right causes images to move left across screen); or the screen cursor may be positioned on an element to cause the selected position to be centered on the screen after a zoom (b). The "sides" method specifies the screen boundaries (c) after manipulation. A horizon may be rotated (d) by drawing a horizon line with the cursor; regardless of the angle between the elements initially, they are redrawn with a horizontal separation and thus a new orientation. For a 3D view of an image, dual screens are used (e): the cursor specifies the eye position relative to each view, and the result appears as isometric projections.

have to be stretched or compressed in one of the dimensions to make it fit into the 4:3 aspect ratio screen; this would distort the geometry of the design. Instead, the computer takes the longest dimension, fits it to the screen, and extends the view in the short direction to meet the 4:3 aspect ratio.

If the design system allows rotation, this too must be interactively controllable. One way to control rotation is through angle key-ins. In many situations, the purpose for viewing a design at an angle is to align a standardized angle with the x or y axis. Rotation angles of 30°, 45°, and 90° are common, and there is no easier way to specify these rotations than by typing them in.

If a display refreshes quickly enough, an interactive device such as a track ball, joystick, or even a potentiometer will work well. If a tablet is used, the "horizon" method shown in Fig. 6-9(d) is appropriate. With this method, the cursor is used to draw what will be the new horizon on the screen (from the new horizon's left, to its right). The display will be rotated accordingly. It is possible to turn images upside down by simply drawing the horizon from right to left instead of left to right.

Tridimensional View Control

Interactively specifying view changes of a 3D design is difficult because display screens, joysticks, track balls, and tablets only have two dimensions of movement. There are two ways to treat view changes and movement in 3D space: either change the viewing angle and location (move the "eye" position), or move and rotate the viewed object. For design systems, the second method works best.

A track ball or joystick can control two dimensions of a 3D display's six movement dimensions ($x, y, z,$ pitch, yaw, and roll), and the user can choose which dimensions they are. A track ball is particularly nice for controlling the rotational variables, because the viewed object spins as the track ball does, and it gives the feeling of almost holding the object. This method only works on systems with quick redraw speeds, however, and most large design systems can't refresh this quickly.

Viewer Point Specification. Viewer point specification is used in systems that have a slow redraw rate. This method requires multiple simultaneous views of the object (a front and side view). When working with 3D designs, multiview displays are common because at least two views are required to visualize x, y and z dimensions on the flat display screen. A center of rotation is first selected with the cursor, as illustrated in Fig. 6-9(e). This point has to be in the center of the object to be rotated on both views simultaneously (multiple cursors are used in 3D, multiview systems). A second point, which defines where the viewer wants to put his "eye" in the new view, is then chosen.

It is easy to get disoriented when viewing a 3D image, especially if it is a wireframe representation. Objects seem to oscillate between their normal and inside-out views, and in many cases become totally unrecognizable in one of the two or three views (when two or more views are displayed simultaneously). It is therefore a good idea to include a "head-on view" command to bring the view back to its original x,y,z aligned direction without having to specify center and eye points.

Automatic View Selection. It's good to give users full control of movement, but an automatic view selection feature also should be incorporated. This system automaticaly adjusts the viewing direction and scale to encompass a whole design in the viewing area. This gives the user a good starting point and avoids the process of trying to "find" the design in space.

DESIGN FILES AND ACCESS

To effectively interact with a design, a design system must be capable of handling large enough designs to fully define and detail objects. Further, the interactive response time must be fast enough so the user does not have to wait between submittal and manipulation commands.

Huge graphic display files (usually stored on high-speed disks) are the hallmark of design systems. When it comes to file size, mapmaking (cartography) is one of the largest users of disk space. Designs of 50 to 100 megabytes are not uncommon (although most systems only pull out a megabyte or two to work with at a time). Large file size naturally works against the goal of fast response time (it takes a long time to search a high-density disk file for a line to be deleted). Efficient file organization, high-performance software, high-speed computers, and special on-the-fly disk scanning hardware are approaches that have been used to solve the problem of response time.

A design is stored on a disk as a design file. This is a list of graphic elements and intelligence information that defines the design. Whenever you add or delete an element from the design, the element is added to or removed from this file. As a design file grows, accessing it and reading through all its elements (a requirement for redrawing the image and finding elements) becomes proportionally slower. At a point, user response time becomes unacceptably slow, and it is at this point, that hardware and software speedups must be made.

High-Performance Computers

A "brute force" way to scan through files faster is to buy a more powerful computer and faster-access disk drives. This is an expensive route to take and is not very cost-effective. A fairly low-performance computer is adequate to perform 90% of a design system's tasks. Adding and deleting elements at a user rate of one every 5–10 seconds puts only a light load on most computers, even if many powerful computations must be performed. The only time the high performance is needed is when redrawing the display file on the screen or when interactively finding an element. In both these cases, the whole file must be scanned. A commendable goal to strive for is to put the computer's idle time (when it is waiting for user input) to use in a way that will speed redraw and finding when the system is asked to perform these tasks. Alternatively, a hardware approach that applies a special piece of hardware that is particularly well suited to rapidly displaying and finding elements could be found.

A faster computer can indeed solve the performance problem, but the final outcome will also include an expensive new computer that is sitting idle 90% of the time.

Disk File Organization

Highly organized disk files can decrease redraw and finding time. It takes more time to enter a new element into a highly organized file structure, but this time comes from the normally idle time between user interactions—precisely where it can be afforded.

Element Separation. A file can be organized by element separation. Instead of using one large file for all graphics and intelligence information, simply create separate files for lines, circles, ellipses, and intelligence information. The finder system then bypasses a lot of disk data which has no chance of containing the element being sought. When a circle is to be found, every file except the circle file can be ignored. Circles normally constitute less than 20% of a total design file size, so a 500% response-time improvement would result.

Separate element files help the redraw rate by bypassing intelligence information. Nongraphic information contributes nothing to the display redraw and would normally be passed over in one large design file.

Geographical Organization. Files can also be "geographically" organized. For example, four files can be set up for the northeast, northwest, southeast, and southwest quadrants of a map. When finding an element, the computer must first determine in which quadrant the cursor lies, then scan the file for that quadrant until it finds the element. Assuming an even distribution of elements across the map, only one quarter of the map's elements would be scanned.

Georgraphically organized files increase redraw rate by scanning only through files that correspond to areas on the screen. A zoom-in view of the southwest, for example, could be redrawn using only the southwest quadrant's file.

Element organization and geographic organization are just two characteristics that can be used to organize a file. Just about any characteristic can be used as an organizational key. A circuit design system may benefit from creating separate files for each circuit board or functional circuit area, while an architectural system could use the rooms of a building as organizational keys.

File Manipulation. Rigid file organization presents a few problems. If multiple files are used, the user must switch back and forth between them. The disk operating system must use a lot of memory for the buffers and control parameters needed to manipulate and keep multiple files open simultaneously. This uses up processor memory space, thereby limiting the size of the rest of the program that can be kept in memory—and design systems need all the memory they can get. The operating system overhead involved in switching between files is also a problem, especially if only one file is open at a time. To switch files, the system has to close

Three-dimensional, shaded graphics with hidden surface elimination (Courtesy Evans and Sutherland and Rediffusion Simulation)

Shadow effects combined with three-dimensional, dynamic graphics (Courtesy Evans and Sutherland and Rediffusion Simulation)

Boeing 757/767 cockpit with EFIS (Electronic Flight Instrument System) and EICAS (Electronic Engine Indication and Crew Alert System) in middle (Courtesy Rockwell International, Collins Division, Cedar Rapids, Iowa)

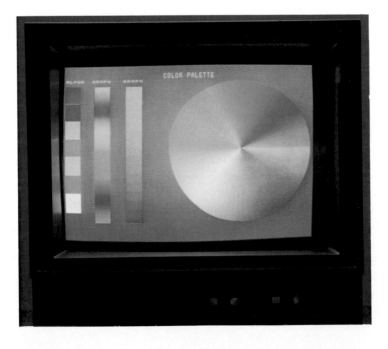

Color palette produced on a 4096-color raster display system (Courtesy Matrox Electronic Systems, Montreal, Canada)

The use of color raster scan graphics in aircraft weather radar (Courtesy Rockwell International, Collins Division, Cedar Rapids, Iowa)

Color keying and shaded graphics used in a demographic mapping application (Courtesy SAS Institute Inc., Cary, NC)

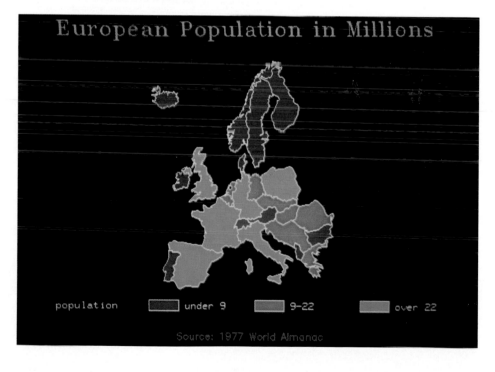

Multiple-font and color usage in a text display (Courtesy SAS Institute Inc., Cary, NC)

Proportional pie-charting graphing technique (Courtesy SAS Institute Inc., Cary, NC)

the current file by writing out the file's temporary data and control buffers that are stored in memory, then it must open the new file by initializing the control buffers and reading in the data buffer from the disk. This can take 500 ms or more.

One way around the file opening and closing problem is to use one big file divided into sections that are treated like small separate files. A whole disk, or even multiple disks, can be accessed as one big file on most operating systems. Disk files are usually accessed using record numbers (were each record consists of 256 bytes, for instance).

Records 1 to 100 may be defined as being the line-string file, records 101 to 200 the circle file, and so on. All is well with this method until one file gets so large that it "bumps into" the adjacent file. This is a standard filing system problem—the kind of problem that the disk operating system is invisibly solving if the operating system is handling multiple files. By dividing the file into subfile sections, however, the user must begin to solve these problems. Essentially, an operating system is being built on top of an operating system.

The use of many files increases disk system performance, but the final design is better stored and transported from machine to machine as one large file. In many systems, the large single file is known as the *design* file, and the many small files are the *working* files. Software that separates design files and merges working files is required to translate between working and design files.

High-Performance Software

Display redraw and finding rates can be improved by decreasing file access time with high-performance file access software. The software that comes with most operating systems (especially those of multiuser systems) is very general in nature. Faster but less flexible disk access routines can be written in assembly language to access the disk controller directly. A simple routine that accepts a disk track, sector, and cylinder number and reads the data directly from disk into a Fortran array (in a design system written in Fortran) avoids the overhead of opening and closing files, operating system checks, and asynchronous requests to a "file manager." It also reads the data directly into the desired array, bypassing the operating system's temporary data buffer from which the data would normally be transferred using hundreds of Fortran read statements in a time-expensive data transfer loop.

Software that gives the user direct control over track, sector, and cylinder number also allows files to be arranged in a strategic manner on the disk. A disk can rapidly move (seek) between adjacent tracks, but it takes a long time to seek between widely separated ones. Files can be placed on adjacent tracks within the scheme of the file organization to further decrease access time.

High-Performance Hardware

Hardware that is dedicated to increasing the design file scanning, finding, and redrawing throughput of a design system can increase performance substantially. Such hardware can also be used to eliminate the need for highly organized and hard-to-work-with file structures. With standard computer hardware, the processor is the limiting performance factor. With high-performance digital hardware (no new mechanical devices), the goal is to make the mechanical disk speed the limiting factor. The object is to pull data off the disk and display it on the fly as the disk spins (at about 3000 rpm).

A *track grabber*—a disk controller that can grab a whole disk track and put it into a buffer memory in one spin—is a good first step. This feature is not built into normal disk controllers. Instead, they read a sector or two, then transfer the data to processor memory using DMA (direct memory access) or PIO (programmed input/output), then wait for the disk to spin around again to grab the next sector. A nice feature about a track grabber is that after the track is read, the disk controller can be instructed to seek to the next track for access. The track data can then be processed while the disk head is moving across the disk to the next track, thus overlapping the seek and processing operations.

If the track processing is done by the time the disk reaches the next track, the next track can be grabbed immediately. But what is involved in the processing of a track?

A cartridge disk with 10M bytes of storage capability is a good choice for a low-end design system, and the following are typical disk characteristics:

Disk drive—Western Dynex Series 6000
Rotational speed—2400 rpm
16-bit words/sector—256
Sectors/track—12
Words per track—3072
Resulting transfer rate—122K words/second
Track grab time—25 ms
Seek time—12.5 ms average
Avg. track transfer time (seek & grab)—37.5 ms
Track density—200 tracks/in.

Assuming that a line element takes 20 words—a realistic estimate when we include line style, range, and double-precision $x, y,$ and z coordinates—153 lines fit on one track. Rotating, translating, and clipping a line requires about 40 multiplications, 10 divisions, and 60 additions and subtractions.

Assuming a complexity ratio of 1, 2, and 0.2 for multiplication, division, and addition, about 72 multiply time periods are required. The data manipulation (miscellaneous buffer moves, comparisons, and branching) could bring this figure up to roughly 100.

A total of 15,300 multiply-complexity operations must be performed. A high-performance microprocessor such as an 8 MHz 68000 microprocessor performs a 32-bit multiply in 35 μs, so track processing would take 535 ms. This does not compare favorably with the 37.5 ms track transfer time, so a more powerful processor or special hardware is needed.

Most of the time is going toward doing the line rotation and projection, so hardware such as matrix multipliers and clipper dividers can speed things up.

Intelligence can be added to the disk controller to determine if a graphic element meets certain display characteristics, such as being a specifically searched-for element or being within the range of the display screen or being nonintelligence information. This hardware is called a *disk scanner*. Disk scanners are much more than simple add-on items. A disk controller must be completely redesigned to incorporate one, and very high-performance logic (usually Schottky TTL or ECL) is required to handle the data in real time.

Peripherals as Files

A design system can be quite complex and may incorporate a few display screens, a large matrix printer (for shaded output), a large plotter (for high-resolution line drawings), multiple input devices (keyboard, tablet, joysticks, or track balls), and miscellaneous alphanumeric terminals. A design system can indeed be a complete computer complex in itself. It is important that the user be able to control all the resources interactively and efficiently.

Disk operating systems on general-purpose computers contain utility programs that allow the operator to move disk files on the disk and to peripheral devices. The famous "PIP" (peripheral interchange program) used on Digital Equipment Corporation computers and later mimicked in other operating systems is a good example. The general idea of these programs is that everything, including I/O devices, is treated as files. A simple command such as filenew.for = fileold.for is used to transfer the data from one file to another. In this case, a Fortran file called fileold.for is copied to a new file called filenew.for. Input and output peripheral devices have standard device names that, when used in a PIP command, channels I/O to them. A user's terminal is referred to as TI: and the line-printer number 0 is LP0:. To look at the filenew.for Fortran file on the terminal, the following command is used:

TI: = filenew.for

To print out the Fortran file on the line printer, the following is submitted:

LP0: = filenew.for

Programs that are similar to PIP can be extended to cover design files and display devices as well as disk files, terminals, and printers. Design files are in fact already disk files. The only additions needed are the device drivers that handle the printers, plotters, and screens.

The following command channels a design file to plotter 1:

PLT1: = mytown.dsn

Menu Method

A multiple-choice menu approach is often used instead of a PIP utility approach. It is probably better suited to people with little programming experience who simply use the system for design work in their own fields. Multiple-choice questions begin the sequence:

1) Create new design file?
2) Use old design?
3) Plot a design?
4) Print a design on the matrix printer?
5) Copy design file to new file?

When an option is selected, more detailed questions about the chosen responses are asked using keyed-in or more multiple-choice responses.

A third way of controlling peripheral data flow on a design system is to use the graphics capabilities of the system to help in the control interaction. A menu of graphics utility functions can be used in the same way graphic elements are submitted. This method is particularly useful for describing system setup information (which screen is displaying what, what the plotter is connected to, etc.), as Fig. 6-10 illustrates.

The user simply points the cursor at the desired graphic function followed by the peripheral device, and the new data flow channel is established. The user can get an overview of system configuration by looking at what is connected to what.

DESIGN SYSTEM SOFTWARE STRUCTURE

There is a lot more to a design system than display hardware backed by a few graphics routines. The heart of a CAD system is its software—the graphics hardware is of secondary importance. And most of the software does not come under the heading of "graphics"—rather, it consists of software for file manipulation, user interaction, and data analysis.

The software for most large design systems is written in Fortran, and a whole system typically has a few hundred thousand lines of Fortran code. The size of the program is somewhat misleading, however, because the "system" consists of hundreds of small routines that perform independent and specialized functions.

Program Library

The core of a design system's software is usually in the form of an *executive*—a program that directs the execution of many smaller, independent programs. The executive continuously resides in memory, and smaller application programs are pulled from the disk as needed.

A memory-resident library of commonly used routines is available to the executive to perform common functions such as multiprecision and floating-point mathematics, basic display generation routines (line drawers, shaders, curve generators), viewing and rotation routines (matrix multipliers, perspective projectors, and clippers), and very importantly, cursor tracking. Figure 6-11 outlines a general design system software structure.

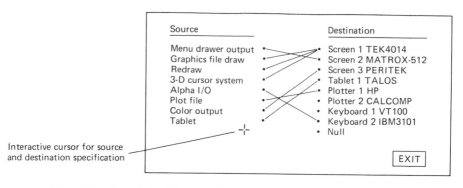

Figure 6-10 Control of peripheral data flow with a menu of graphic functions. The user selects a source with the cursor and then picks an output destination.

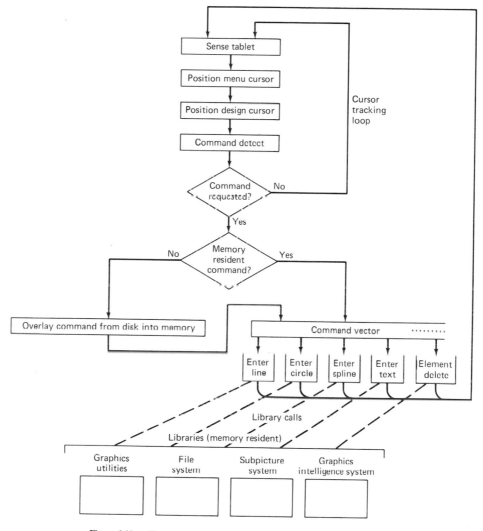

Figure 6-11 Typical software structure of a computer-aided design system.

187

Data Types

Data within a design system is based on a standard data type, and elements within the design all use this data type. Crude systems use 16-bit integers, but this is not enough for serious design work. The two most common data types are 32-bit integer and floating-point. A 32-bit integer gives the user a very wide design range. At first glance, a floating-point capability may seem the ultimate for a design system, because numbers ranging from small fractions to huge values can be expressed. But there is a catch: floating-point numbers have a wide dynamic range, but their precision is less than that of an equivalent bit-sized integer. Floating-point representations are nonlinear. The precision very close to the origin (zero) is very high, but away from zero it decreases. At 25,000 units from zero, a fraction with only 2 decimal digits (25000.23) is the maximum resolution; and at 100 million, the finest resolution is a giant step of 100 units. Moving a 27- by 34- unit rectangle from a location near 0,0 to 100-million, 100-million is possible with a 32-bit integer representation, and the precision at both points in the design space is identical. If the box were moved using a standard translation equation in 32-bit floating point, the box would fold up to a single point at 100-million, 100-million—and all precision would be permanently lost. Floating-point arithmetic is not well suited for design systems or graphics work in general because it does not reflect the resolution linearity of dimensional space.

SIMULATION SYSTEM INTERACTION

The previous discussion described the basic concepts of interaction with a design system, but if real-time graphic simulation is the aim, the rules are totally changed. Design systems use huge amounts of disk storage, relatively slowly drawn displays, long waits between user inputs, and highly fragmented program structures with executive control. Simulations typically use very little disk space or none at all, are very memory-intensive, draw displays at incredibly fast rates, and require instantaneous and continuous user response. Small, totally memory-resident control programs are commonplace.

Simulation software is divided into two segments: the graphics software and the software that actually simulates a physical situation. If the software is running on just one computer, execution alternates between both segments.

INTERACTIVE CONTROL

Finding good ways to interactively control a simulation display is trivial because it is defined by the simulation itself. A flight simulator, for example, requires a control yoke, rudder pedals, and flap, engine, and other miscellaneous controls dictated by the extent of the simulation.

Totally realistic interactive input devices are not always available, and input devices often make good substitutes. Joysticks make excellent devices for controlling aircraft, ground vehicles, and spacecraft—anything having to do with motion viewed from the driver's seat. Track balls are good for control from the observer's viewpoint (controlling the aiming of a gun, for example, or rotating an object in space) and can replace precision mechanical controls such as valves and levers.

When lifelike input devices are not available, it is important that the user get enough feedback from the substitute input device to "close the loop" in the same way the real thing would. Determining exactly what the feedback will consist of is a problem for human-factors psychologists (who can very often be found working around simulation facilities).

Ordinarily, however, it is easy to tell when obvious things are missing. A manual transmission driving simulation may use a joystick to substitute for a gear shift lever. Because the stick has no notch effect, the user may not have a means for knowing exactly which gear the stick is in; so a small indicator on the display screen can be used to show the forward and reverse gears as they are engaged.

SIMULATION SOFTWARE STRUCTURE

Simulation software must perform three tasks simutaneously: display generation, sampling of controls, and the simulation itself. With only one computer available this is not possible, because a computer can only perform one task (actually one instruction of a single task) at a time. The computer has one feature that allows it to compensate for this weakness, however: speed. Real-world events happen very slowly compared to the speed at which a computer can make many small calculations.

Time Interleaving

Simulation software structures are designed to utilize a computer's speed in a way that makes it appear that three tasks are being performed at once. Simulation software makes extensive use of "time interleaving." This process breaks the whole simulation task into several independent programs that each advance their particular task (display, control sampling, or simulation) one small step when called from a control program. The control program cycles through all the small tasks at a rapid rate.

Time interleaving can best be illustrated with an example: Figure 6-12 illustrates a control loop for a video pinball game. This is only a game application, but the components of a more serious simulation are present. When entered, the screen is initialized to look like a pinball game. Simulation parameters such as score, ball count, flipper initial position, and placement of the first ball are performed. Initialization is not time-critical and is usually outweighed timewise by the disk loading time. Initialization procedures are therefore optimized for small memory size rather than speed.

The simulation control loop is then entered. The user interfaces (flipper buttons, striker control, and tilt controls) are sampled. In this case, the flipper buttons are actually pushbuttons that the computer can read as being pressed or released. The striker position is determined by a potentiometer or game paddle, and the tilt key is a keyboard key that has a status bit indicating that they key was pressed and a register that can be read to determine what key was pressed.

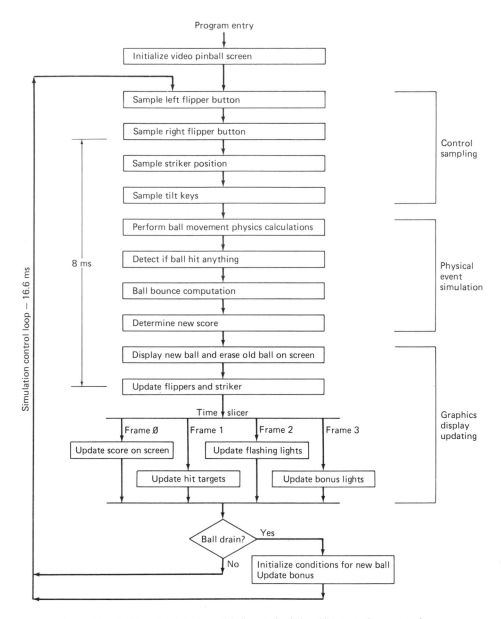

Figure 6-12 In this control loop for a pinball-game-simulating video game, the concept of time interleaving is illustrated. The initialization is optimized for a small memory; following initialization, the control loop samples user interfaces, causes appropriate screen simulations, and updates display and scoring.

The physical events are then simulated. The simulation routines are calibrated to a time scale that corresponds to the display loop cycle time. Each time the routines are called, they assume that one cycle time has passed and perform the ball movement, hit detection, bounce computation, and scoring associated with this time interval.

Finally, the graphic display is updated. The ball can move very quickly in straight lines and arcs across the screen, so updating is required on every control loop cycle for smooth motion. Events such as updating the score, target lights, and bonus lights can be updated less often because they are simply on or off or flash at a very slow interval—these events are *time-sliced*. The time-slicer software counts the number of cycles through the control loop and directs each cycle through one of the time-slice frames. This cuts the processing time to 25% of the time needed to update everything, thus speeding up cycle rate.

Before the loop is again started, the software checks to see if the ball has drained. If so, the system is initialized for the next ball. The reinitialization is outside the simulation loop, so it is not time-critical.

An inexpensive noninterlaced display screen scans at 60 frames per second, so there is no reason to go any faster than this in the display updating. This corresponds to 16.6 ms per control loop cycle.

Response-Time Considerations

Interactive control response time must also be considered. Pressing a flipper button and having the flipper rise half a second later would make the game nearly unplayable. The worst-case control lag is slightly greater than one simulation cycle. If the flipper button is pressed slightly after the button is sampled, the simulation loop will not recognize the press until the next time around. Add the delay from sampling to new flipper generation (8 ms in this case) to obtain worst-case control lag (24.6 ms).

The equations in a simulation model can usually be adjusted to perform incremental updates based on the cycle time interval; but if the interval gets too large, the simulation may not perform properly. This is usually due to quickly responding equations within the simulation that overshoot their proper locations because they would have suddenly slowed or even reversed their direction updates. A rapidly moving ball in a pinball game, for instance, can travel across the pinball machine in 200 ms. If the simulated machine is 128 pixels wide, the ball could travel 10 pixel widths in one 16.6 ms cycle time. The ball could easily pass over a bumper or target, or go through a wall that would have been sensed if movement were restricted to one pixel per cycle. These problems can be solved by (1) damping quickly responding equations, (2) executing the physical event simulation a few times per display loop, and (3) doing quick approximations of intermediate sample points to determine if any abnormal changes occur within the interval. These methods take more software and execution time, but such tradeoffs are always considerations in computer graphics.

Assessing Simulation Update Requirements

It is very important to be aware of situations where overcalculation is taking place. A real-time ship-navigation simulation, for example, hardly requires a simulation rate of 60 updates per second. In this case, it is wise to put the simulation software in one of the time slices to allow more time for display processing. Or better yet, divide the simulation among a few time slices and increase its complexity to simulate the ship that much more accurately.

IMPROVING SIMULATION PERFORMANCE

Overall simulation speed depends on the speed of the simulation software and the graphic routines. Routines for graphics usually account for more than 50% of the simulation execution time, so this is a candidate for software speedups.

The first step is to use the least possible graphics significance, and use the data type that the computer handles most quickly. A precision of 32 bits or floating-point accuracy is rarely required in a real-time simulation. An 8-bit integer for 8-bit microprocessors and a 16-bit integer for 16-bit microprocessors are the best data types for high performance. An 8-bit resolution is not enough for most serious simulations, however, so double-precision integers (16 bits) on an 8-bit processor arethe next best thing.

High-speed addition, subtraction, multiplication, and division routines should be used for mathematical calculations. (These are explained in subsequent chapters.)

To solve speed problems in the most efficient way, they must first be identified. The best tool for doing this is a real-time clock that allows program reset, trigger, and stop under software control. This allows timings to be performed and permits zeroing in on problem areas. The benefits of this tool cannot be overemphasized.

Software typically spends 90% of the time in 10% of the program, and even an educated guess as to where the 10% is would be a shot in the dark. The results of a real-time clock that shows how the time is being used is often surprising. Figure 6-13 presents a real-time clock control program that can be used with the California Computer Systems' programmable timer module for the Apple II microcomputer. It can time events down to the nearest microsecond, and actually counts clock cycles. The programs are totally compensated for their own overhead execution time, and even a single 2-clock-cycle instruction can be timed with 100% precision.

```
; REAL-TIME-CLOCK TIMING SYSTEM

; TO USE:   At beginning of program put TIMINT macro for
;           timer initialization.

;           To reset and start timer use SETTIM macro

;           To sum timer into sum of 32-bit register
;           use SUMTIM  REGNAME   macro.  REGNAME is
;           name of 32-bit register where sum is kept.

;           EXAMPLE: To time routine mltpy
;                 SETTIM
;                 JSR    mltpy
;                 SUMTIM timer1
```

Figure 6-13   (continued)

```
;  TIMER RANGE: Each timer tick is .9778 micro-seconds
;             so RANGE = about 1 hour per 32-bit timer.

;  HARDWARE NOTE: Ground timer input G2

;  6502 INSTRUCTIONS: The mnemonics used here are
;                   modified slightly. An "i" after an
;                   instruction means "immediate":
;                     ldai  0      means    lda  #0

;  MACRO DEFINITIONS:

.define TIMINT =[
           jmp    xxpass
timtmp:  .word  0
timer1:  .word  0,0
timer2:  .word  0,0
timer3:  .word  0,0
timer4:  .word  0,0
xxpass:

           ldxi   15.     ;clear 4 timers
           ldai   0
..lup:   sta    timer1,x
           dex
           bpl    ..lup

           ldai   23h   ;single shot, int. clock, no intrpt
           sta    0c0b1h
           ldai   0ffh       ;latch 2 = ffffh
           sta    0c0b4h
           sta    0c0b5h]

.define SETTIM =[
           php
           pha
           ldai   1
           sta    0c0b0h
           ldai   0
           sta    0c0b0h
           pla
           plp]

.define SUMTIM [reg]=[
           php
           pha
           lda    0c0b4h  ;msb
           eori   0ffh
           sta    timtmp+1
           lda    0c0b5h  ;lsb
           eori   0ffh
           sec            ;subtract-out timer
           sbci   10h     ;software time.
           sta    timtmp
           lda    0c0b1h
..bad:   bne    ..bad   ;timer overflow
           lda    timtmp+1
           sbci   0
           sta    timtmp+1
           clc
           lda    timtmp
           adc    reg
           sta    reg
           lda    timtmp+1
           adc    reg+1
           sta    reg+1
           bcc    ..okok
           inc    reg+2



           bne    ..okok
           inc    reg+3
..okok:  pla
           plp
           ]
```

Figure 6-13   Real-time clock control program for use with California Computer Systems'
programmable timer module for the Apple II microcomputer. (continued)

Chapter 7

Mathematics and Transforms for Advanced Graphics

While it's true that we can create just about any form of computer graphics using the basic methods described earlier, additional concepts that utilize these primitives are good to know. Efficient forms of representation and shortcuts to complex manipulation of data and numbers have evolved over the years through the use of mathematics and matrixing techniques.

MATRIX REPRESENTATION OF GRAPHIC OPERATIONS

All graphics manipulations can be represented in equation form. The problem is that graphics manipulations usually involve many simple arithmetic operations. Whole pages quickly fill with line after line of simple equations that make little sense when viewed at a glance. Matrix representations put all these small equations into a compact form that can be understood at a glance—with a little practice. Due to the multiple numbers associated with graphic elements (a 3D point has an x, y, and z coordinate, for example), it is convenient to handle points and lines as small 3-element entities. Again, the matrix representation is the simplest, cleanest way of doing this. Matrixes are very similar to arrays used in computer programs, so paper representations correlate closely with the final computer program's variable storage.

In many fields, complex mathematical notation is used to impress the reader more than to simplify the task. The use of matrixes in graphics is an exception. Matrixes are used because it's easier and helps get the job done, and that explains why practical programmers and engineers use them extensively in graphics.

VECTOR MATRIX ARITHMETIC

The simplest form of matrix is the row vector. It has two or more elements placed side by side with square brackets around them. The two elements are independent from one another and the brackets simply mark the beginning and end of the elements. We have referred to x, y coordinate points in previous chapters and have often used the notation (x, y) to represent them. The official row vector representation is:

$$[x \ y]$$

This can be extended to three dimensions to fully describe the point in an x, y, z coordinate system:

$$[x \ y \ z]$$

It is often necessary to move up and down rows and columns of a matrix following strict, predefined rules. It's impossible to move up and down a row vector, so when downward movement is necessary, the coordinate point can be expressed as a column vector:

$$\begin{vmatrix} x \\ y \\ z \end{vmatrix}$$

The meaning is the same as the row vector, but it is more convenient in certain applications.

Vector Addition and Subtraction

Offsets must be added to 2- and 3-dimensional coordinate points to move them through space. The 3D concept of point translation reduces to the following equations:

$$x' = x + x\mathrm{T}$$
$$y' = y + y\mathrm{T}$$
$$z' = z + z\mathrm{T}$$

where

(x, y, z) is the original coordinate,

$(x\mathrm{T}, y\mathrm{T}, z\mathrm{T})$ is the x,y,z translation, and

$(x', y' \ z',)$ is the result

The matrix addition method assigns a row vector to the original coordinate, the translation, and the result appears as:

$$[x' \ y' \ z'] = [x \ y \ z] + [x\mathrm{T} \ y\mathrm{T} \ z\mathrm{T}]$$

In vector addition, you simply add the corresponding elements of the two row vectors to get the element in the result row vector. A numerical example helps visualize this:

$$[10 \ 23 \ 5] \ = \ [4 \ 18 \ -3] \ + \ [6 \ 5 \ 8]$$

Vector subtraction is nearly identical in operation. The plus sign is replaced with a minus sign:

$$[4 \ 18 \ -3] \ = \ [10 \ 23 \ 5] \ - \ [6 \ 5 \ 8]$$

Vector Multiplication

In graphics, and in real-world situations in general, it's often necessary to compute sums of products. A good example is the case where you need to determine how many dollars in coins you have. This is a sum-of-the-products case where you multiply the value of each type of coin by how many of them there are and finally add all the products together:

total value of 3 quarters, 7 dimes, and 4 nickels

$$\$1.65 \ = \ (25 \times 3) + (10 \times 7) + (5 \times 4)$$

Row and column vector multiplication is actually more than just multiplication. It is a sum-of-the-products operation designed to handle these real-world situations. The coin example would be expressed as:

$$\$1.65 \ = \ [25 \ 10 \ 5] \times \begin{vmatrix} 3 \\ 7 \\ 4 \end{vmatrix}$$

There are a few things to note about this operation. First, note how the elements have been neatly and logically grouped. The [25 10 5] row vector could be called the "coin value" vector, and the column vector with 3, 7, and 4 could be the "coin count" vector. Also note that the result is not a vector but a single value (a scalar). Finally, the official description of this operation is:

$$a \ = \ [b_1 \ b_2 \ b_3] \times \begin{vmatrix} c_1 \\ c_2 \\ c_3 \end{vmatrix}$$

$$a \ = \ (b_1 \times c_1) + (b_2 \times c_2) + (b_3 \times c_3)$$

Scalar Multiplication

Scaling, like translation, is another common operation that is performed on coordinate points. To make an image defined by points larger or smaller, simply multiply all the x, y, and z coordinates by a scaling factor. The following matrix representation performs this function:

$$[x' \ y' \ z'] = s \ [x \ y \ z]$$

where

> s is the scale factor
> $[x \ y \ z]$ is the original point
> $[x' \ y' \ z']$ is the scaled point

This operation is equivalent to:

$$x' = s \times x$$
$$y' = s \times y$$
$$z' = s \times z$$

RECTANGULAR MATRIX ARITHMETIC

Rectagular matrixes are arrays of numbers that consist of m by n rows and columns. If m equals n, the matrix is square. The matrix itself is simply a rectangle full of numbers. The predefined matrix algebra manipulations that are performed on matrixes give the matrix its meaning.

Rectangular matrix addition and subtraction are performed by adding the elements of one matrix to the corresponding elements of another. Both matrixes must be the same size. This is exactly how column and row vectors (actually small rectangular matrixes with only one row or column) were added and subtracted. Matrix addition in computer graphics is usually limited to row and column vectors that represent points in space. Large rectangular matrix addition is seldom used.

There are two types of matrix multiplication: scalar-by-matrix multiplication and matrix-by-matrix multiplication. As a noun, a scalar is a single number or scale factor that all the matrix elements are multiplied by in scalar multiplication. This is used to scale down all the elements of a matrix in equal proportion. In graphics, this is used on row and column vectors that represent points in space. It moves a point radially toward or away from the origin (0,0,0). This is often done to put the values of $x, y,$ and z within a range that graphics routines can more easily handle, especially when integer arithmetic is being performed.

Matrix-by-matrix multiplication is a sum-of-the-products operation. The result is a matrix. The multiplier, multiplicand, and product matrixes may all be of different dimensions, but their dimensions must match each other in the way shown in Fig. 7-1 (the I, J, K dimensions). This matching corresponds to the way the sums of products are generated from the two matries, also shown in the figure. Small BASIC programs that perform the mathematics are shown to clarify the step-by-step multiplication and addition procedure.

Figure 7-1(b) shows the set of simple equations that correspond to the matrix multiplication. Graphics translations and rotations just happen to take a form that fits precisely into the set of equations; thus, a graphics rotation and translation can be expressed as a matrix. This is the key to using matrixes in graphics.

There are a few more useful matrix properties that are important to know, although their application to graphics may not be immediately apparent.

197

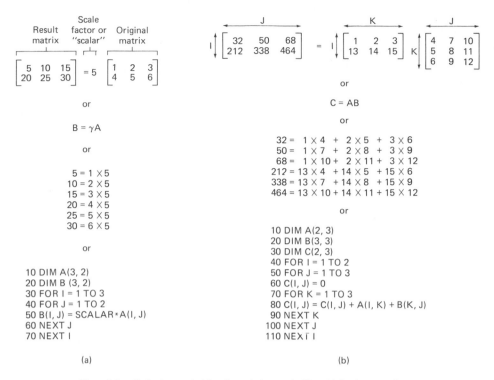

Figure 7-1 Scalar-by-matrix (a) and matrix-by-matrix (b) multiplication procedures.

Matrix multiplication is not *commutative*. Two square matrixes multiplied as *ab* will yield different results than *ba*. Two swapped nonsquare matrixes won't even have the correct *I,J,K* alignment to be multiplied out—the elements won't match.

Matrix multiplication is *associative*. The term *a(bc)* will yield the same result as *(ab)c*. This will be useful in simplifying combined rotations.

A "diagonal matrix" is a square matrix filled with zeros except for entries from the upper left to lower right corner, or *principal diagonal*.

The "transpose" of a matrix is a matrix with identical matrix entries, only arranged in *J,I* instead of *I,J* order. The transpose of a square matrix is thus the original matrix "flipped" around its principal diagonal.

The "inverse" of a matrix is another matrix that "undoes" the operation of the matrix under matrix-to-matrix multiplication. If a matrix represents a 30° rotation about the axis, the inverse matrix represents a −30° rotation about the *x* axis. In general, it is very difficult to arrive at an inverse matrix for any randomly generated matrix, and the concepts of singularity, rank, and the process of Gaussian elimination must be understood; but for special matrixes corresponding to orthogonal space (2D and 3D display space, for example), we fortunately can use much simpler methods.

2D GRAPHICS TRANSFORMS

Chapter 1 presented basics of 2D computer graphics and detailed common transforms in equation form. We now put these transforms into matrix form, which will clear the way for extending them into 3D space.

Translation

Vector addition is used to translate 2D points. A point is represented with a 2-element row vector, $[x\ y]$. The translation displacement is the row vector $[Dx\ Dy]$. The equation is thus:

$$[x\ y]' = [x\ y] + [Dx\ Dy]$$

or

$$PNT1' = PNT1 + Dxy$$

The second form is a symbolic representation that can be understood at a glance. The "PNT1'" term is read as "point one prime."

Scaling

A scalar can be matrix-multiplied by a point to radially scale it toward the origin (0,0). Scaling about the origin is thus:

$$[x\ y]' = scale\ [x\ y]$$

or

$$PNT1' = SCALE \times PNT1$$

Scaling about an arbitrary point other than the origin is common and is performed by shifting the scaling centerpoint to the origin, performing the scaling, then moving it back to its original position. The center of scaling is CENTER in the following equation:

$$PNT1' = CENTER + SCALE \times (PNT1 - CENTER)$$

The preceding scaling equations assumed identical scaling in the x and y directions. For different x and y dimension scaling, a scaling matrix must be used. The equations for x and y scaling are:

$$x' = scalex \times x$$
$$y' = scalex \times y$$

This can be put into the matrix's "product of sums" form by extending the equations to:

$$x' = (\text{scale}x \times x) + (0 \qquad \times y)$$
$$y' = (0 \qquad \times x) + (\text{scale}y \times y)$$

or in matrix form:

$$[x \ y]' = [x \ y] \quad \begin{vmatrix} \text{scale}x & 0 \\ 0 & \text{scale}y \end{vmatrix}$$

or in symbolic form:

$$PNT1' = PNT1 \ SCALEXY$$

Notice that the SCALEXY form is a diagonal matrix. Scaling is an inherent property of diagonal matrixes, and if all elements along the principal diagonal are set to 1 (the scale factors in this example), the resultant form is an *identity matrix,* often referred to as simply " I ". The results of the matrix multipy are equal to the matrix being multiplied by the identity matrix. The identity matrix corresponds to a scale factor of 1, which means original size.

Rotation

The rotation equations derived in chapter 2 fit nicely into matrix form:

$$x' = x \times \cos(\text{angle}) - y \times \sin(\text{angle})$$
$$y' = x \times \sin(\text{angle}) + y \times \cos(\text{angle})$$

in matrix form:

$$[x \ y]' = [x \ y] \quad \begin{vmatrix} \cos(\text{angle}) & -\sin(\text{angle}) \\ \sin(\text{angle}) & \cos(\text{angle}) \end{vmatrix}$$

in symbolic form:

$$PTN1' = PNT1 \ ROT2D$$

Notice how the $-\sin$ term was used to compensate for the subtraction in the equation. The rotation matrix is similar in form to the scaling matrix. For 0° rotations, we have:

$$\begin{vmatrix} \cos(0) & -\sin(0) \\ \sin(0) & \cos(0) \end{vmatrix}$$

or

$$\begin{vmatrix} 1 & 0 \\ 0 & 1 \end{vmatrix}$$

This is the identity matrix. This makes intuitive sense because the resultant point of a 0° rotation will be unrotated and in its original position. Rotation about a nonorigin center may be expressed symbolically as:

$$PNT1' = CENTER + (PNT1 - CENTER) \ ROT2D$$

Derotation

If ROT2D is the rotation transform matrix that rotates a point, then $ROT2D^{-1}$ is the inverse matrix that derotates it. The inverse matrix can be generated the same way the rotation matrix was, only a negative rotation angle will be used to unrotate the point:

$$x = x' \times \cos(-angle) - y' \times \sin(-angle)$$
$$y = x' \times \sin(-angle) + y' \times \cos(-angle)$$

using trig identities

$$\cos(\theta) = \cos(-\theta)$$

and

$$-\sin(\theta] = \sin(-\theta)$$

yields:

$$x = x' \times \cos(angle) + y' \times \sin(angle)$$
$$y = x' \times -\sin(angle) + y' \times \cos(angle)$$

or in matrix form:

$$[x \ y] = [x \ y]' \quad \begin{vmatrix} \cos(angle) & \sin(angle) \\ -\sin(angle) & \cos(angle) \end{vmatrix}$$

Comparing this inverse matrix with the original matrix shows that the inverse or derotation matrix in this case is the rotation matrix transposed. This is more than just coincidence. Advanced rules of matrix algebra state that in an orthogonal vector space, a matrix's inverse is its transpose. Books dealing with advanced matrix algebra or state-space analysis go through proofs of this property. The 2D and 3D spaces we work with in graphics qualify as orthogonal vector spaces, so simple transposes can be used to create derotation matrixes.

Matrix and Transform Concatenation

Scaling and rotation transforms are very similar. In both cases a row vector (the point) is multiplied by a 2 × 2 matrix. In some situations, both scaling and rotation are required. In these cases, the point can first be multiplied by the scaling matrix, then the resulting point can be multiplied by the rotation matrix:

$$PNT1' = PNT1 \ SCALEXY$$
$$PNT1'' = PNT1' \ ROT2D$$

201

This would require 8 multiplications and 4 additions if general matrix multiplication were used. Optimizing for the two zeros in the SCALEXY matrix brings this down to 6 multiplications and 2 additions. Eliminating the intermediate point PNT1 in the equations results in:

$$\text{PNT1}'' = \text{PNT1 SCALEXY ROT2D}$$

Matrix multiplication's associative property allows us to multiply the 3 matrixes in any order. The choices are:

$$\text{PNT1}'' = (\text{PNT1 SCALEXY}) \text{ ROT2D}$$
$$\text{PNT1}'' = \text{PNT1 (SCALEXY ROT2D)}$$

The first way corresponds to the two separate transformations with PNT1′ as an intermediate result. The second way, however, implies that we can combine scaling and rotation into one matrix that, when multiplied by PNT1, will translate and rotate the point in one step. Since both matries are 2 × 2 in size, the resulting matrix would also be 2 × 2; and transforming a point would only require 4 multiplies and 2 additions versus 8 multiplies and 4 additions for separate scale and rotation transformations. This implication is correct, and it can indeed cut transformation time in half.

The process of combining the two matrixes is called "concatenation" and is performed by multiplying the two matries together using matrix muliplication. It actually takes a bit more time to process one point using this method because two 2 × 2 matrixes are multiplied together to form the concatenated matrix (8 multiplies and 4 additions); but in most cases, hundreds of points will be multiplied by the combined rotation–scale matrix, so the concatenation time is actually insignificant overhead.

Transformation Order. In the above example it was assumed that scaling would be performed first, followed by rotation. Perhaps rotation followed by scaling is required. Is the order of transformation important? Will a rotation of 30° followed

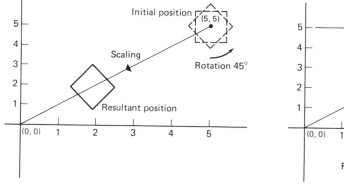

(a) Rotation about 5, 5 followed by scaling about 0, 0

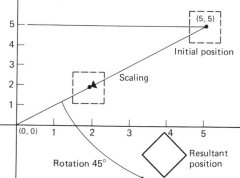

(b) Scaling about 0, 0 followed by rotation about 5, 5

Figure 7-2   The order of transformation can make a difference in the result: with a rotation about 5,5 followed by scaling about 0,0 (a) the result is in a different quadrant than scaling about 0,0 followed by rotation about 5,5 (b).

by a 0.5 scaling produce the same result as scaling followed by rotation? In fact, matrix multiplication is not commutative, so different results *can* occur. In the scaling rotation example, the same center (the origin) is used for both transforms, so the results would be the same; but consider a case where a rectangle centered at 5,5 is rotated about point 5,5 then scaled by 0.5. The results are different from those obtained when scaled first, as Fig. 7-2 illustrates.

Concatenating Translations and Rotations. Rotations followed by translations are often used to position and orient an element in space:

$$\text{PNT1}' = (\text{PNT1 ROT2D}) + \text{DXY}$$

Like regular addition and multiplication, matrix algebra has precedence rules, and combining the DXY and ROT2D terms by concatenation is not possible. The structure of matrix operations allows us to perform translation and rotation in one matrix multiplication by using the " sum " portion of the sum-of-the-products concept to perform the translation addition after the rotation. A few "tricks" are required, however.

The point row vector must have an extra term added to it to allow the consideration of new information in the translation–rotation (TRNSROT) matrix. Translation is the same for every point and is point-independent, so the value "1" will be used on all points. The new point row vector representation is:

$$[x \; y \; 1]$$

Don't confuse "1" with a z value. It simply is a matrix term enabler. The rotation followed by the translation in equation form is:

$$x' = x \cos (\text{angle}) - y \sin (\text{angle}) + \text{D}x$$
$$y' = x \sin (\text{angle}) + y \cos (\text{angle}) + \text{D}y$$

which fits nicely into matrix form as:

$$[x \; y \; 1]' = [x \; y \; 1] \begin{vmatrix} \cos (\text{angle}) & -\sin (\text{angle}) & 0 \\ \sin (\text{angle}) & \cos (\text{angle}) & 0 \\ \text{D}x & \text{D}y & 1 \end{vmatrix}$$

or

$$\text{PNT}' = \text{PNT1 TRNSROT}$$

The new matrix is 3 × 3, but many of the multiplications are trivial 0 × 0 or 1 × 1 cases that take no computation time. The advantage of putting translation and rotation into this form is that the operations are concatenated into a form that matrix multipliers can handle and that other operations (more rotations or scaling) can be concatenated to.

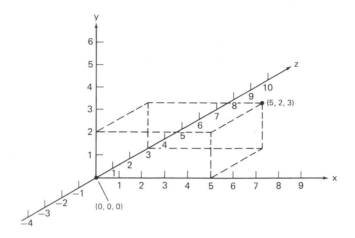

Figure 7-3   The 3D Cartesian coordinate system, in which width, height, and depth are specified in axis order x, y, and z.

3D GRAPHICS TRANSFORMS

Mathematically, 3D graphics are similar to 2D graphics. A new dimension is added (the z or depth dimension), so a totally new procedure to convert 3D representations into 2D screen images is required.

Figure 7-3 outlines the 3D coordinate system used to define graphics transforms. The x and y dimensions correspond to the 2D axes used with 2D graphics. The z axis is depth, and is considered positive as it goes into a 2D viewing screen. This sets up a left-hand coordinate system which many physicists find upsetting, but this convention makes more sense graphically when projecting images on the 2D screen.

Points are specified using x, y, z coordinates. The row vector form is $[x\ y\ z]$.

Translation In Three Dimensions

Moving a point in 3D space requires x, y, and z translation values. The values are added to the original point to obtain the new location:

$$[x\ y\ z]' = [x\ y\ z] + [\mathrm{D}x\ \mathrm{D}y\ \mathrm{D}z]$$

or

$$\mathrm{PNT1}' = \mathrm{PNT1} + \mathrm{DXYZ}$$

Scaling in Three Dimensions

Three-dimensional scaling is a simple extension of 2D scaling: all elements in the row vector are multiplied by a scalar for uniform scaling on all dimensions:

$$\mathrm{PNT1}' = \mathrm{SCALE} \times \mathrm{PNT1}$$

204

For independent scaling on all 3 axes, a 3 × 3 scaling matrix is used:

$$[x\ y\ z]' = [x\ y\ z] \begin{vmatrix} scalex & 0 & 0 \\ 0 & scaley & 0 \\ 0 & 0 & scalez \end{vmatrix}$$

or, symbolically:

$$PNT1' = PNT1\ \ SCALEXYZ$$

Scaling about nonorigin points is performed by moving the scaling centerpoint to the origin, performing scaling, and moving it back to its original location:

$$PNT1' = CENTERXYZ + (PNT1 - CENTERXYZ)\ SCALEXYZ$$

Rotation in Three Dimensions

The simplest form of 3D rotation is that of rotating an element about one of the axes (x, y, or z). Figure 7-4 shows the orientations of these three rotations. Rotations in the 2D case were assumed to be about the x,y origin or some arbitrary x,y point. These were actually rotations about the z axis, which appears as a point on a 2D screen. The values x, y, and z can be switched around to form the equations for rotation about the x and y axes as well:

$$z \text{ axis rotation:}\ \ [x\ y\ z]' = [x\ y\ z] \begin{vmatrix} \cos(angle) & -\sin(angle) & 0 \\ \sin(angle) & \cos(angle) & 0 \\ 0 & 0 & 1 \end{vmatrix}$$

$$x \text{ axis rotation:}\ \ [x\ y\ z]' = [x\ y\ z] \begin{vmatrix} 1 & 0 & 0 \\ 0 & \cos(angle) & -\sin(angle) \\ 0 & \sin(angle) & \cos(angle) \end{vmatrix}$$

$$y \text{ axis rotation:}\ \ [x\ y\ z]' = [x\ y\ z] \begin{vmatrix} \cos(angle) & 0 & -\sin(angle) \\ 0 & 0 & 0 \\ \sin(angle) & 0 & -\cos(angle) \end{vmatrix}$$

These rotation equations assume the origin as the center of rotation; but rotations about parallel axes are also possible by translating the parallel axis to the origin, rotating, and translating back:

$$PNT1' = CENTRXYZ + (PNT1 - CENTRXYZ)\ ROT3D$$

where CENTRXYZ is the translation required to translate the parallel axis to the origin.

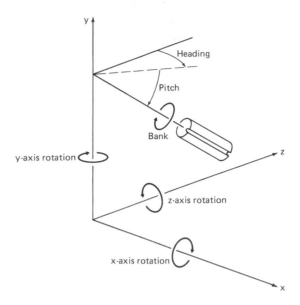

Figure 7-4   Rotations in three dimensions about *x*, *y*, and *z*, and arbitrary axes. The three dimensional rotations correspond to heading, pitch, and bank in aircraft simulations.

Rotations about arbitrary axes are more complex, but are required if an object is to be rotated to any arbitrary orientation. Rotations about arbitrary axes are most easily thought of and performed in terms of rotations relative to one another rather than as absolute components of a rotation vector.

It takes three rotations to fully specify an arbitrary rotation in 3 dimensions, just as it takes three parameters to specify location (*x, y,* and *z*). Figure 7-4 depicts the three parameters that are used to specify orientations of aircraft: heading, pitch, and bank. There are other names for these parameters, such as yaw, pitch, and roll, but the concepts are the same.

Heading is a rotation about the *y* axis. This is absolute rotation with respect to the *x,y,z* coordinate system.

Pitch is a downward rotation. This is with relation to the orientation defined by the heading,

Finally, *bank* is the rotation about the axis resulting from the heading and pitch rotations. If all rotation angles are very small (1 °, for example), these rotations roughly correspond to rotations about *y, x,* and *z* axes for heading, pitch and bank, but they are relative to one another—the relationship gets more complex for larger angles.

Sequentially the rotation operations are: *heading* followed by *pitch* followed by *bank*. The rotations are relative to previous rotations rather than being absolute components of a rotation vector, so equations used to perform the rotation are simplified. First, all the points of the element being rotated are rotated for heading by multiplying by the heading matrix (in this case, the *y*-axis rotation matrix):

$$[x \ y \ z]' = [x \ y \ z] \quad \begin{vmatrix} \cos H & 0 & \sin H \\ 0 & 1 & 0 \\ -\sin H & 0 & \cos H \end{vmatrix}$$

or

$$x = x \cos H - z \sin H$$
$$y = y$$
$$z = x \sin H + z \cos H$$

or

$$\mathtt{PNT1'} = \mathtt{PNT1 \ ROTH}$$

where H = heading and $\mathtt{ROTH}$ = heading rotation matrix.

Next comes pitch, which is a rotation about the x axis. This is not the absolute x axis but the one relative to the heading which we just rotated through. The equation is:

$$[x \ y \ z]' = [x \ y \ z] \quad \begin{vmatrix} 1 & 0 & 0 \\ 0 & \cos P & -\sin P \\ 0 & \sin P & \cos P \end{vmatrix}$$

or

$$x = x$$
$$y = y \cos P + z \sin P$$
$$z = -y \sin P + z \cos P$$

or

$$\mathtt{PNT1''} = \mathtt{PNT1' \ ROTP}$$

where P = pitch and $\mathtt{ROTP}$ = pitch rotation matrix

Finally, roll is accounted for by rotating about the z axis, in reference to the heading and pitch rotations.

$$[x \ y \ z]''' = [x \ y \ z]'' \quad \begin{vmatrix} \cos B & -\sin B & 0 \\ \sin B & \cos B & 0 \\ 0 & 0 & 1 \end{vmatrix}$$

or

$$x = x \cos B + y \sin B$$
$$y = -x \sin B + y \cos B$$
$$z = z$$

or

$$\mathtt{PNT1'''} = \mathtt{PNT1'' \ ROTB}$$

where B = bank and $\mathtt{ROTB}$ = bank rotation matrix

The point is now at its rotated position. Three sets of rotations were required, each requiring 4 multiplications and 2 additions for a total of 12 multiplication and

6 addition operations. Again, matrix concatenation can reduce the number of multiplications used in the rotation. The 3D rotation is combined as:

$$PNT1''' = PNT1 \ ROTH \ ROTP \ ROTB$$

The point vector and 3 matrixes can be multiplied in any order. If three separate rotations are done for heading, pitch, and bank, the order is that shown below:

$$PNT1''' = [[(PNT1 \ ROTH) \ ROTP] \ ROTB]$$

By premultiplying the 3 rotation matrixes (ROYH, ROTP and ROTB), a universal 3D single-rotation matrix results:

$$PNT1''' = PNT1 \ (ROTH \ ROTP \ ROTB)$$

or

$$PNT1''' = PNT1 \ ROTHPB$$

First, ROTP and ROTB can be premultiplied.

$$
\begin{vmatrix} CB & -SB & 0 \\ SBCP & CBCP & -SP \\ SPSB & SPCB & CP \end{vmatrix}
=
\begin{vmatrix} 1 & 0 & 0 \\ 0 & CP & -SP \\ 0 & SP & CP \end{vmatrix}
\begin{vmatrix} CB & -SB & 0 \\ SB & CB & 0 \\ 0 & 0 & 1 \end{vmatrix}
$$

where

$$CB = \cos B, \ SB = \sin B, \ CP = \cos P, \text{ etc.}$$

or

$$ROTPB = ROTP \ ROTB$$

Now, the matrixes ROTH and ROTPB can be premultiplied:

$$
\begin{vmatrix} CHCB+SHSPSB & -CHSB+SHSPCB & SHCP \\ SBCP & CBCP & -SP \\ -SHCB-CHSPSB & SBSH+CHSPCB & CHCP \end{vmatrix}
=
\begin{vmatrix} CH & 0 & SH \\ 0 & 0 & 0 \\ -SH & 0 & CH \end{vmatrix}
\begin{vmatrix} CB & -SB & 0 \\ SBCP & CBCP & -SP \\ SPSB & SPCB & CP \end{vmatrix}
$$

or

$$ROTHPB = ROTH \ ROTPB$$

The ROTHPB matrix may seem quite complex, but once it is calculated, it is simply a 3×3 matrix of 9 numbers that, when matrix-multiplied by a point, rotates that point in 3D space. Point rotation time is reduced to 9 multiplications and 6 additions using this method, but it takes a lot of computations to concatenate the matrix. Unless many points are to be rotated by the same rotation matrix, this method's time savings may not be realized.

Rotational Centers. Rotations are used in two ways in computer graphics: to rotate objects in space, and to rotate space. Single-object rotation is used in design and animation where objects are manipulated and moved. In these cases, translation and rotation are applied to objects.

In typical simulation applications, the objects in space remain static and the viewer (the pilot of a flight simulator, for example) translates and rotates as the simulator moves through space. User movement through a data base is handled by assuming the user to be static and translating and rotating space. All objects in space thus undergo translation based on user movement and rotation about the user based on viewing angle. The world moves and spins around the user.

Figure 7-5 illustrates both rotational philosophies. In a CAD or game system where parts or players and missiles are independently moving (translating and rotating), each object has its own translations, rotation angles, and centers of rotation (the center of the object). In this case the computer must keep track of rotation and translation information for each object. This is usually done by setting up a small memory block or array that holds an object's translation, rotation, projection status, and any other pertinent information concerning the object. Rotation matrixes for each object are different, so many rotation matrixes must be created to rotate all the objects. If the number of elements in each object is very small, the computational effort required to concatenate the three rotational matrixes may not be overcome by the savings realized by the simplified point rotations.

The effect of a user moving through space can be produced by treating the world as one large object consisting of many elements. First, the viewer's movement (translation) is subtracted from all elements in space. Subtraction is used instead of addition because a user moving forward in space is the same as the user standing still and space moving in reverse. Finally, all elements in space are rotated about a common rotation center (the viewer's eye) by the negative of the user's veiwing angle (the user rotating to the right is the same as space rotating to the left). Figure 7-5 illustrates a user moving through space. A single rotation matrix is applied to all elements since they have a common rotation center, and the overhead of matrix concatenation to generate a single rotation matrix is easily outweighed by the time savings in the point rotations of all the objects combined.

Both rotation philosophies can be combined in a single application. A driving simulator that lets a user observe moving traffic is an example where the user moves through space and objects move independently through space. In this case, objects can first be translated and rotated into their proper positions independently; then the reverse of the user's translation and rotation can be applied to simulate user movement. This method is effective but not efficient, because each element must be translated and rotated twice. Matrix manipulations up to this point suggest that the two translations and rotations can be combined to form a single rotation and translation matrix. They can, and the technique is called *nested instancing*. The procedure will be covered shortly.

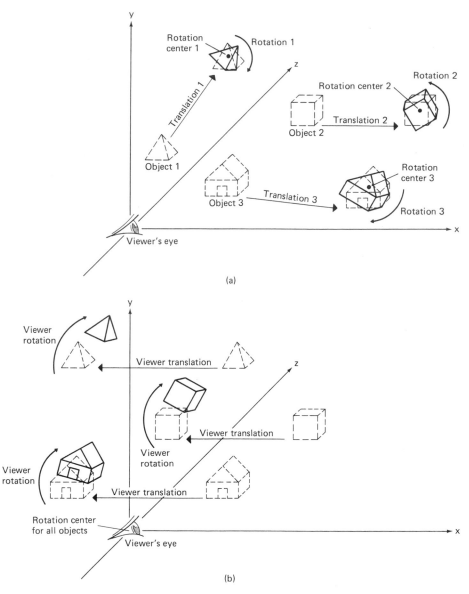

Figure 7-5 Element and user movement and the corresponding centers of rotation: static user-eye locations (a) with independent object movement in space, and the more common approach for simulation (b), where viewer's point of view appears to move through space.

Rotation Order. The order in which heading, pitch, and bank are applied to an object makes a difference. Each of the three subrotations are relative to the rotations preceding it. Figure 7-6 shows identical pitch and bank rotations applied to an object (center of rotation is the viewer's eye location). In the first case the pitch is applied, then the bank. In the second case bank is applied before pitch. The results are different. There is no "correct" or "incorrect" order of application. It is up to

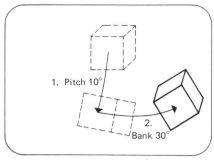

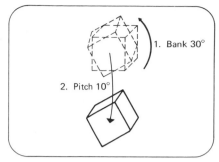

(a) Pitch followed by bank

(b) Bank followed by pitch

Figure 7-6 Order of rotation makes a significant difference in object positioning with a 3D system. A pitch of 10° followed by a 30° bank results in an upscreen movement to the right (a), while the same 30° bank followed by the 10° pitch results in the downscreen display (b).

the user to decide which to apply first, but this must be considered in any case. The concatenated rotation matrix (ROTHPB, for instance) will be different for every application order.

3D TO 2D CONVERSION AND PROJECTION

Matrix methods for translating, scaling, and rotating elements in 3D space work well in three dimensions, but display screens are 2D display devices. Equations for converting or "projecting" the 3D elements on the 2D screen are needed.

Orthographic Projection

The simplest projection method is orthographic projection. The x,y plane of the coordinate system at $z = 0$ is used as a projection plane. The z coordinate of each point in each element is set to zero to project it onto this plane (Fig. 7-7). The result is the sort of figure that would be produced as a shadow if a parallel beam of light were to project a 3D wire frame outline of an object on a wall. The equations are simply:

$$\text{screen } x = \text{space } x$$
$$\text{screen } y = \text{space } y$$

A portion of the x,y plane can be considered to be a display screen or a 2D design space that we can "window-in"on.

The x,y plane borders that are mapped to the edges of the display screen form a rectangular veiwing tube that extends to infinity in the positive and negative z direction, as seen in Fig. 7-7. The depth of the object has no effect on the screen image; cubes look like perfect squares when veiwed head-on.

Orthographic projection is used extensively in design applications where parallel alignment of edges at different design depth must be shown as edges overlapping one another on the 2D projection.

211

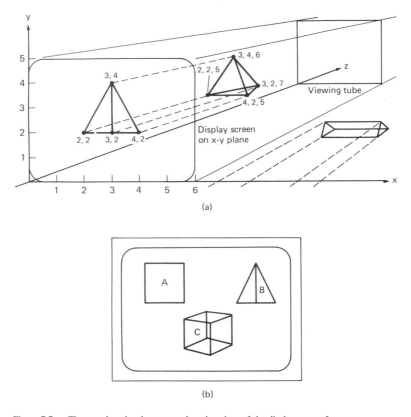

Figure 7-7   The x,y plane borders mapped to the edges of the display screen form a rectangular viewing tube (a) for the orthographic projection. The outline of the objects displayed are similar to that obtained by viewing the shadow of an object projected on a wall with a parallel light beam. Objects labeled A, B, and C on the screen (b) are orthographic projections of a cube (head on), a pyramid, and a rotated cube.

Orthographic projection is simple, but there are a few subtle points that carry over into more advanced projection schemes. The first concept is that of "lines mapping into lines." A straight line in 3D space is represented by its 3D start and end points. Likewise, a 2D screen line is represented by its 2D start and end points. Orthographic projection is performed by eliminating the z component from the 3D space coordinate start and end points, yielding the 2D screen start and end points. A straight line drawn between the 2D screen end points is assumed to be the projection of the 3D line, although none of the intermediate points between start and end point were actually transformed. This is a valid geometric assumption. Straight lines in 3D space always project as 2D screen lines and not curves or other nonstraight elements. Another concept is that of depth information. The viewer has no idea about how deep an element is or how far down the viewing tube an element is because all depth information is removed when z is set to zero.

Perspective Projection

A second common form of projection is perspective projection, which considers element depth and gives more lifelike views that have the familiar "vanishing-point" effect. The most convenient screen coordinate system to use for 3D perspectives is the "origin at screen center" system. Elements shrink toward the origin using this method, and the most desirable screen effect is to have them shrink toward the center of the screen as they get farther away.

Similar Triangles. When viewing objects in the real world, the light rays from the objects within the viewer's field of view enter the eye radially rather than in parallel as in the orthographic projection. The eye is very small compared to the scene it is viewing, and the light rays are projected to the point (the eye) rather than a plane, as Fig. 7-8 illustrates. The equations for the projection are derived using the

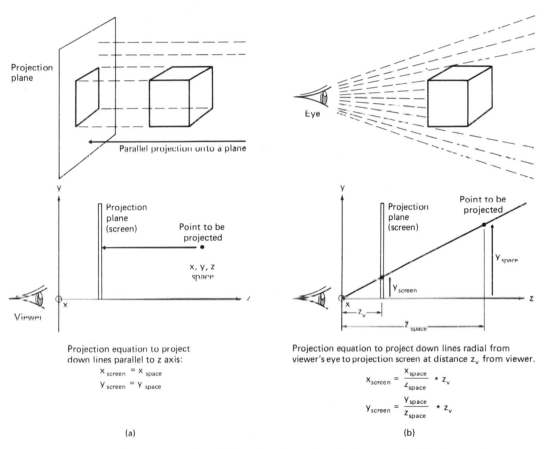

Projection equation to project down lines parallel to z axis:

$$x_{screen} = x_{space}$$
$$y_{screen} = y_{space}$$

(a)

Projection equation to project down lines radial from viewer's eye to projection screen at distance z_v from viewer.

$$x_{screen} = \frac{x_{space}}{z_{space}} * z_v$$
$$y_{screen} = \frac{y_{space}}{z_{space}} * z_v$$

(b)

Figure 7-8   Equation derivations for orthographic projection onto a plane (a) and perspective projection to a point (b).

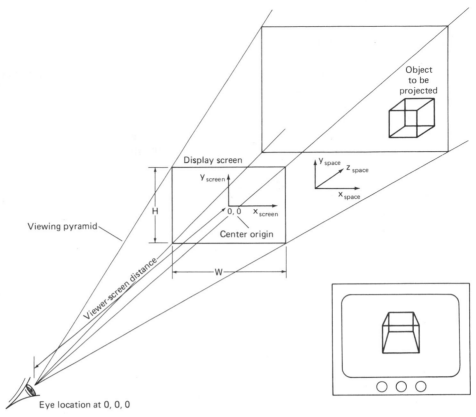

Figure 7-9 Perspective projection and the viewing pyramid (screen image inset shows projected result of viewing cube).

"similar triangles" method, where the triangle formed by the viewer's eye, space z, and space point is similar to that formed by the eye, the screen distance from the viewer's eye, and the screen point. The projection equations are thus:

x screen = (x space / z space) × (viewer to screen / screen width)
y screen = (y space / z space) × (viewer to screen / screen height)

Note: Width and height in this case are distances from screen center to right and top edges of screen.

If distance from screen is assumed to be equal to height and width, then:

x screen = x space / z space
y screen = y space / z space

Notice that the point's depth information is now included in the projection equation. As an object gets farther away (greater z), the x and y screen points get smaller due to division by a larger z. This corresponds to shrinking toward the middle of the screen (0,0 origin) as the object moves away from the viewer. It also means that the rear face of a perfect cube will appear smaller than the front face when projected on the screen because it is farther away. This is the perspective effect.

The display screen edges are the limit of what the user can see, and because points are being projected radially toward the viewer onto the screen rather than in parallel, a viewing pyramid rather than a viewing tube is generated (Fig. 7-9).

214

Assuming that the user is at half the screen width's distance from the screen, the equations of the 4 planes forming this pyramid are:

bottom plane:	$y = -z$	left plane:	$x = -z$
top plane:	$y = z$	right plane:	$x = z$

Viewer Perspective. Perspective-projecting an element onto a 2D screen is easy and only requires two divisions, but coping with the problems of making the projection look realistic on the screen in an actual application is more of a problem.

The perspective projection equations require the parameter of viewer distance from screen. This determines the geometry of the viewing pyramid and how much the viewer will see through the window (the screen). If the viewer is far away from the screen, the pyramid narrows down to a shape approaching that of the viewing tube. The viewer sees less of the scene due to the narrow field of view, and there is less perspective effect. The view becomes nearly orthographic.

If the viewer is close to the screen, the pyramid angles become very steep. This is a wide-angle view. The viewer sees more of the scene; the perspective effect is exaggerated.

The nonsimplified projection equations that include the viewer-to-screen distance, screen width, and height can be used to compensate for viewer distance differences and screen geometries. But this changes the equations of the viewing pyramid planes from their simple $x = z$ forms—which greatly complicates 3D clipping. The preferred way to control field of view is to leave the viewing pyramid at a constant 90° (side-to-side) field of view and "compress" the objects while performing the rotation matrix multiplication. This yields the same geometric results on the screen and reduces clipping complexity, as illustrated in Fig. 7-10. As a bonus, the

Figure 7-10   Field of view and its adjustment: 90° field (a), 33° field (b) with cube projection, and the equivalent of the 33° field of view generated by compressing a cube (c) in the z dimension on a 90° viewing pyramid.

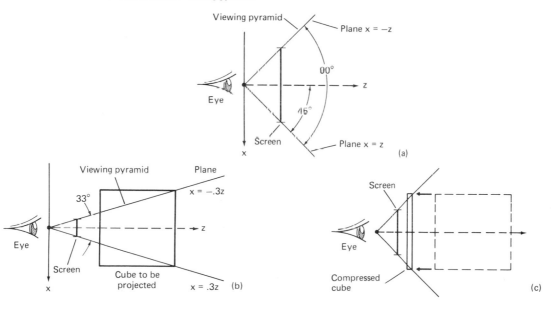

simpler projection equation can be used, resulting in one less multiply operation in the projection.

Space and all the objects in it can be compressed using 3D scaling:

$$[x\ y\ z]' = [x\ y\ z] \begin{vmatrix} \text{scale}x & 0 & 0 \\ 0 & \text{scale}y & 0 \\ 0 & 0 & \text{scale}z \end{vmatrix}$$

This operation is performed after all translations and rotations of individual objects and of space itself (in viewer movement situations).

Since a rotation is usually performed last on an element (before compression and projection), the scaling can be concatenated with the rotation:

$$\text{rotation matrix} = \text{ROTHPB} = \begin{vmatrix} a & b & c \\ d & e & f \\ g & h & i \end{vmatrix}$$

$$\text{scale matrix} = \text{SCALE} = \begin{vmatrix} sx & 0 & 0 \\ 0 & sy & 0 \\ 0 & 0 & sz \end{vmatrix}$$

$$\text{rotation and scale matrix} = \text{RSM} = \text{ROTHPB SCALE}$$

$$\text{RSM} = \begin{vmatrix} a \times sx & b \times sy & c \times sz \\ d \times sx & e \times sy & f \times sz \\ g \times sx & h \times sy & i \times sz \end{vmatrix} = \begin{vmatrix} a & b & c \\ d & e & f \\ g & h & i \end{vmatrix} \begin{vmatrix} sx & 0 & 0 \\ 0 & sy & 0 \\ 0 & 0 & sz \end{vmatrix}$$

The resulting rotation/scaling matrix is simply the rotation matrix with the first column muliplied by the x scale factor, the second column by the y scale factor, and the third column by the z scale factor. This multiplication should be done at rotation matrix generation time—where it is performed once—instead of at element rotation time, where it would be multiplied repeatedly for each element rotated.

Visually, the effect of the 3 scale factors SX, SY and SZ are:

Scale Factor	Result after Increase	Result after Decrease
SX	Objects get wider and field of view gets narrower in x direction.	Objects get narrow and field of view gets wider in x direction.
SY	Objects get taller and field of view gets narrower in y direction.	Objects get shorter and field of view gets wider in y direction.
SX	Field of view gets wider in x and y directions.	Field of view gets narrower in x and y directions.

The SX and SY values can be chosen to match the field of view for the x and y directions, as they are different for nonsquare display screens. The SZ value controls field of view for both *x* and *y* simultaneously, so this can conveniently be used as a zoom control. It is important to note that the sense of field-of-view control is reversed on the SZ value; increases result in a wider field rather than narrower as in the SX and SY cases.

Figure 7-10 illustrates field-of-view concepts and use of *z*-compression to narrow a field of view.

Perspective Anomalies. Field of view can be accurately adjusted based on where the viewer's eye will be with relation to the screen. If all parameters are correctly adjusted, the results entering the viewer's eye will be 100% geometrically correct. In many cases, however, the results will "look" wrong and the graphic system programmer will go scurrying back to the equations to find the error. This is especially true on wide-angle views. The problem lies in the user's interpretation of what is on the screen.

The screen is a window that looks into space, and the idea is to look "through" it. Viewers instead tend to look "at" it. Figure 7-11 illustrates two identical cubes viewed from two different angles. Both cubes project rays that encompass 15°, but

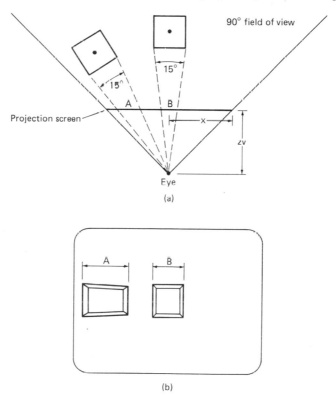

Figure 7-11   Two identical cubes within a 90° field of view (a) appear to be distorted (b) if the viewer looks "at" the screen rather than thinking of the screen as a window to be looked "through." Cube A appears wider. For this 90° field of view, the correct eye position is half a screenwidth from the screen, which translates to no more than a couple of inches from the page.

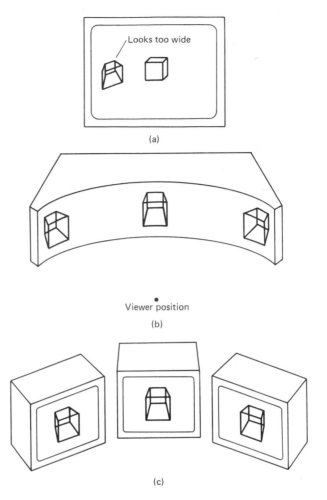

Figure 7-12 The apparent distortion of a wide-angle view on a flat screen (a) could be corrected with a curved screen (b); but since no such screen exists, a multiple-monitor system (c) could be used to depict a more realistic wide-angle view.

this results in two different widths on the display screen. If the viewer's eye is in the correct position, and the screen is treated as a window, both cubes' projections will enter the eye at the correct 15° and the viewer should see two apparently perfect cubes. If the user looks *at* the screen instead of through it, the cube near the screen's edge will appear to be stretched because it takes up a wider area on the screen and is not as tall as it is wide on the screen. This is especially bad in dynamic simulations, because it makes the cube look like it is moving closer to you as it gets near the screen edge, when in fact it remains at a constant distance.

The correct eye position to view a window with such a wide (90°) viewing angle is half a screenwidth from the screen, which is unnaturally close; but the near-the-screen-edge elongation effect is even noticeable on narrower views.

There is no cleancut solution to this problem. Figure 7-12 illustrates a possible solution using a curved screen. The amount of screen area encompassed by a projection is a function of its angular incidence, and a cube appears as a cube no matter where on the screen it falls. But curved screens are not available. One alternative approach might be to use curved-screen projection equations on a flat screen. This can be done by applying a nonlinear scale across the screen coordinate system to compress the edges of the screen. The problem that arises here is that of nonlinear screen coordinates. On such a screen, a "straight" line between two points must be represented by a curve. Also when we view the screen properly (as a window), the image would appear geometrically incorrect.

It's interesting to note that the same problems arise in photographic images. A flat photograph (essentially a window that looks into space) taken with an extremely wide-angle lens tends to bend straight lines at the edge of the picture. Geometric projection equations tell us that lines in 3D space always transform into lines on a 2D projection, so wide-angle lenses actually distort the picture near the edge.

The best way to set the field of view in most cases is through trial-and-error. Small nonlinear scale factors can actually help in some cases. In many applications, a geometrically incorrect representation will work better and look more realistic than a 100% correct projection.

Perspective Clipping. Orthographic projections essentially ignore the z component of elements and treat them as 2D elements, so clipping is identical to the 2D case. After translation, rotation, and projection, the resulting lines can be clipped to the 2D screen boundary using the equations described in chapter 2.

Perspective clipping is much more complicated. Perspective projection divides the x and y coordinates of space points by their depth (z). If everything in space is projected onto the screen plane, a few undesirable side effects occur. First, points that fall behind the viewing pyramid have a negative z value, which changes the sign of the screen x and y output by the projection equations. In visual terms, everything behind the viewer is projected upside-down and backwards. Second, points with very small z values tend to "blow up" and overshoot the integer or floating-point range of the computer's arithmetic system, and points at $z = 0$ result in division by 0; an undefined condition. If all points in an image are guaranteed to be well in front of the viewer, 2D clipping of an image can be performed after translation, rotation, and projection; but in general, clipping must be performed in 3D space before projection. Lines that partially intersect the viewing pyramid must be "pushed" to the pyramid's borders, and lines that fall behind the viewer or outside the viewing pyramid must be eliminated entirely.

Pyramid clipping is performed by pushing lines to the pyramid border planes. This is accomplished by solving the simultaneous equations of the line and the pyramid planes. As with 2D clipping, the line must first be analyzed to determine if it is trivially off the screen; if it is not, a determination must be made regarding which planes to push different points to. A repetitive coding process is probably the most common method. It involves coding the start and end points of lines, analyzing the codes' relationship to one another, and finally pushing the line.

A 5-element code indicates the status of a point in space with relation to the pyramid planes. The code elements are:

$$\text{C0} = 1 = \text{point to left of } z = -x \text{ plane}$$
$$\text{C1} = 1 = \text{point to right of } z = x \text{ plane}$$

$$C2 = 1 = \text{point is above the } z = x \text{ plane}$$
$$C3 = 1 = \text{point is above the } z = -y \text{ plane}$$
$$C4 = 1 = \text{point is above the } z = 0 \text{ plane}$$

Elements 1 to 4 test against the 4 pyramid planes, and element 5 is used to identify points behind the viewer that are trivially invisible. Code C4 is optional but speeds up lines that might otherwise have to be pushed to prove they are not visible.

Once the start and end points are coded, the codes of the two points can be compared. If any corresponding elements of both codes are set to 1 the line is trivially of the screen because it falls entirely to the invisible side of the code's plane. If C1was set in both the start and end point, for example, the whole line falls to the right of the $z = x$ plane and is invisible. This does not necessarily mean that the line falls to the right of the visible screen, however, because points in back and to the left of the viewer also can fall to the right of this plane. It's important to realize that in the 3D case, when a point is behind the viewer, the point can fall on the invisible sides of all planes, and all 5 code elements can in fact be set to 1. Routines that generate codes therefore should not make the assumption that if a point lies to the right of the $x = y$ plane, for it can't possibly also lie to the left of the $x = y$ plane, for it can.

As in the 2D clipping case, if one or both points are off the screen and no two corresponding codes between the elements are both 1, the line may intersect the viewing pyramid; pushing the line to the pyramid is necessary. Figure 7-13 shows the clipping equations which are more complex than the 2D equations. Either point (if both are out of the pyramid) can be pushed first.

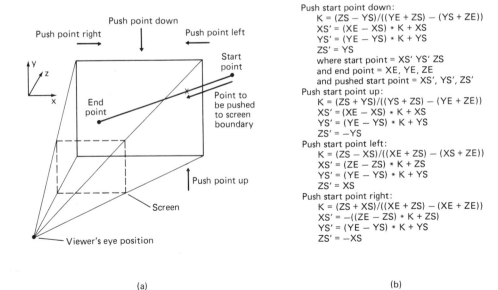

(a)

(b)

Figure 7-13 The start point may be pushed to the viewing pyramid (a) using the clipping equations (b) for perspective projection.

After the push, the pushed point is recoded. The unpushed point's code is still valid. The code comparison and push-if-needed process continues until both points are in the pyramid or the line is found to be off the screen.

After clipping, projection takes place as usual. It takes less calculations to project a line that has been clipped to the edge of the screen because the edge of the screen lies on the $\pm x = z$ or $\pm y = z$ planes. The projection division in these cases yields a 1 or -1. By checking for the edge condition, a division can be saved.

Quaternions. Rotations in 3D space are traditionally performed using the 3-by-3 rotation matrix method previously described. This method is also sometimes known as the direction cosine method because the elements in the matrix are in fact the direction cosines of the rotation angles. A total of nine elements exists in the rotation matrix, but only three parameters (pitch, bank, and heading) are needed to fully specify the rotational position. There is obviously redundancy in the rotation matrix; if some of it can be eliminated, faster rotation computations and more compact storage of rotation matrix information may be possible. One such method uses a 4-element matrix-like operator known as a *quaternion* to pack the rotational information into a compact form. This method finds its greatest use in applications requiring computations based on rates of change of angles rather than absolute rotation angles. In angular rotation situations, it is more efficient than conventional rotation matrix methods. Inertial navigation computers typically use this method to compensate for the earth's rotation. Most graphic systems specify angles as absolute values rather than rotation rates, but a few actually resort to using quaternions to perform rotation.

A quaternion is a 4-element column vector that specifies rotation information, much as a rotation matrix is a 9-element matrix that specifies rotation information. An understanding of complex numbers is necessary to work successfully with quaterions, because 3 of the elements within the 4-element vector are imaginary. Many mathematicians consider the whole quaternion as a single entity which they call a "hypercomplex number" because it has one real and three imaginary components.

The quaternion is thus:

$$Q = \text{quaternion} = Q_0 + Q_1 i + Q_2 i + Q_3 i$$

where

$$i = \text{square root of } -1$$

or

$$\begin{vmatrix} Q_0 \\ Q_1 \\ Q_2 \\ Q_3 \end{vmatrix}$$

Quaternions are best thought of as hypercomplex numbers rather than column vectors, because they cannot be multiplied using standard matrix techniques. Quaternian multiplication of pairs of quaternions are used in rotation, and the rules are as follows:

$$Q = \text{quaternion 1} = \begin{vmatrix} Q_0 \\ Q_1 \\ Q_2 \\ Q_3 \end{vmatrix} \qquad R = \text{quaternion 2} = \begin{vmatrix} R_0 \\ R_1 \\ R_2 \\ R_3 \end{vmatrix}$$

$$S = \text{quaternion multiplication result} = \begin{vmatrix} S_0 \\ S_1 \\ S_2 \\ S_3 \end{vmatrix}$$

Multiplication to be performed is:

$$S = QR$$

or

$$\begin{vmatrix} S_0 \\ S_1 \\ S_2 \\ S_3 \end{vmatrix} = \begin{vmatrix} Q_0 \\ Q_1 \\ Q_2 \\ Q_3 \end{vmatrix} \begin{vmatrix} R_0 \\ R_1 \\ R_2 \\ R_3 \end{vmatrix}$$

or in conventional equation form:

$$\begin{aligned}
S_0 &= Q_0 R_0 - Q_1 R_1 - Q_2 R_2 - Q_3 R_3 \\
S_1 &= Q_0 R_1 + Q_1 R_0 + Q_2 R_3 - Q_3 R_2 \\
S_2 &= Q_0 R_2 + Q_2 R_0 + Q_3 R_1 - Q_1 R_3 \\
S_3 &= Q_0 R_3 + Q_3 R_0 + Q_1 R_2 - Q_2 R_1
\end{aligned}$$

or in matrix form:

$$\begin{vmatrix} S_0 \\ S_1 \\ S_2 \\ S_3 \end{vmatrix} = \begin{vmatrix} Q_0 & -Q_1 & -Q_2 & -Q_3 \\ Q_1 & -Q_0 & -Q_3 & -Q_2 \\ Q_2 & -Q_3 & -Q_0 & -Q_1 \\ Q_3 & -Q_2 & -Q_1 & -Q_0 \end{vmatrix} \begin{vmatrix} R_0 \\ R_1 \\ R_2 \\ R_3 \end{vmatrix}$$

Quaternion rotations require the use of the inverse of the rotation quaternion. The inverse, like a matrix inverse, is the quaternion that yields 1 when multiplied by the original:

$$1 = Q \, Q_{\text{inverse}}$$

This value is generated by changing the sign of Q_1, Q_2, Q_3, and Q_4 and dividing all elements (Q_0 through Q_4) by the "norm." The norm is:

$$\text{norm} = Q_0{}^2 + Q_1{}^2 + Q_2{}^2 + Q_3{}^2$$

Therefore,

$$Q_{inverse} = \begin{vmatrix} Q_0/\text{norm} \\ -Q_1/\text{norm} \\ -Q_2/\text{norm} \\ -Q_3/\text{norm} \end{vmatrix}$$

Although there are other rules for quaternions, multiplication and inverse generation are sufficient to perform rotations.

Rotation can be performed using a direction cosine matrix, expressed symbolically as:

$$P1' = P1 \; ROTPBH$$

where P1 and P1′ are the initial and rotated points and ROTPBH is the rotation matrix.

The same rotation can be performed using quaternions by:

$$P1' = QPBH \; P1 \; QPBH_{inverse}$$

where QPBH is the rotation quaternion.

In the quaternion case, P1 must first be put into quaternion form. This is done by letting the x, y, and z coordinates be elements 1, 2, and 3 of the quaternion:

$$\text{P1 represented as quaternion} = \begin{vmatrix} 0 \\ x \\ y \\ z \end{vmatrix}$$

From this point on, quaternion multiplication yields the result. First, QPBH is multiplied by P1. The result is multiplied by QPBH inverse for the answer.

The rotation quaternion QPBH can be derived using advanced rules of quaternion operations, but the end results are the following simple quaternions for rotation about the x, y, and z axes:

$$\text{QPBH for } x \text{ axis rotation} - \begin{vmatrix} \cos(\text{angle}/2) \\ \sin(\text{angle}/2) \\ 0 \\ 0 \end{vmatrix}$$

$$\text{QPBH for } y \text{ axis rotation} = \begin{vmatrix} \cos(\text{angle}/2) \\ 0 \\ \sin(\text{angle}/2) \\ 0 \end{vmatrix}$$

$$\text{QPBH for } z \text{ axis rotation} = \begin{vmatrix} \cos(\text{angle}/2) \\ 0 \\ 0 \\ \sin(\text{angle}/2) \end{vmatrix}$$

The quaternion method's general-case rotation quaternion is:

$$\text{QPBH for 3-axis rotation} = \begin{vmatrix} \cos\ (\text{angle}/2) \\ \cos\ T_x\ \sin\ (\text{angle}/2) \\ \cos\ T_y\ \sin\ (\text{angle}/2) \\ \cos\ T_z\ \sin\ (\text{angle}/2) \end{vmatrix}$$

where T_x, T_y, and T_z represent the angles of tilt of the rotation axis from the x, y, and z axis, respectively, and the "angle" is the rotation angle about this axis.

The most convenient form of rotation specification is by specifying the angular offset of a rotation axis that the point or element will be rotated about, and the angle of rotation about that axis. This method is much different from the direction cosine method, but it is easier to use in some nongraphic applications (notably inertial navigation).

The quaternion method looks promising in the areas of storage space and computation time. But will the method actually yield any savings? From a rotation-information storage standpoint, only four elements are needed to store the rotation information, as opposed to the direction-cosine matrix's nine. This could be useful in cases where many individual rotations need to be stored on disk or in memory.

Subpictures are often called by specifying an x,y,z offset and rotation angles of where to place the subpicture. Four-element quaternions could be stored instead of pure rotation angles in the subpicture-calling elements, thereby eliminating the need to create a new rotation matrix from the pure angles every time the subpicture is called. This approach does not waste memory as 9-element direction-cosine rotation matrixes would. So the memory savings aspect is definitely an advantage under some conditions.

From a computational standpoint, the quaternion comes in second to the direction-cosine method. It only takes 3 multiply operations to create the rotation quaternion, as opposed to 13 multiply and 4 addition operations to create a direction-cosine rotation matrix; but actual point rotation is computationally expensive. The complicated quaternion multiplication method, plus the fact that we must perform two multiply operations (normal and inverse), results in 24 multiply and 32 add operations versus 6 multiply and 9 add operations for the direction-cosine method. In addition, the inverse quaternion must be generated, and this involves 4 squared terms to create the norm, and 4 divide operations. These multiply and divide operations are seldom required, however, because the norm usually ends up in the form:

$$1 = \text{norm} = \cos^2\ (\text{angle}/2) + \sin^2\ (\text{angle}/2)$$

One final property of quaternions that adds to thier appeal is their "dynamic" character, which can be expressed in rotational rate terms:

$$\text{Rate-oriented quaternion} = \begin{vmatrix} \cos\ (rot) \\ T_x\ \text{angular rate} \times \sin\ (rot) \\ T_y\ \text{angular rate} \times \sin\ (rot) \\ T_z\ \text{angular rate} \times \sin\ (rot) \end{vmatrix}$$

where rot = angular rate $\times$ time / 2.

Creating a rate-oriented generalized rotation matrix would be extremely difficult, especially when expressed in terms on an axis orientation and rotation about that axis.

Quaternions can offer memory storage savings in graphic applications and can make computations easier if we have no objections to specifying element orientations in terms of axis orientation and angle of rotation about the axis. When it comes to use in high-performance applications, this method imposes too much of a computation time penalty to be considered.

INSTANCING

Subpictures and cells were earlier defined as graphic elements or small designs that consist of lines, circles, and other standard elements arranged in an independent coordinate system. To use the small design in the master design, the call is copied into the master database and the subpicture accessed by the database using a subpicture call (similar to a programming language's subroutine call).

When placing a cell or creating a subpicture call, the elements' coordinates in the subpicture or cell's reference frame must be transformed into the master design's coordinate system based on where the user wants to place the subpicture. The user typically specifies one or more orientation points within the subpicture when defining the subpicture, or the origin ($x=y=z=0$) of the cell is assumed as the default placement orientation point. At subpicture placement time, the user specifies a placement point and orientation angle in the master database where the subpicture should appear. Figure 7-14 shows a subpicture being placed in this manner.

INSTANCE TRANSFORM

The subpicture placement and viewpoint specification process is known as *instancing*. The translation and rotation that must be added to the subpicture to instance it into the master design constitute the instance transform. The most convenient way to specify the instance transform is through translation, rotation, and scaling, in that order.

Translation:

$$T_x - P_x - S_x$$
$$T_y = P_y - S_y$$
$$T_z = P_z - S_z$$

where

T = instance translation
P = placement orientation point
S = subpicture orientation point

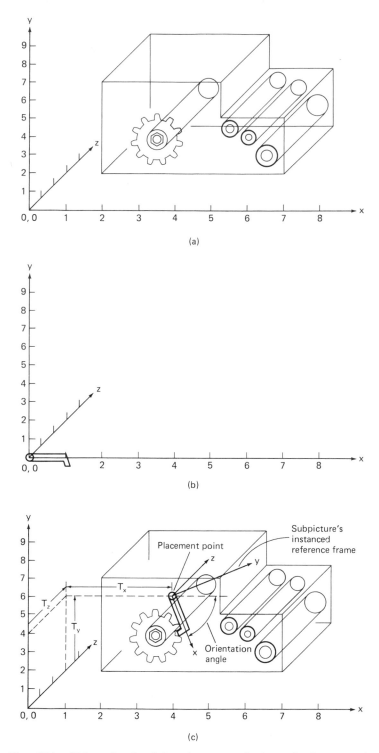

(a)

(b)

(c)

Figure 7-14   3D instancing of a subpicture into a master data base: using the master design coordinate system (a), the user calls the subpicture reference frame (b) and places it into the master design by specifying translation and rotation (c).

Rotation:

Pitch, bank, heading specified at placement time (assuming subpicture orientation is to be 0 degrees = pitch = bank = heading).

or

$$pitch = P_p - S_p$$
$$bank = P_b - S_b$$
$$heading = P_h - S_h$$

where P = rotation defined by vector consisting of two placement orientation points.

S = rotation defined by vector consisting of two subpicture orientation points.

Scaling:

Scale factor (equal scaling on x, y, and z axes) defined by user.

or

$$scalex = scaley = scalez = P/S$$

where P – length of vector consisting of two placement orientation points.

S = length of vector consisting of two subpicture orientatin points.

When copying cells into a database, these transforms are applied to the cell at cell copy time (when the cell is being placed into the database). All the elements' start, end, centers, and other element specifications are transformed, thereby creating a new, transformed set of elements that are copied into the master data base. After placement, the result of the cell placement looks as though it were designed directly in the database.

When specifying subpicture placement, the placement information (translation, rotation, and scaling) is put into a *subpicture call* element in the database. This element is similar to a graphics element; but instead of consisting of graphics element information it consists of data that stipulates where the subpicture's definition can be found (perhaps a call name, code number, memory address, or disk address) and the placement information. When the subpicture call is encountered during display generation, the subpicture definition is found and the placement information is applied to it as it is drawn or plotted.

Cell and Subpicture Placement Considerations

From a display performance standpoint, cell placement presents no problems. The cell must be transformed and copied into the master database once at placement time, but no additional rotations, translations, or scaling need be performed. The cell has been converted to simple elements in the master database and they are processed as quickly and efficiently as any other element. The cell placement software can be very high precision and quite inefficient, yet the picture generation process will not be slowed down.

Subpictures are a different matter. Subpictures are accessed from subpicture libraries and instanced at picture generation time when display speed is of prime importance. The first bottleneck in subpicture generation is accessing the subpicture definition. If a very small number of subpictures are used, all subpictures can be stored in memory and accessed quickly; but in most cases, large subpicture libraries reside on disk. The display software must open appropriate disk files and access the disk for each subpicture call. A master display file is usually stored on disk in a manner that makes access easy (sequential sector and track numbers); but if subpicture calls are encountered while smoothly reading the easy-to-access master display file, the disk may have to move its heads halfway across the disk to access the appropriate disk subpicture library. This nullifies all the advantages of the easy-to-access master file and slows down display rates considerably.

This performance problem is actually a file access problem that is encountered in many forms of data processing—the problem of quickly accessing a small auxiliary file as dictated by a master file. Books on file management and operating systems can be consulted to get ideas about solving the problem, which is similar to the obstacle encountered in high-speed computers that use cache memories (small high-speed computers that are used to increase processor performance) and in large programs that use disk overlays. In both these cases, a program may be running very efficiently out of the high-speed cache memory or processor memory when a small auxiliary subroutine that is not in memory needs to be called. The processor must access slow noncache memory or pull in a disk overlay segment to access the subpicture, thus disrupting the smooth running program.

Storage Considerations

As in the subpicture case, processor memory and cache memory are limited in size, so it may not be possible to store all the subroutines in the cache at once (just as it is not possible to store all subpicture libraries in memory). Computer architects sidestep this problem by carefully controlling what resides in cache memory.

Hardware that determines what subroutines (memory "pages") are currently in the cache and how often they are being used is the way to keep track of what is being used the most. Seldom used routines are swapped out to low-speed memory on a last-used or least-often-used basis, and often used routines remain in cache for quick access.

These methods can be emulated in software in subpicture filing systems. A subpicture is similar to a subroutine. Some subpictures are used once or twice while others are used often. It makes sense to let the often used subpictures reside in memory while leaving the less often used ones on disk.

One approach is to allocate a buffer area in memory for subpicture libraries. A small array can be set up to indicate which subpictures are already in the memory and how many times they have been accessed (this is similar in function to a cache tag memory). When the allocated buffer fills to capacity, the least often used subpicture is replaced by nonmemory-resident subpictures when they are accessed. As the display file is processed, the buffer will eventually contain the most often used subpictures. Display speed can be increased or decreased by allocating more or less buffer space.

NESTED INSTANCING

Can a subpicture call a subpicture? There are certainly many occasions where this capability would be useful. An automobile driving simulation, for example, might show other cars on the road. Other cars (perhaps a few different models) could be stored as subpictures. All the different models, however, could use the same tire subpicture.

There are a few important points to note about the above example. The tires on the cars must be specified with relation to the car's reference frame, not the world's (or master database's) reference frame. When the car moves or turns, the tires must follow. The tires must rotate about their own axes as they spin, yet they must remain attached to the car as it moves. Figure 7-15 illustrates the example.

Nested instancing is the process of subpictures calling subpictures out of their own reference frames. This process can be used in applications like the driving simulation, and is indeed used extensively in engineering simulation graphics.

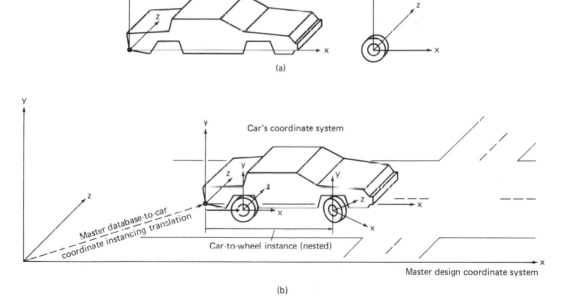

Figure 7-15 The car and wheel subpictures (a) are instanced differently: the car is positioned in relation to the master data base's coordinate system, and the wheels are instanced by nesting (b), using the car's reference frame. This insures that the wheels spin on their own axis while always remaining properly attached to the car.

Displays that use nested instancing look very impressive. Four or five cars independently driving down the road with their tires spinning gives the impression that extremely complex graphics hardware or software is being used. Nested instancing, however, is really quite simple and is all that is required to generate such displays.

The car-and-tire example involves bilevel nesting. The tire is defined as a subpicture in its own reference frame. The car subpicture definition contains a subpicture call to the tire subpicture and specifies where in the car's reference frame to put the tire. Four calls are made for four tires. The master database then calls the car subpicture to project the car onto the display screen. The tires are already placed properly within the car's reference frame and are transformed again (along with all the elements that make up the car) to place it in the master database and thus onto the display screen.

Nesting can go to any depth. A tire valve stem could be defined as a subpicture and called, by the tire definition, yielding trilevel nesting.

Nesting Mathematics

Defining nested subpictures is easy; processing them is difficult, because intermediate results must be stored. The tire on the car can be transformed and placed in the car's reference frame, but the transformed tire elements must then be transformed with all the car elements to instance it into the world data base and finally onto the screen. A small buffer can be used to do this, as shown in Fig. 7-16. Software must keep track of what is in each buffer and where buffers start and end.

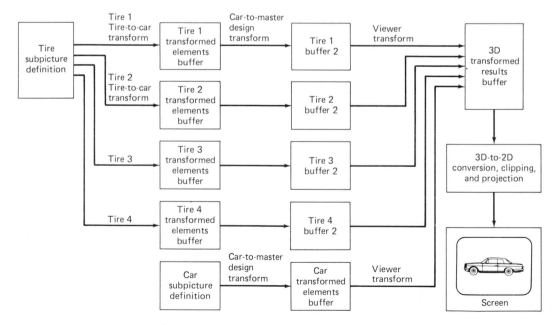

Figure 7-16   Diagram showing processing of nested-instancing transforms into world data base.

Transforming the tire and storing it in a buffer is related to cell placement, where we are making a temporary copy of the instanced tire. This method is also inefficient because the data must be transformed twice: once from the tire to the car reference frame, and once from the car to the world reference frame.

A better way to perform nested instancing is to combine the rotations and translations that transform a nested subpicture through all nesting levels into a single translation and rotation that transforms the subpicture (the tire) directly into world coordinates. This reduces transformation to a single matrix multiplication step and totally eliminates the need for temporary buffers. Projection of subpictures at any nested depth is performed as quickly as projections of unnested elements. All that is needed is the combined translation and rotation matrix.

Nesting Combinations

Matrix concatentation is used to combine nested rotations and translations. Figure 7-17 shows the concatenation process. Translation, rotation, and scaling matrixes are defined for each nested level. These are the subpictures' placement translations, rotations, and scale factors. For representation convenience, 4×4 matrixes are used. It takes 64 multiply and 48 add operations to multiply two 4×4 general-case matrixes, but these matrixes are very sparse and reduce to a few simple add operations in many cases.

$$
\text{T1 = translation matrix} =
\begin{bmatrix}
1 & 0 & 0 & 0 \\
0 & 1 & 0 & 0 \\
0 & 0 & 1 & 0 \\
dx & dy & dz & 1
\end{bmatrix}
\quad \text{or} \quad
\begin{bmatrix}
1 & 0 & 0 \\
0 & 1 & 0 \\
dx & dy & 1
\end{bmatrix}
$$

3D case   2D case

$$
\text{R1 = rotation matrix} =
\begin{bmatrix}
r_1 & r_2 & r_3 & 0 \\
r_4 & r_5 & r_6 & 0 \\
r_7 & r_8 & r_9 & 0 \\
0 & 0 & 0 & 1
\end{bmatrix}
\quad \text{or} \quad
\begin{bmatrix}
r_1 & r_2 & 0 \\
r_3 & r_4 & 0 \\
0 & 0 & 1
\end{bmatrix}
$$

$$
\text{C1 = scaling matrix} =
\begin{bmatrix}
s_x & 0 & 0 & 0 \\
0 & s_y & 0 & 0 \\
0 & 0 & s_z & 0 \\
0 & 0 & 0 & 1
\end{bmatrix}
\quad \text{or} \quad
\begin{bmatrix}
s_x & 0 & 0 \\
0 & s_y & 0 \\
0 & 0 & 1
\end{bmatrix}
$$

$$
\text{P1 = point} =
\begin{bmatrix} x, & y, & z, & 1 \end{bmatrix}
\quad \text{or} \quad
\begin{bmatrix} x, & y, & 1 \end{bmatrix}
$$

P1' = P1(R2   S2   T2) (R1   S1   T1) (TG   RG   SG)

                                 Viewer reference frame

                Subpicture reference frame

    Nested subpicture reference frame

or

P1' = P1   NEST2   NEST1   VIEW

Figure 7-17   3D and 2D mathematics for translation, rotation, and scaling of nested elements.

Matrix multiplication can be performed in any order because it is associative. One convenient order is to premultiply the rotation, scale, and translation for nested levels 2, 1, and the view into three combined matrixes: NEST2, NEST1, and VIEW. Notice that the order of transformation for NEST2 and NEST1 considers rotation first, followed by scaling, and then translation. This is the most common order for describing the placement of a subpicture or cell. First the subpicture is rotated to its proper angular orientation. Then it is scaled to its appropriate size. Finally, it is translated to the position where it belongs in the master data base.

The VIEW transformation specifies the viewer's eye position, viewing angle, and field of view (scale). The order of transformation is translation (to position to viewer in space), rotation (to rotate the viewer to the proper viewing angle), and scaling (to adjust the field of view). Keep in mind that *the order is different from that of subpicture placement;* negative translation values and rotation angles must be used when creating the TG and RG matrixes. Subpicture placement is done from the outside looking in, while viewer direction is specified from the inside looking out.

In practical applications, a graphics data base interpreter program will scan through a data base interpreting and projecting graphic elements on a display screen or plotter. The matrix concatenation method works well in graphics file interpreters. Subpictures can be treated as a subroutine in a computer program. When the interpreter is scanning through the master data base, the VIEW matrix (Fig. 7-17) is used to transform elements.

When a subpicture is encountered, the VIEW matrix can be temporarily stored (pushed onto a stack) the same way program status and registers would be in an assembly language program before a subroutine call. The NEST1 subpicture placement matrix can then be multiplied by VIEW to form the subpicture reference frame matrix, which is applied directly to subpicture data to transform it into screen coordinates.

Deeper nesting is simply a matter of pushing this matrix onto the stack and matrix multiplying by NEST2, NEST3, and so on, for successive nesting levels.

When the subpicture is transformed and a "subpicture return" is performed, the old transformation matrix is popped off the stack and put back into effect as the current transformation matrix. Figure 7-18 depicts the interpretation of a scene with two nested levels of subpictures; it shows how the stack is used to keep track of transformation information while performing nested instancing.

INSTANCING PRECISION

Rotation, translation, and scaling are used to place cells and subpictures. These operations (especially rotation) require a lot of computation time and can slow a display. Reduction in mathematical precision (using 16-bit instead of 32-bit multiplications in a rotation matrix multiply, for example) can speed placement, but it can also create distortion. A goal to strive for is to reduce precision to its minimum value where no distortion occurs.

Cell placement (copying a master cell into a data base) is performed at design time and thus poses no display time problems. Very high precision can be used with no display performance sacrifice. Very high precision is in fact required for cell

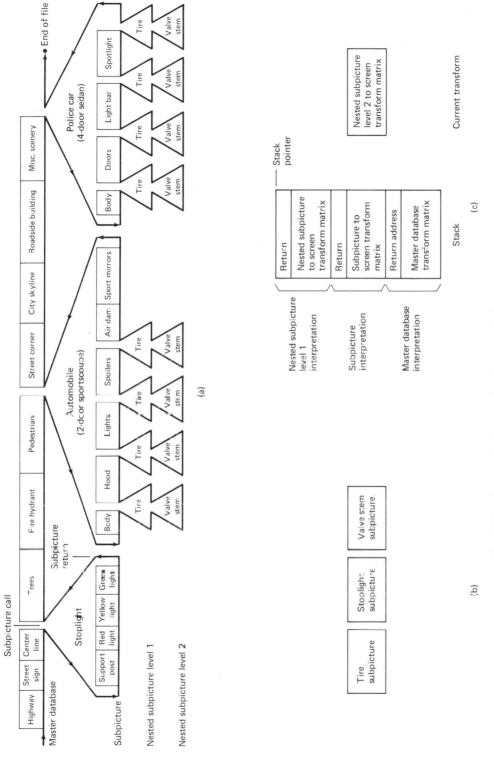

Figure 7-18 Interpretation of a scene from the master data base with two levels of nested subpictures (a), subpicture library contents (b), and representations of the stack and current transform (c) during interpretation of nested subpicture level 2 (the valve stem).

233

placement, especially in CAD applications, because the cell is being rotated and placed directly into a high-resolution data base. If a data base space is defined by 32-bit integers, rotations should use 32-bit integer arithmetic with 64-bit intermediate products.

Subpicture placement requires little precision if the results are being transformed onto a low-resolution (up to 4096 × 4096) display. Precision of 8–12 bits is ultimately all that is required at the display screen level. For translation, rotation, and scaling, 16-bit integer arithmetic is usually sufficient. Even less precision is required in final output projection in the 3D perspective case.

Nested subpictures present larger placement precision problems. Small placement errors at each nested level multiply by one another to form a large cumulative error. Fortunately, subpictures require little precision when being displayed on low-resolution devices, and an adequate precision margin exists in 16- or 32-bit computations to accommodate a few levels of nesting with no noticeable error.

Snapping techniques can be used to more accurately place cells and even nested subpictures. In most precision placement applications, precision is required because end points of existing elements and the cell being placed must meet. For example, resistors and transistors that are defined as cells in a circuit diagram must meet with connecting wires in the diagram. If placement error causes a one-unit variation upon close examination using a zoomed-in view, the wires and circuit components will appear to be disconnected. To get around this problem, orientation points can define critical joining points within the cell.

The user can define the orientation points for proper alignment during cell placement. Or a routine that identifies end points of elements that fall within a prespecified "threshold" distance can identify matchup points. The cell can be placed with 100% precision by snapping the orientation points to the identified placement points. If all orientation points are aligned to their proper placement points, absolutely no cumulative error will be introduced by nested placement using this method.

DIRECT RASTER SCREEN CELLS

Cells and subpictures up to this point have been defined geometrically. Elements such as lines and circles made up the cell. In applications that deal directly with images in screen coordinates on a raster-scan display, the screen memory organization of the raster can be used to define and place cells.

Figure 7-19 shows a raster on which a figure of a house and a tree have been designed. Both images are quite complex if defined geometrically, but both are also small in relation to the screen. A simple way to manipulate small complex designs on a raster display is to define a rectangular subraster and make a copy of the memory it contains in an auxiliary memory (usually in the computer's memory). In byte-oriented displays, the rectangle can be chosen to match byte boundaries, or only the bits within the rectangle can be serially shifted and packed into whatever memory storage form is convenient. No specific information about circles, lines, colors, gray scale, etc., need be considered, because the display memory already contains this information.

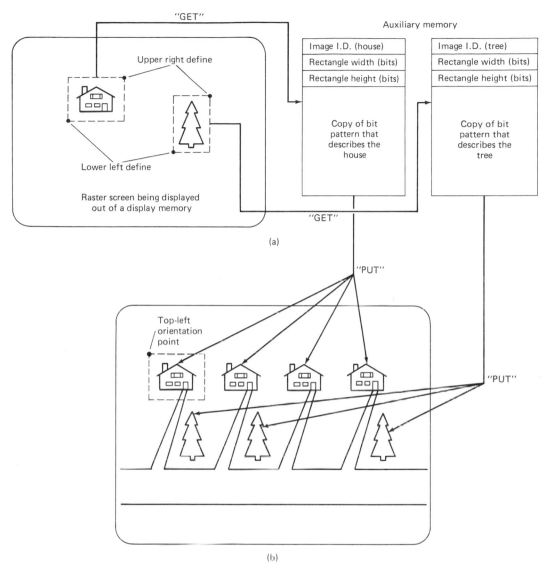

Figure 7-19 Defining subraster cells for auxiliary memory storage (a). The cells are placed with GET and PUT commands (b).

The auxiliary memory can be dumped anywhere on the display to create a copy of the original design. A designated point is used to specify orientation (usually the upper left corner, with rotation assumed to be zero).

The GET and PUT commands in advanced BASIC on the IBM personal computer perform the functions that have just been described. Figure 7-19 illustrates a few houses and trees being placed using direct raster screen cells.

A variation of this method involves placing the bit pattern on the screen at the desired location with exclusive-*or* operations. A second exclusive-*or* of the pattern can be used to erase the image. This makes object movement and animation possible. Large objects and objects requiring rotation (other than the easily accommodated $90°$) and scaling pose problems involving auxiliary memory size and transformation complexity. Conventional cells and subpictures must be used in these cases.

WIRE-FRAME ELEMENT GENERATION

All graphic elements presented up to this point have been either simple points or straight lines. In real-world applications, other elements are often used. Circles, ellipses, parabolas, and general curves are common and must be generated on the screen. The elements must be joined smoothly to form larger images homogeneously.

POINT PLOTTING

Anyone who has studied geometry and trigonometry knows that simple mathematical equations and functions, when plotted on graph paper, can yield curves. The simple equation:

$$y = \sin x$$

yields the familiar sine wave shown in Fig. 7-20(a). Curves of this sort are sometimes required in computer graphics, so this equation may be a good starting point for the generation of such a curve on a graphics screen.

Point-by-Point Parametric Generation

Most display systems are based on Cartesian coordinates and are much like graph paper. When plotting curves on graph paper, we usually select a number of points along one axis (the x axis), plug them into the equation, and plot the resulting y for each x value on the graph. The x parameter is varied and the resulting y parameter plotted. A computer can rapidly calculate thousands of output points for a wide selection of input points. These points can be individually plotted to yield what looks like a fairly smooth curve, as illustrated in Fig. 7-20(b).

There are many equations that yield open curves. Many common closed curves also can be represented mathematically. The circle is a good example:

$$\text{radius}^2 = x^2 + y^2$$

The circle, unlike the sine curve, is limited in its x and y dimensions. The circle in Fig. 7-20(c) can yield no real y value when $z = 5$ is supplied as an input to the equation. The range is limited to the radius of the circle. Another point to note about the circle is that there are two y values generated for every in-range x value submitted. At $x = 0$, y is both 3 and -3.

The limited range and multivalue-result property of close curves (and many open ones) make it difficult to select a good range of input points to yield a smooth-looking curve. Closed-curve equations also tend to yield unequal spacing of output points along the curve if simple "plug in the x and compute the y" methods are

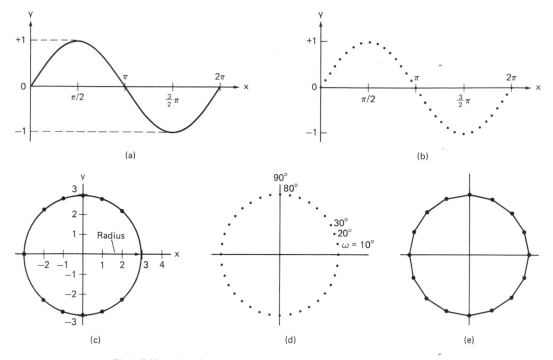

Figure 7-20   Curved-element generation techniques: sine curve of $y = \sin x$ (a) can be represented with a series of plotted points (b). The circle, a closed-curve element, results from the equation $r^2 = x^2 + y^2$, but if "plug-in-the-x-and-compute-the-y" is used (c), unequal point spacing is encountered. The w variable is a parameter that can be used (d) to generate equally spaced points. With fewer points connected by line segments (e) a good representation of a circle can be realized with simplicity.

used as Fig. 7-20(c) shows. Five points are bunched together at the top of the circle while only one is on either side. These points correspond to an equally spaced set of input points (-3 to $+3$).

A curve's equation can be expressed in many forms. It is advantageous to use some of these alternate forms to generate closed curves. We have seen that it is not convenient to generate y values for a circle by submitting x values because of range and unequal spacing problems. It is not convenient to submit y values to generate x values for the same reasons. In cases such as this, it is better to define a curve by using two equations which express the coordinates of points as a function of a third variable:

$$x = \text{radius} \times \cos w$$
$$y = \text{radius} \times \sin w$$

The third variable, w, is called a *parameter*, and the set of equations are the "parametric equations" of the circle. A set of equally spaced input values starting at zero for w generates equally spaced points on the circle until $w = 360°$, as shown in Fig. 7-20(d). Beyond this value, the function simply "goes around the circle" again. There are no range restrictions on w; the smaller the increment used for sequential spacing, the denser the circle gets.

Point and Line Parametric Generation

Curves generated by plotting points look like what they are—a series of dots. There are two ways to smooth the curve into a continuous line.

One way to present a smooth curve is by generating the dots so close together that the distance between them is less than the resolvable distance on the display screen. This involves a lot of computation, however. A circle with a radius of 200 pixels on a 512×512 display, for instance, requires about 1250 pixels, and thus 2500 multiplications and sine or cosine calculations.

A preferable method is to generate enough points to roughly define a figure, then connect them with line segments that are easily generated on the screen using a DDA method. But how many points are enough? The answer depends on the size of the curve, its degree of curvature, and the resolution of the display screen; but the number of points may be much fewer than you might expect. Large 16-point circles such as the one shown in Fig. 7-20(e) look very good, especially on low-resolution raster screens.

GEOMETRIC CONFIGURATIONS

Most equation-based curve generation is performed using parametric generating functions. The following subsections describe generation methods for various geometric configurations and present parametric forms for a variety of curve types.

Automatic Polygons

In cartography and architecture CAD systems it is usually necessary to have the capability to draw "automatic polygons." These are closed elements with an angle at every joined line. The number of sides is up to the designer. The simplest automatic polygon is a rectangle (placed at any angle). These symbols are used for roughly defining the outlines of houses, buildings, swimming pools, and other features on a map.

These elements are generated based on the first line of the polygon submitted by the user. All lines in the polygon that run parallel to the first line have the same slope. All lines that run perpendicular to the first line have a slope that is the negative reciprocal of the first line. If the polygon's sides are to be the same length, the negative reciprocal need not be computed. A perpendicular line can be generated by swapping the x and y value of the original line and negating either x or y, depending on which way the line is to extend.

Limiting an automatic polygon's sides to equal length is usually too restrictive. Allowing only limited proportions of the original line length ("quarter" or "eighth" lengths) however, makes sense. The designer can estimate fairly well where the last point should be to make the polygon close with a final angle. Using quarter or eighth proportions allows the designer to make as many sides as are needed yet maintains the geometry so that all angles will be correct.

Circles

Circles are the elements of a broad class of elements known as conic sections. Circles are more easily specified and generated than other conics (ellipses, parabolas, hyperbolas) because of their x- and y-axis symmetry.

Previous sections discussed how circles can be generated using the parametric equation of a circle:

$$x = \text{radius} \times \cos w$$
$$y = \text{radius} \times \sin w$$

where the w parameter is varied from 0 to $360°$ (0 to 2π radians).

This is a simple but slow generation method. The method can be improved by use of the symmetric properties of the circle. A circle constructed with 12 points is shown in Fig. 7-21. The first point to note is that the points along the circle that fall on the x and y axes will always have x and y coordinates of some combination of 0 and the radius. There is no need to calculate these points using the equations.

Circles are symmetric about the x and y axes. The circle portions in quadrants 2, 3, and 4 are mirror images of the arc in quadrant 1. When a point is calculated in quadrant 1, it can be mirrored to quadrants 2, 3, and 4. In the example of Fig. 7-21(a), $x2$ and $y2$ are computed from the equations, but the corresponding points in the other 3 quadrants are plus and minus variations of the point and need no computation other than sign changes. The performance improvement due to using special properties (on-the-axis points) and symmetry is 570%.

Even more symmetry can be extracted from the circle, as shown in the 8-octant-symmetry example of Fig. 7-21(b). Octant 2 is a mirror image of octant 1 about the $45°$ axis. Coordinates can be mirrored into octant 2 by swapping x and y values of any point. The point for $30°$ is calculated to be (a,b). From this, 7 more points (all combinations of a,b and b,a) can be mirrored for the other 7 octants. The 12-point circle's computation is thus reduced to 2 multiply operations and 2 trigonometric computations. A lot more bookkeeping is required in the program, however, to keep track of the 8 octants.

Circles consisting of computed points connected by line segments are ideal for cases where they are being specified in a large-world coordinate system that will be mapped into screen coordinates. The line segments can be translated, rotated, and clipped using standard line-handling techniques. Circles are so common, however, that direct screen coordinate generation methods are often used. These methods are to the circle as the DDA is to the line.

Instead of relying on equations that use multiplication operations and compute absolute coordinates, differential techniques are used. Small increments are added in special ways to the circle's x and y coordinates as the circle is being generated. These increments are usually based on the standard parametric equations of the circle and are often stored in a table that is sequenced through each time a circle is generated.

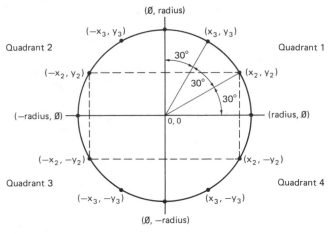

Quadrant 2 — Quadrant 1 — Quadrant 3 — Quadrant 4

(Ø, radius), (−x₃, y₃), (x₃, y₃), (−x₂, y₂), (x₂, y₂), (−radius, Ø), 0,0, (radius, Ø), (−x₂, −y₂), (x₂, −y₂), (−x₃, −y₃), (x₃, −y₃), (Ø, −radius)

Computations required

	Points calculated	sin/cos gen.	Multiplies	Negates	Overall Computation*	Performance*
Standard 2-parametric equations	12	24	24	0	432	1.0
Standard equations and symmetry	2	4	4	4	76	5.7

*Weighted as add or negate = 1, multiply = 8, sin or cos = 10

(a)

(Ø, radius) — Octant 2 — Octant 1

(−b, a), (b, a), 45°, (−a, b), (a, b), (−radius, Ø), (radius, Ø), (−a, −b), (a, −b), (−b, −a), (b, −a), (Ø, −radius)

$a = radius (\cos 30°)$
$b = radius (\sin 30°)$

(b)

Figure 7-21 The use of quadrantal (a) and octantal (b) symmetry in circle generation.

Figure 7-22(a) shows an 8-sided circle drawn using differential techniques. The table of Fig. 7-22(b) reflects the slopes of the segments. This table is precalculated and becomes part of the circle generator routine. The flow chart of Fig. 7-22(c) indicates how computation proceeds for each segment clockwise around the circle until the circle is completed. The following points should be noted:

1 . The circle size and location are specified as START POINT and SIDE LENGTH.

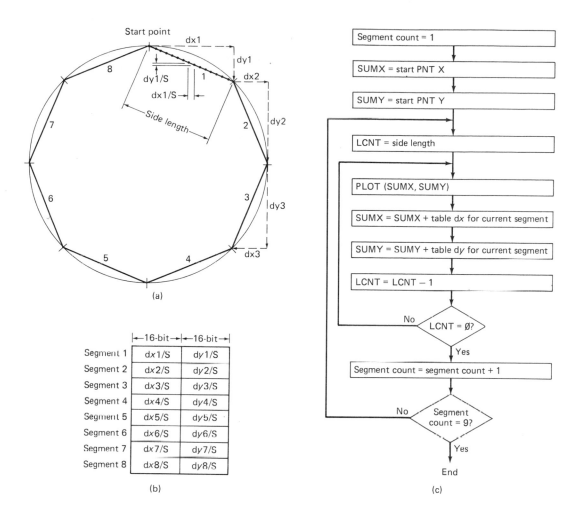

(a)

	←16-bit→	←16-bit→
Segment 1	dx1/S	dy1/S
Segment 2	dx2/S	dy2/S
Segment 3	dx3/S	dy3/S
Segment 4	dx4/S	dy4/S
Segment 5	dx5/S	dy5/S
Segment 6	dx6/S	dy6/S
Segment 7	dx7/S	dy7/S
Segment 8	dx8/S	dy8/S

(b)

(c)

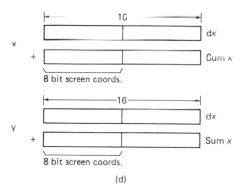

(d)

Figure 7-22 The circle with 8 sides (a) uses the differential-value lookup table (b). The flow chart (c) shows the computation procedure; the summation register bit alignment (d) insures that accurate reflection of x and y locations is maintained.

2. The running sums of the x and y coordinates are 16-bit values. Only the most significant bits are used as coordinate values. The 16-bit registers accurately keep track of small changes in x and y location, even when no x or y screen movement is performed. The bit alignment is depicted in Fig. 7-22(d).

3. The table values are scaled (divided by s) to a small value that will cause points to be placed adjacently on the screen without leaving gaps.

4. The sum of $dx1$ to $dx8$ will be 0. This assures that the circle will close with perfect start/end matchup. The sum of $dy1$ to $dy8$ will also be 0.

This table-oriented differential method can create other closed and open curves as well as polygons. The table controls the slope of each segment, so it can be adjusted to create any figure by adjusting the slopes. An enhancement to this method is to add a segment length multiplicative factor to the table for each segment. Segments would not have to be all equal-sized with this change.

The circle generation methods described above (with the exception of the differential method) assume a center of 0,0. Circles with nonorigin centers are produced by generating the points at the origin and adding the center offset to them. The equations are:

$$x = \text{radius} \times \cos w + \text{centr}x$$
$$y = \text{radius} \times \sin w + \text{centr}y$$

Other conics are centered in exactly the same way.

Ellipses

Conics are derived from a standard conic equation:

$$Ax^2 + Bxy + Cy^2 + Dx + Ey + F = 0$$

The circle was a simple case which reduced to:

$$x^2 + y^2 + (-\text{radius squared}) = 0$$

or

$$x^2 + y^2 = \text{radius}^2$$

The ellipse is a more complex form of the same equation. The A and C terms can be different, thus elongating the ellipse along the x and y axis. Ellipses thus have two axis parameters known as the semimajor (long radius) and semiminor (short radius) axes. The A and C terms of the standard conic equation are specified in terms of the two axes in Fig. 7-23(a).

The parametric equation method is useful for generating ellipses. The figure shows the parametric equations, which differ from the circle equations only because the semimajor and semiminor axes are being substituted for the radius.

242

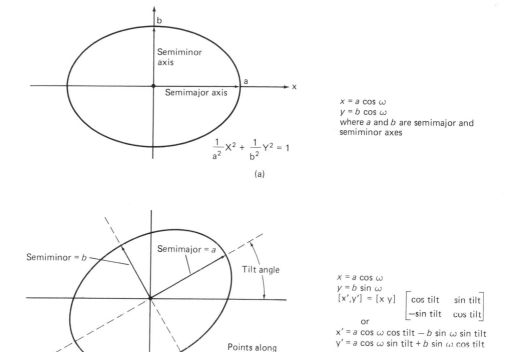

$x = a \cos \omega$
$y = b \cos \omega$
where a and b are semimajor and semiminor axes

$x = a \cos \omega$
$y = b \sin \omega$
$[x',y'] = [x\ y] \begin{bmatrix} \cos \text{tilt} & \sin \text{tilt} \\ -\sin \text{tilt} & \cos \text{tilt} \end{bmatrix}$
or
$x' = a \cos \omega \cos \text{tilt} - b \sin \omega \sin \text{tilt}$
$y' = a \cos \omega \sin \text{tilt} + b \sin \omega \cos \text{tilt}$

Figure 7-23   An ellipse in standard form (a), in which semimajor and semiminor axes align with x and y axes. If a tilt angle is specified (b), the x and y coordinates may be rotated with a rotational-multiply operation.

Tilted Ellipses. The ellipse is not as symmetric as the circle. An ellipse has an orientation angle associated with it. The Bxy term in the standard conic equation controls this orientation. When $B = 0$ the semimajor and semiminor axes align with the x and y axes, putting the ellipse in standard form. Values other than 0 "tilt" the ellipse, as shown in Fig. 7-23(b). In computer graphics it is more convenient to define a tilt angle rather than a B value. If a tilt angle is specified, the x and y coordinates of the standard ellipse can be put through a 2D (or even a 3D) rotation with a simple rotation-matrix multiply operation. This process and the mathematics are shown in Fig. 7-23(b).

Generalized Ellipses. Circle and ellipse segments are often used to form fillets. Both elements have their own characteristic shape that may be appropriate for specific applications. For applications requiring a different fillet shape (usually one that fits more "tightly" into a corner), the generalized ellipse equation can be used. This equation forms an ellipse-like locus, but technically, this is not a conic section. The general form is:

$$1 = \frac{x^n}{a} + \frac{y^n}{b}$$

243

where $n = 1$ for a linear line
$n = 2$ for a normal ellipse
$n = 3$ for third-order general ellipse
$n = 4$ for fourth-order general ellipse

The higher-order generalized ellipses tend to change their directions at their corner more quickly than lower-order ones. It is not always possible to define an ellipse that goes through two points with two specified slopes. But this is not the case with the generalized ellipse. It is always possible to find some power (possibly a noninteger power) that, when substituted as n in the generalized ellipse equation, will match the constraints.

Parabolas

The parabola is a form of conic section that is seldom used by itself in graphics; but it is used to piece other elements together. Sections of general curves and fillets (rounded corners) are often generated using parabolic sections. A parabola is not a closed figure but extends to infinity in the x and y directions.

Figure 7-24 Parabola generation methods. The basic parabola is generated using the standard equation (a), and it may be altered in its angle of orientation (b) by translation and rotation.

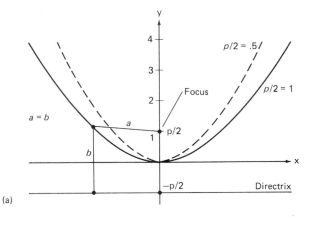

$y = 1/2p \times x^2$
where p = distance from focus to directrix

(a)

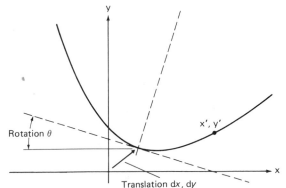

$$[x'\, y'] = [x, y, 1] \begin{bmatrix} \cos\theta & \sin\theta & 0 \\ -\sin\theta & \sin\theta & 0 \\ dx & dy & 1 \end{bmatrix}$$

(b)

The parabola equation is:

$$y = \tfrac{1}{2}p \times x^2$$

where p is distance from focus to directrix of parabola.

Figure 7-24 illustrates parabolas with different focus distances. The points that must be specified to generate a parabola are its focus-to-directrix distance, translation, and rotation. The parabola itself is defined as the locus generated by plotting all points that are an equal distance from the focus and the closest point on the directrix. The y coordinate is easily generated by plugging x values into the equation.

When generating parabolas on a graphics screen, it is important to realize that the degree of curvature is greater near the bottom of the parabola. If the figure is generated by calculating points and connecting them with line segments, points must be spaced at closer intervals near the bottom of the parabola to maintain a smooth curve.

A parabola can be placed at any location and at any angle by applying a translation and rotation matrix to the points generated by the generation equation, as Fig. 7-24(b) shows.

CIRCLE FITTING AND FILLETS

Circles are often used as complete elements in designs; but in many cases, circles and parts of circles are used to form larger curves and to round out corners. The two techniques needed to use circles in these capacities are fitting and partial circle generation.

The easiest way to fix a circle's location is to specify its center and radius. In practical applications this is not always possible. Circles and curves are often described by constraints dictated by the elements they are to intersect or line up with.

Point intersections and tangencies to other lines and circles are the most common constraints. In precision applications such as engineering drawings, a manually specified radius is also a constraint. Enough constraints must be specified to completely define a circle. Three points, three tangents, or a center and and radius are sufficient. Mixed constraints such as tangency to two lines and an intersection point are also common.

A circle specified by its diameter (two points) is a simple constraint from which to calculate center and radius. Two points are usually not enough to specify a single circle, but the context in which they are specified (the fact that they are a diameter) is actually the third required constraint. As illustrated in Fig. 7-25(a), the center is simply the point equidistant between P1 and P2, which can be computed as the average of P1 and P2's x and y coordinates. The radius is the distance from the computed center to either P1 or P2, which is calculated using the Pythagorean rule.

Figure 7-25(b) illustrates a circle defined by three points. There are a few ways to derive center and radius given these three constraints. The most straightforward is to write the equation for the circle with center (h, k) and radius (r) specified as variables. The result is an equation of three variables and three unknowns, which can be solved using simple algebra.

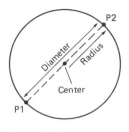

Centrx = (P1x + P2x)/2
Centry = (P1y + P2y)/2
Radius = $\sqrt{(P2x - \text{centrx})^2 + (P2y - \text{centry})^2}$

(a)

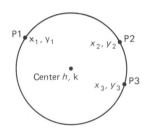

Equations to solve:
$(x_1 - h)^2 + (y_1 - k)^2 = r^2$ (1)
$(x_2 - h)^2 + (y_2 - k)^2 = r^2$ (2)
$(x_3 - h)^2 + (y_3 - k)^2 = r^2$ (3)

(b)

Combining equations (1) and (2):

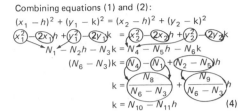

$(x_1 - h)^2 + (y_1 - k)^2 = (x_2 - h)^2 + (y_2 - k)^2$

$x_1^2 - 2x_1 h + y_1^2 - 2y_1 k = x_2^2 - 2x_2 h + y_2^2 - 2y_2 k$

$N_1 - N_2 h - N_3 k = N_4 - N_5 h - N_6 k$

$(N_6 - N_3)k = (N_4 - N_1) + (N_2 - N_5)h$

$k = \left(\dfrac{N_8}{N_6 - N_3}\right) + \left(\dfrac{N_9}{N_6 - N_3}\right)h$

$k = N_{10} - N_{11}h$ (4)

Combining equations (1) and (3):

$k = N_{21} - N_{22}h$ (5)

Using (4) and (5) to solve for center:

$h = \dfrac{N_{10} - k}{N_{11}}$

$k = N_{21} - \dfrac{N_{22} - N_{10}}{N_{11}} + \dfrac{N_{22}k}{N_{11}}$

$k = N_{23} + N_{24}k$

$k = \dfrac{N_{23}}{1 - N_{24}}$

$k = N_{25}$
$h = \dfrac{N_{21} - N_{25}}{N_{22}}$ Center = h, k

(c)

Figure 7-25   The circle can be specified by its diameter (a) or by any three boundary points (b). In the latter case, equations must be employed (c) to solve for circle center.

The solution for the center is worked out in Fig. 7-25(c) to show how a computer might solve the problem. Equations 1 and 2 are combined to eliminate the radius, and the squared differences are quickly broken into single components. When working out solutions on paper, the equation variables (x_1 and y_1, for example) are kept intact as long as possible so their original source is remembered. This is fine from a user standpoint, because it will help during traceback; but the computer has no need to remember where variables came from. Constants and variables are combined and reduced to new constants (n values) as quickly as possible. Notice how quickly the equation reduces to a function of two variables and two unknowns. Equations 1 and 3 are processed in the same way as 1 and 2 were, resulting in a second equation of two variables and two unknowns. The two equations are combined to solve for the center (h, k). The radius is computed using the Pythagorean rule to find the distance from the computed center to any of the three points.

Another method of computing the center relies on the observation that the three lines connecting the three points on the circle are chords of the circle. A line perpendicular to a chord that intersects the chord's center (its perpendicular bisector) also intersects the center of the circle. The intersection of two of these bisectors projected from any of the two chords is the center of the circle. This may seem like a roundabout way of arriving at the solution, but finding centers of lines is easy on a computer because averaging of x and y points is all that is performed Averaging involves a divide-by-2, but this reduces to a fast arithmetic right shift. A time-expensive division is avoided. The exact procedure is:

1. Find the perpendicular bisector of two chords using averaging (for the center) and coordinate swapping (for perpendicular slope generation).
2. Set up the equations for the two lines (bisectors) using the slope and bisector point.
3. Use algebra to simultaneously solve for the intersection of the two lines. This is the center.

Simultaneous equations and perpendicular bisectors are useful in solving more complex constraint problems involving tangents to lines. Figure 7-26(a) shows a

1. Set up equation to find radius from P1 to center

$$r^2 = (C1x - P1x)^2 + (C1y - P1y)^2 \quad (1)$$

2. Set up equation to find radius from P2 to center

$$r^2 = (C1x - P2x)^2 + (C1y - P2y)^2 \quad (2)$$

3. Set up equation of perpendicular line from center to tangent line

$$y = -\frac{1}{M} x + B2$$

where

$$B2 = C1y + \frac{1}{M} C1x \quad (3)$$

to intersect center

4. Set up equation to find tangent intersect point

$$I1y = M\, I1x + B1$$

$$I1y = -\frac{1}{M} I1x + B2$$

therefore –

$$I1x = \frac{B2 - B1}{M + 1/M} \quad (4)$$

$$I1y = M \frac{B2 - B1}{M + 1/M} + B1 \quad (5)$$

5. Set up equation to find radius length to tangent line

$$r^2 = (I1x - C1x)^2 + (I1y - C1y)^2 \quad (6)$$

6. Plug B2 from (3) into (4) and (5) Plug I1x and I1y from (4) and (5) into (6)

7. Equations (1), (2), and (6) are 3 equations of three unknowns ($C1x$, $C1y$, and r^2). Solve simultaneously for result

(b)

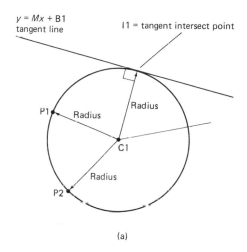

$y = Mx + B1$
tangent line

I1 = tangent intersect point

(a)

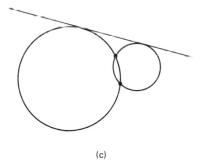

(c)

Figure 7-26 A circle specified by two radial points and a tangent (a) can be computed with a sequence of steps (b) that put the information into an equation with three variables and three unknowns; but two possible circles result from the definition (c).

247

circle defined by two points and a tangent to a line. The center and radius are calculated in the same way as the 3-point case assuming an equal-length radius from the center to P1, P2, and I1 (the center). The computations are complicated by the need to first find the intersection with the tangent intersect point. We base these calculations on the premises that:

1. The radius is perpendicular to the tangent line at the intersection point (by definition of tangency of a circle).
2. The distance from the centerpoint to the intersect point (C1 to I1) is equal to, and is in fact, the radius.

Steps 3 to 6 in Fig. 7-26(a) put this information into an equation of three variables and three unknowns. It is a complicated equation, but variables reduce to constants along the way when actual computation is being performed. Finally, all equations of 3 variables are solved for the center and radius.

The given constraints in this case are not quite adequate because two circles can satisfy the conditions, as shown in Fig. 7-26(b). In practical applications, the graphics system draws both; the user decides which is the correct circle.

As a final example of circle fitting we examine the case of a circle tangent to two lines with a given radius. When circle generation is limited to form an arc to the tangent points, the result is a rounded corner or circular fillet. Figure 7-27 outlines

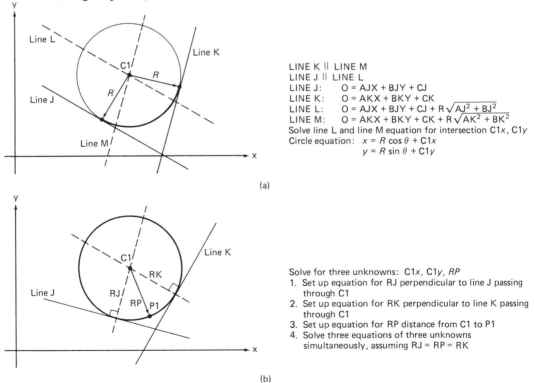

LINE K ∥ LINE M
LINE J ∥ LINE L
LINE J: $0 = AJX + BJY + CJ$
LINE K: $0 = AKX + BKY + CK$
LINE L: $0 = AJX + BJY + CJ + R\sqrt{AJ^2 + BJ^2}$
LINE M: $0 = AKX + BKY + CK + R\sqrt{AK^2 + BK^2}$
Solve line L and line M equation for intersection $C1x, C1y$
Circle equation: $x = R\cos\theta + C1x$
$\qquad\qquad\qquad y = R\sin\theta + C1y$

(a)

Solve for three unknowns: $C1x, C1y, RP$
1. Set up equation for RJ perpendicular to line J passing through C1
2. Set up equation for RK perpendicular to line K passing through C1
3. Set up equation for RP distance from C1 to P1
4. Solve three equations of three unknowns simultaneously, assuming $RJ = RP = RK$

(b)

Figure 7-27 Circle fitting by center determination using parallel lines (a) and solving for unknowns (b) with point on fillet.

248

this situation. The easiest way to solve for the center is to draw parallel lines to the lines of tangency at the radius' distance from them. The intersection point is the center.

In some cases it is easier to specify a point on the fillet than a radius, as shown in Fig. 7-27(b). In this case, three equations of three unknowns that equate the distances from the circle's center to the two tangent lines and the point on the fillet can be set up and solved.

When placing circles and other elements using complex constraints, a lot of calculation is necessary, as the equations are quite complex. The placement calculations, however, are only performed at placement time under operator control. It pays to use all the powerful though slow-running features of a computer language (such as floating-point, trig, squares, and roots) to simplify the placement routines. It makes no difference to the operator whether a circle takes 100 ms or 10 ms to place, and slow calculations at placement time will in no way slow screen drawing time, which is based on simple center and radius circle generation routines.

ELLIPSE AND PARABOLA FITTING

Circle fitting methods make it clear that basic rules of geometry and algebra are all that are needed to fit circles. The same goes for other elements such as ellipses and parabolas that are defined by mathematical equations.

It is not always possible to find an ellipse that fits the four input conditions. For any given point pair, there is a small set of slopes that will have ellipses as solutions. Any software handling ellipse fitting should be able to tell the user the range of slopes for specified points.

There are countless combinations of ways to specify input conditions to fit ellipses, parabolas, hyperbolas, and other conics, but basic rules of analytic geometry and algebra are all that are required. You must select the rules and methods for your particular application. Books on analytic geometry are a great help, as are texts which treat the geometric principles for computer graphics.

Ellipses are usually fitted by specifying the input conditions of two points to intersect along with the desired slopes at these points. Rotation matrix multiplication and translation are used to put the conditions into a position where an ellipse in standard form with its center lying on the y axis can fulfill the conditions. These conditions are:

1. One point on the y axis with slope $= 0$.
2. The other point and slope in quadrant 1.

Analytic geometry is used to solve for the center and major and minor axes. Finally, translation and derotation are applied to place the ellipse into its proper position.

ARC SEGMENT JOINING

Circle fitting methods can be used to create general curves by joining arcs. Arcs (circle and ellipse segments) can be joined using simultaneous equations to solve for radius and center locations. An initial circle or arc is first set up. Then the point at which the next arc is to join is determined. The joining point and the slope of the circle at the joining point are specified as conditions for the next circle (or arc) equation.

An intersection point, another tangential point, a center, or a radius can be used as a final condition to generate the second arc. The process is repeated for the third, fourth, and subsequent arcs in the curve.

BLENDING TECHNIQUES

In most real-world cases, the curves to be represented involve slope variations and radius changes that make them too complex to be generated by simple mathematical functions. While a mathematical function can be found for almost any curve, the functions involve too much complexity to be practical. The most common approach taken to generate generalized curves is to break curves into small segments and find simple mathematical functions to represent each piece. This method is similar to the curve drawing method used by draftsmen. French curves, splines, and compasses are all used to piece together complex curves.

THE BLENDING OPERATION

All the small curved and straight segments in a piecewise curve must be joined together. The curve must be smooth and continuous at the joints. The process of smoothly joining curves together is known as *blending*. Spline curves, Bezier curves, and even curves generated using polynomial fitting are based on simple blending techniques; and in the 3D case, "space curves" are generated using blending.

Averaging

Figure 7-28(a) depicts two straight lines to be blended. The lines are not connected, but rather overlap one another. The goal is to "smoothly" join the lines. It is clear that toward the left side of the figure, line 1 will dominate. Likewise, toward the right, line 2 will dominate. The overlapping area, however, must have a connecting curve or line to join the two lines. In this area, both lines 1 and 2 have an effect on where the connecting line will be placed. A simple way of considering the effect of both lines is to simply take the average of the two lines within this zone. The result is a simple stairstep connection as shown in Fig. 7-28(b); but at least the lines are connected.

This method can be improved upon by using weighted averaging techniques, as illustrated in Fig. 7-28(c). Toward the left side of the center averaging zone, line 1 has more of an effect on the connecting curve than line 2. It makes sense to weigh the average more heavily toward line 1's value. Lines 1 and 2 have equal effects toward the center of the zone, so both lines' y values are weighted equally. In zone III line 2 has a strong influence, so it is weighted heavily. Mathematically, this reduces to:

$$\text{zone I} \quad y = (2 \times y_1 + y_2)/3$$
$$\text{zone II} \quad y = (y_1 + y_2)/2$$
$$\text{zone III} \quad y = (y_1 + 2 \times y_2)/3$$

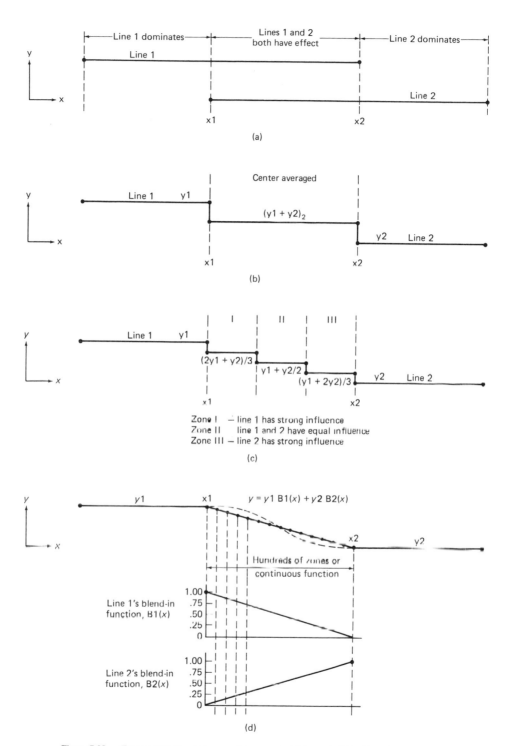

Figure 7-28 Two parallel lines to be smoothly connected (a) may be joined by a blending operation using the averaged center point (b), a weighted averaging of zones (c), or a continuous averaging (d).

251

The 3-stairstep result is slightly smoother than the single step, but there is still room for improvement.

Instead of using just 3 zones for the weighted averaging, a few hundred can be used. The amount of blending of lines 1 and 2 must be defined for each of these zones. The easiest way to accomplish this is to define a separate mathematical function that describes the blend as a function of the zone number. In the example of Fig. 7-28(c) these zones correspond with increasing x values, so the blend functions for lines 1 and 2 are based on the x value of the point being generated. The connecting curve generation equation reduces to:

$$y = y_1 \times B_1(x) + y_2 \times B_2(x)$$

where B_1 is line 1's blend as a function of x
B_2 is line 2's blend as a function of x

The result of the continuous blending functions is a smooth ramp between the lines. The lines are surely blended together, but we may wish for a somewhat different blend that might be preferable. With the continuous blending function, this is easily accommodated. Instead of suddenly and linearly fading in line 2's effect and fading out line 1's effect, we can fade in these effects nonlinearly and gradually. Figure 7-29 illustrates the process.

Blending is conceptually quite simple, but there are a lot of details that add complexity. The various curve generation methods attack these details using different approaches. One detail that all methods contend with is that of axis independence. The examples just blended were special cases where both lines happened to be parallel to the x axis. If the whole blending example figure were rotated 35°, a different connection curve could result if blending functions based on absolute x and y coordinates were used. It is imperative that blended curves not change their geometry when rotated and veiwed or constructed from different angles.

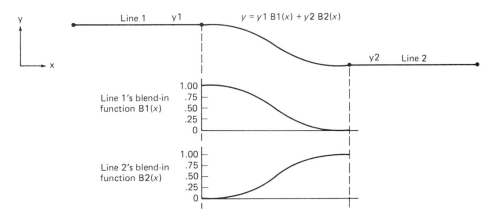

Figure 7-29 The continuous blending operation can be smoothed by rounding through use of the two lines' blend-in functions.

Constraint Matching

When blending lines and curves together, certain conditions must be met. In the example of Fig. 7-28 we stated the conditions:

1. The connecting curve will meet line 1 at x_1, thus making coordinate x_1,y_1 the curve left end point constraint.

2. The connecting curve will meet line 2 at x_2, thus making coordinate x_2,y_2 the curve's left end point constraint.

These were the only constraints put on the curve. Curve start- and end-point matchup are known as zero-order constraints. They deal with x and y position of curves at their end points or at points along the curve.

Slope matchup is another common constraint that often needs specifying. The ramp connection of lines 1 and 2 in Fig. 7-28 is not "smooth" because of the sharp corners at the connection points. End points match up, but the slope suddenly changes from zero to a small negative value, then sharply back to zero again. In the smooth curve of Fig. 7-29, additional constraints were made:

1. The slope of the connecting line at x_1,y_1 must match line 1's slope.
2. The slope of the connecting line at x_2,y_2 must match line 2's slope.

Slope is determined by: $\Delta x/\Delta y$ of a curve at a given point. In calculus, this is the first derivative of the curve at any given point. Slope constraints are therefore known as first-order constraints.

Curves can be constrained even more tightly by specifying matchup conditions for higher derivatives of the curves that meet. Second-order continuity guarantees that the change in the slope is identical for the meeting curves. This is sometimes useful to prevent sudden changes in curvature. Third-order continuity controls changes in the rate of curature. Constraints above the second order get quite abstract and are seldom specified.

Geometry Specification for Smooth Blends

Curves are usually specified by point intersection and slope conditions. Sometimes the rules for point intersection are relaxed and the curve is considered adequate if the curve comes near the point. In the examples just examined two lines were blended with a smooth curve. The specified conditions for blending in Fig. 7-29 were:

1. Intersect at y_1
2. Slope = line 1 slope at y_1
3. Intersect at y_2
4. Slope = line 2 slope at y_2

Smooth blending relies on the fact that an intersection or "control" point will start to exert a strong effect on a line as it nears the point. A smooth blending function must reflect a point's dominance near the point. It must also smoothly increase the point's effect as the line nears a point. Setting aside a zone and saying "this point will dominate in this zone" does not produce smooth blending, because a sudden change in position or slope occurs at the zone boundary.

Polynomial Curves

Powers can be used to create smooth blending functions. Simple algebra shows that the value x^2 rises faster than a constant value of 1, x^3 rises faster than x^2, and x^4 rises faster than x^3, etc. The curves for the functions: constant, x^2, x^3, and x^4 are also very smooth. We can use this property to specify blending functions.

Figure 7-30 illustrates power-based blending functions. The powers are scaled by A_0, A_1, A_2, and A_3 to determine the x values at which their effects will become dominant. The final equation of the line is a combination of all blending functions and is the standard equation for a polynomial:

$$y = A_3x^3 + A_2x^2 + A_1x + A_0$$

The polynomial equation's A_0 through A_3 values can be solved by setting up four equations of four unknowns and substituting the x,y coordinates of points Y_1 to Y_4 into the equations as initial conditions. The result will be a smooth curve passing through all four points.

The polynomial approach may seem like the ideal way to generate curves, but there are many pitfalls. First, polynomials tend to generate curves that oscillate and loop back on themselves. A polynomial of n terms will always go through the n points you specify, but between these points it may oscillate and loop wildly. Another problem is the need for many power terms. A polynomial equation that intersects four points has x^3 as its highest-order term. If 10 points were to be intersected, x^9 would be the high-order term. It's very difficult to solve a ninth-order equation with 10 unknowns.

The number of points to be intersected by a polynomial equation can be traded off for better control of the curve. An nth order polynomial requires $n + 1$ initial conditions in order to be solved. These can be any mix of points positions (y values for a given x) and slopes (slope for a given x). An intersect point and its slope can therefore be specified. Specifying points and their slopes tends to keep a polynomial's curve under tight control, but it also requires more terms per point. A 3-point curve fit would have an x to the fifth high-order term. In practical applications, two points are about the maximum complexity the polynomial can handle. A high-order term of x^3 results in a cubic equation for this case, which is quite easy to deal with.

Spline Curves

Polynomial curves have proven to be quite useless in cases where more than two points are specified, but since they can handle two points nicely, perhaps it is possible to string 2-point polynomial curves together to form larger ones. This is precisely the

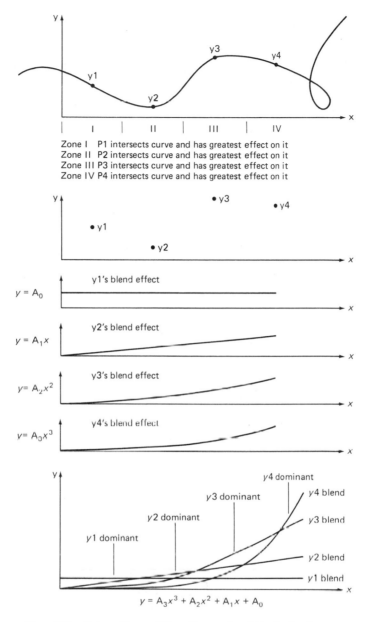

Figure 7-30 Polynomial curve fitting with power-based blending functions.

idea behind *spline* curves, one of the most commonly used general curve generation techniques. It is important to point out that *spline* curves and *B-spline* curves are generated with two nonrelated techniques, which should not be confused with one another.

Figure 7-31 illustrates the spline curve method. The goal is to turn the point string P_1 to P_{10} into a smooth curve that passes through all the points. Cubic equa-

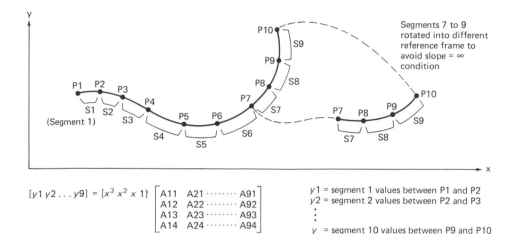

$$[y1\ y2 \ldots y9] = [x^3\ x^2\ x\ 1] \begin{bmatrix} A11 & A21 & \cdots\cdots & A91 \\ A12 & A22 & \cdots\cdots & A92 \\ A13 & A23 & \cdots\cdots & A93 \\ A14 & A24 & \cdots\cdots & A94 \end{bmatrix}$$

$y1$ = segment 1 values between P1 and P2
$y2$ = segment 2 values between P2 and P3
⋮
y = segment 10 values between P9 and P10

Figure 7-31 Spline curve generation (not to be confused with B-spline curve generation). Segments S7 to S9 were rotated for a better angle before solving the cubic to avoid slope blowup; after solving, they were unrotated to return them to proper position.

tions must be set up and solved for each segment. The general form of the equation for the segment S_1 from point R_1 to P_2 is:

$$y_1 = A_{11}x^3 + A_{12}x^2 + A_{13}x + A_{14}$$

The derivative for slope calculation is:

$$M = \frac{dy_1}{dx_1} = 3A_{11}x^2 + 2A_{12} + A_{13}$$

The equations are solved by plugging in the x and y coordinates of points P_1 and P_2 into x and y, and by plugging in the slopes at points P_1 and P_2 into the derivative's slope. The slopes for points P_1 and P_2 can be determined by the method of choice (estimation, slope of line from P_1 to P_2 and P_2 to P_3, etc.). Just be sure to use common slopes at segment joining points when computing adjacent segments; this will insure a smooth transition from one segment to another.

Figure 7-31 shows all nine equations for the nine segments. Segments S_7 to S_9 were found to have overly large slopes, so they were rotated to a more reasonable angle before solving the cubic to avoid any "slope blowups." They were unrotated after the equations were solved to put them back into their proper position.

Bezier Curves

The spline curve generation method works well when slopes are limited to gradual changes and never get too steep. In cases where these conditins are not met, we must rotate pieces of the curve into workable coordinate systems. This requirement can be eliminated, as it was for circles, by putting the generation equations into a parametric form. Unfortunately, it is very difficult to define a series of polynomial curve segments as a simple set of parametrics. The B-spline curve and Bezier curve generation methods take advantage of parametric techniques. These methods, however, are quite different from normal spline techniques.

One way of coming up with a parametric method is to take a standard equation (such as the circle) and derive a set of two equations from it—one that generates x as a function of an input parameter and one that generates corresponding y as a function of the same parameter. Bezier equations for standard generation of Bezier curves were derived using this method in reverse. The assumption is made that a parameter (v for instance) will be varied from 0 to a maximim value of 1 to generate the curve. Bezier curves are specified by a set of control points that "steer" the curve. The curve doesn't usually pass through the control points (except the two end points), but each point bends the curve toward it as the curve gets near it. This is handled mathematically by coming up with a set of blending functions that cause the control points to sequentially have a large effect on the line. For example, if six control points were used for parameter v which varied between 0 and 1, the blending functions would reflect the following:

v	Result
0.0	Point 1 has large effect on curve
0.2	Point 2 has large effect on curve
0.4	Point 3 has large effect on curve
0.6	Point 4 has large effect on curve
0.8	Point 5 has large effect on curve
1.0	Point 6 has large effect on curve

The resulting equations generate x in terms of v and y in terms of v, so axis orientation and steep slopes cause no blowup problems. No power terms are used to blend the points' effects together, so no wildly oscillating or looping curves (as can be found in polynomial curves) are ever generated. Figure 7-32 (a) shows a Bezier curve generated using 6 points. Notice how the curve is affected by these points. It doesn't pass through them but rather is guided by them.

The blending functions are shown in Fig. 7-32 (b). Notice how each control point has more effect (a higher blend value) as v sequentially advances. Points P_1 and P_6 are the end points. They have full effect at the ends of the curve where every other point's effect fades to zero. This property causes the Bezier curve to always meet its end points. The equation for these blending functions is shown in Fig. 7-32 (c). It is this unique blending equation, developed by P. Bezier, that sets the Bezier curves apart from other similarly generated curves (such as the B-spline).

The curve is physically generated by sequentially advancing through v values, plugging them into the blending equation to obtain the six blending functions values for the given v, and plugging the control point x and y values (P_1x, P_1y, P_1z, etc.) along with the blend function values (B_1 to B_6) into the Bezier curve-generation equations. The generated points are connected with short line segments, and the result is a smooth-looking Bezier curve.

257

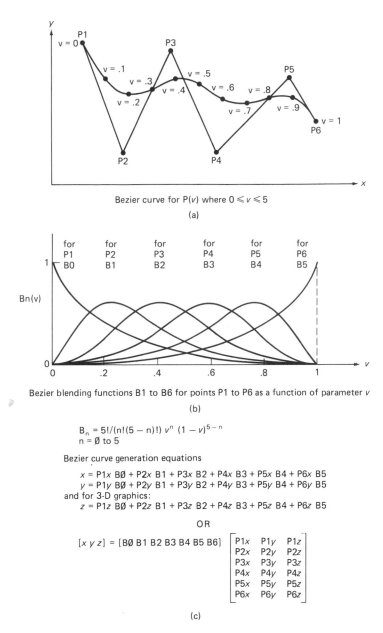

Bezier curve for P(v) where $0 \leqslant v \leqslant 5$

(a)

Bezier blending functions B1 to B6 for points P1 to P6 as a function of parameter v

(b)

$$B_n = 5!/(n!(5-n)!) \, v^n \, (1-v)^{5-n}$$
$$n = \emptyset \text{ to } 5$$

Bezier curve generation equations

$$x = P1x \, B\emptyset + P2x \, B1 + P3x \, B2 + P4x \, B3 + P5x \, B4 + P6x \, B5$$
$$y = P1y \, B\emptyset + P2y \, B1 + P3y \, B2 + P4y \, B3 + P5y \, B4 + P6y \, B5$$
and for 3-D graphics:
$$z = P1z \, B\emptyset + P2z \, B1 + P3z \, B2 + P4z \, B3 + P5z \, B4 + P6z \, B5$$

OR

$$[x \; y \; z] = [B\emptyset \; B1 \; B2 \; B3 \; B4 \; B5 \; B6] \begin{bmatrix} P1x & P1y & P1z \\ P2x & P2y & P2z \\ P3x & P3y & P3z \\ P4x & P4y & P4z \\ P5x & P5y & P5z \\ P6x & P6y & P6z \end{bmatrix}$$

(c)

Figure 7-32 Bezier curve generation using six plotted points (a). The blend functions (b) show how each control point has a higher blend value as v sequentially advances. In the equations (c) the value 5 reflects the 5-sided Bezier polygon.

Computing factorials and powers in the blending function equation take a lot of processing time. The best way for a microcomputer to reduce this problem is to precompute B_n for a sequence of v values and store the result in tables. This effectively precalcutes the blending curves, putting the curve coordinates into lookup tables. Whenever a blending function for a particular v is required, generation is reduced to a simple table lookup.

An examination of the Bezier blending functions in Fig. 7-32 reveals that the blending functions for all six points are nonzero from $v = 0$ to $v = 1$. In graphics terms, all points have a blending effect on the curve throughout curve generation. This results in the very smooth and fluid curve that is typical of Bezier curves. In many applications, however, a curve that fits more tightly into the defining polygon is required. The B-spline curve generation method accomplishes this by limiting the number of points that have an effect on curve bending at any given v parameter value. This is easily accomplished by "sharpening up" the blending functions as shown in Fig. 7-33.

Notice that blending function B_0 is nonzero within the range of 0 to 1. Similarly, functions B_1 to B_5 all have their nonzero ranges. B-splines are described according to the number of points that have an effect on the curve at once. In the example blending functions, three points affect the curve at once, so the *order of continuity* is 3 (often referred to as a B-spline of $k = 3$).

Final curve generation is performed identically to the Bezier method using the standard x, y, and z blending equations, which are shown in matrix form in Fig. 7-33.

The B-spline concept is simple enough, but the mathematics involved in generating the smooth blending curves that are nonzero between specified ranges gets quite complex. Not only do equations for smooth blending curves have to be generated, but a conditional truncation function that forces the curves to zero outside of their range of influence is required. Figure 7-33 goes through the mathematics for $k = 3$ B-splines. The blending function generation method is a step-by-step process.

First, "knot" values are chosen. These specify the range in which the curve blending function will have an effect. This is best illustrated with an example. The knot values in Fig. 7-33 range from 0 to 4. Blending function B_0 has an effect from $v = 0$ to $v = 1$. Function B_3 has an effect from $v = 1$ to $v = 4$. Knot values are used in the generation of blending-function equations to force the blending functions to zero outside of their specified zones. Knots are labeled t_0 to t_8, which are values utilized in the blend equations.

Blend function generation is a three-step process for $k = 3$ curves. This process would have to be extended to more steps for larger k values. The first step results in values of 0 or 1 for functions based on the current range of v. These 1/0 step functions are what forces the blending function curves to zero outside their ranges. The second step uses the standard "B-spline basis function" to define the blending function for $k = 2$. We are interested in the $k = 3$ case, but the $k = 2$ blend function is needed to derive the $k = 3$ result. Blending function generation is a recursive process.

Finally, the $k = 3$ blending function is derived in step 3. Again, the basis function is used, but it is modified for $k = 3$ as marked by asterisks. For higher orders of continuity ($k = 4$ or $k = 5$), a fourth and fifth step using the basis function with modifications for higher order k values would be required.

The best way to handle blending-function generation on a microcomputer is to precompute a table of blend values as was done in the Bezier curve case. Curve

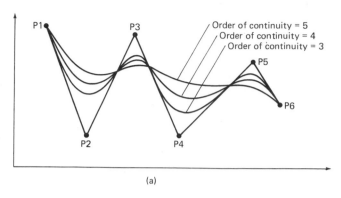

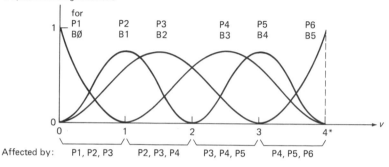

Figure 7-33 B-spline curve generation using six plotted points (a). The overlapping curves represent variations based on order of continuity (the number of points simultaneously affecting the curve). The blending functions (b) show the points affecting the curve over the v range. The mathematics portion of the drawing (c) shows knot values, blend functions, and generation equations.

generation is then reduced to simple table lookups, multiplications, and summations. Bezier and B-spline curves are differentiated only by their blending functions, so a common generation routine can be used for both types of curves. You can in fact precompute a few tables—one for Bezier curves and a few for various orders of B-spline ($k = 3$, $k = 4$, etc.). When a user specifies curve generation, a choice of what type of curve should be available also. The generation routine would evaluate the choice and select the proper blending-function table.

B-splines are useful in tight curve-fitting applications. Their property of using only a few sequential points in the defining polygon can be put to use in making selected corners even sharper. Two or more control points can be placed very close together, or even on top of one another. This area or point will have extremely strong influence when points around this area are being generated. It's even possible to put k points (three in the $k = 3$ example case) on top of one another. Only three points' effects are considered at once on the $k = 3$ case, so when the three overlapping points are considered, the result will be totally dominated by the three identical points. The curve will come up to meet the points, and a sharp corner results. The generation of sharp corners is one of B-spline's advantages. Sharp corners, using any other method, require that curve segments be pieced together.

Closed Curves

B-spline techniques can be modified slightly to allow generation of closed curves. The blending functions of the open spline curve in Fig. 7-33 are said to be uniform nonperiodic. Three points are always considered at any v parameter value, making the function uniform; but the blending functions near the ends of the curve are adjusted to bring the curve to intersection at these points (to start and end the open curve, making it nonperiodic). In a closed curve, there are no start and end points. Any point can be considered the first or last point; there are no distinctions between the way each point affects line generation. It follows that the blending functions for all points should be the same.

Polygons

Figure 7-34 shows the blending functions for a six-point, six-side closed polygon. The functions follow the $k = 3$ B-spline generation guideline that three points affect the line at any v value. This sort of blending function is said to be "uniform periodic" because the blend function repeats itself for each point, then wraps around as the figure closes.

Blending functions for closed polygons are easier to generate than those for open curves. We simply find a symmetric curve that is three units wide on the v axis and then shift it into six positions for blend functions B_0 to B_5. The symmetric B_3 or B_4 curves from Fig. 7-33 can be used as a basis curve, but any curve that meets the range and symmetry test will work. The result will simply have different rates of curvature throughout the curve.

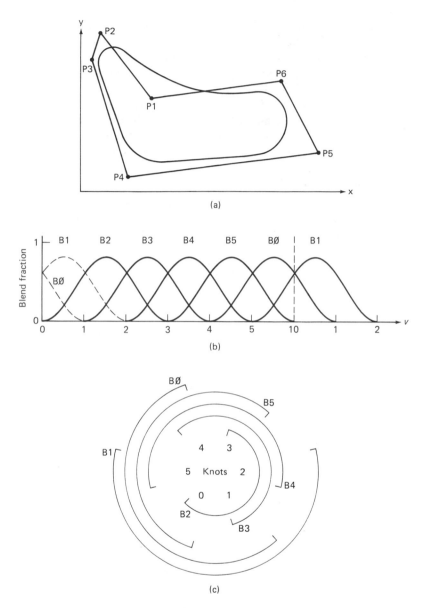

Figure 7-34   Six-point, six-side closed polygon (a) with blend functions (b) and knot values (c).

IMAGE SURFACES

When it comes to display realism in design and animation, you can go only so far with constructions involving line drawings and "wire frames." To achieve the look of solid, realistic images, we must define and manipulate surfaces rather than line-oriented elements.

SURFACE DEFINITION

Surface definition and manipulation encompasses a wide range of graphic techniques. Element groupings and closed polygon generation are used to define surfaces; crosshatching, patterning, and area filling are used to represent them. The advanced techniques of hidden line and surface elimination and incorporation of reflections help add even more realism to a display.

Flat Surfaces

The first step in working with surfaces is defining them. The simplest surface to define is a flat surface. Any closed polygon that lies on a plane can serve as an outline of the surface. There are a number of ways to identify the line segments that make up the polygon as being the border of the surface. A graphic element similar to a line string can be defined. This element can be called a *surface polygon*. This element sequentially defines the first through last point of the polygon's edge. The first and last point are connected by definition. Figure 7-35 shows a pyramid of four flat surfaces. The surface polygon elements are defined for each surface.

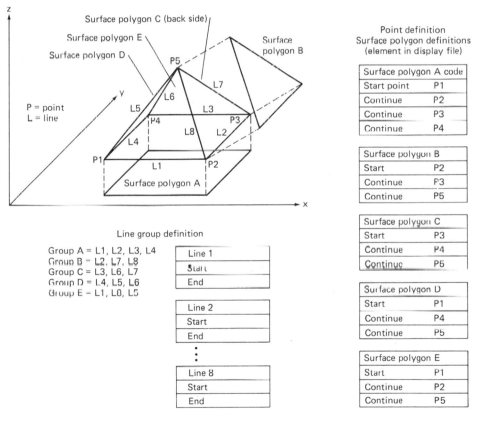

Figure 7-35 Flat-surface polygon definitions based on a simple pyramid. The surface polygon definitions assume wraparound of last to first point for closure.

The pyramid that results from drawing the surface polygons using normal line techniques looks the same as that generated using wire-frame construction, but there is an important distinction in the way the data is organized in the display file. Other subroutines, such as surface manipulators and shaders, have the information they need to identify boundaries of surfaces.

A disadvantage of the point-oriented surface definition is that it does not take advantage of edge commonality. The common edge of polygon A and polygon B in the example pyramid will be drawn twice—once when polygon A is generated and once when B is drawn. Grouping techniques are used to get around this problem and increase representation efficiency. All the pyramid's lines are first defined in a display file. Then grouping elements are set up for surfaces A through E. The surface information is thus available for shading and manipulating subroutines.

This method greatly improves representation efficiency, especially on large objects with many static surfaces. Manipulation of objects stored in this form, however, is not as easy as the point-defined surface polygon, because moving one surface requires an analysis of the situation and possibly the creation of more lines in the display list. Point creation is necessary using the point definition method, but the display list remains the same size (unless more surfaces are intentionally created).

Curved Surfaces

Previous sections show how it is possible to contruct a curve out of many straight-line segments. Likewise, it is possible to construct curved surfaces using many flat-surface polygons. One way to define a curved surface is to manually piece together many small polygons in 3D space coordinates.

Mathematically generated curves can aid us in curved surface definition. Instead of manually piecing small polygons together, mathematial curves (mathematical functions, B-splines, or Bezier) can generate guiding points on which to define surface polygons. A z term can be added to 2D x and y curve equations to define a "space curve." The solution x, y, and z values will lie on this curve. A square grid in the $x - z$ plane can be generated and plugged into the curve equation. The resulting x,y,z coordinate points will form a mesh that nicely represents a space curve.

Figure 7-36 shows a simple space curve. The program that steps through the input grid coordinates generates x,y,z coordinates of the points that make up the space-curve mesh. Simply plotting points, however, yields a nearly unrecognizable curve. Instead, points are connected by line segments. A small additional program is therefore required to keep track of the points from the generation program (after 3D projection) and to finally draw the interconnecting line segments on the screen.

All that has been described about point translation, rotation, scaling, and perspective projection applies to the 3D output points. It is therefore a simple matter of sending the x,y,z coordinates through the proper transform routines to translate and rotate the curve in space. Perspective effects can give the curve the dramatic effect of fading into the distance. Curves can be manipulated and pieced together using translation and rotation.

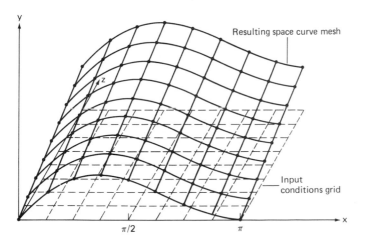

Resulting space curve mesh

Curve equation
  Y = sin X + Z
Input conditions
  X = 0 to π in steps of π/8
  Z = 0 to 8 in steps of 1
Basic program to generate points
  FOR X = 0 TO 3.14 STEP .3925
  FOR Z = 0 TO 8 STEP 1
  Y = SIN(X) + Z
  GOSUB PLOT3D
  NEXT Z
  NEXT X
  END
Note: Subroutine PLOT3D clips
         and perspective-projects the
         point X, Y, Z.

Input
conditions grid

π/2   π

Figure 7-36   Space curve generated from a mathematical function. In the generation program the PLOT3D subroutine is used to cup and perspective-project the *x*,*y*,*z* point.

We can go even one step further with the output of this simple space curve: Instead of simply drawing the interconnection mesh, we can define each mesh square as a flat-surface polygon. This information can be used later in shading and reflection routines to blend the curve into a very realistic appearing hill.

B-Spline and Bezier Surfaces

A simple sine function multiplied by a constant was used as a control function for the generation of the Fig. 7-36 space curve. In real applications, the user requires more control of the surface definition. The B-spline or Bezier curve can replace the sine and additive constant as guiding functions, thereby giving the user interactive control of the shape of the surface.

A single 2D Bezier curve is defined by the number of control points used to generate it. Figure 7-32 depicted a 6-control-point curve. Three-dimensional Bezier curves are a function of two Bezier curves—one for width and one for depth. The two curves may have a different number of control points. A 6-control-point curve may represent width, and a 4-control-point curve may represent depth.

A control-point grid (similar to the input condition grid in Fig. 7-36) is set up. The total number of control points is thus the product of the number of width and depth control points—24 points for a 6 × 4 control-point Bezier surface. The control points needn't be equally spaced in any dimension. They should indeed be moved about extensively by the designer to guide the curve into the desired shape. Like the Bezier curve, the Bezier surface doesn't go through the control points.

Each point on the control grid has its own blending function, which is the product of the two Bezier curves' function for that point (the Cartesian product). The blending functions of the points in the 2D Bezier curve were such that all control points on the curve have an effect on the curve throughout the curve's generation. Points each had their zone where they would dominate the curve, but they also had some small effect throughout curve generation. The same holds true for Bezier surface generation. The blending function of all the control points on the grid have had an effect on every portion of the space curve.

265

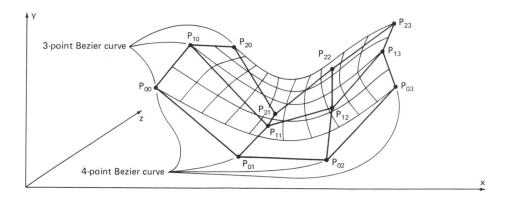

3-point Bezier curve

P_{10} P_{20}

P_{00}

P_{22} P_{13} P_{23}

P_{03}

P_{21}

P_{12}

P_{11}

4-point Bezier curve

P_{01} P_{02}

3-point Bezier curve blending function
$$Bn = 2!/(n!(2-n)!)v^n (1-v)^{2-n}$$
for $n = 0, 1, 2$

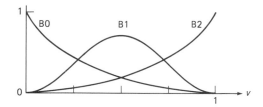

4-point Bezier curve blending function
$$Cm = 3!/(m!(3-m)!)w^m (1-w)^{2-m}$$
for $m = 0, 1, 2, 3$

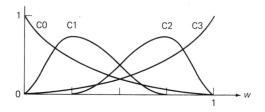

Bezier surface generation equations:

$$x = \sum_{n=0}^{n=2} \sum_{m=0}^{m=3} Px_{n,m}\, Bn\, Cm$$

$$y = \sum_{n=0}^{n=2} \sum_{m=0}^{m=3} Py_{n,m}\, Bn\, Cm$$

$$z = \sum_{n=0}^{n=2} \sum_{m=0}^{m=3} Pz_{n,m}\, Bn\, Cm$$

Example
$v, w = (0, 0), (0, .2), (0, .4), (0, .6)$
$= (0, .8), (0, 1), (.2, 0), (.2, .2)$
$= (.2, .4) \ldots$ etc $\ldots (1, 1)$

Figure 7-37 Bezier space curve generation. The surface points are generated by solving the equations repeatedly as v and w are parametrically increased through their ranges: $v, w = (0,0)$, $(0,0.2)$, $(0,0.4)$, $(0,0.6)$ . . . (see example on drawing).

An example best describes all of these concepts. Figure 7-37 illustrates a Bezier surface generated using two Bezier functions: 3 points deep and 4 points wide. There are thus 12 control points. The blending functions are defined as B and C, respectively. The surface generation equations sum all of the control points' effects to generate *x, y,* and *z* which lie on the curve's surface. Needless to say, this involves a large number of computations that are heavily multiply-weighted—a bad situation for a microcomputer.

As many surface points as desired can be generated by solving these equations repeatedly for a range of *v* and *w* parameter values. The resulting points create a more evenly spaced mesh than the mathematically generated space-curve mesh, because the spacing is proportional to the parameter changes rather than the slope of the surface, as in the mathematical case.

Computations can be reduced, and the space curve can be made to "hug" the control-point hull more tightly by sharpening up the blending functions so control points only have effects over narrow *v* and *w* parameter ranges. What this amounts to is using B-spline curves instead of Bezier curves as generation curves, which is commonly done. B-splines offer the advantage of more control effect in the vicinity of any given point. They also offer the ability to make sharp points by placing multiple control points in identical positions. In contrast, Bezier surfaces offer "fluid" flowing surfaces that avoid sharp corners.

Curves with Edge Constraints

Up until now, our main concern was generating a space curve of any type. In practical applications, however, curves are used to blend flat surfaces and other space curves together to form models of objects in space. The edges of these space curves must match the object outline, and curves that are pieced together must match closely. Edge constraints therefore also must be considered.

Mathematically defined curves can be open or closed. An equation for a sphere creates a closed curve, while the sine curve of Fig. 7-36 is an open curve. The closed curve's boundaries are dictated by the generation equation, and the open curve has no boundaries because it stretches to infinity in all directions. Closed mathematical curves are used when common shapes which they conveniently generate (spheres, ellipsoids, cylinders) are required. Open and semiopen curves (such as the cylinder which stretches to infinity in one dimension) pose problems because it is hard to define edges on the curve at which to truncate them. It is hard to match them to predefined edge conditions.

Bezier and B-spline curves are a bit better in this regard because they are finite curves or "patches" that are limited by their generation parameter sweep ranges. The patches don't always meet the edges that you want them to, but control points can be varied to force them into position; and multiple patches can be pieced together to form the curve you need.

Another approach is available for applications requiring exact edge matching. This approach, pioneered by S.A. Coons, uses defined edges as initial conditions and works backward using blending functions to define the surface. Figure 7-38

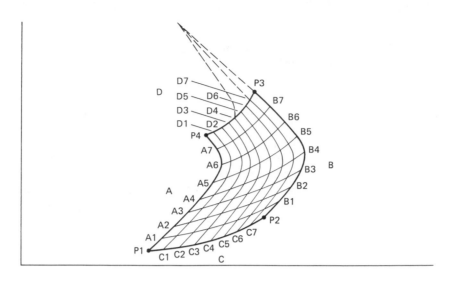

Blending grids

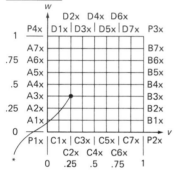

	D2x D4x D6x	
P4x	D1x|D3x|D5x|D7x	P3x

1

A7x		B7x
.75	A6x		B6x
A5x		B5x
.5	A4x		B4x
A3x	•	B3x
.25	A2x		B2x
A1x		B1x

0

P1x \| C1x \| C3x \| C5x \| C7x \| P2x
C2x C4x C6x

0   .25   .5   .75   1

x values at equally spaced intervals
on each arc = A1–A7
B1–B7
C1–C7
D1–D7

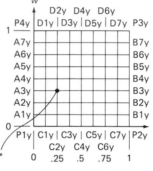

	D2y D4y D6y	
P4y	D1y|D3y|D5y|D7y	P3y

1

A7y		B7y
A6y		B6y
A5y		B5y
A4y		B4y
A3y	•	B3y
A2y		B2y
A1y		B1y

0

P1y \| C1y \| C3y \| C5y \| C7y \| P2y
C2y C4y C6y

0   .25   .5   .75   1

y value at equal intervals
on each arc

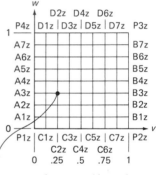

	D2z D4z D6z	
P4z	D1z|D3z|D5z|D7z	P3z

1

A7z		B7z
A6z		B6z
A5z		B5z
A4z		B4z
A3z	•	B3z
A2z		B2z
A1z		B1z

0

P1z \| C1z \| C3z \| C5z \| C7z \| P2z
C2z C4z C6z

0   .25   .5   .75   1

z values at equal intervals
on each arc

*Interpolated point computed using blending function

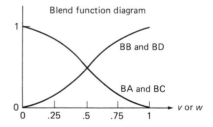

Blend function diagram

Coons blending function

For A interpolation $BA = 1 - (3V^2 - 2V^3)$
For B interpolation $BB = 1 - BA$
For C interpolation $BC = 1 - (3W^2 - 2W^3)$
For D interpolation $BD = 1 - BC$

Coons generation function for example interpolation point

$x = A3x\,BA + B3x\,BB + C2x\,BC + D2x\,BD - P1x\,BA\,BC - P2x\,BB\,BC - P3x\,BB\,BD - P4x\,BA\,BD$
$y = A3y\,BA + B3y\,BB + C2y\,BC + D2y\,BD - P1y\,BA\,BC - P2y\,BB\,BC - P3y\,BB\,BD - P4y\,BA\,BD$
$z = A3z\,BA + B3z\,BB + C2z\,BC + D2z\,BD - P1z\,BA\,BC - P2z\,BB\,BC - P3z\,BB\,BD - P4z\,BA\,BD$

Figure 7-38   Coons function surface patch generation for a motorcycle fairing design. The
defined edges serve as initial conditions, and the blend functions define the surface that fits all
four curves.

shows a curve defined by four general space curves that join at four corners (P1 through P4). The goal is to blend a surface into all four curves. This is done by breaking each of the curves into equal segments along their arc lengths, represented in Fig. 7-38 as A_1 to A_7. The x, y, and z values at these points are obtained. The curves' lengths are normalized to match the v and w parameters' range of 0 to 1, and points across from each other on opposite edges are blended.

This is best represented by the blending grids of Fig. 7-38. Each point on the grid represents an interpolation point. In the example, the x value of the point is a blend of the two sets of opposed-edge points (A_3x, B_3x and C_2x, D_2x) and of the four corner points. The degree of blend for the eight blending terms is controlled by the Coons blending function and the blending equation, as shown. Corresponding x, y, and z points for a representative set of parameters (v and w) are calculated to form the final space curve that exactly matches the edges.

This method is used to match constraints in position only. If many such surfaces are to be smoothly blended together, the slopes at the edges must also match given edge conditions to avoid sharp edges. An enhanced version of this method that defines and interpolates slope is used in these cases.

Cross Sections

As a final example of curve generation and blending techniques, we examine a method that is useful in defining objects that can easily be portrayed by parallel cross-sectional slices. This includes aircraft fuselages, wings, ship hulls, ducts and pipes, etc. This method combines simple blending (but on a radial basis), scaling, and blending functions controlled by the user rather than some mathematical function.

A few representative cross sections of the object to be drawn are set up (see Fig. 7-39). The cross sections are defined radially from a central axis point. This is best done by building a table of values versus sample angle rather than trying to match equations, because any shape can easily be defined in the table. The lifting body in the example is defined by five cross sections (many more would be used in a real application).

A central axis to build the object around is then set up. The designer is given two controls to work with: shape blend and radial scale for each of the cross sections. Object cross sections are generated moving down the central axis based on the amount of blend and the scale factor of each cross section. Figure 7-39 shows the blend and scale diagrams for all five cross sections. Scale is defined only in areas where blend takes place. In other areas, there is no need to define it.

The true power of this method is realized when the defining axis is itself a curve. The duct example in Fig. 7-39 proves this point. From the user's standpoint, object generation is simple. The user defines the central axis to conform to the desired curve (in this case a right angle of fixed radius r, generated using 3D space curve techniques). The cross-sectional blending and scaling functions are then defined, and the figure is generated. The duct example shows a good application of using a radial scale factor. The cross-section diameter reduction from points C to B is easily specified.

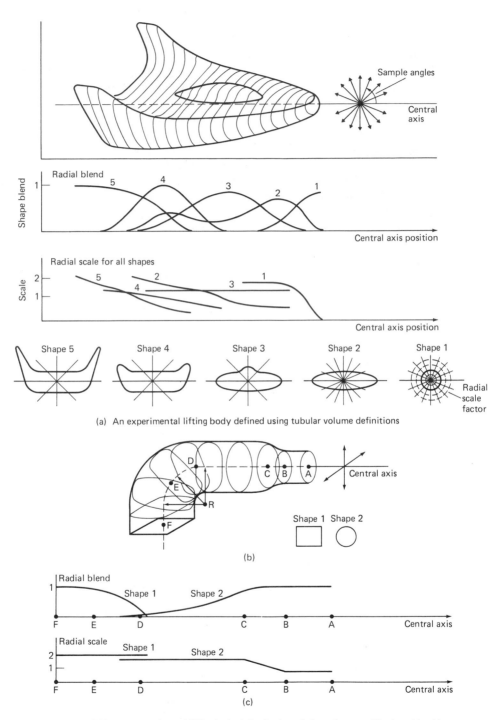

Sample angles

Central axis

Radial blend

Shape blend

Central axis position

Radial scale for all shapes

Scale

Central axis position

Shape 5　　Shape 4　　Shape 3　　Shape 2　　Shape 1

Radial scale factor

(a) An experimental lifting body defined using tubular volume definitions

Central axis

Shape 1　Shape 2

(b)

Radial blend

Shape 1　　Shape 2

F　E　D　　　　C　B　A　　Central axis

Radial scale

Shape 1　　Shape 2

F　E　D　　　　C　B　A　　Central axis

(c)

Figure 7-39　An experimental lifting body defined using tubular volume specifications (a), with five defined cross sections. The defining axis is a curve itself, as shown in the duct example (b). The cross-sectional blend and scale functions (c) apply to the square (shape 1) and the circle (shape 2) of the duct.

SURFACE CLIPPING

Surfaces are defined by closed polygons. The polygons are usually defined in 3D space and are projected onto a 2D screen. As long as the whole polygon falls on the screen, the 2D closed-screen polygon can have surface operations (such as area filling) applied to it. If the polygon falls partially off the screen, however, some of the lines that define it may be totally off the screen, and others may need clipping to the screen boundary. Line clipping poses no problem, but the resulting set of lines may no longer form a closed polygon. Polygon clipping solves this problem.

Standard techniques are used to clip the defining lines to the screen boundaries, and additional analysis is used to synthesize edges to close the one or more polygons that result from a single polygon's clipping.

Figure 7-40(a) shows a fully on-screen polygon and illustrates some of the possible results of polygon clipping. At first glance, polygon clipping seems like an impossibly difficult task. The figure sometimes clips nicely at one edge, but in other cases it breaks into two polygons. All the lines may fall off the screen, but this can mean that the polygon now is either off the screen or totally fills it. Like many other difficult graphics tasks, polygon clipping can be separated into a number of simple operations. Sutherland, for example, attacks the problem by the simple process of clipping to a single edge at a time.

The Sutherland-Hodgman method shown in Fig. 7-40(b) is a point-by-point process. Any screen edge is chosen to clip to. Analysis begins at any point and continues sequentially around the figure, treating each point as a continuation point in a large, closed line string. If a continue point results in a line that crosses the edge, the intersection is computed and stored in a new line string list. If a continuation line goes from the off-screen side of the edge to the off-screen side of the edge, the point that generated it is thrown away. If a line is on the on-screen side of the edge, the point that generated it is added to the new line string list.

Finally, when all points have been considered, the new line string list is sequentially strung together to form a single degenerated polygon that may represent more than one polygon connected together by widthless lines at the screen edge.

Another method, shown in Fig. 7-40(c), is to first determine the line segments that must be added to the polygon components to close them. This is done by clipping line segments and saving all edge intersections. The edge intersections are sorted in terms of increasing x and paired off. The resulting point pairs are the required additional line segments (see the section on area filling for an explanation of why point-pairing works). The new line segments along with the on-screen remains of the clipped lines constitute all the segments we need to piece together the polygons. A small program then analyzes how the segments are pieced together and determines how many polygons result. A table of all the points is set up. Analysis begins at any point. Point-to-point connections are traced around the polygon, and points are "crossed off" on the table until a crossed-off point is reached. This indicates polygon closure, and all the segments that were scanned through are part of that polygon.

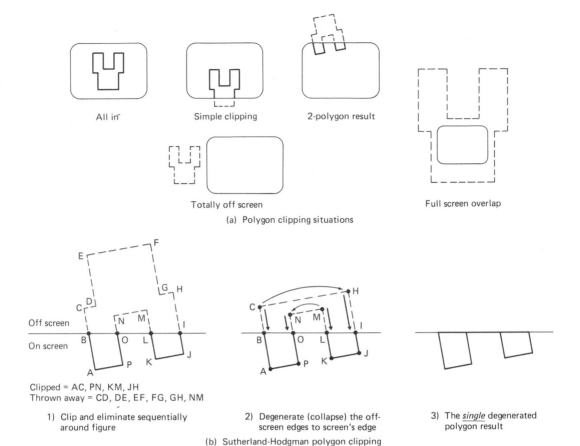

All in

Simple clipping

2-polygon result

Totally off screen

Full screen overlap

(a) Polygon clipping situations

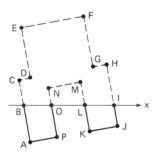

Off screen

On screen

Clipped = AC, PN, KM, JH
Thrown away = CD, DE, EF, FG, GH, NM

1) Clip and eliminate sequentially around figure

2) Degenerate (collapse) the off-screen edges to screen's edge

3) The *single* degenerated polygon result

(b) Sutherland-Hodgman polygon clipping

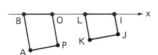

On-screen = AB, OP, IJ, KL
Screen edge = B, O, L, I = 4-points

Pair-off edge crossings
New segments = BO, LI

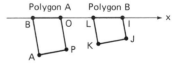

Polygon A   Polygon B

Analyze loops:
A → B → O → P → A = Polygon A closure
But point J not used yet so:
J → K → L → I → J = Polygon B closure
All points used

1) Clip, eliminate and determine on screen line segments and edge crossings

2) Create new segments to close polygons

3) Analyze and identify polygons Two polygon result

(c) Polygon breaker method

Figure 7-40 An object to be displayed may appear fully on-screen, partially off-screen, or fully off-screen, depending on size and position (a). With an off-screen arrangement that ends in two polygons on-screen, the Sutherland–Hodgman clipping method (b) may be used for clipping to one edge at a time. An alternative approach (c) is to clip line segments and save edge intersections using the polygon breaker technique.

The table is then checked. If all points are crossed off, analysis is complete. If some points remain, there must be more polygons. The clipped polygon must have split into two or more small polygons. Any point is chosen and another polygon is analyzed. This process of analyze, piece together, identify, and check for more points continues until all points are exhausted (all polygons are identified). The nice feature about this method is that the resulting polygons are not degenerated cases but the final stand-alone polygons.

This method has a problem in practical implementations. If a polygon vertex falls exactly on the screen edge, a single point (a singularity) results in the edge intersection table. And this "confuses" the routine that pairs off the points. This problem is overcome by having the screen edge identifier specifically watch for this condition and avoid it.

SURFACE AREA CALCULATION

Design systems often need the ability to calculate the area of flat as well as curved surfaces. Surface area can be used to calculate construction cost, aerodynamic response, and weight when combined with surface depth.

A few common area calculation routines should therefore be incorporated into a design graphics system. The following equations are useful for area calculations in a flat x,y plane:

$$
\begin{aligned}
\text{triangular area} &= \tfrac{1}{2} \text{ base height} \\
\text{rectangular area} &= \text{width} \times \text{height} \\
\text{circle area} &= \text{pi radius} \\
\text{ellipse area} &= \text{pi semimajor radius} \times \text{semiminor radius} \\
\text{any polygon } P_1 \ldots P_n \text{ area} &= \tfrac{1}{2}(x_1 y_2 + x_2 y_3 + \ldots \\
&\quad + x_{n-1} y_n - y_1 x_2 - y_2 x_3 - \ldots \\
&\quad - y_{n-1} x_n - y_n x_1)
\end{aligned}
$$

These formulas (especially the last one) will solve almost any area problem in the x,y plane. Unfortunately, curved surfaces consist of many flat planes that are not in the x,y plane. The area of these planes consisting of collinear points P_1 to P_n can be calculated as:

$$
\begin{aligned}
\text{Area} = \text{square root of } (&x \text{ projected area squared} \\
+ \ &y \text{ projected area squared} \\
+ \ &z \text{ projected area squared})
\end{aligned}
$$

where projected areas are calculated using the x,y plane polygon area formula with the values x,y, z,x, and y,z for the x, z, and y projected areas respectively.

SURFACE AREA FILLING

Now that surface definition methods have been covered, we can add the ultimate touch in realism by filling and manipulating the surfaces represented on the monitor screen.

The most common surface operation is area filling. Areas can be filled in on the display screen or plotting device in a number of ways. In raster-scan display systems, solid-area filling is possible. All the pixels within a polygon's boundary can be set to one color to fill the whole area. This capability is raster graphic's prime advantage over other display systems.

In vector-oriented displays, patterning or crosshatching is performed to fill areas. Different patterns identify different surfaces, and variable-density crosshatching combined with color (available on some plotters and matrix printers) can closely approximate solid-area filling.

Raster Filling

Raster filling, also referred to as area painting and solid-area scan conversion, is the process of setting all the pixels in a polygon to one color. The polygon's surface definition is used as the border conditions for the fill.

The *table fill,* the simplest filling method, works well with convex polygons. In the example of Fig. 7-41(a) a "maximum and minimum shading table" is set up. This table has a maximum and minimum entry for every y coordinate on the screen. A 200-pixel-high screen would thus have a table with 400 entries.

The table is initialized. All "min" entries are set to screen maximum x, and all "max" values are set to screen minimum x to indicate that no polygon has intersected any of the scan lines yet. The line segments of the polygon are then drawn. As each pixel of each line segment is plotted, the pixel's x coordinate is compared to the minimum and maximum values in the table's corresponding y coordinate max–min position. If the current pixel is smaller than the minimum or greater than the maximum, it's x value is entered into the appropriate position. The first pixel that intersects an intitialized table entry is entered into both positions because it is smaller than the minimum and greater than the maximum. This sets a reference for future pixels in this scan line.

After all the line segments are drawn, the area filling sequence beings. A routine begins scanning through the shading table. For each scan line, this routine checks the min–max values. Filler or shading lines are drawn between minimum and maximum values according to the following rules:

1 . If max is less than min, draw no filler lines, since this indicates that the line is still initialized and the polygon never crossed this scan line.
2. If min is less than or equal to max, draw a filler line on the current y scan line from min x,y to max x,y.

All the pixels within the polygon are turned on by the filler lines.

The table fill method is limited to convex polygons, except in special cases. The horizontal scan table shades polygons with concave left and right edges nicely, as illustrated in Fig. 7-41(b); but concave top and bottom edges cause the "shadow distortion" shown in Fig. 7-41(c). Vertical-scan shading table methods can shade polygons with concave tops and bottoms, as shown in Fig. 7-41(d), but not concave sides. In applications where areas under curves on graphs and charts are to be

Step 1 Draw outline and build table

Min/max shading table

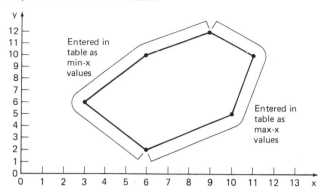

y coord.	Min x	Max x	
0	13	0	
1	13	0	Table initialization values
2	6	6	
3	5	8	
4	4	9	
5	4	10	
6	3	10	
7	4	11	
8	5	11	
9	5	11	
10	6	11	
11	8	9	
12	9	9	
13	13	0	

Step 2 Fill the min to max ranges

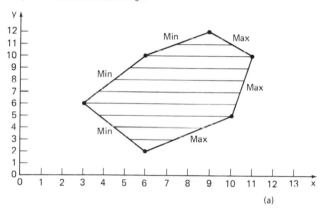

(a)

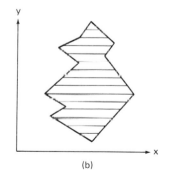

(b)

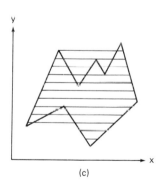

(c)

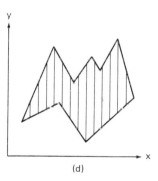

(d)

Figure 7-41   Table-fill polygon shading methods: The first step is to draw the polygon and outline and build the table of minimum and maximum *x* values (a), followed by filling the minimum-to-maximum ranges. A polygon with concave left and right edges (b) is easily filled with the horizontal-scan shading table, but the polygon with concave top and bottom (c) is "shadow-distorted" with horizontal shading, so vertical-scan shading (d) may be used for effective fill.

shaded, vertical scan shading is preferable because charts usually only have concave tops and bottoms. Horizontal scan filling is more easily applied to the hardware in most microcomputer applications, however, because pixels are usually laid out byte-wise in a horizontal manner. A display with 8-bit horizontal bytes can draw filler lines 8 times as fast in a horizontal direction than a vertical direction, and in area filling, speed is of prime importance.

In situations where an area has concave tops and bottoms, or if horizontal scanning's efficiency is opted for in concave-top and -bottom situations, the polygon can be defined as a few smaller convex polygons that can be filled separately. Choosing the correct set of polygons is difficult, especially if the polygons will go through transformations before being projected and filled; but by using the fact that a triangle can never have a concave side no matter how it is transformed, a large polygon can be defined as a large set of small triangles. This definition, though not optimal, is simple and always yields the correct post-transformation results.

Inner Point Determination and Filling

Another way to fill the interior of a polygon is to turn on all the pixels that are found to be inside the polygon, leaving alone those that are outside of it. All the pixels on the screen can be checked to see if they fall within the polygon.

There are two ways to determine if a point is within a polygon. One is to determine if the point is angularly encompassed by all the points in the polygon. This is done by drawing imaginary lines from the point to be tested to all vertex points in the polygon. The angles between the lines must then be added together going around the polygon counterclockwise. If the angle from one point to another sweeps in a counterclockwise direction, it is added to the sum. Clockwise sweep angles are subtracted from the sum. If the final sum is $0°$, the point is outside the polygon; if it is $360°$, the point is inside the polygon.

The second way to determine inner points is the odd–even intersection method. The concept of odd and even edge intersections is used in many other graphics operations, and this is a good time to introduce it. Figure 7-42(a) shows a complex polygon consisting of many edges. Any given horizontal scan line in the image area is crossed by a number of polygon edges. Starting at the left of the screen, moving to the right, the line crosses these edges. Every time the line crosses an edge, it either enters or leaves the interior of the polygon. The line began at the extreme left edge, outside the polygon, so every odd edge crossed (crossing 1, 3, 5, 7, etc.) enters the polygon, and every even edge (2, 4, 6, 8) exits it.

A point can be tested for being inside the polygon by determining how many edges were crossed (from left to right) to reach it. If an odd number of crossings were made, the point is inside; if an even number were made, it is outside.

Now that we have means of determining if a point is within a polygon, we can fill the polygon by testing all screen points for being inside or outside the polygon and turning them on accordingly. This is a slow and cumbersome way to fill an area. It can be made more efficient by limiting the tested pixels to x and y ranges that correspond to the maximum extent of the polygon in the x and y directions; but there are still better ways to fill a surface.

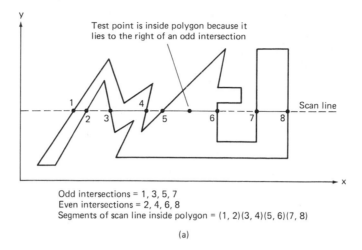

Odd intersections = 1, 3, 5, 7
Even intersections = 2, 4, 6, 8
Segments of scan line inside polygon = (1, 2)(3, 4)(5, 6)(7, 8)

(a)

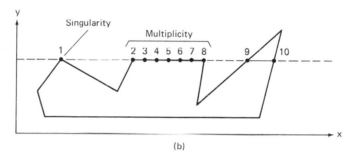

(b)

Figure 7-42   The odd-even method of filling using edge intersections (a) avoids concave-edge problems, but it encounters difficulty from singularities and multiplicities (b) that can confuse the scan algorithm.

Odd–Even Intersection Filling

The inner point determination and fill method may be inefficient, but the odd–even edge intersection method used to determine inner points can be used, in itself, as a filling method. Notice in the diagram that spans between even and odd edges are denoted with broken lines and spans between odd and even edges have solid lines. The solid lines actually represent pixels that must be turned on or filled. And this results in a filling technique the odd–even intersection fill.

A computer would break the filling task into a few simple steps:

1.   Build a table of edge intersections for the current scan lines.
2.   Sort the table into edges of increasing x order.
3.   Pair off the edge intersections (1,2) (3,4) (5,6), etc.
4.   Fill in the pairs on the y scan line: Fill ($1y$) to ($2,y$), ($3,y$) to ($4,y$), ($5,y$) to ($6,y$), etc.

This would seem to be the ideal shading method. It is fast, efficient, simple, and not susceptible to concave-edge problems.

This method does have its problems, though. Vertexes that appear on the scan line can cause *singularities* if they connect a line of rising y to a line of falling y, as shown in Fig. 7-42(b). The single point can confuse the scan algorithm. Lines of zero slope can place all of an edge's points on a single scan line. This causes *multiplicity* problems that also can confuse the scan algorithm.

Routines that watch for singularities are written into odd–even intersection fill programs. Singularities are spotted by watching for a change in y direction. If a singularity is found, it is either eliminated from the edge list or entered twice. Multiplicities are spotted by their zero slope. If the horizontal line connects two lines of increasing y or two lines of decreasing y, the horizontal line marks an entry or exit from the polygon and has its left edge only entered into the edge list. If the horizontal span connects a line of falling y with one of rising y (marking a flat top of the polygon), the start and end points of the horizontal line are entered in the edge list, and all intermediate points are eliminated.

Seed Filling

Seed filling is an interactive method of shading an area within any closed boundary on a raster screen. The user first draws a design using line-drawing techniques. Then areas bounded by lines and curves (they needn't be stand-alone polygons) are chosen for color filling. The idea is to position a cursor inside the area to be filled and instruct the computer to color-fill the area within the bounds. Color filling begins at this user-specified "seed" and spreads throughout the area.

This method is easily implemented on a raster screen that has pixel readback capabilities. Filling starts at the seed's pixel coordinate which is assumed to be within the area enclosed by the polygon. The computer then scans to the right, reading pixels as it goes. If a pixel is currently turned off, it turns it on (or color fills it). If the pixel is already on, a border has been reached and the computer backtracks to the seed and scans to the left until a border is reached. The computer then moves up to the next line (if it can do so without hitting a border) and scans and fills that line. The process continues and the filling spreads throughout the polygon above the seed line. The area below the seed line is then filled in the same way.

Very simple seed filling routines can be used on convex polygons. Complex polygons, however, pose problems for simple seed fill routines because as the routine works its way up the polygon, it may only fill one peninsular section of it. There are two solutions to this problem. This is usually an interactive technique, so the task of finding unfilled polygon sections and reseeding them can be left to the user. The other alternative is to increase the complexity of the seed filling algorithm. Every time the algorithm moves up or down to another scan line, it must check to see if there are other spans on the previous scan line where vertical movement can take place without hitting a border. If so, it must save the coordinate to resume filling when the current peninsular section is filled.

Complex Pattern Filling

The techniques examined to this point have involved solid filling—span lines within polygons have been turned on or off. In many applications, pattern filling is required. At first glance, pattern filling may seem quite complex. A pattern of wavy lines, for instance, must fill the inside of the polygon, and each wavy line must be clipped at all edges. Complex pattern filling on a raster screen, however, is a simple extension of solid filling.

First, a pattern cell of any size is defined. The example in Fig. 7-43 uses a cell of 16 × 16 pixels. The pattern for large areas consists of small pattern cells placed end to end. Elements such as wavy lines that go through cells should be positioned for proper end-to-end matchup. Symbols within cells (such as a set of circles) can also be used as a predefined pattern cell. The result of the end-to-end pattern cells is a pattern plane. A routine that can tell whether a pixel at any specified coordinate of

Figure 7-43   Pattern filling is less complex than it may seem, despite the fact that some instances may require clipping at all edges. A wavy pattern and a dot pattern using pattern cells of 16 × 16 pixels (a) may readily be used to fill a complex polygon (b). With *and*ing of the polygon plane and the pattern plane, the polygon plane acts as a mask through which the pattern plane may be viewed (c), and the approach is applicable to the dot-cell pattern (d) as well.

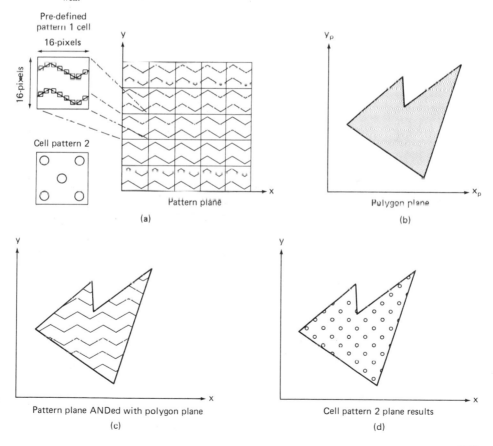

the cell plane is on or off can easily be written. This routine must consider the cell spacing, the specified x,y coordinate, the origin of the first cell, and the internal bit structure of the cell for any given x and y.

The internal polygon patterning is performed by filling the polygon in the normal way using one of the previously described methods (the odd–even intersection method, perhaps), but instead of turning on pixels at each coordinate, the pattern plane for every coordinate is checked. If the pattern plane is on at a coordinate, the polygon pixel is turned on. If it is off, the pixel remains off. The result is a logical *and*ing of the pixels on the two planes. The solid polygon plane essentially acts as a mask that looks through to the pattern plane. The result is a complex-patterned polygon as shown in Fig. 7-43.

Vector Filling and Crosshatching

Vector-oriented displays are at a disadvantage when it comes to area filling. Predefined pixel matrixes that create pure colors when turned on are not available. Area filling can be performed on vector displays by synthesizing a raster and scanning out all the segments that would be turned on in a raster display; but the results usually are poor due to vector bleeding on storage tubes and slightly uneven spacing and flicker on refresh-vector displays. Vector displays are usually only one color, so color distinction between areas is not possible.

A good substitute for solid area filling on these displays is crosshatching, the process of filling an area with equally spaced lines at a preselected spacing and orientation angle. Distinction between areas is possible by varying the distance between crosshatch lines and their angles.

Crosshatching is performed in the same way area filling is performed on a raster screen, but larger y separation between lines is used. The odd–even intersection method words well in crosshatching. Angular orientations other than horizontal are handled by rotating the polygon through the crosshatch lines' orientation angle, performing horizontal crosshatching as usual, and rotating the polygon and crosshatch lines back to the polygon's original position.

Area Filling Priority

Two solid or pattern-filled areas that overlap each other on a display pose display problems. It is up to the user to decide which area will dominate or how the two area colors will mix together. The most common approach to the area fill problem is to let one area dominate another by giving it a higher projection priority. This is easily handled by display hardware and software. The polygons with the lowest priority are projected first, and higher priority polygons are allowed to draw over them.

Display priority capabilities are often included in display hardware. The Texas Instruments 9918 display controller chip, for example, allows different display memory planes to be assigned display priorities. The highest priority memory plane's image dominates in areas where it is turned on. This is particularly useful in game applications where moving players must move in front of background scenery and behind and in front of one another.

HIDDEN SURFACE ELIMINATION

For optimum display realism, solid surfaces must block surfaces that are behind them. Otherwise, viewers may be confused as to which surfaces are viewable and which are masked by other surfaces.

There are many approaches to the hidden surface problem. Some are simple but require huge amounts of memory. Others use less memory but involve considerable computation time. Others are fast, memory-sparing, and simple, but they are limited to usefulness only in special cases. Modern memory technology is making huge amounts of memory available at low cost, so the simple, memory-intensive hidden surface techniques are gaining popularity. These offer the most promising approach to hidden surface elimination today.

Priority Sorts

Object A blocks object B when both objects line up with the viewer's line of sight and object B is farther away than object A. Using this line of reasoning, we can adopt an algorithim that calculates the distance of objects from the viewer's eye, and give closer objects priority in projection to block near objects. This is usually done by calculating each surface's distance from the viewer's eye in the 3D viewing pyramid, and putting all the distances along with surface-identifying tags into an array in memory. The array is sorted using standard sorting techniques, and the surfaces are put in an decreasing-distance sequence. The surfaces are finally projected in the order of decreasing distance, and areas of the screen that are filled by near objects overlap and block far objects. This is the basis of the *priority sort* method.

The many variations of this technique concern the detail rather than the concept. One item of contention is the method for determining how far an object is from the viewer's eye. The simplest approach is to use the z-depth of the centroid of the surface, which is the point on which the surface would balance if the surface were a uniform flat plate. This method is satisfactory for narrow fields of view where small objects have relatively large z-distance variation, but in most cases true distance measurement is required. True centroid distance is measured as:

$$D_c = \sqrt{x^2 + y^2 + z^2}$$

Square roots take large amounts of computation time, so the trigonometry-based alternate form is used:

$$h = z \,/\, [\cos\,[\arctan\,(y/x)]\,]$$
$$C_d = h \,/\, [\cos\,[\arctan\,(x/h)]]$$

This two-step equation can be simplified by setting up a ''$1/\cos\,[\arctan\,(\theta)]$'' lookup table in memory. With such a table, the true distance is found with two divide operations, two table lookups, and two multiplications.

Even when precise distance is calculated, the centroid priority sort has its problems. The centroid is too local an area on which to base priorities of large, odd-shaped, and close-spaced objects. Figure 7-44(a) confirms this point. The centroid priority sort method works just fine for two simple, rectangular planes with relatively large z-separation, but when a large square plane with a small rectangular extension that points in a z direction is placed close to another rectangle at a slightly greater distance, the large rectangle's extension may physically pass behind the small rectangle that the centroid calculation indicates is farther away. The result is the far object blocking the near object and an incorrect projection, as illustrated in Fig. 7-44(b).

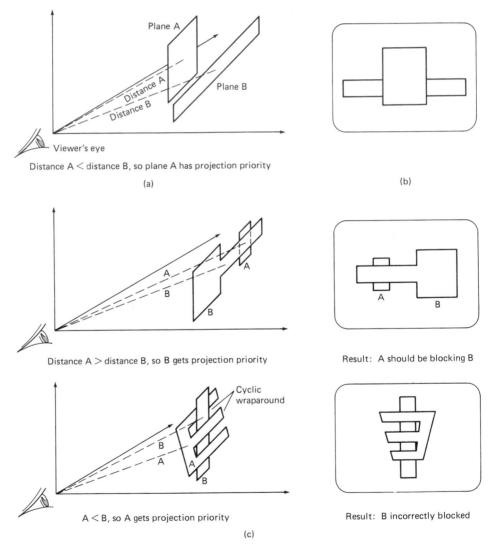

Distance A < distance B, so plane A has projection priority

(a)

(b)

Distance A > distance B, so B gets projection priority

Result: A should be blocking B

A < B, so A gets projection priority

Result: B incorrectly blocked

(c)

Figure 7-44 Hidden-surface elimination with the priority sort: centroid distance calculations (a) and the projected result (b). But some conditions can confuse the priority sort (c).

The priority sort also is based on the false assumption that one surface must totally dominate in blocking—that is, if A blocks B, then B can't block A. In reality, however, this is only true for convex polygons. Odd-shaped concave polygons can in fact block each other. This condition, called *cyclic wraparound,* is shown in Fig. 7-44.

The solution to improper blocking problems is to perform distance calculations at many locations around the polygon and project portions of the polygon based on their own priority rather than the priority of the polygon as a whole. This procedure in effect breaks the polygon into many small polygons with their own centroids.

Back-Side Elimination and Surface Normals

A surface characteristic other than distance can be used to determine the invisibility of surfaces. One such characteristic is the invisibility of the back sides of surfaces. If we look directly at a surface, we see it. If the surface is rotated on the y axis (assume z is depth), its projected area gets smaller and smaller until all we see is the edge. Further rotation exposes the back side of the object. With back-side elimination, projections of back sides are detected and not performed.

This method is particularly applicable to convex closed polyhedra. You never see the back side of any surface in a closed polyhedron because they all face the invisible inside of it. Flat surfaces of a polyhedron also go out of view (by being blocked by other surfaces) immediately after their edge is viewed as the polyhedron rotates. This happens to coincide with the time their back sides would appear, and thus back-side elimination banishes them at just the proper moment.

Back sides are detected by observing the orientation of the *surface normal,* a perpendicular vector extending from a plane. In other words, it's a line sticking straight up from the surface. Assuming an orthogonal projection, the surface is visible when the normal points toward the viewing plane and is invisible when it points away. The pointing direction can be determined by the z component of the normal vector. If it is negative, the normal points toward the view plane; if it's positive, it points away.

A surface normal is best expressed by its direction numbers (a set of three numbers that are proportional to the x, y, and z distance along the normal between any two points). The equation of the plane on which the surface lies must first be derived. The plane equation is expressed as:

$$k = Ax + By + C$$

The values A, B, and C can be solved for by plugging any three surface point x, y, z coordinates into the equation and solving the three equations simultaneously. The normal's direction numbers are simply $[A, B, C]$. In practical applications, the C value's sign would determine whether the normal was pointing toward or away from the view plane.

The back-side elimination method, as a stand-alone hidden surface elimination technique, is only applicable to single closed convex polyhedra; it makes no provisions for multiple polyhedra blocking one another. This would seem to limit its use to special cases only, but as a matter of fact, the technique is often used to boost the performance of other hidden surface methods.

The observation that back sides of surfaces within closed polyhedra (convex or concave) are invisible implies that we can preprocess a data base and eliminate all the rear surfaces that face forward—before sending the surfaces to a hidden surface routine that considers multiple polyhedra blocking. This preprocessing, in many cases, eliminates more than half the surfaces to be considered; and because many hidden surface routines' computation time grows as a square of the number of surfaces (mainly due to the increases in sorting complexity), this can cut computation time by 75%.

Depth Arrays

The priority sort method's results can be improved by subdividing polygons into many small polygons, each with its own depth information. But how small do the polygons have to be to achieve 100% accuracy in the projection? They must be the size at which each polygon fills a single pixel on the display screen. This is very hard to determine at the object itself in the data base's space, but the *depth array* method performs precisely this task in an optimized way.

With this method, a large array in processor memory (or an auxiliary memory) is established with an entry (16-bit integer) for every pixel on the display screen. This is a huge array of 262,144 entries for a 512 × 512 display. Conventional surface projection techniques are used to project and fill surfaces on the display screen, but the depth of the vertexes of the surface polygon are considered in the filling routines. Using vertex depth and linear interpolation (which is valid on a flat surface), the depth of the start and end points of the line span being filled with color can be calculated.

Likewise, the depth of the surface at any pixel on the scan line can be interpolated from the depth at its start and end points. Before the pixel is plotted, the pixel's depth is compared with the information in the depth array for this pixel. If the new point is at a greater depth than the depth buffer value, a closer point on another surface must be closer to the viewer at this pixel location and the new surface is blocked here. The pixel is not filled.

If the new point has a lower depth value than that in the depth array, this surface is the closest one so far and the pixel is plotted (thus overplotting any "old" surface colors at this location).

After all surfaces are projected, a 100% correct 3D hidden surface view is portrayed on the display screen. Even surfaces such as complex space curves that intersect one another at odd angles have their intersection curves displayed with 100% precision (within the limits of the display resolution, of course).

This hidden surface technique has only two drawbacks: memory size and computation time. The memory size problem is rapidly vanishing, however, due to the wide availability of inexpensive 64K and 256K RAM chips. High-performance microprocessors partially solve the processing time problems, but more importantly, this method is so simple and straightforward that dedicated high-performance logic can be built to implement it.

Choosing a Hidden Surface Method

There are many variations of the priority sort, back-side elimination, and depth array surface elimination methods. Most of these attempt to reduce memory requirements by breaking the task into smaller screen area pieces. Others represent an attempt to reduce computations by looking for projection shortcuts in real time. One common shortcut is to look for similarities between scan lines that are adjacent to one another, with the goal of reducing computations.

These optimized methods can speed things in special cases, but under worst-case conditions, their complexity makes them less efficient than depth arrays.

The best hidden surface technique for any given application depends on the complexity of the projection. For simple geometric projections, the back-side eliminator is most appropriate. For relatively easy to resolve multipolyhedra conditions, a back-side eliminator combined with a priority sort is the most time- and memory-efficient way to go. For precision applications of very high complexity, a back-side eliminator combined with a depth array is the best approach.

If computation time is of particular importance, specially optimized hidden surface routines are useful, but only up to a point. The execution times of priority sorts and other back-side elimination methods increases logarithmically with the number of surfaces being processed (a reflection of the sorting steps being performed). Only back-side elimination grows linearly with the number of surfaces being projected, and the depth array's processing time actually decreases on a per surface basis as complexity increases. This is because of the decreased size of many small surfaces on the display screen versus a few large ones. In nearly any situation with more than a few thousand surfaces, the depth array method with a back-side eliminating preprocessor holds a large performance edge.

Hidden Surface Graphs

Manufacturers of graphics hardware often display images on 3D mathematical-function plots with hidden surface elimination as an impressive display that "obviously took a very powerful processor and display system to create." These 3D hidden surface graphs are sometimes used for practical applications as well. It is very easy to generate such graphs because their generation is based around a programming trick that is valuable to know.

Hidden surface elimination becomes a trivial task when the data base to be projected is set up so surface conflicts are easily resolved. An example of this would be a series of plane polygons parallel to the viewing screen at equally spaced increasing depths. Projection would be a matter of projecting the closest polygon, putting its area off limits to other polygons, and moving on to the polygon at the next depth. This is the principle of 3D graphing.

A 3D graph is created by taking an equation with x, y, and z variables and plotting curves of x versus y for a sequence of constant and increasing z values. The result of each x,y plot for a constant z is a polygon in the x,y (screen parallel) plane.

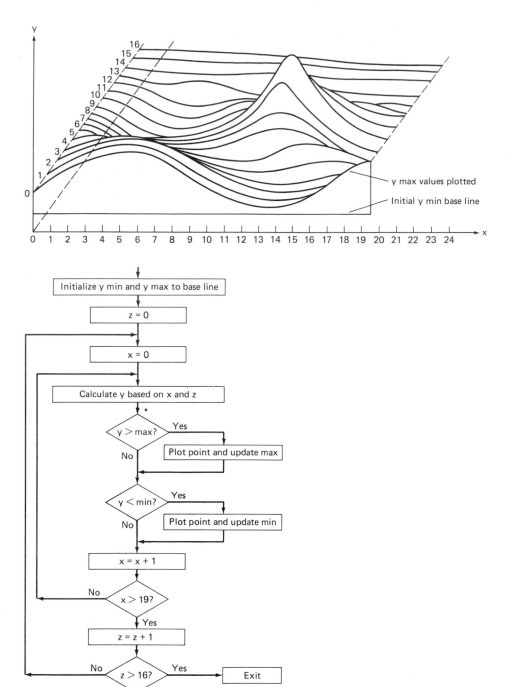

Figure 7-45   Special-case hidden-surface elimination in graphing. To give the graph a rotated look, add current *z* value to *x* and *y* results; the rotation is artificial but effective.

The first z value is chosen for the graph line closest to the viewer. A y minimum–maximum table is set up, and the graph line is plotted for all x values along the graph. As each point is plotted, the minimum and maximum y values in the array are updated according to the y position of the plotted point. The area between the minimum and maximum are off limits to future plotted points, because the area between these points is blocked from view by planes in front of the current plane.

On the second through final z value chosen for the function plot, every projected point must be checked against the table. If it is outside the minimum–maximum range, it is plotted and the maximum or minimum value is updated. If it is within the established range, the point is not plotted and computation moves on to the next point.

In order to achieve a "rotated graph" effect rather than a head-on view, a simple x bias and y bias as a function of z is added to all equation results to "slant" the curve into looking like it has been rotated. This rotation is not the real thing, but rather a special-case trick. Figure 7-45 illustrates 3D hidden surface graphing techniques.

Chapter 8

High-Performance Graphics
and
Animation

The basic graphic techniques and the more advanced mathematics covered in the previous chapters, if put to use in a practical application, are enough to generate technologically up-to-date displays. Anything from simple line drawings to 3D color displays with hidden surface elimination can be projected. This is the point at which users of huge computers can start applying graphic techniques to produce displays. Microcomputer users, however, are likely to be disappointed in the results of their efforts when implementing graphics. The generated images will be the same as those generated on the larger machines (assuming the same-quality display device is used), but the projection rate will be disappointingly low. Microcomputers are limited when it comes to processor speed and memory size.

This does not mean that we must be satisfied with low-performance graphics on microcomputers. A trip to any video arcade will prove that high-performance graphics and animation are indeed possible on microcomputers. Special techniques and a lot of imaginative "gimmicks" are required to achieve these results. This chapter examines many techniques that will aid microcomputerists in achieving state-of-the-art performance as well as superior image quality.

FRAME CONSIDERATIONS IN ANIMATION

Animation is the process of creating dynamic display images with elements that appear to have motion. Animated computer graphics are used in simulating real-life scenes in flight, driving, and other vehicle and engineering simulations. Animation is also used in more artistic ways to create computer movies, to depict processes in a dynamic way, and to create the illusion of motion in computer games. With animated images, the object is to generate images that appear to move smoothly and naturally.

FRAME REFRESHING

Animation technology is much older than computer science. Movies and television have been with us for decades, and these use animation techniques. Movies and television animate scenes by displaying sequences of display frames with minute differences between them. These minute changes from frame-to-frame blend into smooth motion when many frames are sequentially displayed at rates of over 15 frames per second.

The full-frame refreshing technique is ideal for movies and television because of the display hardware involved. A photographic frame can be captured in full color in a few hundredths of a second. This amounts to an incredible data transfer rate. Assuming that film has a color and intensity range expressible by a 16-bit number, and that the resolution is equivalent to a screen of 5000×5000 resolution (good film in 35 or 70 mm widths can easily surpass this), and assuming an update capability of 25 frames per second, this amounts to an incredible 10 GHz bandwidth.

Color television, with its limited screen resolution and color–resolution tradeoffs, is limited in bandwidth to 3–4 MHz. Analog hardware has problems enough working at these high frequencies. Digitally creating animation by totally recomputing every frame in real time on digital hardware such as a 4 MHz microprocessor using 8-bit bytes is simply out of the question.

Full-frame refresh was chosen for movies because that is what is best suited for film. For the best animation with computer graphics, it is important to choose the method that is easiest for the computer to deal with. Computers are good at making decisions and updating only what has changed rather than the whole scene.

Computers are also good at compressing data into compact representations. A line drawing, for instance, is represented by a small display file. Although the drawing may represent an object on the screen that encompasses hundreds of thousands of pixels, the vectors themselves consist of only a few thousand pixels. This representation is so compact that animation using full-frame refresh is possible.

Compact representations, high-performance hardware, high-performance software, and selective updating form the basis for computer animation. All of these items except high-performance hardware can be put to use in a simple microcomputer with graphics capability. In addition, high-performance hardware that boosts performance can be added to most microcomputers by simply plugging in an expansion card such as an arithmetic processor.

DISCONTINUITY AND FLICKER

A frame rate is defined as the total number of complete display frames that are recomputed and projected per second. For conventional motion picture cameras, rates range from 12 to more than 50 frames per second, and can approach the rate of 100,000 frames per second using continuously moving film and rotating projection–mirror techniques for engineering analysis applications.

Television's frame rate is usually said to be 30 frames per second. This includes both interlaced fields. Television's frame definition is different from that of a movie, because all the information for the field is not captured at the same instant; rather, it is spread out over an interval of 1/30 second. The primary frame and its interlaced frame can actually be considered as two different frames spaced 1/60 second apart.

In computer graphics, two important elements enter into frame rate calculations: frame-to-frame flicker and frame-to-frame discontinuity. Flicker is defined as the blinking effect of a display caused by the blank period between screen element erasure and generation. It takes time to erase and redraw a screen image; if the screen off interval is a large percentage of the display interval, flicker will result. Flicker is totally unrelated to animated motion smoothness. Even on static or slowly moving displays such as an animated sequence of a minute and hour hand moving around a clock face, the screen can be flickering badly due to an erase and redraw interval that leaves the screen blank for a period of 30 μs of a 100 μs frame (corresponding to a frame rate of 10 frames per second).

Frame-to-frame discontinuity is defined as the image element's changes in position from one frame to the next. Frame-to-frame discontinuities begin to blend into smooth, realistic motion at frame redraw rates above 15 frames per second.

In cases where only selected screen elements are updated, the term "frame rate" makes little sense. A computerized game in which only the ball and player paddles move, for example, usually displays a static playing field and selectively updates the ball and player paddles only when their positions are changed. The ball may in fact be redrawn at 30 frames per second, but the rest of the scene isn't redrawn at all. In selective erase and redraw cases, display update rates on single elements can be very high with a minimum of computation. Flicker reducing and frame-to-frame discontinuity smoothing techniques apply to single elements in these cases.

FLICKER REDUCTION

Flicker can be caused by an intentional screen erase prior to new screen image generation. If the amount of time the screen remains blank is short compared to the display frame time, flicker can be nearly unnoticeable. Also, if the display rate is extremely high (60 frames per second, for example), the blanking time can be equal to or greater than the display time with the only noticeable effect being the dimming of the display screen. The eyes cannot respond to flickering at such a high rate; instead, the eyes average the duty cycle of the images into a nonflickering image of lower overlap intensity. Microcomputers are not capable of erasing and redrawing whole frames this quickly, so the best way to reduce flicker is to decrease the blank time between frames. There are several ways to accomplish this.

Double Buffering

Some display devices and microcomputers (the Apple II is an example) have more than one "page" of display memory. The display unit can display one image from the first page while the user erases and draws a new image on the second page. When the new image is ready, a display generator command will initiate display of the second page. The transition from one page to the other is performed synchronously in the hardware and results in no screen flicker. The only way to know the frames have been switched is by any frame-to-frame discontinuities in the images. As the second frame is being displayed, the first page is free to use for erasures and image generation.

This technique of "bouncing" between display pages is called *double buffering* or screen ping-ponging. The only disadvantage to this technique is that it requires twice as much memory as would a single buffer display. And the additional memory does not buy any increased color selection or resolution—it simply reduces flicker in animation and allows storage of completely different images that can be switched with a single command.

The Atari 400 and 800 series microcomputers use a programmable display list to instruct the built-in display generator chip which areas of memory to read as it starts each scan line. The display list can be arranged in such a way that only a portion of the screen toggles between two memory areas or pages while the rest of the screen is always read out of one memory area. This saves memory and is useful in situations where a relatively static display (such as an instrument panel) fills half the screen while dynamic animation sequences fill the other half of the screen.

Many higher-level display and image processing systems such as the Comtal Vision /20 have many screen memory planes for image processing data storage. These planes can be used as double-buffer screen pages when the system is used as a display device. Image processing displays have so much memory that more than double buffering, with full color on all pages, is often provided. The Comtal system offers eight pages to work with—enough for a short, cyclic animation sequence in itself.

Intermediate Display File Buffering

When double buffering is not available, the goal is to keep the blanked-screen time to a minimum. This requires extremely high-speed erase software (or hardware) and rapid image generation software. The screen remains blank until the program refills it with a new image.

An animated sequence of screen images can be generated by erasing the screen and then redrawing the image, plotting the elements on the screen as they are transformed, clipped, and projected. When the screen is full, the image can again be erased and the next image drawn. This method has a few problems. Elements plotted on the screen immediately after the erase stay on the screen for the duration of the display frame, but the last-plotted elements are only on the screen for a brief instant before erasure. The first-plotted elements appear to be static and solid, but the most recently plotted elements flicker dimly.

Display flicker can be reduced and display time can be better equalized between display elements by performing rotation, translation, and projection operations on elements and putting the final results (numerical value of start and end points of lines) into a large buffer. While all of this computation is being performed, the lines from the last drawn frame are displayed.

When all the elements are processed, the screen can be erased and the line segments rapidly plotted without any time-consuming rotations, translations, or other calculations being performed between element generation operations.

This procedure improves the animation quality in two ways. There is less time difference between projection of the lines on the screen, so display time differences are reduced; and all elements on the screen remain on the screen for a long duration while computations for the next frame are being performed.

Selective Updating

If only a small portion of an image is changing on each new display frame, it makes little sense to update the whole image. Only the elements that change should be updated.

Selective screen area updating is the simplest form of selective updating. A small rectangular window is chosen to be updated. Everything within this window is erased, and a new image is drawn.

A second selective update method involves moving individual elements. First, the element must be erased from the screen. This can be done using exclusive-*or* drawing techinques. The element is exclusive-*or*ed onto the screen to draw it, and the same image is exclusive-*or*ed to eliminate. The element is then redrawn in its updated location.

Screen erase can be avoided entirely by selectively updating individual elements, but the element must be selectively erased by exclusive-*or*ed redrawing. This takes a lot of time, and the additional drawing time for a large number of selectively updated objects can surpass the time needed for a full screen erase.

Band Flicker Reduction

When selectively updating a small object at a very high rate on a raster screen, an annoying flicker can occur. The flicker is not constant; the small object appears solid at times, and at other times it appears to go black or look like a ghostly image that is hardly there. This phenomenon is known as *band flicker*. The small object is updated by erasing it and drawing a new object. If the object is updated at approximately the monitor's scan rate, the erase portion of the erase-redraw-display sequence will, for brief periods, fall at exactly the same time that the monitor is scanning the band of lines that make up the small object. If this situation occurs for several monitor scan frames in sequence, the object will appear to black out momentarily. Decreasing the erase time will not correct the anomaly, because the problem is not lengthy erase time but rather the synchronization between screen scan and element generation.

To eliminate band flicker, we must erase and redraw the element when the display generator is not scanning those raster lines that make up the element. Most sophisticated graphics generators and some microcomputers (notably the Atari 400 and 800) have registers that can be read by software to determine which line on the display screen is being scanned. Erasing during this scan-line overlap period can be avoided using this method.

Another commonly available signal is the vertical retrace pulse which indicates when the display scanning has reached the bottom of the screen and is retracing to the top. No scan lines are traced in this relatively long interval, and elements can be safely erased and plotted anywhere on the screen without causing band flicker.

DISPLAY GENERATION TIME ANALYSIS

To correct a display rate problem, it is first important to identify where time is being spent in display generation. Where the goal is to improve an existing display, a real-time clock can be used to determine exactly where the time is being spent. Table 8-1 is the result of such a timing. the display process was broken into four steps: (1) matrix generation, (2) translation and rotation, (3) 3D to 2D conversion and perspective projection, and (4) screen line drawing. Matrix generation time is an overhead operation whose percentage of total calculation time drops to nearly zero as the data base grows (only one matrix generation step is needed per display frame), but the percentage is rather large here because the test data base had only one line. For large general data bases, case 5 (see Table 8-1) gives the most realistic time breakdown.

It is interesting to note the reasons for some of the percentage variance in the individual display cases. Screen drawing took only 10% of the total time in case 1, whereas 20% is closer to an average time. This was caused by the program's special-case horizontal line drawer, which plots bytes of 8 pixels rather than single pixels on the screen. Matrix generation time was also low in the horizontal case because the multiply software is optimized to handle special case multiply operations (multiplication by zero or one) quickly. Zero pitch, bank, and heading result in binary numbers for all sines and cosines—and this decreases matrix generation multiply time.

Table 8-1 Typical Program Analysis

Program Tested: Sublogic A2-3D2 Animation Package
Display Method: 3D-to-2D conversion. 16-bit precision database projected
to a 280 × 192 raster display screen
Computer Used: Apple II with 1 MHz 6502 microprocessor
Database: Single line

Case	Line Position	Matrix Generation Time	Translation and Rotation	3D to 2D Conversion and Perspective Projection	Screen Line Drawing	Erase
1	Line Horizontal $P=0°$ $B=0°$ $H=0°$ Line on Screen	27%	33%	29%	10%	
2	Diagonal Line $P=10°$ $B=20°$ $H=8°$	31%	28%	16%	24%	
3	Diagonal Line $P=10°$ $B=6°$ $H=8°$	34%	31%	18%	17%	
4	AVERAGE	31%	31%	21%	17%	
5	AVERAGE Assuming 0 Matrix Time	0%	45%	30%	25%	
6	AVERAGE With 0 Matrix Time and Selective Erase	0%	36%	24%	20%	20%
			Transformation Computations 60%		Image Generation 40%	

In an animation sequence, screen erase also enters into time calculations. Timing case 6 considers selective erase to take the same amount of time as line drawing. Screen line drawing and erasing can be considered *image generation* functions; matrix generation, rotations, projection, and clipping can be considered *transformation* calculations. This breaks the computation time nearly equally (60% vs 40% actually) between these two categories, which is a very representative result for cases where a single microprocessor is performing both transformation calculations and image generation.

Transformation computations require extensive mathematics and decision-making; screen line drawing, filling, and screen erase use data transfer extensively. Methods for improving performance can be concentrated in these two areas.

TRANSFORMATION-COMPUTATION SPEED IMPROVEMENT

The rate at which transformation computations are performed is affected by the arithmetic type (integer, double-length integer, or floating-point), the precision of the calculation, and the inherent capability of the microprocessor (notably whether the microprocessor has multiply and divide instructions).

ARITHMETIC TYPE CONSIDERATIONS

When striving for speed, the goal is to add, subtract, multiply, or divide two numbers as quickly as possible. The time it takes to perform such operations can be found in the specification sheets or programming guides for the microprocessor or computer. Microprocessors—indeed, computers in general—are integer-oriented machines. Floating-point units that effectively add floating-point instructions at an assembly language level exist on many larger microcomputers and on minicomputers, but execution of these instructions usually just initiates a microcode sequence that performs floating-point operations using the processor's standard integer-oriented hardware. The result is increased execution time.

Table 8-2 outlines instruction execution times for integer and floating-point addition, subtraction, multiplication, and division on five popular microprocessors. This table contains much information that bears closer examination. Usually, integer arithmetic is noticeably faster than floating-point, even when high-performance floating-point chips are used. When no floating-point chip is used, floating-point operations can take 10 to 50 times as long to perform as simple 8-bit or 16-bit integer operations.

Another important point concerns integer arithmetic size: A 16-bit machine such as the 8088, LSI 11/23, or 68000 has little edge over simple 8-bit microprocessors when performing simple 8-bit computations. The 16-bit power begins to reveal itself when larger 16-bit and 32-bit simple additions are performed. the 16-bit machines also greatly outperform the 8-bit processors when multiplying or dividing, because they have built-in multiply and divide instructions.

Performing floating-point operations or large integer operations on 8-bit microprocessors and processors without floating-point hardware requires software sequences. These sequences are rarely small enough to insert into the program

Table 8-2   Best Case Arithmetic Execution Time

	6502, μs	Z80, μs	LSI 11/23, μs	8088, μs	68000, μs
Addition[1] *integer 8-bit*	2	1	1.72	0.6	0.5
Addition[1] *integer 16-bit*	8[2]	2.75	1.72	0.6	0.5
Addition[1] *integer 32-bit*	21[3]	11.75	5.16	1.2	0.75
Addition[1] *floating point*	$\approx$100[4]	$\approx$50[5]	37.05	14	
Multiplication *integer 16-bit*	$\approx$200[6]	$\approx$100[6]	24.5	25.6	8.75
Multiplication *floating point*	$\approx$400[6]	$\approx$200[6]	79.95	19	
Division *integer* 32-bit / 16-bit	$\approx$250[6]	$\approx$125[6]	50.62	28.8	17.5
Division *floating point*	$\approx$500[6]	$\approx$250[6]	91.05	39	
Subroutine call & return seq.	12	6.75	14.7	5.4	4.25

[1]Also applies to subtraction and logical (and, or, exclusive or) operations

[2]Software sequence—adc, tay, txa, adc

[3]Software sequence—adc, tay, txa, adc, tax,lda, adc, sta, lda, adc

[4]Software sequence—ADD HL, BC; PUSH HL; LD; LD LH, value; ADC HL, PE

[5]Software sequence—ADD R0,R1; ADD R2,R3; ADC R3

[6]Using inline software sequence with no looping

wherever needed, so they must be turned into subroutines. Subroutine calls and returns use valuable processing time, which in many cases (notably large-integer addition and subtraction) outweighs the computation time itself. The subroutine call and return sequence times in Table 8-2 bear this out.

Generally to increase graphics performance, use integer arithmetic. Also, choose the integer size that is right for the microprocessor. The 8-bit microprocessors handle 8-bit arithmetic very quickly, and on a screen up to 256 × 256 resolution, 8-bit resolution is all that is needed on many calculations. On 16-bit microprocessors, use 16-bit arithmetic. It makes no sense to restrict yourself to 8-bit arithmetic when 16-bit arithmetic is available and can be performed just as quickly.

One other data type, binary-coded decimal (BCD), is used in some high-level computer languages (notably *interpretive BASIC*). It is used primarily for convenience in converting decimal numbers into a computer-usable form. This form of representation, which packs one decimal digit code into each "nybble" (4-bits), should be aggressively avoided in graphics computation.

Most microprocessors have "BCD adjust" instructions that serve to increase efficiency somewhat on addition and subtraction of BCD numbers, but all savings are lost when the first multiplication or division is encountered. If data is presented to a graphics program in BCD form, convert it to integer binary or even floating-point arithmetic as soon as possible.

INTEGER ARITHMETIC TECHNIQUES

Any basic computer science course gives students a ground-level understanding of integer arithmetic. Integers are said to be whole numbers (with no fractional parts) that are represented precisely in binary form within the computer. It is further explained that the range of integers being used in the computer science course's 16-bit computer is − 32768 to 32767, and due to this restricted range and the whole number limitation, floating-point arithmetic is to be used for most computations. In reality, this information just scratches the surface of the capability and versatility of integer arithmetic. A much more thorough knowledge of integers is required to successfully perform integer-based high-performance graphics.

Integers, whether they are used in a high-level language or in assembly language, reflect the binary bytes and words stored in memory and registers in the computer. The computer is capable of adding memory and register locations using binary addition rules. These rules correspond to those of standard arithmetic. An integer can therefore represent a whole number, but an integer is actually open to much wider interpretation than simply whole numbers from 0 to 65,536 (for a 16-bit integer). Interpretations are based on "bit weight," as shown in Fig. 8-1(a).

A bit weight is a multiplication factor. Multiplying this factor by a bit in a specific bit position results in a product that is added to the sum of the bit numbers for the final numeric result. Unsigned integers have weights that basic computer courses teach about: mainly 1, 2, 4, 8, 16, and other increasing power-of-2 values.

With positive weights, only positive values can result. But there are a few ways to generate negative numbers. An assumed bias can be added to every number (called *excess bias* numbering), for example. Or one of the weights can be turned into a sign indicator (+ or −). Or one of the weights can be made negative. Figures 8-1(b) and (c) illustrate the *signed integer* and *two's complement* methods. Two's complement is preferred, because positive and negative numbers can be added together in the normal way to yield the correct result using this weighting. In any two's complement numbering scheme, the most significant bit of the integer is assumed to be a negative value of what would be its normal, increasing power-of-2 weight.

It is often erroneously thought that integers cannot represent fractions. But integers can be treated as fractions simply by moving the "binary point" to the left. Normal decimal fractions are expressed as values such as 675.3298. The decimal point marks the spot where the decimal weights (1, 10, 100, 1000, etc.) to the right of it are negative powers of ten (1/10, 1/100, 1/1000 . . .). Similarly, a binary point is the spot where binary weights to the right of it are negative powers of 2. Figure 8-1(d) shows a number with the binary point between bit positions 3 and 4. This number has a fractional part (the rightmost 4-bits) that can represent fractional parts as small as 1/16.

The binary point can be positioned at any convenient location. It can be all the way to the left, as in Fig. 8-1(e), to indicate totally fractional. Or it can be between 6 and 7, to provide a two's complement fractional value with a range of − 1 to almost + 1, as shown in Fig. 8-1(f). Fractionals, and especially two's complement fractionals, are used extensively in graphics, signal processing, and in any application where sines and cosines that range from 1 to 0 are involved.

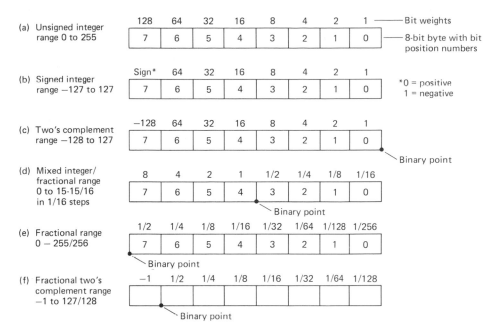

Figure 8-1 Byte representations of fractional and integer quantities: unsigned integer (a), signed integer (b), two's complement (c), mixed integer and fractional (d), fractional (e), and fractional two's complement (f).

Assuming that the binary point stays to the left of the word (or one bit inward, if a two's complement fractional is used), increasing the number of bits in the word does not increase its range. Instead, the precision is increased. An 8-bit fractional integer has a range of -1 to almost $+1$ in $\frac{1}{128}$ unit steps. A 16-bit fractional integer has the same range but in $\frac{1}{32768}$ unit steps.

One problem with using fractional two's complement integers to represent sine and cosine values is that there is no value of 1. There is a negative one; and there is $\frac{32767}{32768}$, which is almost a 1, but a pure 1 is not possible. In most situations, however, this doesn't matter. For graphics and signal processing, $\frac{32767}{32768}$ is close enough. If total perfection is desired, the binary point can be moved one more position, to make the range -2 to $1\frac{32767}{32768}$. This complicates multiplications and other processing, however.

Integer Sign Extension

To keep calculations efficient, a few different sizes of integers can be used. Byte-size integers are fine for low-resolution screen coordinates, while large 16- or even 32-bit integers are used to perform data base level calculations. Sooner or later, a large integer will have to be added to a small one. The smaller integer must first be converted to a large one so it has as many bits to add. Figure 8-2(a) shows how this is done with positive values, and Fig. 8-2(b) shows the procedure with negative values. A small two's complement integer with its binary point at the least signifi-

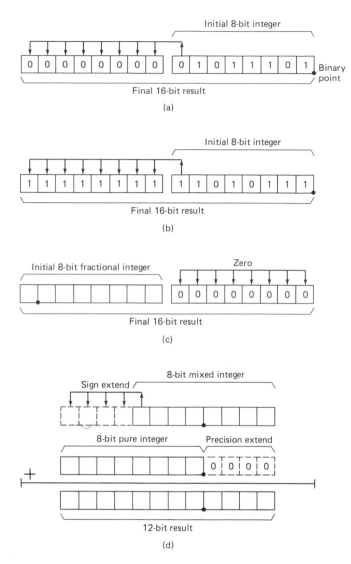

Figure 8-2 Sign extension techniques for two's complement integers: Conversion of 8-bit to 16-bit positive-value (a) and negative value (b) two's complement integer using sign extension; conversion of 8-bit to 16-bit fractional two's complement integer by appending zeros (c); and integer addition (d) of pure, mixed, and fractional integers.

cant position (to the right) can be converted to an arbitrarily large two's complement interger by "extending its sign" into all the added bits. Sign extension is necessary because a large integer has its negative weight in a bit location different from that of the small integer.

Increasing the number of bits in a fractional integer is more straightforward. The negative weight remains in the same position in the initial and final result, so bits can be added in positions of lesser significance by appending 0s, as shown in Fig. 8-2(c). No sign extension is necessary.

Integer Addition

Pure integers, fractional integers, and mixed integers with pure and fractional parts can be added together with no problems using conventional addition, as long as all the binary points are aligned and all the integers are sign-extended properly before the addition. Figure 8-2(d) illustrates addition between two numbers with different binary point locations. The mixed integer is sign-extended, and the pure integer is precision-extended to align the binary points. The result is a 12-bit value.

Integer Multiplication

Multiply instructions and software that performs multiplication on computers that have no multiply instruction (a program will be described shortly) are almost universally integer-oriented (with the exception of multiply instructions in dedicated signal processing computers). Two pure integers (16 bits, usually) with binary points at the right are assumed to be the input. A 32-bit two's complement result is produced. A 32-bit result reflects the maximum value of the multiplication, but an overflow flag is often set if the result exceeds 16 bits of precision (sensed by the top 16 bits not all being the sign extension of the bottom 16-bit value). This indicates overflow to users trying to limit their range to a 16-bit value. Figure 8-3(a) shows an 8-bit pure integer multiply.

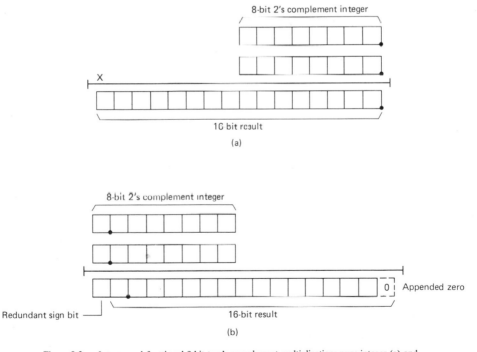

Figure 8-3 Integer and fractional 8-bit two's complement multiplication: pure-integer (a) and fractional-integer (b) 8-bit multiply operations.

299

Fractional multiplication on a binary level is identical to pure integer multiplication and can in fact be performed by an integer multiply instruction; but binary point positioning is a bit tricky. Two fractional integers, when multiplied in a conventional way, produce a redundant sign bit. If two 8-bit fractions are multiplied, a 16-bit result is created, but the result must be shifted to the left by one bit to get the correct answer, as shown in Fig. 8-3(b).

This characteristic can best be explained by considering the input values, each effectively having 7 bits of precision and 1 bit of sign information. When two 7-bit precision positive integers are multiplied, the maximum result is contained in a 14-bit field (7 + 7 precision fields). The final result needs a single bit of sign information, so all the precision of the multiply can be expressed by the 14 precision bits and the single sign bit—for a total of 15 bits. The result, however, is 16 bits. The extra bit is redundant, and it comes from the input sign bits. Only one is needed, so the other is discarded. The least significant bit is precision-extended with a 0.

Pure integers cannot overflow in a multiply operation, but a flag is set when values become so large that they can't fit in a 16-bit field. This flag is meaningless in fractional multiplies. An appropriate flag for a fractional multiplier would be one that indicates when the least significant 16 bits of the answer are not zero. This would indicate a precision underflow. No extraordinary action would need to be taken if this flag were set, however, because the most significant 16 bits of the result are always used as the result anyway, and these bits can never overflow.

What happened to the redundant sign bits in the pure integer multiply? The fact is, they do exist, but they are no problem because they occur in the most significant bits—away from the binary point, which remains properly aligned. The redundant sign bits automatically sign-extend the result to the 16-bit field width. They are useful for this reason.

The only time the redundant sign bits in an integer or fractional multiplication are not both the same is when a full-scale negative number is multiplied by a full-scale negative number (-256×-256, for example). The result in the pure integer case is a number so big that no product of two full-scale positive numbers could have generated it (255×255 would be a maximum value in the above example). In the fractional case, the result is a positive one, which is not representable in a purely fractional result. No special routines to adequately handle this special case need be taken, however, since it is a quirk of the two's complement numbering system and may be considered an overflow condition.

Integer Division

Integer division instructions and software are usually arranged to perform a multiplication in reverse. A 16-bit integer divide instruction usually expects a 32-bit dividend and a 16-bit divisor. The 32-bit number is divided by the 16-bit number for the 16-bit quotient. Bit alignment for fractional integers must be compensated for using the method outlined in the integer multiply description.

Bit Capacity. Instructions and software usually have 32-bit dividend capability because it essentially comes "with the territory" in the standard division algorithm. In high-level languages, little use is made of 32-bit outputs from multiplication and

32-bit inputs into division instructions, but on the assembly language level, there are ways to put these capabilities to good use.

Any situation where a number is multiplied by a variable, then divided by another variable is a prime candidate for the 32-bit capability. The standard 3D perspective equation is a good example:

$$\text{screen } x = \text{screen width} \times \text{space } x \: / \: \text{space } z$$

The screen width can be multiplied by space x without regard for overflow of the 16-bit field. The 32-bit result is the intermediate product and can be divided immediately by space z without worrying about truncation problems and precision loss. A 32-bit intermediate product was used, and it cost nothing, memory or timewise.

In many cases where sums of products are calculated and very high precision is required (an example is nested-instancing rotation-matrix concatenation), the 32-bit products can be summed. Precision is maintained in the 32-bit intermediate additions. The final sum can be rounded to a 16-bit value.

Roundoff Bias. The result of a division is usually presented as two parts: the quotient and the remainder. Many computer divide instructions are designed to maintain truncation symmetry about the 0 point by presenting the remainder as the same sign as the dividend. In other words, if the result was 2.85, the quotient would be 2 and the remainder would be 0.85 rather than the quotient being 3 and the remainder being -0.15. Likewise with negative numbers, a result of -2.85 would yield a quotient of -2 and a remainder of -0.85. The quotient is effectively truncated toward 0. Everything slightly above 1 is truncated to 1, above 2 to 2, and so on.

In the negative direction, everything just slightly below -1 is truncated to -1, below -2 to -2, and so on. Every number on the number line then has a 1-unit "distance" associated with it that anything falling within will be rounded down to. There is one exception to this rule: the value 0. All values from 0 to 0.99999 will be rounded to a 0 quotient with a positive remainder, and all values from 0 to -0.99999 will be rounded *up* to zero with a negative remainder. Everything in the span from -0.9999 to $+0.9999$ is truncated to 0.

Where division is used most frequently in graphics is in clipping and in final projection. In clipping, the roundoff bias is not a problem because this sort of rounding tends to balance out bias problems in systems of equations; but in final projection, the pixels are "crushed" by one unit toward the center of the screen in the x and y directions. This is due to the leftward truncation of positive values and rightward truncation of negative values toward 0. While the effect is hardly noticeable, it should be eliminated. Subtle perfections add up to a graphics system that presents a quality image. The solution to the problem is to monitor the division's remainder: If it is negative, subtract 1 from the quotient.

Integer Arithmetic Instructions

Computer instruction sets often have instructions that can really aid a programmer in working with integers. These are particularly useful with fractional integers and when matching short and long integers. One such instruction is the arithmetic right and left shift.

Arithmetic shifts are defined as instructions that move each bit of a byte over by one bit position. This is useful for shifting bits to the left or right to align their binary points. There are three basic shifts: logical, arithmetic, and cyclic. The differences lie in the way they handle (1) what falls off the end of the word and (2) what shifts into the other end when a shift is performed. *Cyclic shifts* makes the byte ''wrap around'' on itself and shift the ''dropped'' bit into the bit that is shifted into the byte. *Logical shifts* ignore dropped bits and shift in a 0. *Arithmetic shifts* ignore dropped bits and shift in a 0 for left shifts; for rights shifts, they shift in whatever the sign bit previously was. This essentially performs automatic sign extension. A left logical and left arithmetic shift are identical. Arithmetic right and left shifts can safely be used to align integers without worrying about sign extension—the sign is extended automatically with this instruction.

Another useful instruction is the *sign extend*. Advanced microprocessors such as the LSI 11 (SXT instruction) and 68000 (the EXT instruction) incorporate this. This instruction automatically checks the sign of the byte or word you want to sign-extend and fills the extension register or memory location with all 1s or 0s based on the sign bit result.

Software Multiplication Routines

Multiplication is the most frequently used higher-order mathematical operator in graphics, and unfortunately most 8-bit microprocessors (8080, 6502, 6800, Z80) don't have a multiply instruction. For graphics operations, a subroutine that performs multiplication must be written—and it must be written to perform multiplication as quickly and efficiently as possible.

Repetitive Adder. The simplest form of software multiplier is the *repetitive adder*. We can multiply 123 by 482 by adding 482 to a sum 123 times—but this method is too inefficient to be considered. The most common multiplication scheme is the shift-and-add method, which performs multiplication the same way humans do with normal decimal arithmetic using pencil and paper, only on a binary basis.

Figure 8-4(a) shows the process. The multiplicand is considered a bit at a time, starting with the rightmost value. If the bit is 1, the multiplicand is added to the sum. If it is 0, it is not added. the partial products are shifted over one place with each successive mutiplier bit test to account for the heavier weight of the new bit. Registers are used to store the multiplier and multiplicand, and a double-width sum register is used to accumulate the results.

First, in step 1 of Fig. 8-4(b), the multiplier is shifted to check its least significant bit. If it is 1, the multiplicand register is added to the most significant part of the sum register. On the next add, the multiplicand would normally be moved to the left one place, but instead, the sum is shifted to the right for the same effect. After all multiplier bits are shifted out and considered (8 cycles through steps 1, 2, and 3 for an 8-bit multiply), the sum register contains the result. The pencil-and-paper multiply method has thus been implemented directly in the software (or hardware).

A close examination of the register arrangement in the multiplier reveals that an optimization can be made. The sum register is initially empty, and multiplicands are only being added to its left half. Every shift fills one more bit in the right half of

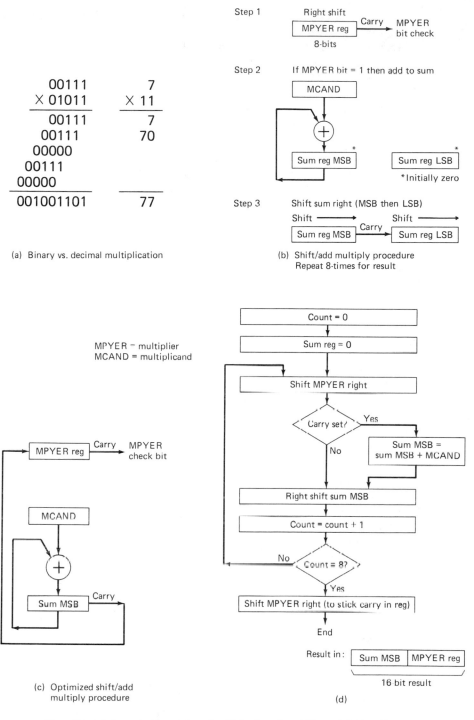

Step 1   Right shift

MPYER reg → Carry → MPYER bit check

8-bits

Step 2   If MPYER bit = 1 then add to sum

MCAND

(+)

Sum reg MSB *   Sum reg LSB *

*Initially zero

Step 3   Shift sum right (MSB then LSB)

Shift ——→   Shift ——→

Sum reg MSB → Carry → Sum reg LSB

```
00111        7
X 01011     X 11
─────      ────
00111        7
00111       70
00000
00111
00000
─────────   ────
001001101    77
```

(a) Binary vs. decimal multiplication

(b) Shift/add multiply procedure
Repeat 8-times for result

MPYER − multiplier
MCAND = multiplicand

MPYER reg → Carry → MPYER check bit

MCAND

(+)

Sum MSB → Carry

Count = 0

Sum reg = 0

Shift MPYER right

Carry set? —Yes→ Sum MSB = sum MSB + MCAND

No

Right shift sum MSB

Count = count + 1

Count = 8? —No

Yes

Shift MPYER right (to stick carry in reg)

End

Result in: | Sum MSB | MPYER reg |

16 bit result

(c) Optimized shift/add
multiply procedure

(d)

Figure 8-4   Software implementation of multiplication using addition and shifting: binary vs decimal multiplication (a), shift-and-add multiply procedure (b), optimized shift-and-add procedure (c), and flowchart for optimized shift-and-add (d).

303

the sum register. In step 1, each shift empties one bit of the multiplicand shift register. The carry from the shift in step 3 can be stuck in the multiplier shift register as it shifts out the next multiplier bit, as shown in Fig. 8-4(c). This saves a shift into the sum register LSB. The multiplier register in effect doubles as the sum register LSB. The LSB of the result will found in the multiplier register when the multiplication is complete.

A flowchart for the optimized method is shown in Fig. 8-4(d). Notice that a variable called COUNT is set aside to count how many times the loop has been cycled through.

In graphics applications, multiplications are so common that it pays to optimize the multiplier even further. An in-line multiply routine can be used. To put this routine in in-line form, the count variable is eliminated and the shift and add steps are repeated in the software eight separate times. This takes up much more memory than the loop multiplier, but loop counting and branching are totally eliminated.

Booth Multipliers. The shift-and-add multiplication scheme works very quickly for multipliers with large strings of 0s because the addition steps are avoided. The routine therefore slows down proportionally to the number of 1s in the multiplier. Logically, large strings of 1s in a multiplier can be reduced to a single add by adding a value one power of 2 higher than the highest one in the string and then subtracting the multiplicand corresponding to the lowest bit in the string of 1s. In other words, the value of binary 11111111 can be represented by 100000000 − 1. A multiplication method developed by Booth uses this fact to reduce the overall number of additions in a multiply.

In Booth's algorithm, scanning of the multiplier starts at the right as usual, shifting the sum register accordingly. When the first 1 is encountered, the multiplicand register is subtracted from the sum. Scanning resumes until the end of the string of 1s. When a 0 is encountered, the multiplicand register is added to the sum. No additions or subtractions are necessary within large strings of 0s or 1s.

Implementations of Booth's algorithm on microprocessors can improve multiplier performance slightly; but more importantly, it equalizes multiplication time between different input values. This algorithm also automatically takes negative numbers into consideration. Normal shift-and-add multipliers must consider sign separately or perform multiplicand sign extension throughout the multiply and perform a subtract instead of an add in the final "addition" step.

Large Product Generation. In some cases, a multiply instruction is available, but the product capacity is inadequate. The 6809 microprocessor, for example, has an 8 × 8 multiply instruction, but in graphics applications, at least a 16 × 16 bit multiply is needed. In situations such as this, two 16-bit values can be broken into four 8-bit values so that partial products can be generated and added together. The following factoring is used:

Multiplier = M15 to M0 16-bit number
Multiplicand = N15 to N0 16-bit number

where 15 to 0 represent bit positions.

$$\begin{array}{r} M15\ldots M0 \\ \times \quad N15\ldots N0 \\ \hline P31\ldots\ldots P0 \end{array} \quad = \quad \begin{array}{r} M15\ldots M8 \quad M7\ldots M0 \\ \times \quad N15\ldots N8 \quad N7\ldots N0 \\ \hline PPA15\ldots\ldots\ldots\ldots PPA0 \\ + \; PPB15\ldots\ldots\ldots\ldots PPB0 \\ + \; PPC15\ldots\ldots\ldots\ldots PPC0 \\ + \;\; PPD15\ldots\ldots\ldots\ldots PPD0 \\ \hline P31\ldots\ldots\ldots\ldots\ldots\ldots\ldots\ldots P0 \end{array}$$

where

$$PPA15\ldots PPA0 = \underset{\text{unsigned}}{(M7\ldots M0)} \times \underset{\text{unsigned}}{(N7\ldots N0)}$$

$$PPB15\ldots PPB0 = \underset{\text{signed}}{(M15\ldots M8)} \times \underset{\text{unsigned}}{(N7\ldots N0)}$$

$$PPC15\ldots PPC0 = \underset{\text{unsigned}}{(M7\ldots M0)} \times \underset{\text{signed}}{(N15\ldots N8)}$$

$$PPD15\ldots PPD0 = \underset{\text{signed}}{(M15\ldots M8)} \times \underset{\text{signed}}{(N15\ldots N8)}$$

When generating and combining partial products in this way, it is important to perform signed and unsigned multiplies at the right times and to align all results correctly before adding partial products. Signs must be extended on PPB and PPC partial products before final partial product addition; but sign extension isn't necessary on PPA because the product of two unsigned numbers is always positive. If the most significant 16 bits of the result are all that are required and an error of one or two units is acceptable, the PPA multiplication and addition can be eliminated entirely. Also, check to see if a shift-and-add multiplier can equal or exceed the performance of combined partial products. The time required for the combining process plus the small partial product multiply may be greater than that for a straight shift-and-add operation or a Booth algorithm.

Software Division Routines

The shift-and-add method is the standard multiply algorithm, so it's not surprising that the shift-and-subtract method is used for division. Again, division is performed as we would in decimal using pencil and paper, but it's done in binary. Figure 8-5(a) outlines the steps.

First, the dividend is compared to the divisor (using subtraction or a compare instruction). If the dividend is larger, it "goes into the dividend," so to speak, and the divisor is subtracted from the dividend. A 1 is shifted into the quotient to indicate that the subtract operation was performed. The dividend is then left shifted to decrease the significance of it by a factor of 2 for the next compare–divide step.

The subtract-and-shift process continues until as many bits of quotient as needed are available. In a final division in the screen projection equation, an 8-bit result would be sufficient for 256-pixel resolution. The remainder, at any time, resides in the dividend registers.

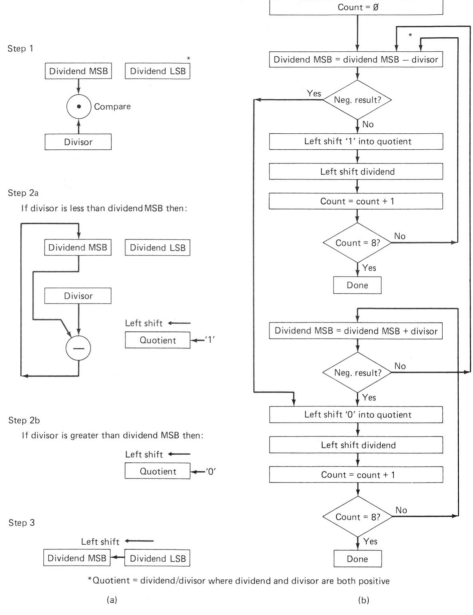

Step 1

Dividend MSB → ● Compare ← Divisor

Dividend LSB *

Step 2a

If divisor is less than dividend MSB then:

Dividend MSB   Dividend LSB

Divisor

−

Left shift ← Quotient ← '1'

Step 2b

If divisor is greater than dividend MSB then:

Left shift ← Quotient ← '0'

Step 3

Left shift ← Dividend MSB ← Dividend LSB

*Quotient = dividend/divisor where dividend and divisor are both positive

(a)

Count = Ø

Dividend MSB = dividend MSB − divisor

Neg. result? — Yes

No

Left shift '1' into quotient

Left shift dividend

Count = count + 1

Count = 8? — No

Yes

Done

Dividend MSB = dividend MSB + divisor

Neg. result? — No

Yes

Left shift '0' into quotient

Left shift dividend

Count = count + 1

Count = 8? — No

Yes

Done

(b)

Figure 8-5   Software division using subtraction and shifting: normal subtract-and-shift divide operation (a), and nonrestoring divide (b).

One of the main bottlenecks in this routine is the need to do the comparison. The comparison is a subtraction that is performed again in step 2 if conditions dictate. An alternative is to perform the subtraction in step 1 instead of the compare. The problem here is that if the result is negative, we must restore the dividend to its presubtraction value because that subtraction should not have been performed.

The solution to the double-subtract problem is the nonrestoring divide. A flow chart of this method is shown in Fig. 8-5(b). The divisor is subtracted, whether it should be or not. If the result is negative, a 0 is shifted into the quotient, but instead of restoring the value to its presubtracted value, we begin to add the divisor to the negative dividend. Whenever the resulting dividend is negative, a 0 is shifted into the quotient and an add is performed. Whenever the dividend is positive, a 1 shifts into the quotient and a subtract operation is performed. Double subtractions are avoided entirely.

Nonrestoring methods are computationally faster than the restoring method, but the value in the dividend is only a valid remainder if it is positive. In most graphics applications, however, the quotient is computed to the number of bits needed and any remainder is ignored, so this poses no problems.

Special-Case Multiplication and Division Operations

Arithmetic shifts are in themselves special-case multiply and divide instructions. A left shift multiplies a register by 2, and a right shift divides by 2. In power-of-2 multiplications and divisions, a series of shifts—or a multiple-bit shift instruction such as the SAL (shift arithmetic left n places) on the 8086—can improve computation speed dramatically.

When multiplying by a constant, the constant should be checked. If it is nearly a power of 2, a few shifts and adds may be combined to generate the desired results. To multiply a number by 5, for example, left shift it two places (to multiply it by 4) and add the original number to it (to bring the multiplier up to 5).

Special-case multiplies and divides can even save time on high-performance processors with multiply and divide instructions.

Trigonometric Functions

Sines and cosines are used in rotation matrix generation, which is usually performed only once per display frame (unless rotated cells are being processed); thus, slightly less than 100% efficiency is acceptable in calculating sine and cosine values. Most standard sine and cosine algorithms, however, take so long to execute that rotation matrix generation time can grow to be a major percentage of the computation time, even when large data bases are projected. Efficient sine and cosine routines are important for computer graphics programs.

Power Series Expansion. One way of calculating trigonometric functions is to expand their defining power series. The formulas are:

$$\sin x = x - 1/3! \, x^3 + 1/5! \, x^5 - 1/7! \, x^7 + \ldots$$
$$\cos x = 1 - 1/2! \, x^2 + 1/4! \, x^4 - 1/6! \, x^6 + \ldots$$

Each of these series yields 100% correct results if expanded sufficiently, but expanding a series to many terms takes many calculations. The factorials and powers involved also get rather large, which puts them out of reasonable-size integer ranges. With limited expansion, these equations give reasonable results for small x values, but large x values cause very large errors.

Arithmetic processor chips (such as the Advanced Micro Devices 9511) get around this problem by using Chebychev polynomials in series expansions. This technique minimizes errors and evenly distributes the small errors within a wide computation interval. A mathematics handbook or a differential equations text should be consulted for the procedures for using Chebychev polynomials.

Every term that a power series is expanded to requires two multiplies. The factorial terms and division can be precalculated and stored in a table. Calculation is still time-expensive due to the large number of multiplications that need to be performed. Creating a rotation matrix requires three sine and three cosine computations. If 20 multiplies are required for each sine or cosine, 120 multiplications would be required. This adds up to 24 ms on a 1 MHz 6502—an unacceptably long time.

Lookup Table Storage. The fastest way to generate sines and cosines is to precalculate cosine values and store them in a lookup table. Linear interpolation can be used for values between table listings. It's surprising how accurate the results of such interpolation can be. As an example, assume that a table with cosine values for 0 to 90° has been precalculated in 1° increments. We need the value for 43.712°:

$$
\begin{aligned}
\text{Desired cosine angle} &= 43.712° \\
0.731353702 &= \cos (43°) \\
0.7193398 &= \cos (44°) \\
0.012013901 &= \text{cosine } \Delta \text{ between } 43° \text{ and } 44° \\
0.722799804 &= 0.731353702 - (0.012013901 \times 0.712) \\
&= \text{interpolation} \\
\\
0.722822432 &= \text{exact cosine} \\
0.000022628 &= \text{error} \\
0.003\% &= \text{percentage error}
\end{aligned}
$$

This small an error works out to be one part in 31,943—the accuracy is good to almost 16 bits. The errors will be greatest at the point in the function where the second derivative of the function (its change in slope per change in x) is the highest. For cosines, this is at 0 to 1°. Accuracy can be improved using denser tables and increasing table density in areas where the most interpolation error will result.

Tables for cosines need only span the range from 0 to 90°. Values for 90–360° can be solved through symmetry using the 0–90° tables. Sines can be computed from cosine tables by making use of the trigonometric identity: cosine $(x - 90°) = \sin (x)$.

The Value of 1. Sine and cosine functions have ranges of -1 to $+1$. Fractional arithmetic can be used to express the range, although the precise value of 1 is not expressible. For graphics applications, a value that is close ($\frac{32767}{32768}$, for instance) is usually good enough. In head-on views and views rotated about just one axis, 1s appear in the rotation matrix. If software multipliers are used, this, combined with the $\frac{32767}{32768}$ representation of the value 1 can slow down processing. The value $\frac{32767}{32768}$ is a string of fifteen 1s. This is the worst-case situation for a normal shift-and-add multiplier. There are two solutions to this problem. A Booth algorithm multiplier that handles large strings of 1s as easily as large strings of 0s can be used. Another possibility is to check for multiplier values of 32767. If one is found, it can be assumed to represent the value 1 and the other operand being multiplied by it can be returned as the result.

Pseudodegrees. Circles are traditionally broken into either radians (2π per circle), degrees (360 per circle) or grads (400 per circle). Unfortunately, none of these graduations is a power of 2. In simulation applications it is advantageous to work with a circle graduation method that works more harmoniously with the byte and word ranges used in the rest of the simulation. One approach taken on some simulation is the use of *pseudodegrees*. A pseudodegree is $\frac{1}{256}$ circle, and a double-precision pseudodegree is $\frac{1}{65536}$ circle. These numbers correspond to the ranges of 8- and 16-bit integers. The pseudodegree system's advantage is its wraparound characteristic. Advancing past 255 pseudodegrees causes 8-bit overflow and a resulting value of 0, but this is the point on the circle that returns to 0 pseudodegrees. No range checks need to be made when computing with pseudodegrees because cyclic overflow causes circle wraparound.

Another pseudodegree advantage is that maximum precision per byte or word of data is obtained. If normal degrees were specified in a single byte, the value of $2°$ per unit could be chosen to keep the value within 8-bit range. The result would be 180 two-degree steps. Seventy-six units of the 256 are wasted. Pseudodegrees use all 256 units to represent the circle.

Precomputation

In high-performance graphics, four time periods must be considered: (1) compilation or assembly, (2) initialization, (3) overhead, and (4) real time. In many cases, computations can be done at any one of these times and yield identical numerical results. The rate at which the computation is performed—especially within a repetitive display loop—can vary dramatically, depending on the time period in which the calculation is performed.

As a somewhat artificial example, assume that a data base has an unwanted x bias on all the coordinated points. This bias must be subtracted before projection. There are a few ways to do this. The bias could be subtracted in real time as each point is processed on each frame. If eliminating the bias took 5 μs per point and there were 5000 points in the data base, total processing for bias correction would take 25 ms per display frame. The more points in the data base, the longer the processing takes.

This processing time is excessive. Another way to perform the same task is to adjust the translation value by subtracting a bias from it when the translation and rotation matrix is computed. This would compensate for the bias in the overhead part of the program. The translation and rotation matrix for a display frame is calculated only once per frame, so the time it takes to adjust the translation factor (perhaps 10 μs) is amortized over all the real-time projected points. Any number of points can be projected with no additional bias correction time penalty.

A time requirement of 10 μs per frame is very reasonable, but it can be even better. A small subroutine that executes when the simulation is first turned on can scan through the 5000-point data base, subtracting the x bias from all the points. This procedure may take 10 μs per point (for a 50 ms total), but this procedure is performed in initialization time, at system startup. The user will have to wait 50 ms longer to begin using the simulator, but in a two-hour simulation, this could scarcely be considered consequential. Time consumed in real-time and overhead-time frames is zero.

We can't do better than zero time (assuming that initialization time is unimportant), but the bias correction routine still uses up memory, a very valuable commodity in a consumer video game. The routine can be totally eliminated from memory by performing the bias correction at compilation time. The bias value can be subtracted from the data base coordinates when the program is put together by the assembler or compiler. This increases the complexity of the source listing and may increase assembly or compilation time slightly, but it totally eliminates the bias problem and associated solution software from the final program. Zero time and memory is used in the simulation software to solve the problem. The goal is to squeeze as many of the computations as possible from real time and perform them using overhead time, initialization time, and compilation time.

Never compute a result if it can be precomputed at a less critical level. This rule applies to bias and prerotations, groups of constants that can be precombined, and matrixes that can be concatenated in the overhead instead of in real time. Table lookup methods fall into the precomputation category and are useful in sine and cosine as well as in generation of other trigonometric functions. They are also useful in curve generation where complex blending functions can be precomputed at compilation time and stored in lookup tables.

IMAGE GENERATION SPEEDUP TECHNIQUES

When a single microprocessor is performing both graphics calculations (rotations, clipping, and projection) and image generation (line drawing, area filling, screen erasing), some 40–60% of the time is usually spent performing image generation. Image generation speedups thus have a major impact on overall display performance.

The functions on which image generation time is spent depends on the display device. On raster displays, significant time is spent performing screen erases. On a vector display, time is often spent waiting for vectors to slew across the screen. Raster-scan graphics are most common in microcomputer applications, so this section focuses on raster-scan image generation speedups.

FAST ERASE

Before a display is drawn, the screen must be erased. In frame-by-frame animation, the screen must be erased between frames. Many displays have built-in hardware that erases the screen by a single command from the computer. These systems usually take about 30 ms to erase the screen, because they perform erase by zeroing out pixels as the display screen is scanned. This erase period works out to 30 erases per second. If a display rate of 15 frames per second is desired, half the display system's time will be used erasing the screen.

Erase Loops

Display devices that share memory space with the microprocessor's memory space (including those on most personal computers) perform screen erase under microprocessor control. The screen is erased by setting all bytes in the screen memory to 0. A small software loop to zero out blocks of memory locations is easy to write, and a small simple loop is usually all that is used in simple graphics commands found in high-level languages with built-in graphics functions (such as graphics-oriented BASIC found on many microcomputers). Simple erase loops are notoriously inefficient and perform very slow erases. For every byte zeroed, the address counter that points at screen memory must be incremented and checked to see if the full screen is erased yet. A low-resolution display screen of 256 × 256 resolution contains 8192 bytes of memory, so the memory address updating, checking, and zeroing must be performed thousands of times. Figure 8-6(a) flowcharts a simple erase loop.

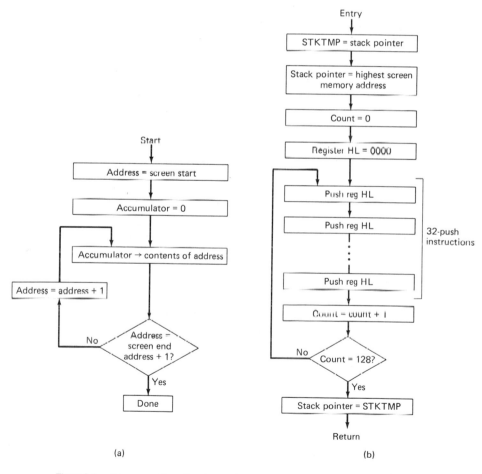

(a)

(b)

Figure 8-6   Screen erase-loop flowcharts. The simple erase loop (a) must be repeated 8192 times for a 256 × 256 screen; the reverse-push method (b) can erase an 8192-byte screen.

311

Stack Operators vs. Instructions

The first step in optimizing a software erase loop is to find the computer's fastest memory-filled instruction. The standard *store accumulator* instruction is rarely the optimal instruction. A few of the instructions on the 8085, for instance, are:

Store accumulator (byte)	13 clock cycles
Store accumulator indexed	7 clock cycles
Store HL reg. pair (2 bytes)	16 clock cycles
Push reg. pair onto stack	12 clock cycles

The fastest memory filling instruction on a time-per-byte basis is the PUSH instruction, at 6 clock cycles per byte. Upon closer examination, the PUSH also automatically updates the address (autodecrements it) when a push is performed. This eliminates the need for us to do it manually and thus saves even more time. This is a typical result.

Stack operators (PUSH and POP) can, on most processors, sequence through, load, and unload memory faster than any instruction, and as a bonus they have autoincrement capabilities. If it is possible to position the stack pointer at the display screen memory, the PUSH is the best choice in a rapid memory filling subroutine.

The theoretically fastest screen erase subroutine is one that consists of a long string of the fastest memory filling instruction followed by a RETURN. For an 8192-byte memory, the erase routine would consist of a stack pointer LOAD (to point the stack at the screen) followed by 4096 PUSH instructions (remember, PUSH pushes 2 bytes at a time). There is rarely enough memory space for such long erase programs, so an erase loop must be used. Instead of putting a single PUSH inside the loop, however, a string of perhaps 16 or 32 in a row should be used. This cuts the loop counting time down to $\frac{1}{16}$ or $\frac{1}{32}$ of its single-PUSH loop value, amortizing loop overhead of 32 or 64 bytes of erase. With a 32-PUSH loop, an erase rate of 96% of the theoretical maximum can be reached on the 8085.

Figure 8-6(b) flowcharts the REVERSE PUSH screen erase method. Small details such as saving the stack pointer are included to make the program work. Speedwise, this method can easily outperform erase hardware. An 8 MHz 8085 can erase a 256 × 256 screen in 6.4 ms—almost 5 times as fast as standard "zero as you scan" hardware erase systems.

SPEED AND RESOLUTION TRADEOFFS

Increased resolution is advantageous from an image fidelity standpoint, but higher horizontal and vertical resolution also means more pixels on the screen and slower element generation time. Erase time and area fill time increase as the square of the resolution, and line generation increases linearly with resolution increase. In situations where limited processing power is available (mainly in microcomputer systems), it may be wise to trade off some resolution for increased projection speed.

Decreased resolution offers more advantages than increased animation speed. Microcomputers usually offer wide color selections in lower resolution modes while sticking to monochrome in the highest resolution mode.

One other thing to keep in mind about decreased resolution is that graphic resolution is not as critical for dynamic displays as it is for static displays. Image movement and varying edge intersections tend to bring out details beyond the resolution of the display screen as the elements move across the screen.

RESOLUTION TRUNCATION MAPPING PROBLEMS

Many display systems and display controller chips offer a wide selection of display modes and resolution. While all the modes, color selections, and resolutions add versatility, they also increase the burden on the software that must support all the modes. In many instances, a high-resolution monochrome mode will have a half-resolution equivalent mode that presents a single pixel for every 2 bits instead of the normal single-bit monochrome pixels—the 2-bit code is used for color. Separate line drawers for each mode take up a lot of memory (not to mention the time taken to write them), so line drawers that can successfully operate in a number of modes are opted for.

One multimode line drawer that designers sometimes use is the high-/low-resolution line drawer. The high-resolution monochrome mode and the half-resolution color mode are addressed nearly identically. Designers reason that by simply truncating the least significant bit of the x and y high-resolution address and plotting 2-bit color codes instead of single-bit pixels, the high-resolution line drawer can be used as a low-resolution line drawer. This is very tempting to hardware designers also, because it involves the addition of only one gate to mask the least significant bit. Truncation-based line generators work, but the line quality is poor due to resolution truncation mapping problems.

Figure 8-7 illustrates this effect. A high-resolution 8-octant DDA algorithm is used to generate a line on the high-resolution display, as in Fig. 8-7(a). The line has evenly spaced segments with identical overlap (none) at their edges. The least significant bit is then truncated, and the results are used on the half-resolution bit map as in Fig. 8-7(b). If a high-resolution pixel occurs in a low-resolution cell, the low-resolution pixel is turned on (set to the appropriate color). Notice the unevenness of the line. Line overlap is zero in some cases and one unit in others. The problem occurs because a single pixel from a high-resolution line can barely skim the corner of a low-resolution pixel cell, and the whole low-resolution pixel is turned on. This "corner skimming" effect tends to put blotches along the side of an otherwise nicely drawn line.

For the lower resolution case, a separate line drawer should be used, or perhaps the high-resolution line drawer can be modified so all bits of significance except the most significant bit (which would be outside the range of the horizontal pixel count) are used, but the line drawer output's least significant bit should never be truncated.

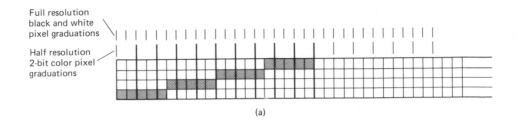

Full resolution
black and white
pixel graduations

Half resolution
2-bit color pixel
graduations

(a)

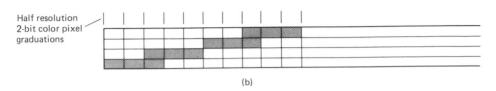

Half resolution
2-bit color pixel
graduations

(b)

Figure 8-7   The effects of mapping-truncation distortion caused by mapping to a lower resolution: line segment plotted in high resolution by high-resolution line drawer (a), and an uneven line segment plotted in half-resolution color mode (b) using the high-resolution line drawer with the least significant bit truncated.

HIGH-SPEED VECTOR GENERATION

The general-direction line is one of the primitive drawing functions on most systems, and it pays to optimize the line drawers for high-speed operation. The 8-octant DDA described in chapter 2 is a good algorithm for high-performance use because it draws fewer pixels than the 4-quadrant DDA and other line generation methods with overlap at the ends of line segments.

Line drawers should be implemented in assembly language. Fast-executing add and subtract instructions are used to update the ERROR parameter and x and y pixel plot position, but time-intensive conditional jumps are used to test if the line is through being drawn. It is good practice to optimize these jumps by putting them into positions where they take the place of unconditional jumps. When an x and y movement are made between plotting two pixels, both Δx and $-\Delta y$ must be added to avoid two separate adds for every diagonal pixel movement. Finally, display device I/O should be optimized, especially if low-speed communication lines to the display device are used. In the example in Fig. 8-8(a), the device requires x and y coordinates and an intensity bit of 1 or 0 to set or reset the pixel at x,y. In the regular octant 1 DDA, x and y information is sent for every pixel. In the optimized equivalent of Fig. 8-8(b), which includes the optimizations just discussed, a new y value is sent to the device only if y has changed.

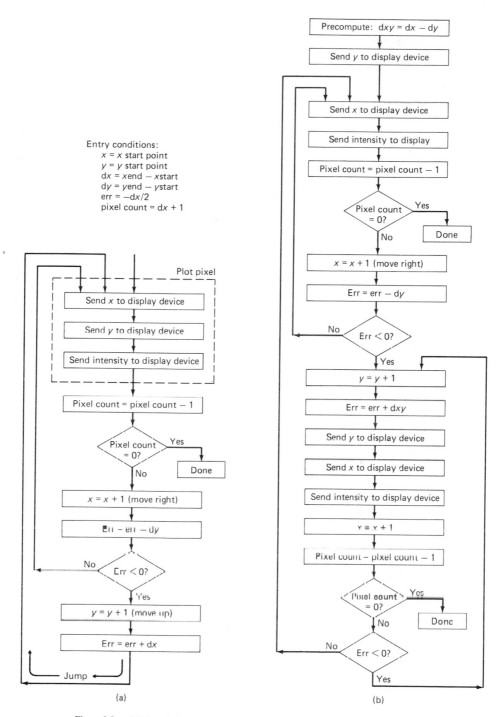

Entry conditions:
$x = x$ start point
$y = y$ start point
$dx = x$end $- x$start
$dy = y$end $- y$start
err $= -dx/2$
pixel count $= dx + 1$

(a)

(b)

Figure 8-8 DDA optimization through jump overhead reduction and minimized device output: octant 1 DDA line generator (a) and its optimized equivalent (b).

315

Preferential Direction Line Drawers

Horizontal, vertical, and 45° lines are special-case lines that require little computation for pixel coordinate generation. Horizontal lines start at the left point and advance to the right (incrementing the x coordinate) until the end point is reached, or more efficiently, until the change in x between the start and end point is counted down. Vertical lines are generated in the same way, only movement is in the $+$ or $-$ y direction. Diagonal lines move one x and one y for every new pixel. The Δx or Δy can be used as a countdown value to determine when the proper number of pixels are plotted.

These lines are so easy to generate and are so common in some forms of graphs (business charts, scientific graphs, and horizontal lines in area fill routines) that special "traps" in the general line drawer should be included to test for these conditions. In an 8-octant line drawer, when a Δx value of 0 is computed, the program should trap (jump) to a vertical line drawer. When a Δy value of 0 is sensed, a horizontal line drawer trap should occur. When determining if a line in a quadrant falls in one of two octants, Δx is compared to Δy. If Δx equals Δy, the line is a 45° line drawer. In graphics that use many of these special-case lines, the speed improvements will be dramatic.

Memory-Map Line Drawers

The line drawers discussed to this point fed x and y coordinates directly to a display device. Many display devices, and all processor-shared displays, don't accept x and y coordinates; instead, they require bits within bytes at specific addresses to be turned on. These device interfaces complicate point plotting and line generation considerably.

Coordinate Conversions. A pixel's x and y coordinates can be converted to an address and mask using software that performs shifts and bit manipulations as dictated by the Martin diagram for the specific display mapping. The mask is a byte with 1s in the bit positions that are to be plotted. For high-resolution displays, usually only one bit is set to indicate the single pixel bit within the bute. This bit can be *or*ed into memory at the proper address to set the pixel, or the byte can be complemented (all bits inverted) and *and*ed with the memory at the address to turn the bit off.

In displays of lower resolution, where multiple bits per pixel are used, the mask must have bits set to 1 for all the bits defining the pixel. To place a color code into the mask position, the byte at the screen address must first be *and*ed with the complement of mask to set any bits within the pixel off. The mask must then be *and*ed with the color byte (a byte with proper bits set to give the desired color in all the pixel positions of the byte) to create a color mask that affects only the selected pixel. The color mask can be *or*ed with the memory at the screen address to drop the color code into the zeroed-out pixel.

A line drawer like that of Fig. 8-2 can be used to draw lines on memory-mapped displays, but the *plot pixel* section must be replaced with a call to a subroutine that takes the *x* and *y* coordinate and performs the proper address and mask generation and the plotting in screen memory.

Optimizing Pixel-Plotting Routines. Line drawers that call a mapping and point-plotting routine for every generated pixel are quite inefficient. Memory-mapped display characteristics can be taken into account to optimize these line drawers.

Bits within bytes represent single pixels on a memory-mapped high-resolution display. Adjacent bits represent adjacent pixels (usually). By *or*ing a mask with a screen address calculated using a Martin algorithm, the pixel at the desired *x,y* location will turn on. If the mask is right-shifted one place and *or*ed with the screen memory, the next pixel to the right will turn on. If the mask is right-shifted again, the next pixel will turn on, and so on. We are thus making right pixel movements without calling any mapping routine.

When the mask bit shifts off the end of the byte, it indicates that the next byte to the right must be masked. This byte is usually at the next sequential address in memory, so we simply increment the address and start a new mask with the mask bit in the MSB position. We can continue plotting pixels toward the right until we reach the end of the screen if we want to.

One way to avoid checking for mask bit overflow is to perform cyclic rotations of the mask so it wraps around on itself. When a bit shifts out the right end of the old mask, the new mask with a 1 at its left end is ready for use. Also, add the carry bit (by performing an ADD WITH CARRY IMMEDIATE ZERO instruction) to the address after every mask shift. If the mask didn't cause overflow, the carry bit is 0 and the address remains the same. If the mask wrapped around, the carry bit is set and the ADD WITH CARRY will automatically increment the address to the next byte!

Memory-mapped displays usually have characteristics that allow *y* moves to be made without calling a mapping subroutine. Again, a study of the mapping scheme will bear these methods out. On the IBM personal computer color graphics card, for instance, a pixel can be plotted below the current even-value *y* pixel by adding 8192 to the address. (For odd-value *y*, add 80 and subtract 8192 from the address.) The masks in either case remain the same as the original mask because all bytes are aligned in vertical columns.

These memory-map characteristics should be incorporated into high-speed line drawers to increase performance. One call to a mapping routine is necessary to generate the start-point pixel's address and mask, but from that point on, wherever we would have incremented *x* to move to the right, we rotate the mask instead. Where we would have incremented *y*, add 8192 to the screen address instead. When it is time to plot the pixel, simply *or* the mask onto the byte at the screen memory address. This technique completely eliminates the need to call a point mapping and plotting subroutine repeatedly.

Vectorized Line Drawers. The optimized memory-map line drawer just described makes line generation become so fast and efficient that most of the time is spent accessing screen memory rather than doing mapping functions. Screen memory bytes that are pointed to by a screen address that is in some memory location or index register are accessed using indexed instructions. Indexed addressing modes require more processing time than direct access because the processor must first fetch the address and then fetch the byte from the address. A close examination of the optimized line drawer reveals that when we are plotting a string of single-bit pixels in a single horizintal byte, the screen byte is repeatedly loaded into a register, *or*ed with the mask, and stored at the screen address. Loading and storing is performed with time-wasteful indexed addressing.

Vectorized line drawers reduce the number of screen memory accesses by treating each byte as a small 8-bit vector. A copy of the screen byte is loaded into a register and the mask is *or*ed with it, but the byte is not returned to memory until all pixels in that byte have been plotted. In other words, a copy of the screen byte is temporarily stored in a rapid-access register. When all pixels are plotted within the byte (sensed by mask bit shift-out or any vertical or horizontal move that causes a change in screen memory address), the register is stored in memory. A short horizontal vector consisting of all pixels in that byte appears on the screen in one store instruction time. This method greatly improves line drawer speeds for lines consisting of large, horizontal spans. Vectorizers can be written into octants 1 and 8 of 8-octant DDA routines. Octants 2 and 7, however, derive no benefit from vectorizers because a *y* movement is performed and a new address is used for every pixel in the line generation.

Lines at angles between 35° and 45° (horizontal-to-vertical pixel movement) should not be vectorized, because more time is wasted in determining when to load and store bytes than is saved by reduced screen memory access.

IMPROVING IMAGE QUALITY

At first glance, it would seem that stairstep lines are the best lines that could be drawn on a raster-scan display system. In 3D hidden surface elimination projections, one would think that solid surfaces of the specified color are the best possible projections. In these two, and many other cases, special techniques can be used to improve the image to a degree that might seem beyond the capability of the display device.

EDGE SMOOTHING

The stairstep approximation of a line is one of the most annoying aspects of lines generated on raster-scan bit maps. The stairsteps can be made smaller by increasing the resolution; this alleviates the problem to some degree, but resolution can only be increased so far. A vertical limit of about 200 pixels (400 pixels on interlaced standard monitors) is a limiting factor in most microcomputer applications. If a bilevel (monochrome pixels only) display is used, the stairstep line is the best that can be generated. Slight overlaps of stairstep segments help to some degree. If multiple intensity levels are available for individual pixels, however, the corners of the stairsteps can be filled in with low-intensity gray shades or dim colors. This takes the sharpness out of the step and blends the line segments together due to the limited response time of the monitor. The resulting line is, signal-wise, very much like the image that would be generated if the diagonal line were being viewed through a television camera.

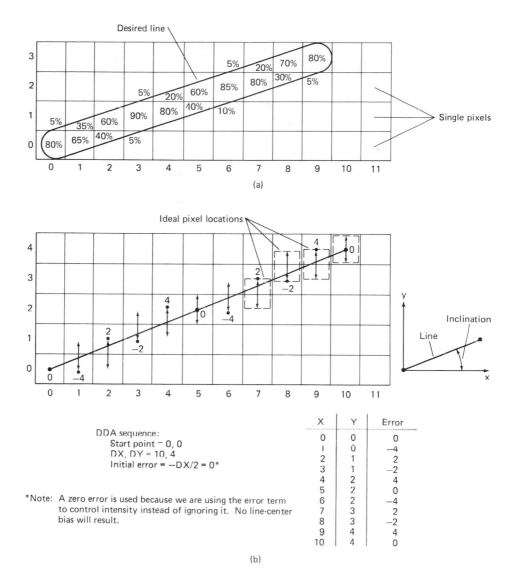

Figure 8-9 Edge smoothing using variable pixel intensities, with pixel/line area overlap (a) and with the error term used as an intensity factor (b).

On a conceptual level, stairstep corner filling or "edge smoothing" is easy enough to understand. Practical implementations are a bit more tricky. Figure 8-9 illustrates two methods for determining pixel intensity. For 100% correct edge smoothing, pixel intensity must be based on the percentage of a pixel that is overlapped by a line. Think of the line not as a one-dimensional entity but as an element having length and width. Pixels must be considered as small squares or rectangles. Polygon clipping and area computation methods can be used to determine the percentage of the area of each pixel covered by the line, as shown in Fig. 8-9(a). Pixel intensity can be set based on (1) the area percentage and (2) the nonlinear intensity characteristics of the monitor being used. This method is very involved and requires too much time to perform in real-time applications.

Approximation methods that work quite well, especially on display devices with a limited set of gray shades, are more appropriate for practical applications. Figure 8-9(b) shows a practical method. The ERROR value in a DDA indicates the variance of a plotted pixel's position from the ideal position of the pixel. A better line could be generated if we could slide the pixel up or down to bring the error value to zero; but on a bit map, this is impossible. It *is* possible, however, to divide the intensity between the two adjacent pixels that are overlapped by the computed "ideal" pixel. The intensity can be based on the error value, and the sum of the intensities of the two pixels spanned by the line width should be:

$$\text{sum of pixel intensities} = \text{line width}/\cos(\text{inclination})$$

This equation compensates for the decrease in line intensity as the line's angle gets steeper and the line gets longer, yet the line retains the same number of pixels. The method just described applies to the 8-octant DDA. Rules for other line generation methods are similar.

SURFACE SHADING BASED ON NORMALS

The shade and intensity of a viewed color surface depends on the light with which it is illuminated. Surface shading and reflection can be considered in computer image generation to present more lifelike views.

Before such shading can be performed, the reflective characteristics and the illuminating light sources must be considered. The color of objects in the real world is determined by their surface reflectivities. A red object, for instance, has a high red reflectivity but no green or blue reflectivity. A dull, grayish red object would have a low red reflectivity with no green or blue. Surfaces in a computer data base can have their color defined by reflectivities in the same manner. Red, green, and blue reflectivity constants with ranges of 0 to 1 (0–100% reflection) can be specified. This method's advantage over specifying colors absolutely is that surfaces can be "illuminated" with different colored light. A green object illuminated with red light, for example, will appear black on the screen because it has no red reflectivity. This corresponds to the real-life situation.

There are a few ways objects can be illuminated. Diffuse or ambient light illuminates an object from all directions. This kind of light is caused by light from many sources and by light reflected from many other objects. Highly directional light may also illuminate an object. This light is caused by strong, single light sources. Diffuse light tends to light surfaces evenly, regardless of their orientation toward the viewer. Diffuse reflections are depicted on the screen as a single shading color and intensity, no matter how the surface is turned toward the viewer.

Highly directional light sources cause surfaces to encounter and thus to reflect more light as they turn toward the source.

One final illumination source can be the fluorescence of the object itself. Light can be considered to emit from the object's surface or perhaps from a light source underneath a semitransparent object. Fluorescence acts like diffuse reflection. The angle of view makes no difference in the shading intensity. Unlike diffuse reflection, external illumination has no effect on the result. A red-hot glowing cube would still appear red, even when illuminated with purely green light.

The color and intensity of a surface is computed as the sum of the diffuse, directional, and fluorescence effects. In equation form:

Definitions:
RI,GI,BI = red, green, and blue diffuse illumination intensity.
RK,GK,BK = red, green, and blue surface reflectivity constants.
RDI,GDI,BDI = red, green, and blue directional illumination intensities.

Diffuse Reflection:
RDR = red diffuse reflection = RI × RK
GDR = green diffuse reflection = GI × GK
BDR = blue diffuse reflection = BI × BK

Directional Reflection:
RSR = red directional reflection = RDI × RK × cos (*ni*)
GSR = green directional reflection = GDI × GK × cos (*ni*)
BSR = blue directional reflection = BDI × BK × cos (*ni*)

where *ni* is the angle between the surface normal and directional light illumination source.

Fluorescence:
RF = red fluorescence
GF = green fluorescence
BF = blue fluorescence

Total Color:
Red Intensity = RDR + RSR + RF
Green Intensity = GDR + GSR + GF
Blue Intensity = BDR + BSR + BF

The directional reflection was computed as a function of the angle between the surface normal and the light illumination source. This angle can be found using the simple analytic geometry techniques on the surface normal calculated for hidden surface elimination and the vector extending from the center of the surface to the center of the light source. The light source is assumed to be far enough away that the incident angle is nearly the same for the whole surface. If it is not, the surface should be broken up and small sections treated separately. A very close light source will produce a bright spot on a single flat surface below it.

321

VERTICAL BLANKING SYNCHRONIZATION

Erasing, redrawing, and ping-ponging between images at a random but steady interval produces smooth animation when the rate is fast enough. This statement is 100% correct for film and animation on vector refresh screens, but another factor enters into smooth animation on raster screens: the inherent scan rate of the display system and monitor. The following should be kept in mind when performing animation on raster screens:

1. Frame rates above the display refresh rate (30 frames per second) are of no benefit because they outrun the raster screen's refresh frame rate. This is particularly important when selectively updating objects.
2. Frame rates that do not multiply evenly into the raster screen's refresh rate cause frames to be split between screen scans. A display rate of 20 frames per second, for example, doesn't multiply into a 30-frame refresh rate—1½ screen scans will occur for each frame update. The image on every other scan will thus be split between two frames. A slower rate of 15 frames per second that allocates two screen scans per frame gives smoother-looking animation.
3. Changing display frames in the middle of a screen scan can cause an annoying glitch on some systems, and it results in an unrealistic picture on all systems.

To generate smooth, realistic image sequences, the display generation must be synchronized with screen scanning. Many display controllers have a computer-readable status signal called VERTICAL BLANK that indicates when the screen scan has ended and the beam is retracing back to the top of the screen. This marks the beginning of a new frame and gives a few milliseconds of time when the screen can be ping-ponged to a new display frame or a new image can be generated. Synchronizing a display to the vertical blank interval will provide smooth animation with no screen glitches.

It is best to update the display at the screen refresh rate. If the microcomputer is not capable of generating an image this fast, two or more scans per frame can be used. If the frame rate doesn't multiply into the scan rate evenly, either slow the rate or show one frame for two scans and the next frame for one scan. The result of mixing the number of scans per frame can be observed by watching a filmed motion picture on television. Scan combinations such as two scans for one frame and three scans for the next are often used to synchronize film projection with television scan rates.

SPECIAL-CASE SOFTWARE PERFORMANCE BOOSTERS

There are several noteworthy special-case gimmicks that can be used in microcomputer displays to take advantage of properties of graphics projection and human perception. Some of these "tricks" might be ideal for giving a marginal-performance application just the quality boost it needs.

FRAME SYNTHESIS AND MOVEMENT EXTRAPOLATION

Many graphics techniques rely on *coherence,* the property of elements near one another having computationally usable similarity. In hidden surface elimination, span coherence—the property of many adjacent pixels being similar enough to project or eliminate as a whole—speeds up hidden surface removal. Most coherence in graphics is related to element position. In animation, sequential frames are usually very similar in content. Even at long intervals of 500 μs or so, very little change occurs. Elements can move far enough in 500 μs, however, to jump noticeably if the frame rate is only 2 frames per second. In cases where extensive processing is going into projection calculations and little time is being spent on image generation, display frames can be synthesized between two calculated frames to smooth out the animation.

Frame synthesis is performed by interpolating line segments between the positions of a line in two sequential frames. Figure 8-10(a) outlines the procedure. The start and end points of a line segment on two adjacent frames are subtracted from one another to get the change in screen (not data base) position. The values $\Delta P1$ and $\Delta P2$ are divided by the number of lines to be projected minus one. This division value should be a power of 2 so division can be performed by multiple right shifts. The resulting Δ values are added to the first frame's screen point coordinate to generate the interpolated screen points. Synthesized lines are drawn between the corresponding screen points.

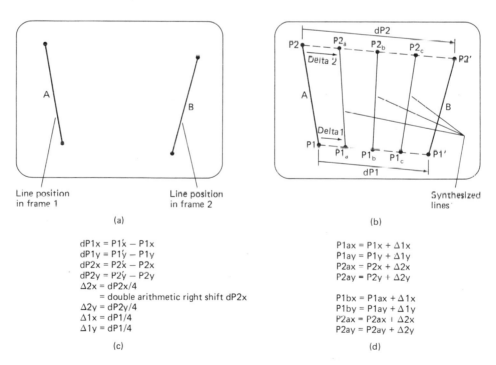

Line position in frame 1
Line position in frame 2

(a)

Synthesized lines

(b)

$$dP1x = P1\acute{x} - P1x$$
$$dP1y = P1\acute{y} - P1y$$
$$dP2x = P2\acute{x} - P2x$$
$$dP2y = P2\acute{y} - P2y$$
$$\Delta 2x = dP2x/4$$
$$= \text{double arithmetic right shift } dP2x$$
$$\Delta 2y = dP2y/4$$
$$\Delta 1x = dP1/4$$
$$\Delta 1y = dP1/4$$

(c)

$$P1ax = P1x + \Delta 1x$$
$$P1ay = P1y + \Delta 1y$$
$$P2ax = P2x + \Delta 2x$$
$$P2ay = P2y + \Delta 2y$$

$$P1bx = P1ax + \Delta 1x$$
$$P1by = P1ay + \Delta 1y$$
$$P2ax = P2ax + \Delta 2x$$
$$P2ay = P2ay + \Delta 2y$$

(d)

Figure 8-10 Frame synthesis using line interpolation: line positions in frames 1 and 2 (a), three synthesized lines (b), delta value computations (c), and synthesized points computation (d).

323

No multiplications or divisions are performed, and all mathematics are of screen coordinate precision (usually 8 bits on a microcomputer). Practical implementations require that buffers be set up to hold the two frames' coordinate points and computed Δ values. The Δ values for elements that move very short distances (2–3 pixels) often reduce to zero when two or more right shifts are performed. Cumulative error caused by successive additions of truncated Δ values can be minimized by retaining intermediate shift results and using them to generate synthesized points where appropriate. The x value for point P2b in Fig. 8-10(b), for example, should be calculated as $\Delta P2/2$ instead of $\Delta P2/4$ added to $\Delta P2/4$. The equations in Fig. 8-10(b) and (c) show computation requirements for Δ values and synthesized points.

Synthesized displays lag one frame behind the most recently generated true frame because the most recent frame's values are needed to begin synthesis of the frame immediately following the preceding true frame. Display response lag can pose major simulator control problems. The cases where frame synthesis' use is considered, usually in already slow displays, have very little margin for lag to begin with.

Control input extrapolation can be used to help solve this problem. A program to sense directional and rotational viewer position changes can extrapolate ahead to where the viewer will be one or two frames from the current position. The display can be generated based on this information, and the display lag will cause the proper scene to appear at about the right time. There is no way to anticipate sudden and abrupt control input changes, but as soon as they are sensed, the routine can immediately overcompensate for a few frames to get the display scene anticipator extrapolating correctly again.

CLIPPING WITHOUT DIVIDING

Time studies of 3D and 2D microcomputer graphic programs show that a large percentage of the processing time goes toward 3D and 2D clipping. One of the reasons for this is the need to perform multiplication and division in the clipping equations—division is especially costly in terms of processing time. Perhaps the clipping equations can be optimized. Two-dimensional clipping equations take the following form:

$$x_2' = x_1 + (x_2 - x_1) \times (y_b - y_1)/(y_2 - y_1)$$
$$y_2' = by$$

where

x_1, y_1 is on-screen point
and x_2, y_2 is off-screen point
and y_b is border y value
and point x_2, y_2 gets pushed toward y border.
x_2', y_2' is pushed point.

Rearranging equation terms yields the following equation:

$$x_2' = x_1 + (y_b, y_1) \times (x_2 - x_1)/(y_2 - y_1)$$
$$= x_1 + (y_b - y_1) \times \Delta x/\Delta y$$
$$= x_1 + (y_b - y_1) \times \text{line's slope}$$

Line clipping can take many iterations, especially in the 3D case. The line may be below the bottom border and to the left of the left border. Two pushes may be needed to clip the line to the screen's edge. On every PUSH iteration, the off-screen point "slides down the line" to the border it is clipped to.

The point position may change for every iteration, but the line's slope and thus the $\Delta x/\Delta y$ term in the clip equation does not. This means that once the slope has been calculated in a clip routine, it does not have to be recalculated for every PUSH. This observation can in itself halve the time spent on division in a clip routine.

Using the common-slope method, the number of divisions per line clipped is reduced to one. The number of divisions can be reduced all the way down to zero in some cases. One example is when no rotations are performed, such as when panning a window through a data base. As long as the window's angular orientation to the data base does not change, neither will any of the slopes of the lines being viewed.

If all the slopes are precalculated and stored (perhaps in an allocated section of the element definition), there is no need to calculate the slope at clip time. Thus, all division is eliminated from the clipping process.

This method can even be used when a data base is rotated. The computer can go through the data base on the first after-rotation display frame (or during a processor idle time when the system operator is not performing any graphic function), performing clipping using division to recalculate lines' slopes. The slopes can be updated in the data base at this time. Subsequent frames can use the previous clip's precalculated slopes.

TEXT TRANSFORM SPEEDUP

Vector text consists of large numbers of line segments that form characters. These line segments, and thus the text itself, can be translated and rotated in two or three dimensions by performing ordinary translations and rotations on the individual line segments. This takes an enormous amount of time, especially for long text strings composed of complex font characters.

Text strings are arranged in horizontal rows with equal character spacing, as shown in Fig. 8-11(a). The characters are usually defined on submatrixes of a standard size (a 16×16 coordinate character matrix, for instance). This rigid organization can be put to use to speed text generation. The "text placarding" process of Fig. 8-11(b) makes use of the organization by defining a "text placard" with a coordinate system based around the character cell x and y spacing. Letter slots are allocated for all characters in the text string.

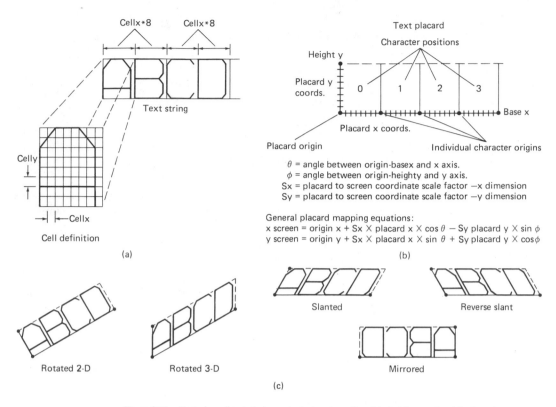

θ = angle between origin-basex and x axis.
φ = angle between origin-heighty and y axis.
Sx = placard to screen coordinate scale factor —x dimension
Sy = placard to screen coordinate scale factor —y dimension

General placard mapping equations:
x screen = origin x + Sx × placard x × cos θ − Sy placard y × sin φ
y screen = origin y + Sx × placard x × sin θ + Sy placard y × cos φ

Figure 8-11 Text placarding techniques: typical vector cell and text string spacing (a), placard definition and equation (b), and example placard placements (c).

Placard coordinates are mapped to screen coordinates using the placard equations which map x and y movement on the placard to x and y movement on the display screen. Notice that pure x movement on the placard can result in both x and y movement on the screen. This would occur if the placard were slanted.

The placard equation's trigonometric and scaling terms are generated by relating how the placard's three positioning points (origin, basex, and heightx) relate to the screen coordinate system.

The scaling factors, sines, and cosines can be calculated and combined in text placard projection overhead. This reduces point mapping to 4 multiplies, an add, and a subtract at a screen precision level (8- or 16-bit arithmetic). This is the same number of arithmetic operations required of a 2D point rotation but at a lower precision than that of the data base.

This calculation requires much less time than performing a 3D mapping of a point to the screen. The multiplications can be reduced to simple shifts due to the highly organized placard structure and the power-of-2 character cell matrixes, reducing computations even further.

A placard is placed on the display screen by mapping its three positioning points (origin, basex and heightx) from the data base onto the screen. From this point on, all generation is performed on the placard in screen coordinates. Figure 8-11(c) shows some examples of the way a placard might map to a screen in 2D and 3D cases.

ARTIFICIAL SCREEN MEMORY READBACK

Some graphics display devices have no pixel readback capabilities. Stand-alone terminals and some plug-in graphics boards for popular microcomputer buses use I/O port addresses instead of shared memory addresses to receive x, y positioning and intensity information in one direction only. Seed area filling, hidden surface elimination, and exclusive-*or* pixel projection rely on screen pixel readback. Screen memory readback can be simulated on nonreadback devices by setting up an area in processor memory to look like a display screen of the same resolution as the nonreadback display device. Pixels plotted on the display device should also be plotted in this screen memory. The screen pixels can be read back from the duplicate screen memory.

All pixel plotting operations must be performed twice using this method. The additional time required is not overly large on a percentage basis, however, because pixel plotting within line drawers takes a very small portion of the processor time. Screen erase does take substantially longer if the device must be erased by zeroing out all memory locations under processor control; but devices that communicate unidirectionally (stand-alone graphics terminals) usually have built-in erase hardware that requires a single erase command. Erase hardware typically takes 30 ms to erase the screen, so the duplicate screen memory that was set aside for screen readback can be zeroed out while the real display is going through its erase cycle. An efficient REVERSE PUSH (as an erase routine) can easily outrun the display device's erase time.

INCREMENTAL FILL

Area filling takes a lot of time on a high-resolution display system. Computations are not too extensive, but the sheer number of pixels that must be turned on (hundreds of thousands for large surfaces on a dense screen) slow display rates. Area fill can add realism to simulations. A flight simulator with a solid blue sky and green ground looks better than a simple line drawing of a ground grid and a horizon line. Unfortunately, large area fills performed by speed-limited microprocessors make large area shading and smooth animation a mutually exclusive proposition.

A close examination of situations where large-area shading is used shows that large color-filled areas seldom change position and size in large steps from frame to frame. The flight simulator display with blue sky and green ground, for example, remains almost the same from frame-to-frame. If the aircraft noses up or down, the horizon (the point where blue meets green) moves upward or downward and a very narrow band of color changes from blue to green or vise versa. If the aircraft banks, two pie-shaped slices of the screen change color—one from green to blue, and one from blue to green.

Solid area fill can be incorporated in animation if only the filled areas that change from frame to frame are changed on the screen. Implementations of this procedure are called incremental filling methods. The incremental fill concept is easy to understand, but implementing it poses problems. The areas that must be

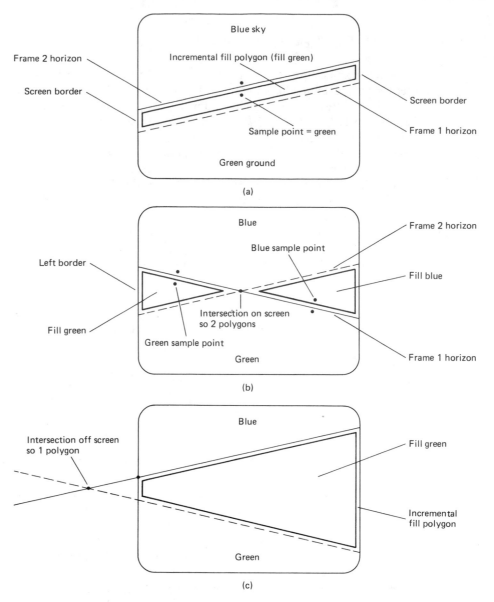

Figure 8-12 Incremental filling methods: simple-case parallel incremental polygon (a), two incremental polygons (b) caused by rotation, and single incremental polygon (c) caused by rotation.

refilled (the incrementally changed areas) are not represented as elements in a data base and must instead by generated as elements and fed to an area fill routine in real time.

Color surface borders must be sampled for two sequential frames and pieced together to determine which areas have changed color. Figure 8-12(a) illustrates how two frames' color areas are analyzed. In the flight simulator example, the horizon combined with the screen edges form blue and green polygons that define the ground and the sky. When the horizon changes between frames, a new polygon consisting of the new and old horizon lines (and the two screen borders they intersect) is formed. This is the area of color change. Any point inside the polygon is then sampled. The color inside the incremental polygon must change, so it can simply be filled with the color opposite to that which was sampled.

The horizon can move in many ways, making a wide range of incremental polygons. Rotation always causes pie-shaped polygons to form, but whether two pie-shaped polygons or only one will be on the screen depends on the combination of translations and rotations through which the line goes. In Fig. 8-12(b) and (c), two cases are depicted with different results. In one case, the intersection of the horizon lines falls on the screen. This indicates that two polygons have been formed and should be filled separately with different color. In the second case, the intersection is off the screen so only one on-screen polygon results.

Incremental fill routines are combinations of analytic logic, polygon clipping, and area filling, and they are hard to write in a way that lets them handle each and every incremental fill case. These routines must be pieced together and optimized for the situation at hand.

RESERVED POINTS

Solid objects created from line segments joined in space typically have many more line segments than vertexes. A cube, for instance, has 8 corner points that interconnect to form 12 line segments. A complicated connection structure such as a cube with crosses on each face has an even higher line-to-point ratio. In these situations, specifying the object by describing line segments individually is wasteful. A great deal of memory is required to store all the line segment definitions, and considerable time is required to process the line segments. All that is really required to store and project the image is a list of the eight corner points and some interconnection information. The eight points can be transformed from 3D to 2D space, and interconnecting lines can be added; this avoids 3D-to-2D transformation of a much larger number of line segments.

Reserved points are used to handle cases like these. A point in space is specified as a "reserved point" and is given an identification number. Line segments can be specified by indicating the joining of reserved points. In the cube example, the following information would sufficiently define the cube:

Reserved point 1 = 0,0,0
Reserved point 2 = 5,0,0
Reserved point 3 = 5,5,0
Reserved point 4 = 0,5,0
Reserved point 5 = 0,0,5
Reserved point 6 = 5,0,5
Reserved point 7 = 5,5,5
Reserved point 8 − 0,5,5

Interconnections:

1-2, 2-3, 3-4, 4-1, 4-5, 5-6,
6-7, 7-8, 1-5, 2-6, 3-7, 4-8

329

Reserved points are desirable on a user interaction level as well. Designers often depend on arbitrary points to which they make repeated references and connections. If a user is allowed to set aside a set of reserved points that can be referred to by name or number instead of snapping to them or respecifying them, design effort can be reduced.

SPACE FRAMING AND 3D INTERPOLATION

Flat surfaces are often represented in vector form using a grid in data-base space. A flat, square grid with 17 lines running in one direction and 17 lines running in a perpendicular direction can be defined with 34 line segments. This means that 68 points that define the line segments must be translated and rotated from 3D data base to 2D screen coordinates. The number 17 was chosen in this example because this number of grid lines breaks the grid into 16 equally spaced bands in each dimension. This power-of-2 division lends itself to the powerful optimization technique of *space framing*.

A point equally spaced between two other points in 3D space can be calculated by averaging the *x, y,* and *z* coordinates of the two points it is between. This amounts to adding the coordinates and dividing the results by 2 with a quick arithmetic right shift. This averaging can be performed before or after the points have been translated and rotated to their final 3D space position (just prior to projection), and the resulting points will still be precisely placed between the two defining points.

The four points equally spaced between the four corner points of the grid happen to be the start and end points of the grid's centerline. The points between the centerline points and the corners represent the start and end points of the quarter-grid division lines. The consequence of this observation is that a grid can be defined by its corners in 3D data-base space. The four points can be translated and rotated into their final 3D position, and all the intermediate grid lines' end points can be correctly synthesized using adds and shifts for averaging between points. The number of grid lines must be a power of 2 to take advantage of shifts as divisions by 2.

The example grid's 64 rotations and translations are thus reduced to just four rotations and translations—a sizable savings, especially for a microcomputer without a multiply instruction. The points that form the corners of the grid make up the space frame, and all internal points (the other grid lines' start and end points) are interpolations within this space frame. There is no reason why space frame extrapolation cannot also be used.

BOOSTING PERFORMANCE WITH SPECIAL HARDWARE

If all the special software techniques and tricks have been exhausted and higher performance is still needed, high-performance hardware may be just the ticket. A system based around a latest-generation microprocessor that has overall high processing power is one solution. And peripheral processors and special graphics processors can be added to systems to boost their power. These and a few other options bear some examination.

SCROLL AND ZOOM DISPLAYS

Hardware scrolling and zooming are included in many of today's display systems. These features can reduce the need for incremental filling in shaded animation. Solid filled areas can be drawn on the memory map, and scrolling can be used to roam over the areas without having to change the image in memory.

Zoom also reduces the need for incremental filling by letting the hardware zoom-in on selected memory map areas instead of expanding them and refilling them using hardware.

MULTIPLIERS AND ARITHMETIC PROCESSORS

The 8-bit microprocessors found in most popular microcomputers rarely have multiply instructions, and those that do are ususally limited to 8 × 8-bit multiples. Multiplication and division are used extensively in graphics, so performance can be boosted by using external hardware that can perform these operations more quickly than software. Arithmetic processors should be considered as add-ons to existing systems only. They typically cost must more than high-performance 16-bit processors (due to limited demand and production). The latest high-performance microprocessors offer better performance and lower price if a new system or new product is being bought or designed.

Among the most popular arithmetic processors are the Advanced Micro Devices 9511 and 9512 arithmetic processing units (APUs), the TRW MPY-8, MPY-12 and MPY-16 multiplier chips, and the Intel 8087 used in conjunction with an 8086 or 8088 system (a socket for this chip exists in the IBM personal computer). The 9511 and 8087 are true arithmetic processors. They perform floating-point as well as integer operations, and calculate sines, cosines, logarithms, powers, roots, and other high-level math functions. Table 8-3 shows the operations and execution times of the functions.

The arithmetic processors offer excellent performance in generating trigonometric functions, especially considering the precision to which these calculations are carried out; but calculation still takes a long time (up to several milliseconds). For graphics applications, the high precision is not needed and table lookup methods combined with interpolation can yield usable sines and cosines more quickly.

Arithmetic processors can be added in a number of ways. In some cases, a socket is provided within the computer for APU chips. The chips themselves, however, must be bought separately because they are so expensive. Unlike memory and popular microprocessor chips, the price of APUs does not drop quickly with time.

It is also possible to buy plug-in cards that have APU chips. The California Computer Systems 7811 board, for example, is an arithmetic processor that plugs directly into the Apple II microcomputer.

Table 8-3 Operation Time

	5 MHz 8087	4 MHz 9511	MPY-16
16 bit multiply	26.6¹ μs	23 μs	0.18 μs²
16 bit divide	32.4¹ μs	23 μs	
32 bit multiply		52 μs	
32 bit divide		52 μs	
Floating point add	18 μs	92 μs	
Floating point multiply	27 μs	42 μs	
Floating point divide	39 μs	46 μs	
Floating point:			
Power		3000 μs	
Exponential	100 μs	1218 μs	
Log		1783 μs	
Natural log		1739 μs	
Square root	36 μs	217 μs	
Sine		1201 μs	
Cosine		1219 μs	
Tangent	90 μs	1471 μs	
Arcsine		1984 μs	

¹Performed by 8086 microprocessor
²High performance multiplier only

HIGH-PERFORMANCE MICROPROCESSORS

One way to increase display system performance is to take the brute-force approach and use a high-speed computer. Advanced high-performance microprocessors of current vintage offer excellent opportunitites to do this.

Selection Criteria

When choosing a high-performance microprocessor, the instruction set should be considered. The three features that will improve graphics performance the most are these:

1. The ability to move data within a large block of registers and to memory very quickly (judge performance based on microseconds rather than clock cycles).
2. The availability of multiply and divide instructions.
3. The ability to work directly in the data type (16-bit integer, for example) of your intended application.

Four microprocessors that fulfill these requirements are the National Semiconductor INS 16000, Motorola M68000, Intel 8086/8087, and the Zilog Z8000. These chips are available from second-source manufacturers as well.

Processor Flexibility

There is more than one way to upgrade to a high-performance processor. An original system based around the selected microprocessor can be purchased. An alternative method is to switch processors on an existing system. This is a lot easier than it sounds. Many plug-in boards for common microcomputer buses (notably the S100 and SBC bus) based around these high-performance processors are available.

Switching processors is as simple as plugging in a new board. Software and hardware incompatibility with peripheral cards already in the system can complicate the changeover, but bus standards such as the IEEE 696 (the official S100 standard) have reduced these problems.

Alternate processor boards that plug into and take control of small microcomputers that are not even meant to have a processor card are also available. The "CP/M Softcard" from MicroSoft is a Z80 processor card that plugs into and takes control of the Apple II 6502-based microcomputer. The Z80 is used more for software compatibility with CP/M operating system software than to improve performance, but other cards that similarly take control with 68000 and 8086 microprocessors are also available.

Memory Access Speed

Microprocessors of a given type come in a variety of clock speeds. The MC68000, for example, comes in 4, 6, 8, and 10 MHz speeds. Higher clock speeds mean higher program performance, but only if the memory being accessed is fast enough to keep up with the high clock rate. Memory cards that plug into computers often contain slow-speed memory and "wait state" generation hardware that causes a fast microprocessor to wait while data is fetched out of the low-speed memory on the card. Using this type of memory with a high-speed microprocessor defeats the purpose of the high clock rate, especially in memory-intensive graphic applications.

A well balanced system should have memory speeds to match microprocessor speeds. This does not mean that a 10 MHz microprocessor requires 10 MHz (or 100 ns) memory because many processors use two or more clock cycles to access memory. Manufacturer's literature tells how fast memory access and cycle time must be to run without wait states. Information that comes with high-performance plug-in CPU cards also states this information.

BIT-SLICED MICROPROCESSORS

Designing a whole computer system using these chips may be too much of an undertaking, but graphics peripherals such as clipper dividers, vector generators, and shaders can be built and added onto a more conventional computer system.

One final alternative is to use multiple standard microprocessors, each on its own plug-in card with its own memory to perform specialized graphics tasks. Multiprocessing is particularly well suited to graphic applications because graphics tasks, unlike standard tasks, partition so nicely. A graphic display system's capabilities increase linearly with the number of processors used.

Chapter 9

Business
Graphics

The term "business graphics" may conjure an image of pie charts and bar charts on display terminals. While pie and bar charts definitely fall under the category of business graphics, the field encompasses a much wider range of capabilities and applications. Report and presentation graphics; computerized typesetting and handling of photographic images in advertising; and the retrieval of demographic, area sales, and distribution information from computerized data bases using graphics keys for selection . . . these all fall into the business graphics category. The most recent trend is toward "office automation," which encompasses typical office functions from typing to report generation and document filing. Office automation systems usually make extensive use of graphics to identify and select functions as well as to mimic the conventional look of the noncomputerized offices they replace. This chapter examines common uses of business graphics and describes how to implement them using the graphics methods described in this book.

CHARTS AND GRAPHS

Charts and graphs are used to more effectively communicate information that normally appears in large tables of data. Charts help point out overall trends and sudden changes that might go unnoticed while scanning over a table of numbers. Graphs and charts also let a user visualize data which makes the data, or at least the important trends it represents, easy to remember.

Charts and graphs fall into three broad categories: line graphs such as the one shown in Fig. 9-1, which trace the progress of one or more parameters with a series of line-connected data points, histograms or bar graphs such as that shown on the screen in the photo of Fig. 9-2, which show parameter values with sets of proportionally large bars or 3D square columns, and divided-area graphs that show relative quantities of parameters by breaking up a standard-shaped area into parameter-proportional pieces (the familiar pie chart is an example).

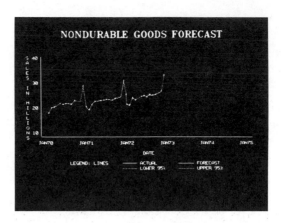

Figure 9-1 Black-and-white photographic reproduction of a multicolor chart display in which green, red, and yellow lines are used to plot value changes over time. (Courtesy SAS Institute Inc., Cary, N.C.)

Figure 9-2 Bar charts such as the one displayed on the screen in this photo offer a means of conveying complex comparative data to users at a glance. (Courtesy Hewlett-Packard.)

Computer graphs are similar to manually drawn graphs, but the generation process is faster and easier, and the final results are of publication quality if generated by the proper software on high-quality display equipment.

335

SOFTWARE CHARACTERISTICS

Computer graph generation software handles many of the numerical chores that are time-consuming in manual graph layout. Special features are often included to aid the chart designer, typical of which are autoscale, curve fitting, smoothing, and color filling.

Autoscale

Before the chart or graph is made, all numeric data is considered and ranged with autoscale. The chart is arranged so the whole graph fits nicely into the allocated chart space. Room for text headers at the tops, sides, and bottom are also accounted for in the data ranging process.

Curve Fitting

With curve-fitting features, various mathematical curve-fitting criteria can be applied to data before it is plotted. This is an excellent utilization of a computer's number-crunching capabilities combined with computer graphics. The user is not faced with the chore of tabulating data, fitting it, and plotting the fitted as well as the data points on the graph. Chances for errors are reduced essentially to zero.

Smoothing

Sharp corners on line charts can be rounded using user selectable rounding techniques. The resulting rounded curve is smoother, and segments of it blend together more smoothly than they would on a manually drawn graph.

Color Filling

Solid, uniformly filled areas can be specified by the user and generated by the computer. Bar areas and pie areas can be filled and patterned with the precision otherwise attainable only by an artist or skilled draftsman.

Three-Dimensional Graphs

These can be generated with total perspective accuracy. The computer can watch for and correct situations where a bar or other 3D chart element overlaps and obscures another portion of the graph.

SOFTWARE IMPLEMENTATION

Charting and graphing capabilities can be added to a computer by either writing subroutines that can draw charts or graphs, or by purchasing a commercially available graphics package that contains such routines.

Such software packages as *Tell-A-Graf* by Integrated Software Systems Corporation and *PLOT 50* by Tektronix are primarily meant for minicomputers and large mainframes. Packages with less sophistication are also available for microcomputers. *Visi-Plot,* a program by VisiCorp, is a graph-plotting package that takes data from the popular *VisiCalc* spreadsheet computation program and presents it in graph form on popular microcomputers.

For users who don't want to get too involved with the graphics generation process and would rather stick to the business application at hand, commercially available packages are certainly the way to go. Users who are willing to get involved with programming, at least on a high-level-language basis, can easily write their own small plotting packages that perform the graphing functions they need.

In writing a plotting package, it is best to take advantage of the graphics functions that already exist in the computer's language. Advanced *BASIC* on the IBM personal computer, for instance, has the commands:

```
CLS — clear screen
CIRCLE — draw a circle
COLOR — set the display color
DRAW — draw a line string
GET — store a screen cell in an array
LINE — draw a line
PAINT — fill an area surrounded by lines with color
PRESET — turn a pixel off
PSET — turn a pixel on
PUT — place a cell stored by the GET command
SCREEN — set display mode to alpha or graphic
```

In addition, text commands can be specified in the graphics mode. These commands are:

```
LOCATE — place the text cursor at an x,y position
PRINT — print a text string
WIDTH — sets line length limit
WRITE — print the values of variables on the screen
```

The graphics and text commands can be combined in a plotting subroutine to generate graphs based on arrays of data presented to them.

The simplest graph is the line chart. A subroutine to plot a simple line chart could accept the following variables as arguments:

```
NDPTS = number of data points
SDPTS = spacing between data points (x axis)
DXVAL = x axis value change per data point
VALAR = value array that gives values of data at the data points
NAME$ = text string that tells the chart's name
XNAM$ = text string to label the x axis with
YNAM$ = text string to label the y axis with
```

The plotting subroutine would perform the following steps:

1. Range the data. Assuming that we want line graphs to be 200 pixels wide starting at $x = 50$ on the screen (origin = 0,0 in upper left corner), the spacing between the data points would be:

$$XSPACE = 200/NDPTS$$

Assuming that we want the maximum data point to be at 50 and the x axis to be at 170 (remember, y values increase toward the bottom of the screen), the input data scaling factor would be:

$$YSCALE = (50-170)/ \text{ maximum-value } y \text{ data point}$$

The maximum value y data point must be found by scanning through the VALAR array with a small loop program to find the maximum value:

```
MAXVAL = 0
FOR I = 1 TO NDPTS
IF VALAR(I) > MAXVAL THEN MAXVAL=VALAR(I)
NEXT I
```

2. The second step would involve drawing the chart's borders and labeling the axes. The x axis is at $y = 170$ in this case and stretches from 50 to 300. The y axis is at $x = 50$ and stretches from 50 to 170. The axes are thus drawn as:

```
LINE (50,170)-(300,170)
LINE (50,50)-(50,170)
```

Axis labeling can be performed using the WRITE command to generate the text, and the LOCATE command to position the text-generation cursor. The LOCATE command takes parameters as in a "row, column" format where the screen contains 25 rows and 40 columns. To properly position text at graphic coordinates, the text coordinates must be calculated from screen coordinates by dividing x and y by 8. A small loop to generate the x axis values can be written:

```
XVAL = 0
FOR I = 1 TO NDPTS
TCRSX = (I*XSPACE + 50)/8
TCRSY = 180/8
LOCATE TCRSX,TCRSY
WRITE XVAL
XVAL = XVAL + DXVAL
NEXT I
```

The x-axis labels will appear on line 180, right below the $y = 170$ x-axis line. Labels will start at zero and advance by DXVAL for each label. The y axis labels can be plotted in a similar way.

3. Finally, the chart line can be plotted. This is a simple matter of sequencing through the value array for sequential *x* values and connecting the *x,y* data points using the line command:

```
X = 50
Y = 170
PSET (X,Y)
FOR I = 1 TO NDPTS
X = I*SPACE + 50
Y = VALAR(I)*YSCALE + 170
LINE - (X,Y)
NEXT I
```

This procedure produces a very simple line chart. Complexity can be added as desired. The color specifier in the LINE command can be used to make axes different colors. The graph can be named. The final graph point can be connected to the *x* axis and the PAINT command can be used to shade the area under the graph.

Bar charts and pie charts are just as easy. Simply use existing graphics commands to create a crude program that begins to perform the desired task. Then add enhancements until the complexity satisfies the requirements.

MIXED GRAPHICS AND TEXT

Reports often contain graphs, charts, illustrations, and photographs. An intelligent computer graphics system can be used to manipulate these reports. Computer graphics can generate the charts and illustrations, and photographs can be digitized and stored on a computer disk. Finally, formatter programs can arrange text as well as all graphics information into a final, combined report form

Most of today's microcomputer software divides the tasks of text editing (entering written material), text processing (formatting text into even columns and leaving "holes" for graphics material), and interactive graphics into separate programs. Sophisticated editors and text processors are widely available for all popular microcomputers. Separate software packages that save graphic images on a disk are also available, but general-purpose merging and formatting programs that combine text, illustrations, and digitized photographs are nearly nonexistent. Complete office automation systems, however, usually have these merging features built into a complete system operating environment.

PRESENTATION GRAPHICS

Slides, posters, and transparencies have been used for years in conventional sales, training, and report presentation, and this is one area where computer graphics can be quite useful.

Static presentation materials such as slides, film strips, and large posters and charts can be designed using interactive computer design systems. The results can be fed to media generation hardware, and traditional slides, film strips, posters, and transparencies can be produced. The process requires special hardware and software.

Interactive design terminals such as the Tektronix 4027 raster-scan unit, combined with some sort of input device such as a joystick or graphics tablet, are used to design presentation material. The operator uses the terminal and its supporting computer to "build" images on the screen. When the desired image is built, it is saved on a disk. The image file can then be processed by the host computer or another machine with media generation hardware for the final result.

Special design software such as that supplied by Tektronix or Dicomed Corporation give the designer a set of tools to aid in design. Various text fonts, cell libraries, and geometric shape generation commands give the designer all the capability of a traditional graphic artist. The design time is less than that required using conventional methods because of the computer's ability to align, shade, and manipulate elements at very high speeds with superb precision.

Final paper output is generated on color matrix printers or multicolor pen plotters. Pen plotters supplied by companies such as Calcomp, Hewlett-Packard, Zeta, and Gerber can produce presentation materials of any required size (up to more than 10 ft wide by hundreds of feet long), and special felt plotting tips can create results that look hand-produced. Smaller, less expensive flat-bed plotters can plot on transparent Mylar, which can be used on a conventional transparency projector for presentations.

Display file output can also be recorded on 35 mm slides or on microfiche using a film recorder. These recorders have small, extremely high-resolution display screens (usually monochrome) that project images onto slide film in a multistep process using high color-fidelity filters. The results of a slide created using a film recorder are far better than could be achieved using a color display screen and a camera.

The film recorder can also produce microfiche directly from a computer data base. This makes it convenient to access text and graphics information at remote sites without computers while avoiding the necessity of manually converting design graphics and text into document form.

A replacement parts inventory system, for example, could be totally computerized. Engineering drawings could have part numbers linked to them using CAD and intelligent data base techniques. Pricing information based on materials and labor cost could be computer-generated from cost data input from each production run of new parts. Finally, microfiche could be produced using a film recorder, and all regional warehouses and service centers could receive up-to-date copies of the latest inventory and pricing information to be conveniently accessed using a low-cost microfiche machine. Keeping inventory and part placement information on microfiche can also save a lot of space. Rows of shelves of cumbersome notebooks can be replaced by a case of microfiche the size of an index-card box.

Large plotters and film recorders are very expensive; not many businesses have enough graphics output to justify owning one. The need for limited business graphics is filled by service bureaus that own such equipment and process designs overnight. A small company can own its own design work station which is relatively inexpensive, and can send its designs on disk or tape to a service bureau for processing. Large plotters and film recorders are sensitive pieces of equipment that require a trained staff of operators and repair personnel, so the service bureau approach relieves the small business of the resulting staffing requirements of such machines as well.

INTELLIGENT GRAPHICS DATA BASES

One of the most powerful aspects of CAD graphics is the ability to attach intelligence information to elements in a design. This same power can be used in business graphics.

Intelligence can be added to a graphics data base by attaching meaningful information to elements in the image in the data base. In the case of engineering drawings, the type of material and the stress the material could take might be attached to a structural member shown in the drawing. With any design, the inventory, supplier, delivery dates, and cost must also be considered, and there is no reason why this kind of information can't be attached to elements in a design as well.

Commercially available systems for data base management, such as "Datatrieve," can be used to scan through the intelligence files of an intelligent graphic data base and tally the costs, number of parts, shipping weight, and even the expected delivery dates based on the longest lead-time item. And no cost or high lead time will be missed or go unnoticed. The computer's throughness can help avoid schedule slipping and cost overruns.

Intelligent data-base capabilities are mostly available in large, expensive CAD systems designed for engineering use. As time goes on, especially with the push toward office automation, data base intelligence will become more available and should certainly be utilized when it does.

OFFICE AUTOMATION

Computers and mass memory storage have finally evolved to the point where nearly every business can afford to own a business system. With the huge potential business market, and the knowlege that businesses of the future will require computers just to be competitive, large and small computer companies are scurrying to meet that market.

The focus of many of the computer companies' efforts is on incorporating nearly all office tasks from typing to scheduling, interoffice mail, file handling, accounting, and document generation. The term used to describe this type of task merging is "office automation."

Office automation systems are using graphic techniques to present information to the user in familiar forms. Screen cursors and input devices such as joysticks, combined with easy-to-use menus, are typical system input devices. The output devices in these systems are terminal screens, but they are a new generation of screens. Text appears on the screen in black on a white background. The characters on the screen are formed in standard print fonts instead of in the familiar computer styles. Gray shades are used to specify border areas. The result looks like a crisp photograph of a piece of paper with typeset printing and illustrations set against a gray surface (perhaps the top of a desk).

The Xerox Star system is a prime example of a state-of-the-art office automation computer. This system has a graphics terminal with a 90 MHz bandwidth that fully refreshes 39 times each second.

The Star makes extensive use of graphics and windows on the display screen. Functions are selected by pointing a cursor at the desired function on the screen and pressing a cursor button to submit the command. The goal in this design was to relieve the user from having to remember the computer's commands and from having to type them. All the commands appear on the screen and the user makes selections by pointing to them.

CAD systems have shown that for beginning users, such a simplified input scheme is superior to type-in commands; but more experienced operators still seem to prefer short type-in commands and would rather not scan the screen for the option they need. Today's office automation systems may be a bit too "point-and-press" oriented, especially for the day-to-day user, but the right mix of typed-in commands and pointed-at commands will evolve over time, just as it has in the CAD field.

Familiar shapes are also used in the Star system. In and out bins and mailboxes are graphically represented on the screen as small bins and mailboxes. Files are

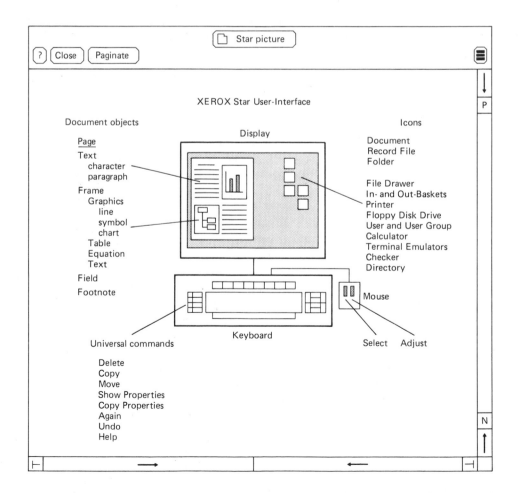

shaped as standard file folders with small tabs on them. And callable functions such as the operations of a calculator are selected by pointing to a small drawing of a pocket calculator. Figure 9-3 illustrates a portion of a typical Star screen image. This is the Star Desktop. Keep in mind that the image shown is not just an artist's depiction of what would normally go on a green-on-black display screen, but is rather a photograph of the screen exactly as you would see it black on white with crisp, high resolution.

Office automation, static and dynamic presentation graphics, graphics intelligence, and graphics–text mixing in computer-generated reports are truly at the forefront of business graphics. This overview of the business graphics field certainly shows that there is more to business graphics than just pie charts.

Appendix A

Foreign and Domestic Television Data

INTERNATIONAL TELEVISION STANDARDS

Lines per Frame: 525 Field Rate: 60 Hz Color Coding: NTSC	Lines per Frame: 625 Field Rate: 50 Hz Color Coding: PAL		Lines per Frame: 625 Field Rate: 50 Hz Color Coding: SECAM
Antigua, West Indies	Algeria	Sweden	Afars and Issas
Bahamas	Australia	Switzerland	Arab Republic of Egypt
Barbados	Austria	Tanzania	Bulgaria
British Virgin Islands	Bahrain	Thailand	Czechoslovakia
Canada	Bangladesh	Turkey	East Germany
Chile	Belgium	United Arab	France
Costa Rica	Brazil (525/60)	Emirates	Greece
Cuba	Brunei	United Kingdom	Haiti
Dominican Republic	Denmark	Yugoslavia	Hungary
Ecuador	Federal Republic	Zambia	Iran
El Salvador	of Germany		Ivory Coast
Guatemala	Finland		Iraq
Japan	Hong Kong		Lebanon
Mexico	Iceland		Luxembourg
Netherlands Antilles,	Ireland		Mauritius
West Indies	Italy		Monaco
Nicaragua	Jordan		Morocco
Panama	Kuwait		Poland
Peru	Malaysia		Reunion
Philippines	Netherlands		Saudi Arabia
St. Kitts, West Indies	New Zealand		Tunisia
Samoa (U.S.)	Nigeria		USSR
Surinam	Norway		Zaire
Province of Taiwan	Oman		
Trinidad, West Indies	Pakistan		
Trust Territory	Qatar		
of Pacific	Singapore		
United States	South Africa		
of America	Spain		

MONOCHROME STANDARDS

	U.S. Broadcast	European Broadcast	U.S. Closed-Circuit	U.S. High-Resolution
Lines/Frame	525	625	525	—
Field Rate (Hz)	60	50	60	60
V-Interval (μs)	16,667	20,000	16,667	16,667
V Blanking (μs)	833	1,200	1,250	1,250
V-Sync Pulse (μs)	190.5	192	150	150
H-Interval (μs)	63.5	64	63.5	—
H Blanking (μs)	11.4	12.8	10	—
H-Sync Pulse (μs)	5.1	5.8	4.8	2.8

U.S. HIGH-RESOLUTION STANDARDS

Lines/Frame	Active Lines	H-Interval	H-Blanking
675	650	49.5 μs	7 μs
729	702	45.7 μs	7 μs
875	842	38.1 μs	7 μs
945	909	35.3 μs	7 μs
1023	985	32.5 μs	7 μs

STANDARD PHOSPHOR IDENTIFICATION AND CHARACTERISTICS

"P" Number	Persistence*	Fluorescence	Phosphorescence Color	Refresh Rate (No Flicker)	Composition	Uses
P1	M	YG	YG	32 Hz	Zn_2SiO_4/Mn	Oscilloscopes; radar
P2	M	YG	YG		ZnS/Cu	Oscilloscopes
P3	M	YO	YO			
P4	MS	W	W		ZnS/Ag	Television; monitors
P5	MS	B	B			Photography
P6	S	W	W			
P7	MS(B) L(Y)	B	Y	29 Hz	ZnS/Ag ZnS-CdS/Cu	Oscilloscopes; radar
P8						Replaced by P7
P9						Replaced by P7
P10	VL					Radar
P11	MS	B	B		ZnS/Ag	Photography
P12	L	O	O			Radar
P13	M	RO	RO			Radar
P14	MS(B) M(YO)	B	YO			Radar
P15	VS(UV) S(G)	UV	G			Flying-spot scanners (FSS)
P16	VS	UV	UV		$Ca_2Mg_2Si_2O_7$/-Ce	FSS; photography

Continued on next page

"P" Number	Persistence*	Fluorescence	Phosphorescence Color	Refresh Rate (No Flicker)	Composition	Uses
P17	S(B) L(Y)	B	Y			Oscilloscopes; radar
P18	M/MS	W	W			Projection TV
P19	L	O	O	18 Hz		Radar
P20	M/MS	YG	YG		ZnS-CdS/Ag	Storage tubes (high-efficiency)
P21	M	RO	RO			Radar
P22	MS	R,G,B	R,G,B			Color television
	1 ms	Red	Red		Y_2O_2S:/Eu	
	60 μs	Green	Green		ZnS-CdS/Ag	
	22 μs	Blue	Blue		ZnS/Ag	
P22GLP	150 ms	YG	YG		Zn_2SiO_4/-Mn/As	Long-persistence color graphics
P23	MS	W	W			Television
P24	S	G	G			Flying-spot scanners
P25	M	O	O			Radar
P26	VL	O	O	17 Hz		Radar
P27	M	RO	RO			Color TV monitors "European amber" monitors
P28	L	YG	YG			Radar
P29	(P2 and P25 stripes)					Radar
P30	(Canceled)					
P31	MS	G	G	55 Hz	ZnS/Cu	Oscilloscopes; bright TV (high-efficiency) Green monitors
P32	L	B	YG			Radar
P33	VL	O	O			Radar
P34	VL	BG	YG			Oscilloscopes; radar
P35	MS	G	B			Oscilloscopes
P36	VS	YG	YG			Flying-spot scanners
P37	VS	B	B			FSS; photography
P38	VS	O	O			Radar
P39	L	YG	YG		Zn_2SiO_4/-Mn/As	Radar; low-frame-rate displays; monitors
P40	MS(B) L(YG)	B	YG			Radar
P41	VS(UV) L(O)	UV	O			
P42	M	YG	YG		ZnS/Cu/-Zn_2SiO_4/Mn/As	Slow-scan TV; high-brightness displays
P43	M	YG	YG		Gd_2O_2S/Tb	Visual displays
P44	M	YG	YG		La_2O_2S/Tb	Visual displays
P45	M	W	W		Y_2O_2S/Tb	Visual displays
P49	M	YG	RO		Zn_2SiO_4/Mn YVO_4/Eu	Penetration-color displays

Colors: B = blue; P = purple; Y = yellow; R = red; G = green; O = orange; W = white

*Decay: VS = <1 μs (time for light to fall to 10% of initial value)   M = 1 ms to 100 ms
        S = 1 μs to 10μs   L = 100 ms to 1 s
        MS = 10 μs to 1 ms   VL = > 1 s

Appendix B

Graphics on the Apple II Microcomputer

The Apple II microcomputer, developed by Apple Computer Inc. of Cupertino, California, is one of the most popular and versatile microcomputers. Its 1977 design, which was based on experience gained on the Apple I, was clearly ahead of its time. The cost of 16K dynamic memories in 1977 was certainly out of reach of the average Apple II owner, yet the machine was designed to accommodate a full 48K bytes of 16K rams. High-resolution graphics based on the availability of at least 16K of memory, and the machine's ease of use and program debugging capability (due to the ROM-based debugger, assembler, and disassembler) are the elements that set this machine apart from others.

The Apple II has three primary screen modes:

1. Text (40 columns by 24 rows).
2. Low-resolution 16-color graphics (40 × 48 pixels).
3. High-resolution 280 × 192 monochrome (with nonsuppressed color burst) or 40 × 192 6-color (two palettes of 4 colors each, where palettes are selectable on a screen byte basis).

The display generator produces colors using artifacts. No interlace is used, and the image refreshes at a 60 Hz rate, making the image very solid.

MODE CONTROL AND MEMORY AREAS

Four areas of memory in the processor's address space are used for display generation. Two 1K areas are allocated as text pages. Each byte in the text page represents a character. The two text pages can also be used as low-resolution graphics pages. Each character byte is split into two 4-bit nybbles, each representing a 16-valued color code corresponding to two color pixels, one above the other at the character location.

Two 8K areas are allocated as high-resolution graphic display pages. Seven bits of each byte represent single pixels on the display screen. The remaining bit controls the color palette of the byte.

Any one of the four screen areas can be fully displayed on the screen. A "mixed mode" allows the four bottom character lines of the text page to be displayed with the top 160 lines of the high-resolution page. This allows the user to run a debugger or other text-oriented software using the bottom four lines for text output while working with high-resolution graphics on the graphics page. This is a very convenient debugging feature.

The display pages occupy the following areas:

Text/low-resolution graphics page 1 = 400 to 6FF hex
Text/low-resolution graphics page 2 = 800 to bFF hex
High-resolution graphics page 1   = 2000 to 3FFF hex
High-resolution graphics page 2   = 4000 to 5FFF hex

Page and mode selection and switching are controlled by reading specified memory locations. Writing into these registers is not necessary. The simple act of reading them is decoded as the control signal to set the proper mode-setting flip-flops. The memory location controls are in the device control memory area at:

Address	Function
0C050 hex	Set low-resolution graphics mode
0C051 hex	Set low-resolution text mode
0C052 hex	Clear mixed (160 line high-resolution graphics 4-line text) mode
0C053 hex	Set mixed mode
0C054 hex	Select display page 1 (affects low- and high-resolution pages)
0C055 hex	Select display page 2
0C056 hex	Select text/low-resolution page for display
0C057 hex	Select high-resolution page for display

TEXT AND LOW-RESOLUTION MEMORY MAPPING

The Apple II's screen memory does not map linearly into the screen scanning. Memory location 400 of the text page corresponds to the upper left character; subsequent memory locations represent characters sequentially to the right. When the end of the 40-byte text line is reached, the next sequential memory location wraps around to the left of the screen, but eight lines down (1/3 of the way down the screen). This line wraps around 8 lines below it (2/3 down the screen). This line ends 120 character addresses (3 rows of 40 characters) higher than 400 hex where the upper left began. The eight bytes after these 120 character bytes are invisible and off the screen. This aligns the address with a power of 2 (128) and lines begin again at location 480 hex (128 decimal greater than 400) which corresponds to the second text line from the top of the screen. This "display a line and drop 1/3 down the screen" sequence continues until all screen text lines are filled in.

This addressing scheme makes byte-locating based on x,y position a difficult chore. The best way to handle this is to use a lookup table that returns the start address of the line corresponding to the specified y value. The x value can be added directly to the value because the display is linear on a single-line basis starting with 0 on the left side.

Low-resolution addressing is the same as text addressing. Each text position's byte is interpreted as two pixels, one above the other. The top pixel's color is controlled by the least significant 4-bit nybble, and the bottom pixel's color is controlled by the most significant 4-bit nybble. Figure B-1 shows the low-resolution mapping.

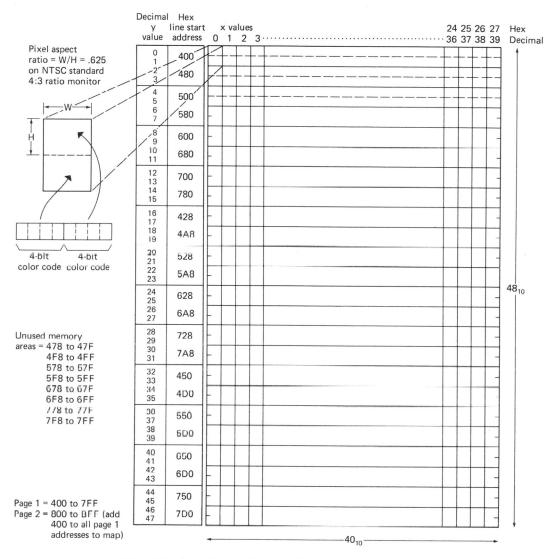

Figure B-1 Apple II low-resolution graphics screen. Page 1 addresses are 400 to 7FF, and page 2 addresses are 800 to 8FF (add 400 to all page 1 addresses to map).

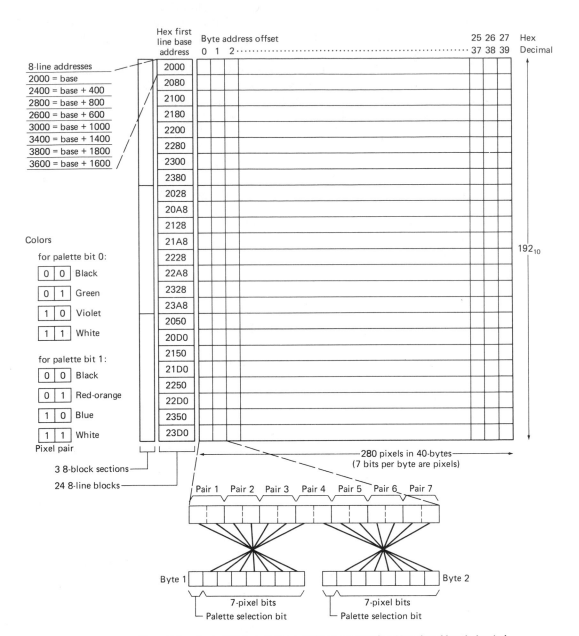

Figure B-2 Apple II high-resolution graphics screen mapping. Note that although the pixel pair that produces white is the same for palette bit 0 and 1, the white produced is slightly different; thus the whites on the two palettes will not precisely match if palettes are mixed, especially on short horizontal spans.

HIGH-RESOLUTION MODE

Each high-resolution page has 8192 bytes of memory allocated to it. Of these, 7680 are displayed on the screen. The other 512 bytes are scattered throughout the memory as 64 blocks of 8 bytes each that are totally unused by the screen display.

MEMORY MAPPING

Mapping is similar to the low-resolution mode in that bytes progressing sequentially through memory correspond to bytes on the screen moving to the right across scan lines. When ends of scan lines are reached, the bytes resume on the left side of the screen, 1/3 of the screen distance down from the current position. Figure B-2 illustrates the high-resolution graphics screen mapping.

This is a very complex mapping, and there are many important subtleties. The y coordinate to start of line address mapping is so entangled that the best way to handle it is with a lookup table that contains all the starting addresses for all 192 rows. The byte offset from the beginning of the line is obtained by dividing the x coordinate by 7. This is not a power of 2, so simple shifts can't be used. The best way to generate the offset is with another lookup table relating x position to byte offset for all 280 x values. This lookup table essentially is a divide-by-7 table for values 0 to 280. The line address table and x-offset table will occupy 664 decimal bytes. This is a lot, but routines to decode the coordinates into an address would take quite a lot of memory anyway.

On a monochrome basis, the screen has 280 × 192 resolution. The color burst is always on in the high-resolution mode, so images drawn using 280 × 192 resolution will generate color artifacts on color monitors. *Even* horizontal pixels generate violet or blue colors, and *odd* pixels generate green or red colors (depending on the palette bit's setting in the byte). The row in which the pixel appears has no effect on color.

MONOCHROME MODE

In the monochrome mode, each horizontal row can be thought of as containing 40 bytes of 7 pixels each. The least significant 7 bits in the byte represent 7 pixels. The least significant bit corresponds to the leftmost pixel, so the bit order is swapped compared to the way bytes are laid out.

The most significant bit in the byte is the palette bit. On a qualitative basis, this bit selects the color of the bit pattern of the color-pair pixels in the byte. In the 280 horizontal mode, colors are not used, so this bit does not act as a pixel color selector (although it will determine which artifact colors are produced). On a waveform basis, the most significant bit phase-shifts the waveform by one-half pixel width for all pixels in the byte. It therefore moves all the pixels in the byte over by one-half pixel. This effect should be remembered if precise pixel alignment is important.

The monochrome mode, when displayed on a high-resolution black-and-white monitor, yields sharp 280-horizontal-pixel resolution. Character sets and complex drawings that utilize 280 resolution will appear with sharply defined individual pixels. The 280 horizontal mode, when viewed on a color monitor, translates single pixels on even x coordinates into green or red pixels, pixels with odd x values into violet or blue, and adjacent pixels into wide white spans.

If pixels weren't arranged for color generation, the screen will show random mixed colors. This effect can be eliminated by turning the color control on the monitor down to zero. The resolution of color monitors, even with their color controls turned all the way down, is not high enough to distinctly show every pixel. Two white pixels surrounding a black pixel will appear as one large white pixel, or at best a white pixel with a slight gray spot in the middle. Dense text and graphics that rely on single pixels and especially single black pixels on a white background, will not produce good results on color monitors.

Finally, the monochrome mode is really not different from the high-resolution color mode. All control registers are at identical settings in these two modes.

SIX-COLOR MODE

The six-color mode is identical to the monochrome mode; but instead of the screen having 280 individual pixels across, it is thought of as having 140 pixel pairs. These pairs can be set to 0,0; 0,1; 1,0; or 1,1 to produce 4 distinct colors (actually two colors plus black–white). The seventh bit determines whether the two colors other than black–white will be violet and green or blue and red for the pixels in the current byte.

Word Division

From a memory-mapping standpoint, it is best to break horizontal display lines into 20 individual 16-bit words. Each word controls 7 pixel pairs. Words are chosen over bytes because one of the pixel pairs splits between two bytes. The color phasing between adjacent bytes is thus backwards. The value 55 in byte 2000 will produce 3.5 green pixels while the value 55 hex in byte 2001 will produce 3.5 violet pixels. Words, however, act the same as one another. The word 552A hex at address 2000 produces seven green pixels, as does the word 552A at location 2002.

Monochrome and Color Masks

Turning individual pixels on and off requires more than an address. A "mask" that specifies which bit for monochrome and which pair of bits for color is required.

A monochrome mask has one of its 7 pixel bits turned on to represent which bit in the byte is to be toggled to affect the desired pixel on the screen. The mask can be *or*ed with screen memory at the looked-up address to turn it on or the complement (binary inversion) of the mask can be *and*ed with the screen memory byte to turn the pixel off. An exclusive-*or* of the mask onto the screen will toggle the bit to invert it. The possible masks are thus:

$$\begin{aligned}
\text{binary } 0000001 &= \text{leftmost pixel mask} \\
0000010 &= \text{next right pixel} \\
0000100 &= \text{next right pixel} \\
0001000 &= \text{next right pixel} \\
0010000 &= \text{next right pixel} \\
0100000 &= \text{rightmost mask}
\end{aligned}$$

The fastest way to generate a mask is with a table. A mask should be assigned to the 280 x coordinate locations in the table.

Color masks are more complex than monochrome masks. One out of every seven color pairs are split between two bytes. This means that a single-byte color mask cannot represent a true color mask. A 16-bit color mask is necessary. Two bits in the mask word must be turned on to represent which two bits the color code will be placed in.

Colors can be plotted by setting up a color pattern byte that represents a 7-pixel row of the solid color. The pixel mask that defines which two bits the pixel represents is *and*ed with the pattern to create a 16-bit color mask. The screen memory is *and*ed with an inverted copy of the pixel bit mask to create a 2-bit "hole" in the memory. The 2-bit color code is then "dropped into the hole" by *or*ing the color mask with the screen memory. Figure B-3 illustrates the process.

Pixel bit masks can be generated from x values using a lookup table of 140 16-bit masks. A savings of 70 bytes can be realized by using the most significant bit of the mask byte to indicate that two bytes must be *and*ed and *or*ed. The masks would thus be:

$$\begin{aligned}
\text{binary } 00000011 &= \text{pair 1 mask} \\
00001100 &= \text{pair 2 mask} \\
00110000 &= \text{pair 3 mask} \\
11000000 &= \text{pair 4 mask (msb indicates lsb in next byte)} \\
00000110 &= \text{pair 5 mask} \\
00011000 &= \text{pair 6 mask} \\
01100000 &= \text{pair 7 mask}
\end{aligned}$$

The high-resolution mode officially has only 6 colors: black, green, violet, red, blue, and white. A color monitor's interpretation of these colors, especially on many adjacent pixels of alternating colors, tends to produce different shades of colors that don't fall within the spectrum defined by the hardware. Artistic design software that makes use of these monitor distortions to produce hundreds of shades of colors are now available.

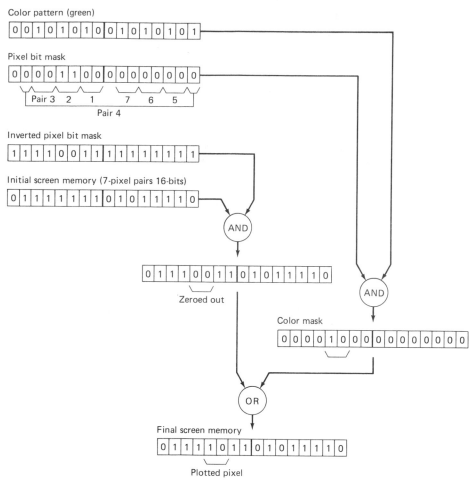

Figure B-3 Apple II color masking: First, create "hole" at pixel location, then create 16-bit single-pixel color mask. By *or*ing the color mask with the screen memory, the 2-bit color code can be dropped into the hole created by the zeroed out bits.

480 HORIZONTAL RESOLUTION

The half-pixel phase shift caused by setting the most significant bit in the screen byte can be put to use in the 240 horizontal resolution mode to move pixels over by one-half pixel. This can only be done on a byte (7-pixel) basis, but in some cases such as a single screen line at 85°, where every pixel is on a different byte, higher horizontal resolution (480 across) can be obtained.

A full 16K 480 × 192 screen can be synthesized by using display page 1 with all palette bits set to 0 and page 2 with all palette bits set to 1. Page 2 will thus be shifted to the right by one-half pixel with relation to page 1. By toggling rapidly between pages, the out-of-phase bits can perform interlacing on a horizontal basis, giving 480 horizontal resolution. Unfortunately, the Apple II has no provision for sensing the vertical blank interval which makes it nearly impossible to switch from one page to the other at the screen scan rate. Some users attempt to sense the current scan position by reading memory locations where no memory exists to hopefully catch the data left over from the display generator's scanning of the screen memory that occurs on the same bus. This method can work, but the practicality is questionable. Higher resolution requires better monitors, scan synchronization is unreliable, and interlace flicker of the same kind introduced by higher vertical resolutions all enter into the picture.

ORANGE SQUEEZEOUT

The most significant bit of each pixel controls the byte's color palette. Color palette selection is implemented by using this bit to move pixels one-half pixel to the left on the screen when the bit is turned on. This results in a different color phase with relation to the color clock, so a different color is generated.

A conflict exists at the border of a byte with zero phase shift and a byte with a ½-pixel left phase shift. The byte that is left phase-shifted "bumps into" the non-shifted byte. This results in one-half pixel overlap between the two bytes.

The Apple II display generator handles this by chopping off half the left-shifted pixel. This leaves only 1½ pixels for the first color pixel pair in the shifted byte. If the bit closest to the edge is 0, no harm is done because the black interval just gets a bit narrower. If both bits are 1, the 2-pixel-wide pulse reduces to 1½ pixels in width, which isn't too noticeable. If the bit nearest the edge is 1 and the other bit in the pair is 0, however, the only 1 bit in the color pair gets cut in half—and this is visually noticeable. On high-resolution monitors, the color pixel will appear half as wide as it should, and it will be half as bright as it should be. Low-bandwidth monitors are unable to handle such a quick pulse and consequently ignore the color altogether.

This phenomenon only occurs on the color orange-red. The effect is especially distracting on near-vertical orange lines. The stairstep that happens to fall on an "orange squeezeout boundary" causes a dim spot or total dropout of this portion of the line. There is little that can be done about orange squeezeout except to avoid generating it.

FAST ERASE

The 6502 microprocessor cannot use REVERSE-PUSH stack techniques to quickly fill memory and erase the screen, because the stack is at a fixed location (100 to 1FFH). Other methods must be used to erase the screen. Looking through the 6502 instruction set reveals that the quickest memory filling instruction is "store accumulator direct" which takes 4 clock cycles. The theoretical limit on screen erase speed is 30.720 ms with a 1 MHz clock rate. The erase program would consist of 7680 STA instructions and would be 23000 bytes long—excessive for a simple screen erase.

The only way to access changing memory address locations other than direct addressing is indexed addressing. The fastest indirect addressing instruction is STORE ACCUMULATOR ABSOLUTE-INDEXED OFF THE X REGISTER. This adds the specified direct absolute address to the x register and stores data at that location. Changing the absolute address within the instruction itself as memory is erased would take too much time and would result in an instruction modifying code (which is undesirable). The only alternative is to index through memory using the x register as an increment. The x register has only a 256-address range, so 32 instructions that each index through a 256-address range is the solution. The 32 instructions also amortize the index increment and loop time among themselves, reducing erase time still further. The resulting program to erase high-resolution page 1 is thus:

```
; Screen Erase Program
; From A2-3D1 Animation Package
; copyright 1979 by SubLogic Co.
;
ERASE:   LDX   #0
ERLOOP: STA   2000h,X
         STA   2100h,X
         STA   2200h,X
         STA   2300h,X
         .
         .
         .
         STA   3C00h,X
         STA   3D00h,X
         STA   3E00h,X
         STA   3F00h,X
         INX
         INX
         INX
         BNE   ERLOOP
         RTS
```

This program does a triple increment of the x index register instead of a single increment. This causes a more even distribution of the erase areas on the screen and causes it to fade out as a checkerboard pattern instead of in bands on the screen. This is much less annoying to the eye. There are an odd number of increments, so the x register cyclically overflows without ever being 0 on the first and second countups. Two INX statements instead of three would result in only half the screen's area being erased.

SCREEN PING-PONGING

One of the features that has made the Apple II so popular for animation is its ability to "ping-pong" between pages 1 and 2. This is accomplished by reading the proper page select register. Page changeover is smooth, rapid (a few microseconds), and glitch-free. While the screen is displaying one page, a user can be erasing and getting the next image ready on the undisplayed page. When it is ready, a toggle is called for. (The section in chapter 8 on display smoothing goes into this and other smoothing methods in detail.) An Apple II must contain at least 24K of memory to perform ping-ponging on the high-resolution graphics pages due to the memory location of high-resolution graphics page 2.

Appendix C

Graphics on the
IBM Personal Computer

The IBM personal computer is unique in that its display generator system is a plug-in card that is separate from the main computer board in the machine. This allows various display cards to be plugged in and allows easy expansion to high-performance graphics cards as they become available. The two most popular plug-in display generator cards for the IBM personal computer are the *IBM monochrome display and parallel printer adapter* and the *color/graphics monitor adapter*. The monochrome card is a text generation card that can generate high-resolution text at a higher than standard scan rate (720 × 350 resolution at 50 Hz refresh rate). The output is not compatible with standard NTSC monitors and must drive the *IBM monochrome display*, which is a monitor that is specially designed for it.

The color graphics card is similar to the display generators found in other microcomputers. It generates standard NTSC output and can drive any standard monitor or rf adapter. It also has RGB outputs so it can drive a color RGB display.

The display generator is based around the Motorola 6845 display generator chip. This chip is designed for "alphanumeric and limited graphics generation." The color graphics card, however, has much external circuitry that provides alphanumeric and full color graphics capability. Graphics as performed on the color/graphics monitor adapter is addressed in this appendix.

MEMORY AREAS

The color graphics generator is a memory-mapped device. The memory resides in the 8088's address space at location B8000 to BBFFF hex. Unlike other popular microcomputers that use valuable processor memory for display, the color graphics card has its own on-board 16K of display memory and uses none of the processor's main-board 64K memory.

MODE CONTROLS

The 6845 CRT controller chip is a programmable device. It has 19 internal registers: one that is loaded with a value from 0 to 17 to point at the internal register to be accessed, and 18 that control display generation functions. This would seem to give unlimited flexibility to the graphics programmer, but most of these control registers have low-level functions that contribute little to graphics flexibility. These registers include horizontal sync pulse position, vertical sync pulse position, horizontal bytes displayed, vertical rows displayed, and other display generator functions (see Fig. C-1).

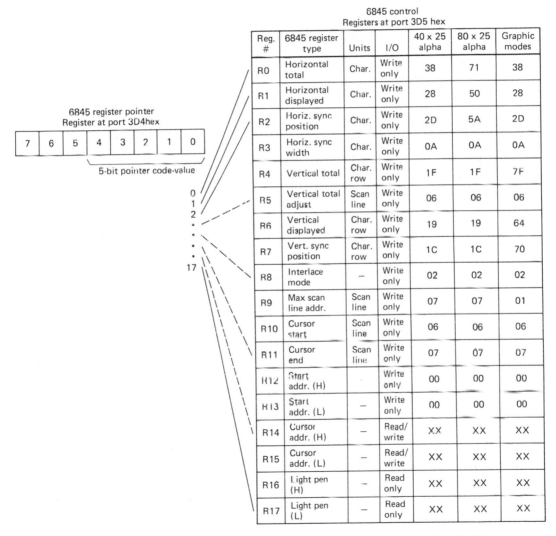

6845 register pointer
Register at port 3D4hex

7	6	5	4	3	2	1	0

5-bit pointer code-value

0
1
2
.
.
.
17

6845 control
Registers at port 3D5 hex

Reg. #	6845 register type	Units	I/O	40 x 25 alpha	80 x 25 alpha	Graphic modes
R0	Horizontal total	Char.	Write only	38	71	38
R1	Horizontal displayed	Char.	Write only	28	50	28
R2	Horiz. sync position	Char.	Write only	2D	5A	2D
R3	Horiz. sync width	Char.	Write only	0A	0A	0A
R4	Vertical total	Char. row	Write only	1F	1F	7F
R5	Vertical total adjust	Scan line	Write only	06	06	06
R6	Vertical displayed	Char. row	Write only	19	19	64
R7	Vert. sync position	Char. row	Write only	1C	1C	70
R8	Interlace mode	–	Write only	02	02	02
R9	Max scan line addr.	Scan line	Write only	07	07	01
R10	Cursor start	Scan line	Write only	06	06	06
R11	Cursor end	Scan line	Write only	07	07	07
R12	Start addr. (H)		Write only	00	00	00
R13	Start addr. (L)	–	Write only	00	00	00
R14	Cursor addr. (H)	–	Read/ write	XX	XX	XX
R15	Cursor addr. (L)	–	Read/ write	XX	XX	XX
R16	Light pen (H)	–	Read only	XX	XX	XX
R17	Light pen (L)	–	Read only	XX	XX	XX

Figure C-1   Control register types and capabilities in the 6845 CRT controller. The 5-bit pointer code value, from 0 to 17, indicates the register number for display.

There are five additional registers that are not on the 6845 chip. Two of them (at output port addresses 3Db and 3Dc hex) are light pen registers that are not used unless you are working with a light pen. The other three are:

Port	Register Function
3D8	Mode control register (write only)
3D9	Color select register (write only)
3DA	Status register (read only)

Figure C-2 shows the bit assignments of the mode and control registers. The status register only has 4 status bits. Bits 1 and 2 are light pen bits. Bit 0 is a "display enabled" bit. In 80 × 25 alpha mode, this bit should be a 1 before writing into

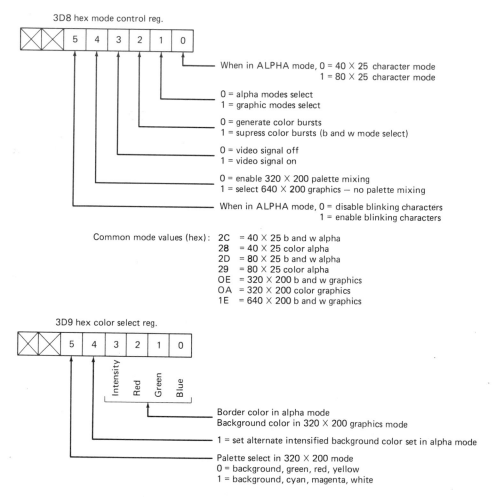

Figure C-2 IBM personal computer bit assignments of mode control and color select registers.

display memory to avoid memory conflict screen glitches. Bit 3 reads video bits from the video signal in alpha mode to be sure that video is being generated. The status bits are not used in the graphics mode unless you are using a light pen.

MEMORY MAPPING

The color graphics card's memory is mapped quite linearly. Address B8000 holds the first 8 pixels at the top left of the screen in left-to-right order just as they are laid out in the byte itself. As the address is increased, bytes and pixels are generated toward the right of the screen. When the end of the line is reached, display generation continues two lines down. In other words, all the even screen lines (0 to 198) are generated first. The even lines (100 lines of 80 bytes each) occupy 8000 sequential bytes of memory from B8000 to B9F40.

The addresses for the odd scan (1 to 199) lines start 192 bytes later at BA000 hex. Another field is then addressed-out sequentially for the odd lines (another 8000 bytes total). There are therefore two blocks of 192 bytes each on the card that go unused. The two fields (odd and even lines) interlace each other on a memory address basis. This should not be confused with display scan interlacing. The color graphics card generates a 640 × 200-pixel noninterlaced display at the monitor level.

USING THE DISPLAY MODES

Graphics generation is no problem on the color graphics card. Almost linear mapping makes line drawing and area filling simple and straightforward, and the 8088's ability to point the stack at the display memory allows fast REVERSE-PUSH screen erase routines to be used. The graphics user may spend more time, however, deciding which display mode to use.

For very dense drawings and text, the 640 × 200 mode can be used. A horizontal resolution of 640 pixels is beyond the resolution limits of anything except high-resolution black-and-white monitors and RGB color monitors (which the card can drive directly).

For color graphics, there are many possible modes. IBM defines medium-resolution modes as those having 320 pixels per line. Each byte on the line is broken into four 2-bit color codes. Masking and addressing methods can be programmed as described in Appendix B (Apple II graphics). There are two palettes from which to choose:

Code	00	01	10	11
palette 1	backgnd	cyan	magenta	white
palette 2	backgnd	green	red	yellow

The palette is selected by bit 5 in the color select register. The background color is also determined by the color register (bits 3, 2, 1, 0). One of the following 16 colors can be chosen for background color:

Color Code				Color
I	R	G	B	
0	0	0	0	black
0	0	0	1	blue
0	0	1	0	green
0	0	1	1	cyan
0	1	0	0	red
0	1	0	1	magenta
0	1	1	0	brown
0	1	1	1	white
1	0	0	0	gray
1	0	0	1	light blue
1	0	1	0	light green
1	0	1	1	light cyan
1	1	0	0	light red
1	1	0	1	light magenta
1	1	1	0	yellow
1	1	1	1	bright white

Notice how the second set of eight colors is an intensified version of the first set due to the intensity (I) bit being set.

Another standard IBM mode is the low-resolution mode. This mode is not supported in ROM. It has a resolution of 160 × 100 with 16 colors per pixel. Bytes are divided into two nybbles, each containing a 4-bit color code.

Another way to get 16 colors with a standard supported mode is to go into text mode. Colors can be specified for any character, and the character set includes codes for all pixels in character cell off and all pixels on. A matrix of 80 × 24 color cells which can be mixed with characters is thus available. This is poor in resolution but is fine for color charts mixed with alphanumerics.

NONSTANDARD MODES

The 6845 registers and the mode and color select registers can be programmed to generate many nonstandard modes. One of the most versatile of these is the 160 × 200 16-color mode. The mode is selected as 640 × 200 black-and-white, but the color burst (bit 2 in the mode register) is set to 0 to turn the color burst on. This gives the programmer complete control of color artifact generation.

Each byte covers two color clock cycles, so a color pixel is defined by one color clock cycle or 4 bits. Each byte is broken into two pixel nybbles. Since these four bits all fall along different areas of the color clock cycle, different combinations produce different artifact colors. In this mode, the color select register acts as a bit mask on the color nybble. The background color bits in the color register (bits 0 to 3) should all be on. Pixels can be masked out on a whole-screen basis by manipulating the background color bits. They have the effect of color filters being placed over the screen.

SCREEN PING-PONGING

The color graphics display card has a single 16K buffer that is totally used in the 640 × 200 or 320 × 200 color modes. This leaves no room for another display page. The 6845 can be programmed, however, to start its address scanning on locations other than 0 (6845 registers number 12 and 13). Any mode that only requires 8000 bytes of memory can be assigned two display pages by simply changing the scan start address.

RGB COMPATIBILITY

One problem with custom modes is that there is no guarantee that they will work correctly when displayed through an RGB monitor. Colors generated using artifacts will not be portrayed correctly on an RGB monitor due to the way the card encodes the RGB signals.

Another problem with RGB graphics is that most color monitors have no intensity input. They can be driven by the red, green, and blue inputs only and a color picture will appear, but all the intensified colors will come out looking identical to their nonintensified versions. Dark blue writing on a light blue background—which looks fine on a composite video monitor—will simply vanish on an RGB monitor that doesn't use the intensity input. Black boxes that synthesize intensity-corrected R,G, and B signals from R,G,B and I inputs are an alternative to upgrading to an RGBI monitor.

Index

D

Tridimensional view control, 180–81
Trigonometric functions, 307–9
2D graphics transforms, 199–204
Two-step clipping, 36–38

U

Uniform text, 153–54
Units of resolution, 168–69
User query design element location, 158

V

Value of 1, 308–9
Vector definition, 56–57
Vector displays, 14, 17, 122
Vector filling and crosshatching, 280
Vector generating devices, 138
Vector generation, high-speed, 314–18
Vectorized line drawers, 317–18
Vector matrix arithmetic, 195–97
Vector tracking noise, 101–2
Vector tracking problems, 104
Vertical blanking synchronization, 322
Vertical line generation, 17–19
Vertical-scan shading table methods, 274–76
Vertical scroll address manipulation, 76, 77
Video bandwidth, 82–85
Video modulators, 98–99

Video noise, 99–104
Video signals:
   color, 88–99
   monochrome, 81–87
Video voltage, polarity, and impedance, 86–87
Viewer and element manipulation commands, 59
Viewer perspective, 215–17
Viewer point specification, 180
Viewing, 178–81
Viewports, 38, 39
Voltage, video, 86–87, 91, 92

W

White erase, 45
Windows, 38, 39
Wire-frame element generation, 236–50
Word-oriented erase and fill, 45
Working coordinates, 38, 39
Working files, 183
World coordinates, 38, 39
Wraparound, 32, 33
Writethrough mode, 123, 149

Z

Zoom, 45, 331
Zoom address manipulation, 77–79